Programming the Web Using XML

Programming the Web Using

Ellen Pearlman
Columbia University

Eileen Mullin

Boston Burr Ridge, IL Dubuque, IA Madison, WI New York San Francisco St. Louis
Bangkok Bogotá Caracas Kuala Lumpur Lisbon London Madrid Mexico City
Milan Montreal New Delhi Santiago Seoul Singapore Sydney Taipei Toronto

PROGRAMMING THE WEB USING XML

Published by McGraw-Hill Technology Education, a business unit of The McGraw-Hill Companies, Inc., 1221 Avenue of the Americas, New York, NY, 10020.

This book is printed on acid-free paper.

domestic 1 2 3 4 5 6 7 8 9 0 DOC/DOC 0 9 8 7 6 5 4 3
international 1 2 3 4 5 6 7 8 9 0 DOC/DOC 0 9 8 7 6 5 4 3

ISBN 0-07-284550-3

Editor in chief: *Bob Woodbury*
Publisher: *Brandon Nordin*
Senior sponsoring editor: *Donald J. Hull*
Developmental editor: *Lisa Chin-Johnson*
Marketing manager: *Andy Bernier*
Executive producer: Media technology: *Mark Christianson*
Project manager: *Kristin Puscas*
Senior production supervisor: *Sesha Bolisetty*
Lead designer: *Pam Verros*
Senior supplement producer: *Rose M. Range*
Senior digital content specialist: *Brian Nacik*
Cover design: *Adam Rooke*
Typeface: *10/12 New Baskerville*
Compositor: *Black Dot Group*
Printer: *R. R. Donnelley*

Library of Congress Cataloging-in-Publication Data

Pearlman, Ellen.
Programming the Web using XML / Ellen Pearlman, Eileen Mullin.
p. cm. – (Web developer series)
ISBN 0-07-284550-3 (alk. paper) – ISBN 0-07-121504-2 (international : alk. paper)
1. XML (Document markup language) 2. Internet programming. 3. World Wide Web. I. Mullin, Eileen. II. Title, III. Series.
QA76.76.H94P43 2004
006.7'6–dc22

2003066462

INTERNATIONAL EDITION ISBN 0-07-121504-2

www.mhhe.com

McGraw-Hill Technology Education

At McGraw-Hill Technology Education, we publish instructional materials for the technology education market, in particular computer instruction in post-secondary education—from introductory courses in traditional four-year universities to continuing education and proprietary schools. McGraw-Hill Technology Education presents a broad range of innovative products—texts, lab manuals, study guides, testing materials, and technology-based training and assessment tools.

We realize that technology has created and will continue to create new mediums for professors and students to use in managing resources and communicating information to one another. McGraw-Hill Technology Education provides the most flexible and complete teaching and learning tools available as well as offer solutions to the changing world of teaching and learning. McGraw-Hill Technology Education is dedicated to providing the tools for today's instructors and students, which will enable them to successfully navigate the world of Information Technology.

- McGraw-Hill/Osborne—This division of The McGraw-Hill Companies is known for its best-selling Internet titles, Harley Hahn's *Internet & Web Yellow Pages*, and the *Internet Complete Reference.* For more information, visit Osborne at www.osborne.com.
- Digital Solutions—Whether you want to teach a class online or just post your "bricks-n-mortar" class syllabus, McGraw-Hill Technical Education is committed to publishing digital solutions. Taking your course online doesn't have to be a solitary adventure, nor does it have to be a difficult one. We offer several solutions that will allow you to enjoy all the benefits of having your course material online.
- Packaging Options—For more information about our discount options, contact your McGraw-Hill sales representative at 1-800-338-3987 or visit our web site at **www.mhhe.com/it**.

McGraw-Hill Technology Education is dedicated to providing the tools for today's instructors and students.

Preface

To the Student

This book gives a simple but extensive introduction to XML with its many derivations. The textbook contains everything necessary to learn XML and build on that basic understanding to understand how many different aspects of the Web and other display and nondisplay devices XML encompasses. If you are a Web developer, database administrator, graphic designer, system administrator, or even a computer-science pundit, this book is essential for you to grasp both the subtle and wide reach of XML in today's dynamic and changing technology environment.

Initially the Web dealt primarily with plain text and images through the use of HTML. The necessity for working with data in any form other than straight pages of typed information was an afterthought. XML has taken the art of data in its many forms to a new level. All student levels should be able to comprehend how XML newly defines data and how that data can be put to new and varied uses. After comparing HTML, XHTML, and XML, this book looks at creating Document Type Definitions and schemas and examines checking that information through the use of XML parsers and the expanded role of the multilingual capabilities of Unicode. It examines the role of the Document Object Model and then shows how to style basic XML though Cascading Style Sheets, eXtensible Style Sheets, and the linking of documents. The last section of the book examines the more complex subjects of Scalable Vector Graphics, Synchronized Multimedia Integration Language, databases, and, finally, the expanding use of Web Services. After completing all the chapters, exercises, and projects, you not only should be knowledgeable about XML, but also should be able to begin implementing it in your own projects.

The basic structure of XML and the enthusiasm with which the software development community has welcomed it makes XML certain to be around for many years. Whether you are working with only raw data or sophisticated media presentations, XML is certain to be involved with some part of your project planning. XML statements can be written in a simple text editor or in a sophisticated editor such as XML Spy. Many software vendors are integrating XML into their new releases in new and unexpected ways. The examples, exercises, projects, and code samples in this book will give you a solid foundation to understand any new uses of XML that will show up in the future, knowledge that will not become irrelevant after just a year or two.

To the Teacher

The students do not need a programming background to begin to grasp the concepts and uses of XML, though they do need to understand how to navigate and use the Web. After the core components of elements and attributes are understood, a student can begin to make rudimentary statements. Because XML touches on so many areas, students who are not computer science majors can greatly benefit from this book as well as those starting out in that field.

Each chapter breaks down into fundamental programming concepts about a specific aspect of XML, something that was unimaginable just five years ago, when XML was just emerging as a standard. Using the coding examples, students will very quickly learn how to code and correct their mistakes. The Hands On Projects at the end of the chapters build on the core concepts developed in the chapter and real-world examples are also used to illustrate more sophisticated uses in a business or enterprise environment. This book is an overview of many aspects of XML but does not delve too deeply into the technical side, as there are other texts designed to do that. What it does do is give a thorough introduction to XML and allow students to use that knowledge to build on.

Each chapter leads to the next and there are always examples from real life to reinforce the lessons. Each chapter highlights key vocabulary terms and also asks relevant questions, points out technical tips, and supplies specialized alerts and advice.

Following is a short outline describing the contents of all of the chapters.

- Chapters 1, 2, and 3 go over the basic structure of XML and show how to write simple XML statements. The chapters then go on to compare and contrast XML, HTML, and XHTML. Chapter 1 discusses the history of XML and how it works with multiple platforms and devices to share content. Chapter 2 shows how XHTML documents differ from HTML and investigates namespaces. Chapter 3 shows the overall structure of an XML document; looks at the difference between well-formed and valid XML; and examines elements, attributes, entities, and comments within the context of Document Type Definitions. After completing these chapters, students will be familiar with SGML, XHTML, DTDs, well-formed and valid XML, simple DTDs, elements, attributes, entities, and comments.
- Chapters 4, 5, and 6 cover how to build a Document Type Definition and related XML Schemas and how these files are parsed though different editors. They also look at XML's multilanguage capabilities though the use of Unicode. Chapter 4 shows the basic function and syntax of a Document Type Definition and its internal and external subsets, how elements work, and when to use them with attributes. Although the book does not

set up universal standards for Document Type Definitions, it enables the student to quickly comprehend and read these statements. Chapter 5 expands on the structure of an XML statement and explores schemas, an expanded alternative to Document Type Definitions. It defines schema namespaces and shows the difference between `simpleType` schema data and `complexType` schema data. It then shows how child elements and minimum and maximum occurrences of those elements are set. Finally, it explains how to make intelligent choices when designing a schema. Chapter 6 illustrates how an XML statement is parsed and looks at a variety of different programs and how they can treat the exact same statement differently. It briefly looks at the multilingual capabilities of Unicode and explores the different character sets and typefaces that are available to use with it. After completing these chapters students will be familiar and comfortable with markup, structure, and editing XML, and will understand the importance of rigorous coding. Students also will have a simple framework to build XML statements and a clear picture of the importance of step-by-step coding.

- Chapters 7, 8, and 9 are primarily concerned with the simple design and linkage of XML, and show how some of the same principles that apply to HTML can be relevant for styling XML. Chapter 7 covers CSS stylesheets and how they are used with XML documents and explains the difference between CSS and XSL formats. Chapter 8 shows how XSL can transform XML documents into HTML and how templates govern these transformations. It also examines the three components of XSL: XSLT, XPath, and XSL Formatting Objects. Chapter 9 explains how to link specific parts of XML documents using XLink and how single-direction and multidirectional links can be built. Finally, it shows how to use XPointer to point to any section of a target document on either a local or remote Web Server. After completion of these chapters, students will have a basic understanding of how to style XML documents with coding and templates, and how to link those documents to each other and to servers. In addition, students will understand how basic styling of XML documents works and how these documents can be linked to themselves and other documents.

- Chapters 10, 11, and 12 increase in complexity and cover scripting with the Document Object Model, as well as introducing graphic and media uses of XML vis-à-vis SVG and SMIL. Chapter 10 shows how elements and attributes can be represented as objects and how XML data can be loaded and displayed using simple JavaScript statements to make a site work with on-the-fly interactive capabilities. Chapter 11 shows the benefits of coding visual objects in SVG to save bandwidth and make editing of visual information simpler than editing in Flash. Chapter 12 shows how SMIL is now being deployed in multimedia presentations and discusses the critical differences between SMIL 1.0 and SMIL 2.0. After completion of these chapters, students will be ready to design, program, and view simple visual examples of the visual representations of XML.

- Chapters 13 and 14 take XML into even more complex terrain by showing how XML is used with databases and Web Services. Chapter 13 explores how XML is used with a relational database and discusses when to use a native XML database. It gives the student an overview of how database vendors use XML. Chapter 14 explains how XML underlies Web Services and looks at the three components of Web Services—SOAP, UDDI, and WSDL—and shows how they are used to "publish, find, and bind." The student will learn in these chapters how to go on to the next level of whatever subgroup of XML they intend to specialize in, and will have a thorough understanding of how to integrate XML within their own programming specializations.
- There are also lists of questions, exercises, and code examples from all the chapters as well as alerts and advice, tech tips, and hands on projects. The appendices provide additional information to supplement your lessons.

Acknowledgments

My eternal thanks to the McGraw-Hill team: Lisa, Dan, and all the other editors and diligent production staff who worked so thoroughly to make sure this book got out on time. Special thanks go to Dan Silverburg, who initially acquired and shepherded the project, and Lisa Chin-Johnson, who took it over and skillfully managed it. The entire team, from tech editing to proofreading to production, was extraordinarily helpful. The academic reviewers and professional programmers who reviewed each chapter offered many suggestions that made this a better textbook and showed infinite patience in the process.

Hats off to Dennis Green, Director of the CTA (Computer Technology and Applications) Program at Columbia University, for letting me first teach XML before it achieved its raging popularity, as well as Sven Travis at Parsons School of Design, M.A. Program in Digital Design for allowing initial forays into SVG and SMIL and Michael Randazzo and Zee Dempster at the New School University Computing Center for taking the XML leap in 1999.

Bob Albert, of RealNetworks, Inc. Strategic Relations Group for helping with conversion codes as well as Erika Shaffer, Director PR, RealNetworks for taking me through the maze, and Tina Eisinger, Marketing Manager at Altova GmbH, the XML Spy Company for complete, for copies of XML SPY.

To the members of the "Web Cabal" a.k.a. Link Tank, for thoughts on future uses of XML and beyond. Enormous and eternal thanks to Ken Jordan for being a great friend and initiating the collaborations with the VAN (Virtual Arts Network), the Walker Art Museum and the Ford and Rockefeller Foundations for having the foresight to fund the VAN studies.

Also to Jonathan Spira and David Goldes of Basex, Inc. experts in collaborative business knowledge for supplying underlying technologies and expertise. Finally, eternally and always thanks to David Fugate at Waterside Productions, my agent who, through the entire hand holding is, simply and always, the greatest!

—Ellen Pearlman

For Ross, from four to forever

> **"Let us dedicate ourselves to the task of simplifying the Internet's interfaces and to educating all that are interested in its use."**
>
> —Vinton Cerf, The Internet Is for Everyone

I'm most grateful to my family, friends, and colleagues who help me dedicate my time in a small way to these tasks.

I'm obliged to the students (kids and grownups alike) and parents at GenuineClass who continually remind me of the joys of teaching and learning about technology. Instructors Russell Dale, Josh Kaden, and Chippy deserve special thanks for helping me do what I do by doing what they do.

I'm grateful to Adam Chng, Titu Sarder, Russell Sarder, and the extended team at Netcom Information Technologies for their support and resources as I juggled writing, teaching, and entrepreneurial angst.

Warmest thanks go to my parents, Eileen and Jim, my siblings and their spouses, and my nieces and nephews, who graciously understood that I wouldn't be using their photos this time for the book. I'm grateful to my extended family—including Irene, Nat, Jared, Bari, and the whole Terry clan—for always lending a collective sympathetic ear.

I owe a debt of thanks to my dear friends Neil deMause, Mich Nelson, Lee Steele, Jonathan Cott, and my sister Kathleen for always letting me vent and then making me laugh.

My sincerest thanks go to Developmental Editor Lisa Chin-Johnson for her eagle-eyed attention and supportive e-mail during the writing and editing stages. I'm also grateful to Sponsoring Editor Don Hull, Project Manager Kristin Puscas, Production Supervisor Gina Hangos, Technical Editor Sal Rodriguez, and the copyediting and design teams for the final good-looking results.

The biggest family-sized bucket of thanks goes to Ross, my husband and true companion. The Kodak moments and major life events we went through together while this book was being written really take my breath away, just like he always does.

—Eileen Mullin

Brief Contents

Contents

CHAPTER 14

Programming the Web Using 

CHAPTER 1

An Overview of XML

LEARNING OBJECTIVES

1. To learn the history of XML.
2. To gain an understanding of XML's importance working with multiple platforms.
3. To learn about content and data sharing with XML.
4. To learn how to use XML.
5. To learn the drawbacks of XML.

Data are now managed across diverse platforms such as Linux, DOS, or Mac, or in networked environments like a business enterprise. If you include browsers and devices such as mobile phones or a PDA, another layer of complexity is added. Finally, if different foreign languages, which all of these user interfaces are capable of displaying, are added, there has to be a way to accommodate this intricate data seamlessly. This has led to the accelerated development of XML, which stands for Extensible Markup Language.

Learning the History: The Many Incarnations of SGML into XML

Underlying the alphabet soup of Web dialects found in HTML, XHTML, and XML is the underlying concept of markup languages—the "ML" that ends each of these acronyms. Markup languages contain not only the codes that enable computers to interpret data, but also descriptive information to help humans understand the function of each element in a document. Markup languages have indicators called **tags.** Tags are first read and then processed by an appropriately enabled processor. Researcher Charles Goldfarb coined the term "markup language" in the late 1960s while developing a project at IBM to automate the processing of legal documents. IBM adopted GML (Generalized Markup Language) and used it to build **mainframe**-based publishing systems that were widely used to produce technical documentation across the firm. This helped popularize GML's approach to generating automated documents, and eventually led to the development of Standard Generalized Markup Language (SGML).

SGML is actually a **meta-language,** that is, a language that describes other text markup languages. XML's function as its own meta-language allows it to create XML-based languages that create either documents or files used by a variety of organizations, developers, and consolidated industries. While not a markup system in and of itself, SGML is a programming language used to build working languages. The grammar of such a language is called its **Document Type Definition (DTD)** and contains its parts of speech. XML refers to these parts of speech as the attributes, entities, elements, and notations, something we will look at more closely in Chapter 3. Also, parts of the speech of XML can be further extrapolated in a structure called a **schema,** a more sophisticated and inclusive type of DTD, which we will examine more closely in Chapter 5. For now, just note that a markup language's DTD is used to provide information about that document's structure and formatting. Furthermore, elements in these documents are often allowed to contain other elements, a feature known as a **hierarchy.** This type of element hierarchy also can be envisioned as a branching tree diagram as shown in Figure 1.1.

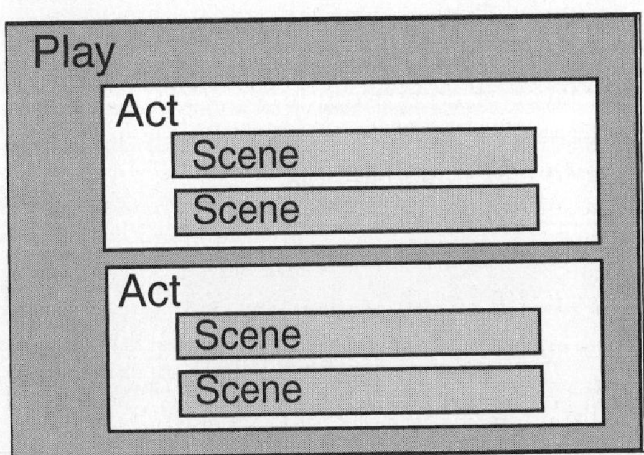

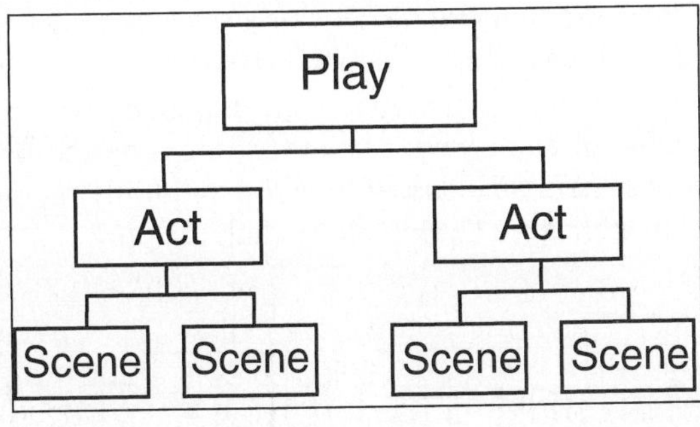

FIGURE 1.1 Tree Hierarchy

Grammatical mistakes made while using a markup language—much like those in a spoken language like English—immediately make their presence known. Elementary school teachers nationwide wince every time they hear a child say "I didn't do nothing" or "I ain't got my homework." Similarly, the grammar of a markup language must be followed, or else the software tools used to interpret the markup may not comprehend the message at all.

XML itself is also a meta-markup language, and one of its derivatives such as SVG (Scalable Vector Graphics) is written in an XML-derived syntax. SVG is its own markup language, and one we will examine more closely in Chapter 11. There are many XML subset languages. For a current list go to

http://www.w3.org

and look on the left-hand side of the page, as new XML derivatives are being added there all the time. W3 is the World Wide Web Consortium, or three W's. And remember that an XML document, in and of itself, isn't capable of doing anything. It needs a program of one type or another to interact with.

To make sure the grammar of a markup language is correct, a **parser** is used. A parser is a grammar checker for markup languages. A parser compares an HTML or XML, or even SVG, document against the grammar (the DTD or even the schema, depending on the parser used) in a process called **validation,** to ensure there are no mistakes. If a document follows the rules listed in its DTD (or schema), then it is said to be *valid.* If the document has markup errors that contradict the rules of the DTD (or schema), then it would be labeled *invalid.* We will investigate different types of parsers more extensively in Chapter 6.

As an example, consider the following XML tag:

```
<team>Yankees</team>
```

If you made a typographical error while typing this line, the tag and its contents might erroneously appear as

```
<team<Yankees</team>
```

This would be an invalid tag, because an XML tag requires a beginning (<) and ending (>) bracket, known as a **delimiter,** surrounding the tag name. Since the ending delimiter does not appear where it should, the tag will not be recognized correctly by an XML parser.

The major breakthrough ushered in by SGML was that it offered a series of rules for making documents publishable across different media—whether print or CD-ROM, for example—and across different computer platforms. In addition, SGML supports very powerful searching features, letting large information repositories be rearranged into individual documents and used for different purposes. These capabilities were immediately of interest for large corporations and agencies that produced large quantities of documents and could sustain using a single standard format internally. Besides IBM, early participants in developing applications using SGML included the U.S. Department of Defense and the Association of American Publishers.

> **Tech Tip**
>
> You can create SGML, HTML, or XML files by typing in a simple text editor, or by using software tools that take care of much of the manual effort for you.

Developed in 1974 and ratified by the International Standards Organization (ISO) in 1986, SGML remained largely unchanged during its first decade in use. Although it's a tribute to the robustness of SGML that so much time passed before even minor revisions were considered necessary to the specification, the very power of SGML hindered the development of SGML-aware applications because of the extent of the programming required to ensure compliance.

The time line in Figure 1.2 shows how many document markup programs and publishing standards took off after the advent of SGML.

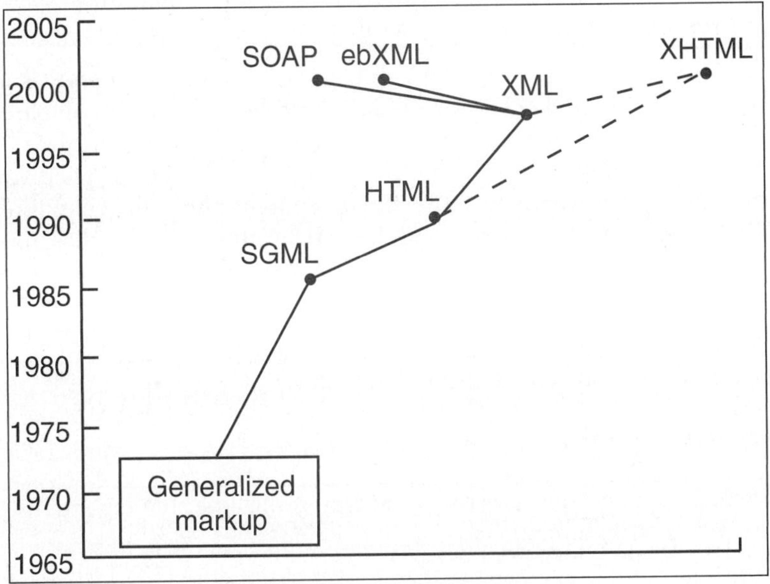

FIGURE 1.2 Advances in Markup Languages over Time

By the early 1990s, the Internet was already an established medium for information retrieval and communication. It provided a ready platform for a hypertext mechanism, but a tagging language was needed to provide a linking mechanism as well as basic text formatting. Toward this end, in 1991 researcher Tim Berners-Lee at the European Laboratory for Particle Physics (CERN) released a hypertext markup language called **HTML** using SGML syntax. In its original incarnation, though, HTML did not fully implement SGML principles; only over time was HTML revised to a fully SGML-compatible application.

XML itself became a full W3C recommendation in February 1998, written by Tim Bray and teams from Sun Microsystems, Microsoft, and the University of Illinois at Chicago. It was originally developed by the XML Working Group in 1996, chaired by Jon Bosak. It created its syntax by making a subset from SGML (ISO 8879: 1986(E)). It also uses the associated standards of Unicode (ISO/IEC 10646) and other ISO standards for language and country name codes. XML documents contain either parsed or unparsed character data. Some of the data is composed of characters and some is composed of markup. Markup itself describes the way information is laid out and its inherent structure.

However, there were some very significant differences between XML and HTML. HTML had a certain set of predefined tags, which were augmented in subsequent versions, until it morphed into an application of XML with **XHTML.** HTML displays information. XML can supply its own tags and lets developers structure and define what type of information goes into their documents. Its primary focus is to describe data or information.

The ultimate goal with all of these standards is to make machine-understandable data on the World Wide Web fully sharable by automated programs and people. This means the Web needs to have the ability to scale, or grow larger or smaller based on the needs of the user. It also means that as new programs are written, older programs can be integrated into newer versions. This overall need is being investigated by W3C with an activity group called the Semantic Web, to make sure there is coherence in the way information displays, automates, links, and is reused across the Web and beyond.

Creating One Document for Multiple Platforms and Devices

XML is an **open standard** that very clearly spells out data structures and their associated content. It does not overload applications with legacy, or leftover data, nor does it depend on a proprietary or specialized system. A **proprietary** system means it is accessible only to a special group or uses a special kind of technology. XML does streamline data exchange, making it cheaper and faster.

In the past, getting into a **database,** or a computer-coded information storage retrieval system, required development skills using high-level database programming languages such as **SQL.** It was very confusing to keep track of different field names and make them relate to one another. XML cut through all those complexities. Its structure is defined by its DTD, explaining both the content in the data and the types of names used to define the data. XML documents must have a DTD associated with them. This means, in a simple sense, XML must define the ingredients allowed inside. If you were making a cake, you would be allowed to put in sugar, but you would not be allowed to put in cough syrup—unless you wanted to make a cake no one could eat. Of course, converting **legacy data,** or data from older systems, into a format XML can use presents a challenge, but there are many developers working on these older systems to bring them up to speed.

However, even as XML 1.0 was being written in February 1998, it became clear to its developers at W3C (World Wide Web Consortium) that the syntax and structure of a DTD was limited. They were already creating a Schema Recommendation to set the framework of a new modeling definition, called the XML Schema Definition Language (XSD) as part of their XML Activity Group. In XML, a schema is used to define a class of XML documents, and so the term *instance document* is often used to describe an XML document that conforms to a particular schema. The first working draft was released in April 2000, and a Candidate Recommendation followed in October 2000 divided into schema structures and datatypes. In May 2001, the W3C's XML Schema Part 1: Structures and XML Schema Part 2: Datatypes became official W3C recommendations. We will examine schemas in depth in Chapter 5.

For example, if you wanted to write a DTD about automobiles, you would have to make a separate DTD for each category such as SUV, compact, station wagon, hatchback, two door, and so forth. Schemas allow all variations of a DTD to be incorporated for reuse and sharing between common standards. Another example is in the United States, where a date is written in the form 05-22-2004, but in Europe the same date is written 22-05-2004. An XML schema could easily interpret a date in both ways. However, schemas are not easy to write, and tend to contain enormous amounts of information that is difficult to track and follow.

HTML (Hypertext Markup Language) delivers images and text to a browser, but that is all it does. XML works *only* with data, though that data now consists of voice, images, and even wireless frequencies. For example, think about a library having a million books. Without a card catalog, you wouldn't know where anything was located, and neither would the librarian. A card catalog is an agreed-upon system that all librarians make use of with what is called the Dewey Decimal System. What if every chapter or even every paragraph could be cataloged, categorized, and accessed electronically in every document somewhat in the same way? This would allow the ability to search individually on the **content** of a page, not just its subject title. It would mean you could conceivably mark up a simple document, or a structured record like an invoice or contact card or an object with data. But the use of that kind of markup is larger than that. You could even mark up methods used by a **Java object** (a Java-coded programming object), as well as an actual data record that answers a specific query in a database program.

In order to deliver information to multiple platforms, there is usually one centralized database where the information is stored. These databases are accessed either through a Web browser or a proprietary application interface, built with either **Visual Basic** or some other programming language such as SQL. Think of an article displayed on a Web page that contains a clickable link to a larger story. On the Web the clickable link is displayed on the screen in front of you. What if you are using a mobile phone or a **personal digital assistant (PDA)** that has a limited display screen? Probably only the headline will display on a small handheld device. The problem is to feed this information out to different environments at the same time where it will make sense in terms of the limits of the display devices and their corresponding bandwidth requirements.

Once properly coded, this allows tremendous reuse of the same data in different ways, also called **repurposed.** The ability to repurpose data is one of the best features of XML, as shown in Figure 1.3.

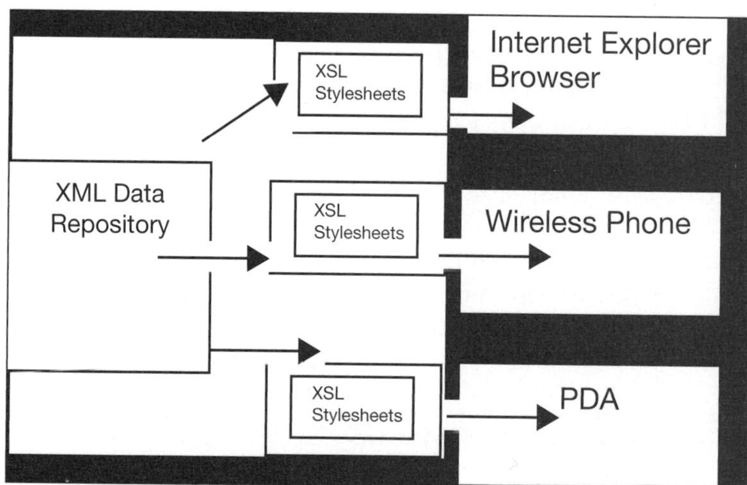

FIGURE 1.3 Repurposing Information

What would be a very simple example of this? Think of a news site. Suppose the Yankees are in the World Series (Go Yankees!). All the relevant information, stats, video clips, history, and player bios are in the XML Data Repository, or database that the Yankees homesite keeps on their database server. The server has coded information on how to display a Web page in Internet Explorer or Netscape. This Web page has relevant links and information that connects to everything a Yankees fan could want to know. Another **stylesheet** could be set up to only pull information about the current game, a live time score, and perhaps a player's basic statistics, useful for people who live in low-bandwidth areas and can't load all the eye-popping graphics. The PDA

IMPORTANT

You can use XML data again and again, once you set up a basic definition (DTD).

stylesheet might be set up to display in color, and even have a small area to view the scores of other baseball games that are going on simultaneously (like the Mets!).

Using XML for Data Exchange

Advice

Data can be words, pictures, sound, moving images, pure information, and data that remains invisible to the user or is mined for information.

Data in this context is information that has been digitized in order to move it across a network. The words you are reading right now are data when they are written on a computer and sent to the publisher of this book over the Internet. But that's not all. Pictures, and even moving images, can be data. There is pure data that does not necessarily need to be displayed, such as large records of payroll or financial information. There is data that is "mined," or remotely examined for information, such as who might want to subscribe to *Baseball Magazine* since they spend all that time on their PDA following the ball scores. But how can all of this data communicate with itself over such different devices and platforms? And how can it all make sense?

XML addressed this issue right from the start. It has divided basic sets of information into DTDs, or Document Type Definitions. We will examine DTDs extensively in Chapter 5 but in Figure 1.4 you can see how extensive the cate-

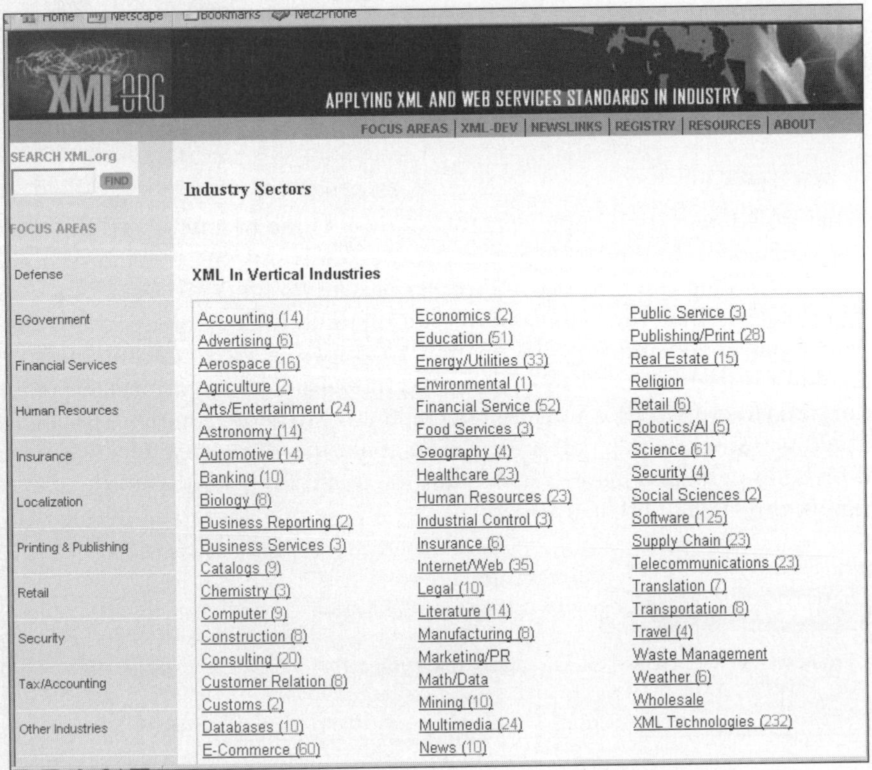

FIGURE 1.4 XML.org Web Site Showing Different Categories of XML by Industry

gorization is within the world of XML. So let's use our baseball fan as an example. Since XML is a markup language that describes data, our baseball fan is in for a treat. She especially likes to follow Derek Jeter. So a made-up XML tag might look something like this:

```
<sport>baseball
  <team>Yankees</team>
  <player>Derek Jeter</player>
  <stats>
    <numbhomeruns>45</numbhomeruns>
  </stats>
  </sport>
```

Here we have our first XML statement. In order to create different definitions, it is necessary to use tags. Every tag starts with a beginning (<) and ending (>) delimiter and each tag has a beginning and end tag (</>). With a real XML document, definitions must be well-formed and valid, something we will look at more closely in Chapter 3. Well-formed basically means that all tags are balanced and have end tags, and that there are openings and closings for all definitions. Valid means that the tagging system and definitions in the DTD are all in compliance. The definitions of the DTD are specified in the official recommendation maintained by W3C. That means, if you say your cake can contain sugar, and by accident you put in hot chili paste, it would not be valid because your recipe does not allow for hot chili paste. And neither does your tongue.

Tech Tip

< opens an XML tag.

>closes an XML tag.

<>encloses an opening XML statement.

</> encloses an ending XML statement.

This is a hierarchical list where the type of sport is used as our first characterization. Then, after we establish the sport is indeed baseball, we have divided baseball further into team, player, and stats (statistics). Under stats we have chosen to highlight, or discuss, only the number of homeruns. Of course, we could use any statistic—RBIs, fouls, whatever. The stats and sport tags are then closed. Now think of multiplying all of this information by the dozens of teams and hundreds of players and thousands of categories and many years of statistics and it becomes rather overwhelming.

On the Web, every statistic about Derek Jeter might be instantly accessible, whereas on a wireless cell phone, our intrepid Yankees fan might have to go into each menu item one hierarchical level at a time by pressing only one button on the receiver of the phone. At this point, there is no definition of how to display the raw information. That comes later with **Extensible Stylesheet Language (XSL)** and **Cascading Style Sheets (CSS),** both of which are XML-compliant. For a more in-depth explanation of what these are, see Chapter 8 for XSL and Chapter 7 for CSS.

This example discusses a server (where the information is kept) to browser (where it is displayed on the Web) or handheld device display (like a cell phone), but XML can pass data just from application to application and from only platform to platform. It is completely database-neutral, which means any database can access it. This ability allows batch processing, something formerly done only with the complex and cumbersome system of **electronic data interchange (EDI). Batch processing** is when you process large amounts of data all at once, such as when a utility company issues all their bills at the same time. In fact, there is a large consortium of XML and EDI developers who are working together to make EDI convert to and be compatible with XML. For an in-depth look at this, point your Web browser to http://www.geocities.com/WallStreet/Floor/5815/guide.htm. In order for all this to work smoothly, specialized industry vocabularies have to be created (i.e., Human Resources, with specific tags such as `<datehired>`). Information can be pulled out precisely on an as-needed basis such as "how many home runs did Derek Jeter hit in 2003"? A tag like `<amountofhomeruns>` can be set up to integrate perfectly with HTML, now renamed in its newest version to XHTML, to comply more closely with XML's underlying structure. And remember, it is a language human and machines can both understand. Best of all, it works with **metadata,** or data about itself, which means it can know when to link to other like-minded pages if necessary (How many home runs did Sammy Sosa hit?). The best way to think of metadata is to think about our analogy of the card catalog. It contains information that points you toward the information you are looking for, but is not the actual information itself. That is metadata.

The data can then be filtered by the appropriate application, because the XML structure has defined the appropriate category, and the designer or developer can choose how much information to actually display. This process allows seamless integration with complex middleware architecture. **Middleware** is an overall term that defines any programming that mediates between two separate and different programs. It also provides ways in which the different layers can communicate through messaging services. When middleware ties together many different systems in an organization or enterprise, it is called **enterprise application integration (EAI).** It also can, when written into an XML schema, reposition itself to work with Java classes and hierarchies, part of the **Java** programming language.

Content Sharing with XML

The Web has allowed communications to go global and become cheap. But, in order to work effectively, standards must match up worldwide. Otherwise, how would Japan talk to Spain or the United States to Egypt or Russia to Ghana? The way content appears to the end user on the Web, like you or me is visual, and uses specific standards like HTML, **Graphics Interchange Format (GIF), Joint Photographic Experts Group (JPEG),** and others. This allows a designer or developer to create a page once and display it on the browsers of thousands of different users at the same time.

But, as mentioned previously, these standards are insufficient to represent actual data and its associative content. What is the difference between content and data? Data is raw information; it is not assembled, edited, presented, or analyzed. Content provides us with information that is useful for our work and lives.

The *Wordsmyth* dictionary defines content as

> 1. the language accompanying a particular word or phrase and thus often influencing its meaning or effect, 2. The set of circumstances or events in which a particular event occurs; situation.

This means content needs a context. Managing and categorizing that much information necessitate a **taxonomy** (from Greek *taxis,* meaning arrangement or division, and *nomos,* meaning law). This is part of what XML developers are doing: creating and categorizing information guided by input from many specific industries. Taxonomies are usually created by a combination of methods including working with real people like librarians, users, and analysts in the field. Taxonomies also use automatic **spidering** of terms (searching the Web with an artificial agent) and finally the use of sophisticated linguistic analysis tools. There is a big difference in meaning between "great" and "grate" besides the obvious spelling differences, and tools, especially those that will be used with **VoiceML,** or XML for voice, must be programmed to understand those differences. Various other standards written in XML need the help of taxonomies, but not the **XML standards** themselves such as those we will look at in Chapter 9 like Xlink, XPath, and so forth.

Sharing content, then, can happen in many ways. Some of the most important ways to share content is across different platforms and different devices. Repositories of many sources can be searched simultaneously, including proprietary sources if permissions are granted by the person or organization that holds that information. This means that if you performed a search on Derek Jeter, not only could you view news stories on him, but if the Baseball Hall of Fame allowed access, you could go into their archives as well and see, for example, what team was playing against what other team 50 years ago today. Usually these data repositories are made up of numerous incompatible formats, but XML has the ability to convert this legacy, or older, information to a format that can be used by many sources, if it is scripted correctly.

Actually, this is one of the Web's largest faults. Think of it this way. If your doctor writes a prescription for you, currently he or she writes it with a pen on a prescription pad and then you bring it over to a pharmacy to be filled. But what if your doctor wrote it on a PDA and it immediately went into a database that could be accessed by any pharmacy? And you could have your choice of where to fill it, all without paper? This ability already exists with a system that uses iPaq handhelds with software from Allscripts Healthcare Solutions, a company in Chicago.

Of course, the downside of this revolves around privacy concerns, accuracy, and the right to not have your information placed into a database, issues each and every one of us should thoroughly consider.

The implications of having this ability are far-reaching. For instance, one college course could be written on different levels: one for a state college and others for different community colleges tiered for different levels of understanding (see Figure 1.5).

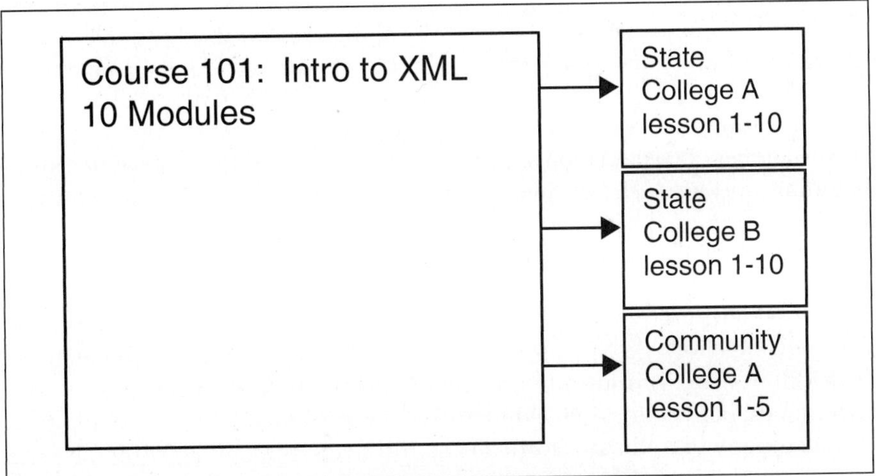

FIGURE 1.5 Same Information Sent to Three Different Colleges

In this example, the same course is sent out to two state colleges in its entirety of 10 weeks and to one community college as a mini five-week course. The information, therefore, does not have to be written and rewritten, but can be reused in however many sections as is necessary. Technically speaking, the same course could even be used for different languages, and a Spanish language edition could be made available as well.

On a more sophisticated level, there is a lot to be thought through in content management. Managing content and searching through that content require the use of different software, but essentially the tasks are related. There are two basic ways to search through enormous amounts of Web content. The most common is where a spider or artificial intelligence preprogrammed **bot** is used that **trolls,** or crawls over, a Web site and indexes it according to a preset algorithm and presetup static index. This is the method used by Google, Hotbot, Lycos, Yahoo, and other common Web search sites. Another approach, not normally mentioned, is a more dynamic one. The search is actually turned into a database query submitted to an underlying database and the results are received in HTML format that are then displayed to the end user.

Good sites to investigate this further can be found at

http://www.bottechnology.com/latest_articles/index.html
http://www.robotstxt.org/wc/faq.html

If wireless, faxes, HTML, and call processing can all talk to each other with a common standard, this means that almost every device is being set up to talk to almost every other device and platform. But remember that XML is still an evolving standard. As more and more people think of more uses with more standards, who knows, maybe one day you could turn on and off your TV at home via your cell phone. Actually, that is a reality now, with a company that is marketing a product that lets college students check the availability of washing machines in their dorm. To read about it, go to

http://www.ibm.com/news/us/2002/09/032.html

So how does this manifest in the real world? *PC World* magazine runs a Web site called *PC World Online*. The site is 8,000 pages deep and averages nine million page viewers a month and must constantly update and refresh its site. This means it has to obtain information from various sources and those sources are in a number of different formats.

For example, in the case of the featured article of the month from the print version, it is up to 10 pages long and has many sidebars, charts, screen shots, and graphic images. It is designed using Quark Express. It must then be converted to HTML for the Web and have a subset of licensee-specific formats. There must be a similar look and feel between the Web version and the print version of the magazine. The online editors also deliver special content that is not in the print version.

All of this content has to be fed out to different sources. There are special email-only editions of subscriber-specific information covering, for instance, flash memory. Licensee information has to be modeled in ASCII and Quark. On the Web, the HTML is divided into at least five different channel streams and sections, and has to allow itself to be printed from the browser. Plus the content has to be set up so it can be used in the future, in wireless delivery, for example.

Traditionally, the magazine had used a simple template tagged to a database. But that was no longer sufficient both because that information could not be transformed easily into Web content and because it allowed only one database "field" for text, so larger articles spilled over on the Web.

The editors at *PC World* created their own DTD that had definitions for their specific needs, such as the parts in an article with headlines, paragraphs, "tips" section, and product reviews. Using a third-party vendor's software, they converted their Quark document markup to XML, and then the XML complied with their DTD. They also allowed a URL definition to be included in the DTD so links to other sites were allowed. Then article information could be retrieved on an as-needed basis, either as just a headline or a full article.

The articles are stored in special XML-enabled databases. When someone wants to view the article, a specific styling template is called up if appropriate (XSL) and translates the XML into, for instance, HTML for viewing on the Web. It can even be displayed as an insert on someone else's Web site, such as Dow Jones or *The Wall Street Journal*. So this is a good example of "reuse" of the same information. *PC World* can also, using XML, tag product reviews to specific requests, or tailor requests one at a time to the needs of a specific user. *PC World* has said that using XML cut down the time of going from print to the Web from two days to two hours. That is because the editors actually enter their copy into XML-enabled sections, and programs on the resident server create the HTML output. And server software can hone search capabilities within each article. With the use of XSL style sheets, XML can go directly to XML-enabled browsers and let the browsers themselves format the article.

Advice

XML is great for reusing or repurposing data, and different stylesheets can display the same data different ways. Also remember that XML is database neutral.

Limitations of XML

XML does not solve all problems for all situations. DTDs were the original way to describe the structure of information within an XML document and language, and as we saw above, they were derived from the structure of SGML. But W3C had already realized the limitation of DTDs when the first edition of XML 1.0 was accepted in February 1998. W3C was already creating a Schema Recommendation to set the framework of a new modeling definition, called the XML Schema Definition Language (XSD). The problem with DTDs is that their syntax is not particularly flexible. Documents in XML follow one syntax and DTDs follow another. It's hard to read attribute list declarations and it is very difficult for many organizations that use precise pattern data to share that data because oftentimes it cannot be defined in exactly the same way. Sophisticated descriptions and shared markup vocabularies are not allowed to mix in a DTD. Plus XML has no native data transformation facilities, and usually a third-party vendor has to develop those facilities, making for a costly transformation of both legacy data and data that has to be filtered.

Both DTDs and Schemas perform validation against data, but DTDs are not capable of complying with C++ and Java classes, also referred to as instance documents. Schemas can comply. Many businesses still use one type of XML category DTD to describe their goods and services. The most difficult aspect of a DTD is that it employs its own syntax, which is not the same as XML syntax. DTDs can't describe the actual data contained in elements. There is no way in a basic XML statement to combine all categories. This is the reason the XML Schema Definition Language was created. It can accommodate combining different categories. In Figures 1.6 and 1.7 you can see a list of different categories, including DTDs, schemas, and the **Semantic Web** that W3C is working on.

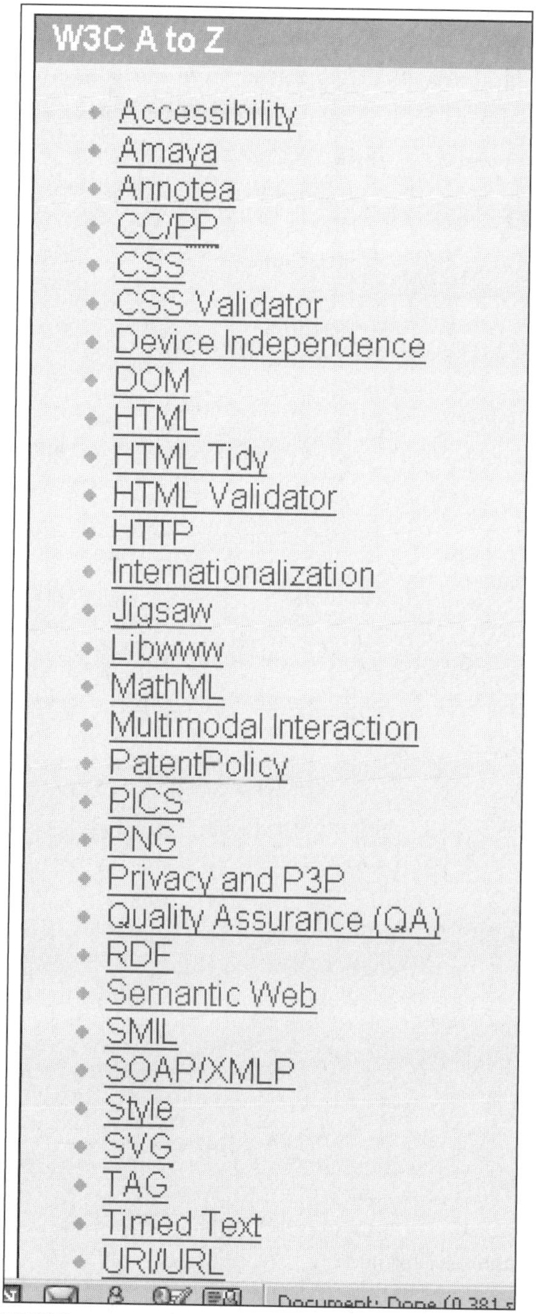

W3C A to Z

- Accessibility
- Amaya
- Annotea
- CC/PP
- CSS
- CSS Validator
- Device Independence
- DOM
- HTML
- HTML Tidy
- HTML Validator
- HTTP
- Internationalization
- Jigsaw
- Libwww
- MathML
- Multimodal Interaction
- PatentPolicy
- PICS
- PNG
- Privacy and P3P
- Quality Assurance (QA)
- RDF
- Semantic Web
- SMIL
- SOAP/XMLP
- Style
- SVG
- TAG
- Timed Text
- URI/URL

Document: Done (0.381 s

FIGURE. 1.6 Categories of XML Development from W3C

- Voice
- WAI
- WebCGM
- Web Services
- Web Ontology
- XForms
- XHTML
- XLink
- XML
- XML Base
- XML Encryption
- XML Key Management
- XML Query
- XML Schema
- XML Signature
- XPath
- XPointer
- XSL and XSLT

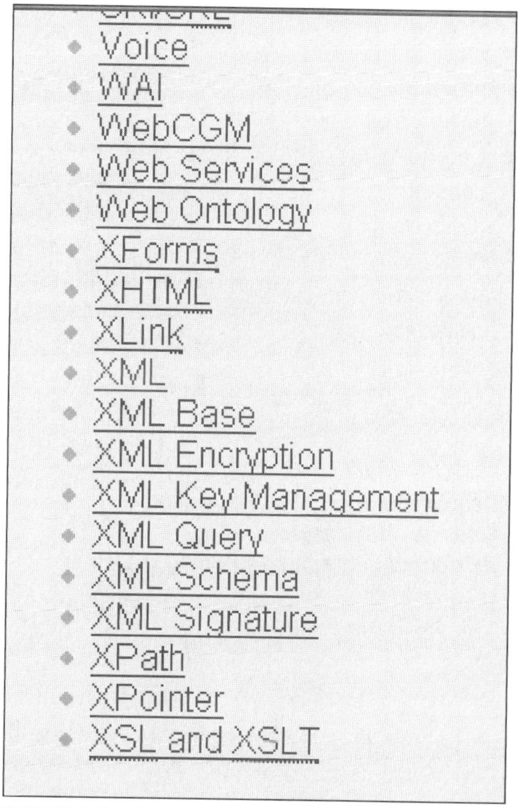

FIGURE 1.7 Categories of XML Development from W3C

Key Terms

batch processing
bot
browsers
business enterprise
Cascading Style Sheets (CSS)
content
cross platform
data
database
delimiter
devices
Document Type Definition (DTD)
DOS
electronic data interchange (EDI)
enterprise application integration (EAI)
Extensible Stylesheet Language (XSL)
full-field searching
Graphics Interchange Format (GIF)
hierarchy
HTML
Java
Java object
Joint Photographic Experts Group (JPEG)
key field
legacy data
Linux
Mac
mainframe
metadata
meta-language
middleware
open standard
parser
personal digital assistant (PDA)
platforms
proprietary
repurpose
schema
Semantic Web
spidering
SQL
stylesheet
tags
taxonomy
troll
validation
Visual Basic
VoiceML
XHTML
XML standards
XSL

Review Questions

1. Why was it necessary for XML to come into existence?
2. What does “ml” stand for?
3. What is a tag and what does it do?
4. What is a meta-language?
5. What is a DTD and what does it contain?
6. What does W3 stand for?
7. What does a parser do?
8. What is the relationship between HTML and XML? What are their differences?
9. What is a proprietary system?
10. Define legacy data.
11. What is XSD?
12. What is the difference between content and data?
13. What does repurposing data do?
14. What can data consist of?
15. Simply stated, what is the difference between valid and well-formed?
16. What is batch processing?
17. What is middleware?
18. What is a taxonomy and why is it important in the development of XML?
19. What is XSL?

Case Study

Go to http://www.ebxml.org/, the site for Electronic Business XML sponsored by the United Nations (UN/CEFACT) and Oasis, the standards body that runs XML.ORG, a noncommercial portal that delivers information on XML. Clink on the "Presentations" link on the left-hand side, and read though the e-government and European Electronic Market articles. Feel free to read any other articles on business protocols and ebXML.

Go to http://www.voicexmlcentral.com/, a site for a voice XML–enabled search engine, and read about the developments in VoiceML.

Hands On Project

Inktomi has created an enterprisewide XML-enabled search engine. To read about it, go to http://xml.coverpages.org/InktomiSearchToolkit200205.html. Then point your browser to http://www.inktomi.com/products/search/nativexsdk.html. Scroll down the page and look at the technical specifications and see how many of them you recognize from this chapter. Discuss the ones you don't recognize in class with your instructor.

IBM has joined with "Hard to Find Auto Parts," a multinational conglomerate, and illustrates, in a very simple visual example, how XML is used to locate difficult-to-find auto parts and supplies for a global market. Go to http://www-106.ibm.com/developerworks/education/xmlintro/xmlintro-4-6.html.

Using the example from above with Derek Jeter and the Yankees, write an XML statement using the new tags listed below:

```
<sport>baseball
   <team>Yankees</team>
   <player>Derek Jeter</player>
   <stats>
      <numbhomeruns>45</numbhomeruns>
   </stats>
   </sport>
```

sport: baseball

team: San Francisco Giants

player: Barry Bonds

numbhomeruns: 46

CHAPTER 2

Comparing HTML, XHTML, and XML

LEARNING OBJECTIVES

1. To trace the effect that the Web's immediate popularity had on the development of HTML, XHTML, and XML.
2. To learn about the XML compatibility requirements that differentiate an XHTML document from earlier HTML ones.
3. To discover how namespaces are used by XML and XHTML documents.
4. To learn about how XML manages documents and data.

XML has had a substantial impact on HTML, the primary language used to construct Web pages and sites. The most recent version of the HTML specification is known as XHTML. XHTML is an updated version of HTML that is written according to the rules of XML. In this chapter, we'll cover what you'll need to know about using XML and HTML together—through XHTML—in your Web projects.

From HyperText to XHTML

The concept of **hypertext**—electronic linking between documents stored on computer systems—has been around nearly as long as computer systems themselves. As the Internet became a popular medium for exchanging information in the scientific and military communities, it became a natural candidate for supporting its own hypertext system. A graphic or text link on a Web page that opens another Web page or document is known as a **hyperlink,** and the act of following a link to the intended destination is called *hyperlinking.*

The main purpose of **HyperText Markup Language (HTML)** is to display Web documents and hyperlink among them. HTML was originally created by Tim

Berners-Lee, a physics researcher at the European Center for Nuclear Research (CERN). HTML was initially designed to be a simple application for physicists to maintain research abstracts and cross-reference their documents on the Internet.

Berners-Lee built a program to allow these documents to be viewed and hyperlinked to each other; programs like this are now known as Web **browsers.** Berners-Lee also designed a set of instructions (called a **protocol**) to tell a browser what Web document to retrieve, how to obtain it, and how to display it. This protocol is called **http** (for **HyperText Transfer Protocol**) and constitutes the beginning part of most Web addresses (or **URL**—short for **Uniform** or **Universal Resource Locator**). For example:

http://www.ibm.com/
http://www.cnn.com/
http://www.mhhe.com/

are the URLs for the Web sites for IBM, CNN, and McGraw-Hill Higher Education, respectively.

HTML documents are also commonly called Web pages. The main entry point on an individual or organization's Web site is called the **home page,** and usually takes as its filename index.html or index.htm. These file extensions (.html and .htm) tell the Web browser that the file should be viewed as a Web page using a Web browser, in the same way that a file ending with .doc is an indicator that the file is a word processing document that should be opened with Microsoft Word.

Similarly, an HTML document can reference other file formats that are recognized by Web browsers. Over time, these formats have come to include images, Java applets, and Adobe PDF files, among others.

The Limitations of HTML

Tim Berners-Lee had no idea how popular his invention would prove to be. Dubbed the World Wide Web, the system quickly grew from the initial server based at CERN to over a billion documents in just over 10 years. Given the potential uses envisioned for the Web by business leaders, advertisers, publishers, marketers, and researchers, the limitations of HTML quickly made themselves known. The language designed to index physics papers was woefully inadequate to play host to multimedia, games, animation, and forms processing (used for all kinds of interactive capabilities, from guestbooks to online shopping carts).

A committee of dedicated researchers convened the **World Wide Web Consortium (W3C)** to develop the next incarnation of the language, HTML 2.0, which was published in November 1995. The major additions at this stage included tables (which provided some rudimentary layout control) and basic form processing. The browser wars reached a fever pitch in 1996 as Microsoft and

Netscape lobbied heavily for their proprietary tags to be accepted by the nonproprietary HTML protocol.

The driving forces behind the next major release, HTML 3.2, published in January 1997, included enabling scripting and extended functions known as "third-party plug-ins"—such as Shockwave games or Adobe PDF (Portable Document Format) files—that made Web browsers useful for much more than viewing hypertext documents. New tags were added to the language to promote these components.

To accommodate continued user demands for typographic and presentation controls, the **Cascading Style Sheets (CSS)** standard was introduced. This was designed to separate presentation (such as the way colors, fonts, or backgrounds displayed) from content (the information contained in a document). However, the W3C concluded that CSS would not ultimately solve what were seen as deep, structural problems within the HTML protocol. Since the demands of the Web were too diverse for one language to fulfill, the argument went, what Web developers truly needed was a meta-language—a language for writing new Web languages. This effort was what led to the creation of XML.

In the meantime, HTML 4.0 was issued as a W3C Recommendation in December 1997. HTML 4.0 addressed the issue of separating presentation from content by creating what were called flavors of HTML. Strict HTML 4.0 eliminated elements and attributes that focused on presentation (such as the `<font>` tag and color attribute), relying instead on CSS. Transitional HTML 4.0 continued to support those presentational elements for legacy purposes; this was only meant to be a stopgap measure until Web browsers could fully support HTML Strict and CSS. Finally, Frameset HTML 4.0 is largely identical to Transitional HTML 4.0 but supports framed Web sites, which were not standardized prior to HTML 4.0.

Much of HTML's initial broad appeal was that anyone with a rudimentary understanding of HTML could be a publisher to a worldwide audience. Over time, the additional complexity added to the HTML language threatened to put the language out of the reach of nonprogrammers. HTML 4.0.1, a release that provided minor updates over HTML 4.0, was released in December 1999.

The Emergence of XML

The W3C decided to develop a streamlined version of SGML (which you read about in Chapter 1) to serve the purpose of linking many kinds of computer languages together with a single tagging system. Named the **Extensible Markup Language (XML),** it was designed to parallel HTML but would let developers create and specify new tags, structures, attributes, and other Web language elements.

Figure 2.1 shows a brief side-by-side example of how both HTML and XML could be used to format a memo.

Tech Tip

XHTML documents, like earlier HTML documents, must be named with a .html or .htm extension.

HTML	XML
<HTML> <HEAD> <TITLE>Memo</TITLE> </HEAD> <BODY> <H2>To: Dorm Residents</H2> <H2>From: Resident Advisor</H2> <H2>Date: 11-17-03</H2> <H2>Subject: Fire Hazards</H2> <P>Boxes should not be stored in hallways, stairwells, or against doors. These areas must be clear at all times.</P> </BODY> </HTML>	<?xml version="1.0" encoding="UTF-8" ?> <!DOCTYPE correspondence SYSTEM "Memo_template.dtd"> <html xmlns="http://www.w3.org/1999/xhtml"> <FILENAME>111703 Memo</FILENAME> <TITLE>Memo</Memo> <TO>Dorm Residents</TO> <FROM>Resident Advisor</FROM> <DATE>11-17-03</DATE> <SUBJECT>Fire Hazards</SUBJECT> <MESSSAGE>Boxes should not be stored in hallways, stairwells, or against doors. These areas must be clear at all times.</MESSAGE>

FIGURE 2.1 Comparing HTML to XML

At first, you might think that HTML looks a lot like XML. However, there are some subtle underlying differences that demonstrate XML's potential for exchanging data in a much more powerful way.

Notice how the HTML version uses the <H2> tag in several lines of code. In HTML, <H2> represents a second-level heading tag, which has some implications on the size of the letters used to display the text it contains. The lettering will be smaller than text marked by <H1> tags and larger than text marked by <H3> tags; but other than this, there's no real connection between the tag and the text that it contains. Since the <H2> tag doesn't really describe the data within it, the memo includes extra information like the words To:, From:, Date:, and Re: to add more context.

Tech Tip

Descriptive HTML Tags
There are several HTML tags that are notable for describing specific kinds of content. These include <ADDRESS>, used to denote an e-mail address as a sort of signature; <CITE> for citations; or <BLOCKQUOTE> to indent a quote on a page. But most HTML tags do not describe what kind of content they contain. Tags like <BLOCKQUOTE> are also frequently used for other purposes—say, to indent any amount of text, not necessarily a quote.

Let's take a look at the XML version of this memo on the right-hand side of Figure 2.1. Here, the tags <TO>, <FROM>, <DATE>, and <SUBJECT> readily explain the purpose of the data contained within them. As a result, we don't need to include descriptors like the words To: in the text as well.

The fields used in a memo are easily understood. But you may produce documents that contain kinds of information that are specific to a certain industry. Book publishers track individual book titles by ISBN number, for example, and music companies track their CDs by ASIN numbers. In XML, you might use tags like <ISBN> or <ASIN> to designate this content. Within your XML documents, you can decide what your tags should stand for and what data they should contain.

In short, although HTML can display your data, it really doesn't indicate what the information means or how to use it. XML, on the other hand, is a markup language that classifies the data it contains. You can use XML to describe any data that appears in a repeating form, such as a class schedule, course listings, invoices, product directories, restaurant reviews, flight schedules, or hotel room reservations.

Tech Tip

All tags in an XHTML document should appear using lowercase letters (as in <body>).

One caveat is that XML is much stricter than HTML about how well you code your markup. XML dictates that you use well-formed tags, also known as **elements,** in your documents. An opening tag (such as <SUBJECT>) must be matched by a closing tag (such as <SUBJECT>); even the upper- or lowercase letters in your tag names must match in the opening and closing tags.

HTML is much more forgiving; you can use an opening <P> tag without a matching closing tag (</P>) and not experience any adverse results in your page display. Whether your code's tags are in uppercase, lowercase, or mixed case is not important in HTML; you can use an opening <H2> tag and match it with a closing </h2> tag.

After its initial release in February 1998, XML was not immediately embraced as HTML had been. This can be attributed to several factors. For starters, designing a new Web language, as XML demanded, is a much more substantial challenge than creating Web pages with a handful of established HTML tags or with HTML publishing tools (such as Microsoft FrontPage), as many nontechnical Web designers did. More significantly, no Web browser supporting XML natively was released until nearly a year and a half after the XML specification was written. Since its results couldn't be seen or utilized by most Web visitors, XML was hardly likely to be adopted and widely used.

While XML did not initially gain the popular support that HTML had, it spurred development of a number of robust technologies, including

- **Extensible Stylesheet Language (XSL),** for transforming one flavor of XML to another.
- **XML Schema,** for defining the structure of an XML framework.
- **XPath,** a language that defines parts of an XML document.

These XML technologies will all be described in the chapters ahead. When the W3C decided it would reformulate HTML based on XML rather than previous versions of HTML, it led to the renaming of HTML as **Extensible Hypertext Markup Language (XHTML)**.

Taking the Mid-Road with XHTML

XHTML was first released in early 2000 to meet the needs of XML within Web pages. It lets you create sets of markup tags for new purposes. There are several benefits to creating Web pages with XHTML, even if you're already familiar with HTML.

One benefit of separating presentation markup from content. Controlling a Web page's presentation—that is, how its fonts, borders, colors, and other visual elements will look—can be difficult, at best, since the same page can display differently depending on a reader's browser, device, and screen resolution. The W3C has devoted much effort to ensuring that XHTML (and HTML before it) can help make the Web more accessible to people with disabilities. You can store presentation information (such as colors or fonts) for your XML documents using either Cascading Style Sheets (CSS) or the Extensible Stylesheet Language (XSL), which you'll learn about in Chapters 7 and 8, respectively.

Working with XHTML documents also enables you to use XML tools and technologies in extending your Web site's capabilities. These include both XML editors and XHTML editors, and online validators. Some XHTML editors include templates for creating documents more quickly; others are full-fledged HTML authoring environments that have been extended to support XHTML. Macromedia Dreamweaver MX, Macromedia Homesite, Microsoft FrontPage, and BBEdit are all Web authoring environments that feature XHTML support in their latest versions. The online resources page for this chapter includes links to these and other XHTML tools.

Tech Tip

Since all attributes in XML tags must be enclosed within quotes, you need to take extra steps if you need to enclose content that contains quotes as part of the text. You may use single quotes instead if the content contains double quotes as part of the text:

```
<piechart diameter='3'">
```

If both single and double quotes are used in the content, you can replace a single quote with the code ' and a double quote with ":

```
<board length="6&quot;">
<board length='3&apos;6"'>
```

Finally, the most recent version of XHTML (XHTML 1.1) is **modular,** which means that the parts of an XHTML document can be divided into separate modules and added or removed. In practical terms, it is used to add a new XML vocabulary to an XHTML document. In this way, for example, you can create an XHTML document that also utilizes the vocabularies of both MathML and Scalar Vector Graphics (SVG) at once. Other XML vocabularies, such as RSS (commonly used in news feeds) and VoiceXML (for online audio communications), are gaining increasingly greater popularity as well.

XML's Compatibility Requirements

As an XML-based language, XHTML has strict rules regarding its syntax. If you make mistakes in creating HTML code, most Web browsers will strive to display the page as best as possible anyway. XHTML, however, may remind you of a strict English teacher who insists on absolute adherence to all rules of grammar. If you make a mistake, your page will not display at all within an XML-enabled browser. Luckily, the syntax and coding rules of XHTML are very easy to learn, and are truly not that different from those of HTML. The ultimate purpose of these rules is to ensure that XHTML files work well with XML technologies. Table 2.1 shows some of the basic ways that an XHTML document differs from earlier flavors of HTML documents.

Creating an XHTML Document

If you're already familiar with creating HTML documents, you'll see that creating your first XHTML document is not a vastly different process. If you're new to creating Web pages, don't worry—we will look at each part that differentiates this XHTML document in turn.

TABLE 2.1 Differences between XHTML and Earlier Versions of HTML

Feature	HTML (4.0 or earlier)	XHTML
Case sensitivity	Not case-sensitive. The `<body>` tag may also appear as `<Body>` or `<BODY>`	XML is a case-sensitive language. Since the W3C designated lowercase letters for XHTML tags, only tags in the form of `<body>` are permissible.
Interpretation of invalid tags	Although some HTML 4.0–aware browsers are less forgiving than others (especially on the Macintosh), most browsers will forgive invalid HTML (such as a missing `</body>` tag or improperly nested tags) and display the Web page as intended anyway.	XHTML-compatible browsers tend to be much less forgiving than their predecessors and fail to display any element they cannot parse properly. A missing `</body>` tag could cause a Web page to display entirely blank, for instance.
Empty elements (tags that do not require a closing tag)	Some HTML tags do not require a closing tag, for example: ` `	XHTML requires some indication that a tag does not have a separate closing tag. As a result, you add a space and an ending slash (/) to the empty element: ` `
Quotes in attribute values	Quotation marks are optional. Both of the following tags are valid: `<table width=100%>` `<table width="100%">`	Attribute values must be placed within quotations marks. `<table width="100%">` is a valid XHTML statement. `<table width=100%>` is invalid in XHTML.

Now let's take a look at the sample XHTML document shown in Figure 2.2.

Most of the tags shown in Figure 2.2 do not differ greatly from ones you might see in a regular HTML document. Figure 2.2 points out the tags that are needed in an XHTML-enabled version of this Web page:

- **XML declaration,** for indicating to the Web browser what version of XML is at work here.
- `DOCTYPE` **declaration,** which appears only in a document that uses a **document type definition (DTD).** A DTD can be used to describe the structure of a document; XHTML documents use one of several XHTML DTDs, which you'll read about a little later in this chapter. The DOCTYPE declaration acts as a container for the assigned DTD.
- **XML namespace,** for helping the browser keep track of the vocabularies of element and attribute names used in your documents.

Let's take a look at each of these elements next.

Tech Tip

Ensure that you are using an XML-friendly browser by consulting the list at http://www.xmlsoftware.com/browsers/.

XML declaration — DOCTYPE Declaration — XML namespace

```
<?xml version="1.0" encoding="UTF-8"?>
<!DOCTYPE html PUBLIC "-//W3C//DTD XHTML 1.0 Transitional//EN"
   "http://www.w3.org/TR/xhtml1/DTD/xhtml1-transitional.dtd">
<html xmlns="http://www.w3.org/1999/xhtml">
<head>
<title>As We May Think</title>
<link rel="STYLESHEET" type="text/css"
   href="/util/css/vb_abstract_stylesheet.css">
</head>
<body>
<h1>As We May Think</h1>
<b>by Vannevar Bush</b>
<p>
This has not been a scientist's war; it has been a war
in which all have had a part. The scientists, burying
their old professional competition in the demand of a
common cause, have shared greatly and learned much. It
has been exhilarating to work in effective partnership.
Now, for many, this appears to be approaching an end.
What are the scientists to do next?
</p>
.
.
.
</body>
</html>
```

FIGURE 2.2 A Sample XHTML Document

Tech Tip

Although this example doesn't show it, an XML declaration also can show a third piece of information: A `standalalone` attribute can take a value of "yes" or "no." This is used if the XML processor should look at an external file to find entity references, which let you make substitutions for text or markup. You'll learn about entity references in Chapter 4.

XML Declarations

All XML and XHTML documents begin with an XML declaration that signals to XML-compliant tools like editors and browsers that they can process this document.

```
<?xml version="1.0" encoding="UTF-8"?>
```

Since this is the first line of XML code we've shown in this chapter, let's examine its structure in detail. The syntax of `<?xml` at the start and `?>` at the end identifies this line as the XML declaration. The version number (1.0) indicates what version of XML is used in authoring this document. This value will have greater significance as future versions of XML are developed. The value of UTF-8 with the `encoding` attribute represents the **character encoding** that is used. XML supports the Unicode character set, which provides multilingual capabilities in your XHTML or XML documents. UTF-8 is one method of encoding Unicode characters.

`DOCTYPE` Declaration and Document Type Definition (DTD)

Since XML is a markup language used to create other markup languages, it therefore can use a DTD as a tool to create and describe the language. The **DOCTYPE** declaration immediately follows the XML declaration. It's a standard component of older HTML pages as well, but here it will point to an XHTML DTD instead of an HTML one.

```
<!DOCTYPE html PUBLIC "-//W3C//DTD XHTML 1.0
  Transitional//EN" "http://www.w3.org/TR/xhtml1/DTD/
  xhtml1-transitional.dtd">
```

Let's examine the structure of this tag as well. After the opening character string (<), an exclamation mark precedes the `DOCTYPE` entry. The next word, `html`, tells the browser or parser to treat the document as a Web page. Each DTD may be recognized by a public identifier; in the example above, the text following the word `PUBLIC` refers to version 1 of the W3C's XHTML DTD. This is followed by a space, then the URL for this DTD (recognizable by the file extension .dtd). The public identifier and URL for the DTD are enclosed by quotes. Finally, the tag ends with a closing character string (>).

Tech Tip

Note that the `DOCTYPE` declaration is the only tag in an XHTML document that does not take a closing tag.

The most recent version of XHTML, called XHTML 1.1, uses a single XML document type, which also is called XHTML 1.1.

XHTML 1.0 uses three XML document types that correspond to three DTDs: Strict, Transitional, and Frameset. This convention was carried over from the three flavors of HTML 4.0, which you read about earlier in this chapter. XHTML, like earlier versions of HTML, is actually an SGML application. Since SGML applications are defined using DTDs, each of these different XHTML flavors is, accordingly, based on a separate DTD.

The Strict version of XHTML 1.0 has removed all presentational elements (such as `<font>`) and attributes (like `bgcolor`). To restore presentation features, you could link to a CSS **stylesheet.**

In practice, you will most likely use only the XHTML 1.0 Transitional DTD. You would insert a `DOCTYPE` declaration in your XHTML document immediately after the XML declaration. Here's how the first two lines of your XHTML might look together:

```
<?xml version="1.0" encoding="UTF-8"?>
<!DOCTYPE html PUBLIC "-//W3C//DTD XHTML 1.0 Transitional//
  EN" "http://www.w3.org/TR/xhtml1/DTD/xhtml1-transitional.
  dtd">
```

Table 2.2 shows the at-a-glance differences between the three XHTML 1.0 DTDs and the one used with XHTML 1.1.

XML Namespaces

An XML namespace lets you distinguish which definition you mean when you use certain tags. For example, if you are tagging a listing of library records or furniture inventory, you might naturally want to label content using the tags `<title>` or `<table>`, respectively. Since `<title>` and `<table>` are tag names already used by HTML, though, specifying an XML namespace is the way to avoid any confusion about what is meant by each tag name.

TABLE 2.2 Differences between the XHTML DTD Standards

DTD Name	Value	Description
XHTML 1.1	`<!DOCTYPE html PUBLIC "-//W3C//DTD XHTML 1.1//EN" "http://www.w3.org/TR/xhtml11/DTD/xhtml11.dtd">`	This is a modular version of the Strict XHTML 1.0 document type shown below. Use with HTML documents that do not define any presentation formatting.
XHTML 1.0 Strict	`<!DOCTYPE html PUBLIC "-//W3C//DTD XHTML 1.0 Strict//EN" "http://www.w3.org/TR/xhtml1/DTD/xhtml1-strict.dtd">`	Use with HTML documents that do not define any presentation formatting. All formatting should be provided by Cascading Style Sheets.
XHTML 1.0 Transitional	`<!DOCTYPE html PUBLIC "-//W3C//DTD XHTML 1.0 Transitional//EN" "http://www.w3.org/TR/xhtml1/DTD/xhtml1-transitional.dtd">`	Can be used with HTML documents that exert some control over presentation formatting. All the tags in HTML 4.0 are permitted. Can also be used to support older browsers that don't understand Cascading Style Sheets.
XHTML 1.0 Frameset	`<!DOCTYPE html PUBLIC "-//W3C//DTD XHTML 1.0 Frameset//EN" "http://www.w3.org/TR/xhtml1/DTD/xhtml1-frameset.dtd">`	Use whenever your HTML markup uses frames to partition the browser window into two or more content areas.

Tech Tip

To learn more about creating your own XHTML-compatible pages, we recommend *Programming the Web Using XHTML and JavaScript* by Larry Randles Lagerstrom (New York: McGraw-Hill, 2003).

In the example below, we define the XHTML namespace within the document's opening `<html>` tag. The `xmlns` attribute points to the URL for the page where the W3C defines the XHTML namespace:

```
<html xmlns="http://www.w3.org/1999/xhtml">
```

Since browsers are limited in terms of their ability to deal with elements from other namespaces within XHTML documents, you'll need to work with full-fledged XML documents in order to truly take advantage of the other XML vocabularies that enjoy their own namespaces. More details appear a little later in this chapter in the section on "Deciding When to Use XHTML or XML."

Reformulating an HTML Document into XML

If you have already created Web pages that are compliant with earlier versions of HTML, you can convert them to work with XML. Listing 2.1 shows an example of an ordinary, if brief, HTML page.

LISTING 2.1

```
<!DOCTYPE HTML PUBLIC "-//W3C//DTD HTML 4.0
  Transitional//EN">
<html>
  <head>
    <title>Registration Roadblock</title>
  </head>
  <body>
    <p>You must register in order to access this site.
      Please fill out our <A HREF=regform.html>
      registration form</a>.
  </body>
</html>
```

There are several changes we must make to ensure that this page will comply with XML standards. We need to add an XML declaration as the first line. We also need to change the designated DTD to point to an XHTML DTD rather than an HTML DTD. We also need to specify the XML namespace. Finally, we need to make some syntactical corrections that were acceptable under HTML but would not be to an XML parser. The `<p>` tag now requires a closing `</p>` tag. The `<A HREF>` tag should appear in lowercase as `<a href>`. Further, the page referenced by the anchor tag should be enclosed in quotes (`"regform.html"`). The corrected, XML-compliant version appears in Listing 2.2.

LISTING 2.2

```
<?xml version="1.0" encoding="UTF-8"?>
<!DOCTYPE html PUBLIC "-//W3C//DTD XHTML 1.0
  Transitional//EN" "http://www.w3.org/TR/xhtml1/DTD/
  xhtml1-transitional.dtd">
<html xmlns="http://www.w3.org/1999/xhtml">
  <head>
    <title> Registration Roadblock </title>
  </head>
  <body>
<p>You must register in order to access this site. Please
  fill out our <a href="regform.html">registration
  form</a>.</p>
  </body>
</html>
```

Let's reformulate another sample HTML document to make it XHTML-compliant. Listing 2.3 shows what we have to work with.

LISTING 2.3

```
<html>
  <head>
    <title>Halfhearted HTML</title>
```

```
  </head>
  <body>
<div>Make sure that you nest tags <strong>properly</div>.
  </strong>
And remember closing elements:
<OL>
<li>For some HTML elements, closing tags are optional.
<li>In XHTML, though, you'll want to remember to include
  the closing tag.
</ol>
<br>
<br>
Leave some extra space here. Here's a picture from one of
  my favorite Web sites:
<br>
<br>
<img src=http://www.google.com/images/logo.gif width=276
  height=110 alt="Google">
  </body>
</html>
```

There are quite a few things to fix in order to make this document XHTML-compliant. First, we'll need to add an XML declaration as the first line in the document. We also need to add a `DOCTYPE` declaration to point to an XHTML DTD. Then, we need to specify the XML namespace. We also have a few fixes to add to clean up the HTML. For starters, the `<div>` and `<strong>` tags are not nested properly. Since the `<strong>` tag should be nested inside the `<div>` tag, the `<strong>` tag needs to be closed before the `<div>` tag is. Next, the opening and closing ordered list tags do not have matching case. In our new version, we'll change the opening `<OL>` to `<ol>`. Next, the list item tags (`<li>`) do not have corresponding closing tags in the HTML version, but we'll need them in an XHTML-compliant document. The `<br>` tags and the `<img>` tag are empty elements, and so should properly be displayed as `<br />` and `<img />`. Finally, in XHTML, quotes are required on attributes, so these need to be added to the `src`, `width`, and `height` attributes in the `<img>` tag.

Listing 2.4 shows what our XHTML-compliant document looks like with the revised tags in place.

LISTING 2.4

```
<?xml version="1.0" encoding="UTF-8"?>
<!DOCTYPE html PUBLIC "-//W3C//DTD XHTML 1.0 Transitional//
  EN" "http://www.w3.org/TR/xhtml1/DTD/xhtml1-transitional.
  dtd">
<html xmlns="http://www.w3.org/1999/xhtml">
  <head>
    <title>Halfhearted HTML</title>
```

```
    </head>
    <body>
  <div>Make sure that you nest tags <strong>properly</strong>.
    </div>
  And remember closing elements:<
  <ol>
  <li>For some HTML elements, closing tags are optional. </li>
  <li>In XHTML, though, you'll want to remember to include
    the closing tag. </li>
  </ol>
  <br />
  <br />
  Leave some extra space here. Here's a picture from one of
    my favorite Web sites:
  <br />
  <br />
  <img src="http://www.google.com/images/logo.gif" width="276"
    height="110" alt="Google" />
    </body>
  </html>
```

Tech Tip

As a preparation for ensuring XML compliance, run your existing Web pages through a freely available program called HTML Tidy (http://tidy.sourceforge.net/).

Choosing to Use XHTML or XML

Note, though, that XHTML does not extend to you the full potential of XML. As Figure 2.3 depicts, XHTML represents just one vocabulary of XML. XML has the ability to dynamically describe the data that it transmits. Other languages and tools are then needed to display and reformat an XML document on the Web, or to share its data with other applications.

Table 2.3 shows some at-the-ready criteria you can use to determine whether XHTML will suffice for your Web project or if you'll want to take advantage of a full-fledged XML implementation.

Going Further with Namespaces

Earlier you saw how to specify the XHTML namespace when you create or format an XHTML document. But now let's consider what to do when we want to utilize more than a single vocabulary in the same document. Listing 2.5 shows how a home furnishings catalog might begin compiling a structured document detailing its offerings.

LISTING 2.5

```
<?xml version="1.0" encoding="UTF-8"?>
<furnishings>
<table>
<tr>
```

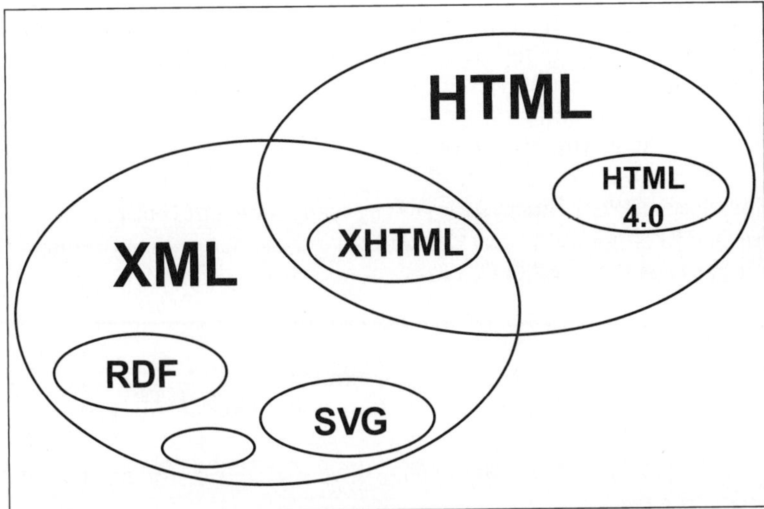

FIGURE 2.3 XHTML Only Represents Part of What You Can Accomplish on the Web with XML

TABLE 2.3 XHTML versus XML: Choosing the Right Language for the Job

Use XHTML . . .	Use XML . . .
. . . when you're creating a display-only or brochure-type Web site.	. . . when you need to dynamically generate your content's presentation using different layouts and forms.
. . . when you want to quickly publish your documents on the Web.	. . . when you need to store your documents and data in a format that's searchable, reusable, and cross-platform.
. . . when you're redesigning a large set of existing static HTML pages.	. . . when you want your data to be able to interact with applications.
	. . . when you're pursuing a "knowledge management" strategy to make your organization's information accessible on demand.

```
<td><table material="walnut" type="dining"/></td>
<td><chair material="beech" type="dining"/></td>
<td><lamp material="iron" type="floor"/></td>
</tr>
</table>
</furnishings>
```

What's immediately apparent, though, is that there are two different elements called `table` that have different meanings. This demonstrates why you need two different namespaces—the kind of table that's described in a home furnishings context is different from the spreadsheet type of table defined in the XHTML namespace. Listing 2.6 corrects this by defining the namespaces needed here, and adding a prefix to each element name to denote which vocabulary is being used where.

LISTING 2.6

```
<?xml version="1.0" encoding="UTF-8"?>
<furn:furnishings
xmlns:furn="http://genuineclass.com/xml/homefurnishings/"
  xmlns:xhtml=http://www.w3.org/1999/xhtml">
<xhtml:table>
<xhtml:tr>
<xhtml:td><furn:table material="walnut" type="dining"/>
  </xhtml:td>
<xhtml:td><furn:chair material="beech" type="dining"/>
  </xhtml:td>
<xhtml:td><furn:lamp material="iron" type="floor"/>
  </xhtml:td>
</xhtml:tr>
</xhtml:table>
</furn:furnishings>
```

A simpler way to display this is through the use of a **default namespace,** if one vocabulary is used far more extensively than another. You define a default namespace by using the `xmlns` keyword in the document element, but you omit the prefix. Using the home furnishings example from Listings 2.5 and 2.6, you could define the home furnishings–related vocabulary as the default namespace with a line of code that looks like the following:

```
<furnishings xmlns="http://genuineclass.com/xml/
  homefurnishings/" xmlns:xhtml=http://www.w3.org/
  1999/xhtml">
```

You then won't need to use a prefix for the default namespace, as shown in Listing 2.7. The furnishings-related tags (like `<table>`, `<chair>`, and `<lamp>`) no longer take a prefix, while the XHTML-related ones (like `<table>`, `<tr>`, and `<td>`) still do.

LISTING 2.7

```
<?xml version="1.0" encoding="UTF-8"?>
<furnishings xmlns="http://genuineclass.com/xml/
  homefurnishings/" xmlns:xhtml=http://www.w3.org/
  1999/xhtml">
<xhtml:table>
<xhtml:tr>
<xhtml:td><table material="walnut" type="dining"/>
  </xhtml:td>
<xhtml:td><chair material="beech" type="dining"/>
</xhtml:td>
```

```
<xhtml:td><lamp material="iron" type="floor"/></xhtml:td>
</xhtml:tr>
</xhtml:table>
</furnishings>
```

In later chapters, you'll see how you'll need to change the namespace again when you want to incorporate other kinds of XML-related technologies, such as SVG or Synchronized Multimedia Integration Language (SMIL).

Data and Metadata

One conclusion you can draw from Table 2.3 above is that there are really two purposes for XHTML and XML: managing documents and data. The difference between the two is not always clear, but, broadly speaking, documents are much like their physical, paper counterparts: books, articles, and so on. In many cases, XHTML will be sufficient for publishing static, brochure-type documents on the Web. Data applications, on the other hand, can include a much wider assortment of uses, and require XML's flexibility.

You can use XML, for example, to store inventory information or incorporate it in any application where you might otherwise have used a small spreadsheet or database. Later, in Chapter 10, we'll discuss how you might use XML with either an existing database or a content management framework, which is used for managing large text documents.

Today, we rely on the Web largely as a global directory of resources for information and entertainment. But one of the biggest problems the future may hold for the Web is growth. It's difficult enough today to search for information online; how will we manage to organize and process information in the future when the amount of information that's available online only continues to grow? One of the technologies currently in development by the W3C to address this question is an XML vocabulary called the **Resource Description Framework (RDF).**

RDF is an XML-based language for expressing **metadata,** which is data about data. One example of metadata could be the table of contents for this book. The table of contents describes the contents of each chapter. The purpose of RDF is to provide an XML-based method of describing online information so that different kinds of Web resources can be referenced consistently—thus making information easier to catalog and easier to find.

Summary

As you can see, using XHTML is only the tip of the iceberg that comprises the XML syntax. Using XHTML is a means of readying your Web pages for the next generation of Web browsers. As long as you have an audience that's using older browsers, you'll still need to make sure your XHTML pages work well (or "degrade gracefully," as Web developers say) with older Web browsers by validating your Web pages. Making your data available to other applications will require you to work with XML, rather than just XHTML.

This brief overview of XML and its relationship to HTML and XHTML was designed to familiarize you with the structure and syntax of HTML and XHTML documents, and XML documents in general. You also saw that XML is comprised of a number of vocabularies—including XHTML, SVG, RDF, and a host of other technologies we haven't even mentioned by name yet—that fit together to deliver on XML's promise of sharing data and enhancing accessibility and usability.

In the chapters ahead, you'll discover the details of the building blocks of XML—and learn how to create your own individual XML documents and manipulate data within them.

Key Terms

browser
Cascading Style Sheets (CSS)
character encoding
default namespace
DOCTYPE declaration
document type definition (DTD)
element
Extensible Hypertext Markup Language (XHTML)
Extensible Markup Language (XML)
Extensible Stylesheet Language (XSL)
home page
hyperlink
hypertext
HyperText Markup Language (HTML)
HyperText Transfer Protocol (http)
metadata
modular
protocol
Resource Description Framework (RDF)
stylesheets
Uniform (Universal) Resource Locator (URL)
World Wide Web Consortium (W3C)
XML declaration
XML namespace
XML Schema
XPath

Code Summary

1. **A sample XML document:**

```
<?xml version="1.0" encoding="UTF-8"?>
<!DOCTYPE correspondence SYSTEM
"Memo_template.dtd">
<html xmlns="http://www.w3.org/1999/xhtml">
<FILENAME>111703 Memo</FILENAME>
<TITLE>Memo</Memo>
<TO>Dorm Residents</TO>
<FROM>Resident Advisor</FROM>
<DATE>11-17-03</DATE>
```

```
<SUBJECT>Fire Hazards</SUBJECT>
<MESSSAGE>Boxes should not be
stored in hallways, stairwells,
or against doors. These areas must
be clear at all times.</MESSAGE>
```

2. **A sample XHTML document:**

```
<?xml version="1.0" encoding="UTF-8"?>
<!DOCTYPE html PUBLIC "-//W3C//DTD XHTML 1.0 Transitional//EN"
  "http://www.w3.org/TR/xhtml1/DTD/xhtml1-transitional.dtd">
<html xmlns="http://www.w3.org/1999/xhtml">
<head>
<title>As We May Think</title>
<link rel="STYLESHEET" type="text/css"
  href="/util/css/vb_abstract_stylesheet.css">
</head>
<body>
<h1>As We May Think</h1>
<b>by Vannevar Bush</b>
<p>
This has not been a scientist's war; it has been a war
in which all have had a part. The scientists, burying
their old professional competition in the demand of a
common cause, have shared greatly and learned much. It
has been exhilarating to work in effective partnership.
Now, for many, this appears to be approaching an end.
What are the scientists to do next?
</p>
.
.
.
</body>
</html>
```

3. **Enclosing content that contains quotes within attributes:**

```
<board length="6&quot;">
<board length ='3&apos;6"'>
```

4. **An XML declaration:**

```
<?xml version="1.0" encoding="UTF-8"?>
```

5. `DOCTYPE` **declarations for the XHTML 1.0 DTDs:**

```
<!DOCTYPE html PUBLIC "-//W3C//DTD XHTML 1.0 Strict//EN"
  "http://www.w3.org/TR/xhtml1/DTD/xhtml1-strict.dtd">
<!DOCTYPE html PUBLIC "-//W3C//DTD XHTML 1.0 Transitional//EN" "http://www.w3.org/TR/
  xhtml1/DTD/xhtml1-transitional.dtd">
<!DOCTYPE html PUBLIC "-//W3C//DTD XHTML 1.0 Frameset//EN" "http://www.w3.org/TR/xhtml1/
  DTD/xhtml1-frameset.dtd">
```

6. `DOCTYPE` **declarations for the XHTML 1.1 DTD:**

```
<!DOCTYPE html PUBLIC “-//W3C//DTD XHTML 1.1//EN" "http://www.w3.org/TR/xhtml11/DTD/
   xhtml11.dtd">
```

7. **Listing an XML namespace (here with the XHTML vocabulary):**

```
<html xmlns="http://www.w3.org/1999/xhtml">
```

8. **Defining two namespaces in an XML document:**

```
<?xml version="1.0" encoding="UTF-8"?>
<furn:furnishings xmlns:furn="http://genuineclass.com/xml/homefurnishings/"
   xmlns:xhtml=http://www.w3.org/1999/xhtml">
<xhtml:table>
<xhtml:tr>
<xhtml:td><furn:table material="walnut" type="dining"/></xhtml:td>
<xhtml:td><furn:chair material="beech" type="dining"/></xhtml:td>
<xhtml:td><furn:lamp material="iron" type="floor"/></xhtml:td>
</xhtml:tr>
</xhtml:table>
</furn:furnishings>
```


Ensure that you are using an XML-friendly browser by consulting the list at http://www.xmlsoftware.com/browsers/.

Properly nested tags are strictly enforced in XHTML documents. If you fail to properly close one tag before opening another, your content may not display at all.

XHTML documents, like earlier HTML documents, must be named with a .html or .htm extension.

All tags in an XHTML document should appear using lowercase letters (as in `<body>`).

Ensure that you use consistent upper- and lowercase in naming and using your XML element names, since these are case-sensitive—a name like HeaderXLarge is different from headerxlarge.

You can use a plain text processor, such as Notepad on a Windows machine, to create and edit your Web documents. Avoid using Microsoft Word, which will attempt to display your pages the way a Web browser would.

If you use an HTML authoring tool to create and edit Web documents, you'll need to make sure it can create well-formed XML. You can download a free validation program called HTML Tidy from http://tidy.sourceforge.net/ to check this.

Always use self-descriptive names for your elements to readily describe their contents.

Since all attributes in XML tags must be enclosed within quotes, you need to take extra steps if you need to enclose content that contains quotes as part of the text. You may use single quotes instead if the content contains double quotes as part of the text.

Use empty elements to merge the opening and closing tags of an element containing no data into a single tag (as in `<br />`).

Review Questions

1. How does XHTML differ from earlier versions of HTML?
2. What is the main purpose of HTML?
3. What is the main purpose of XML?
4. Name some of the markup conventions that XHTML observes that HTML is less strict about.
5. What does it mean to say that XHTML 1.1. is modular?
6. What purpose does a DTD serve?
7. Why are namespaces defined, and how are they used?
8. Besides XHTML, what are some other XML vocabularies?

Case Study

Compare and contrast the differences that XML makes by pointing your Web browser to the Chapter 2 Case Study page listed in this chapter's online listing of URLs (to come). From here, you can click to an HTML, XHTML, and XML with CSS version of the same page (see Figure 2.4). Note that each page uses the same content. The XML version of this page utilizes metadata and a structure that's unavailable in the HTML version. You will need MS Internet Explorer 5.5 or later to view the XML version. You also may find that the HTML and XHTML renditions will look similar in any version of MS Internet Explorer or Netscape Navigator browser at version 4 or later.

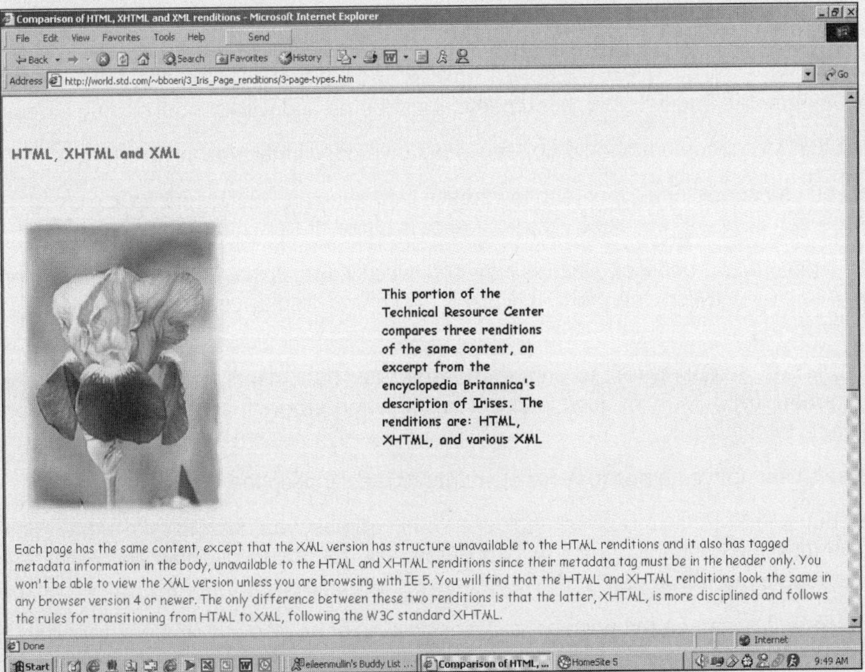

FIGURE 2.4 Comparison of HTML, XML, and XHTML Renditions

Create a new XHTML document:

1. Open Notepad (or whichever plain text processor or Web authoring tool you're using instead) and create a new Untitled document.
2. Type in the XHTML code shown in Figure 2.2, but use your own title and a personal message instead. Don't forget to close all tags and nest them properly!
3. After you have typed in this code, save the document with a name such as firstpage.html.
4. Now that you have saved your source code, launch your Web browser. If you're using MS Internet Explorer, make sure you're using at least version 5.5.
5. Within Internet Explorer, choose `Open` from the `File` menu and then click on the Browse button. Toggle through the directories on your hard drive to find your new Web document.
6. Now return to Notepad (or other text editor) and open your firstpage.html document. Add some additional text of your choosing. Experiment with adding the `<br />` tag and opening and closing `<p>` tags to create additional paragraphs. Be sure to save your work at regular intervals.
7. Take note that if you leave off a closing tag, your content may no longer display the way you intended. For example, if you omit a closing `</a>` tag, the text that follows will now display as hyperlinked text.

Transform a simple HTML document into XHTML:

1. Open Notepad (or whichever plain text processor or Web authoring tool you're using instead) and create a new Untitled document.
2. Type in the HTML code shown below:

```
<html>
   <head>
      <title>My First Transformed Document</title>
   </head>
   <BODY>
<p>The W3C's Web site includes information about the
   <strong><a href=http://www.w3.org/MarkUp/#xhtml1>XHTML recommendations
   </strong></a>. Here is some information about the W3C.
<UL>
<LI>The mission of the W3C's HTML Working Group is to develop the next
   generation of HTML as a suite of XML tag sets>
<LI> W3C produces what are known as "Recommendations." These are specifications
   that are developed by W3C working groups, and then reviewed by members of the
   W3C.
</UL>
<br>
<br>
If you validate your XHTML documents with the W3C's <a href=http://validator.
   w3.org/">Markup Validator Service, you can publish this icon on your Web pages:
<br>
```

```
<IMG src=http://www.w3.org/Icons/valid-xhtml10 width=88 height=31 alt="Valid
   XHTML 1.0!">
   </body>
</html>
```

Consider using the free W3C Markup Validation Service to ensure that your XHTML pages are valid. Visit http://validator.w3.org/, shown in Figure 2.5.

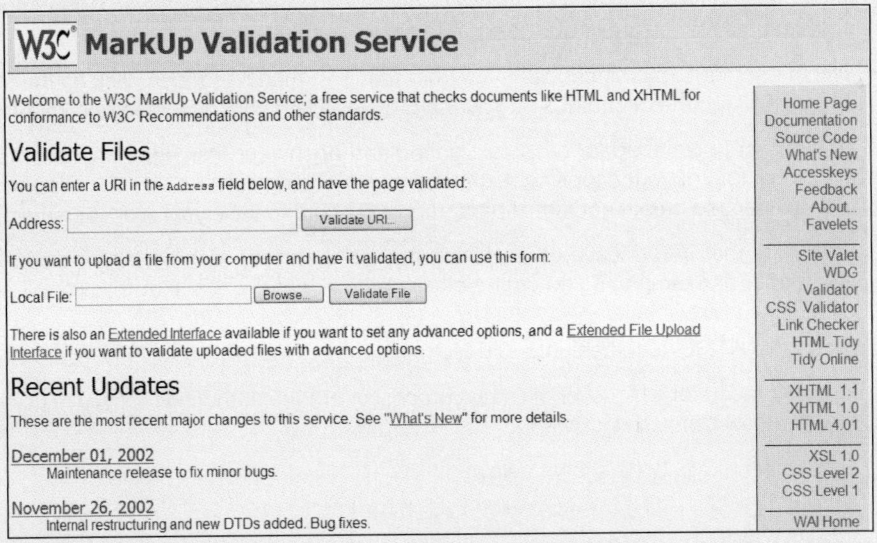

W3C MarkUp Validation Service

Welcome to the W3C MarkUp Validation Service; a free service that checks documents like HTML and XHTML for conformance to W3C Recommendations and other standards.

Validate Files

You can enter a URI in the Address field below, and have the page validated:

Address: [Validate URI...]

If you want to upload a file from your computer and have it validated, you can use this form:

Local File: [Browse...] [Validate File]

There is also an Extended Interface available if you want to set any advanced options, and a Extended File Upload Interface if you want to validate uploaded files with advanced options.

Recent Updates

These are the most recent major changes to this service. See "What's New" for more details.

December 01, 2002
Maintenance release to fix minor bugs.

November 26, 2002
Internal restructuring and new DTDs added. Bug fixes.

Home Page
Documentation
Source Code
What's New
Accesskeys
Feedback
About...
Favelets
Site Valet
WDG
Validator
CSS Validator
Link Checker
HTML Tidy
Tidy Online
XHTML 1.1
XHTML 1.0
HTML 4.01
XSL 1.0
CSS Level 2
CSS Level 1
WAI Home

FIGURE 2.5 The W3C Markup Valiation Service, a free online service from the W3C.

3. Correct the tags shown above so that they conform with a valid XHTML document. Check back in the section titled "The Emergence of XML" and Table 2.1 to see what these requirements include.

CHAPTER 3

Understanding How XML Works: The Fundamentals

LEARNING OBJECTIVES

1. To understand the overall structure of an XML document.
2. To gain a familiarity with basic EBNF characters.
3. To know the difference between well-formed and valid XML.
4. To make a simple XML file.
5. To look at a simple DTD.
6. To look at elements, attributes, entities, and comments.
7. To decide between elements and attributes.

Before beginning to model XML documents, you will need to understand the basic physical structure of an XML document. This means having an overview of processing instructions (PI), elements, attributes, entities, and their details, syntax, and logical structure. In the most simplistic terms, an XML document consists of a prologue, the root element, and its sub elements. Of course, there is more to it than that, and this chapter will introduce you to the core concepts that you will need to build intricate XML statements.

Before getting started, ensure that the Web browser you're using offers native support for XML; use at least version 6 of either Microsoft's or Netscape's Web browser. Microsoft Internet Explorer 6, for example, has built-in capabilities for transforming XML into HTML either inside the browser or at the server before pages are displayed. MSIE 5.5 ships with an out-of-date XML parser, but the browser can be upgraded to replace the XML parser. Netscape Navigator 6 uses a different XML parser, one that relies on using XML with CSS.

IMPORTANT

A regularly updated listing of XML-compatible Web browsers is available at http://www.xmlsoftware.com/browsers/. We will examine editors in more depth in Chapter 6.

Steps to a Basic XML Document

- Write the statement in an editor such as **Notepad** for PC Users or, for Mac users, **BBEdit**. Save the document with an ".xml" extension.
- Have the .xml document read by an **XML-compliant browser**.
- Display the .xml document to the user.

Each one of these processes is completely separate from the other process and the only thing that connects them is the actual XML document. Remember, the user might be viewing the document over the Internet, or on a mobile phone's tiny screen (see Figure 3.1). When the .xml document is read by an XML-compliant browser, it will often be associated with a **stylesheet**. A stylesheet helps regulate formatting and display issues. We will examine stylesheets more in Chapters 7 and 8.

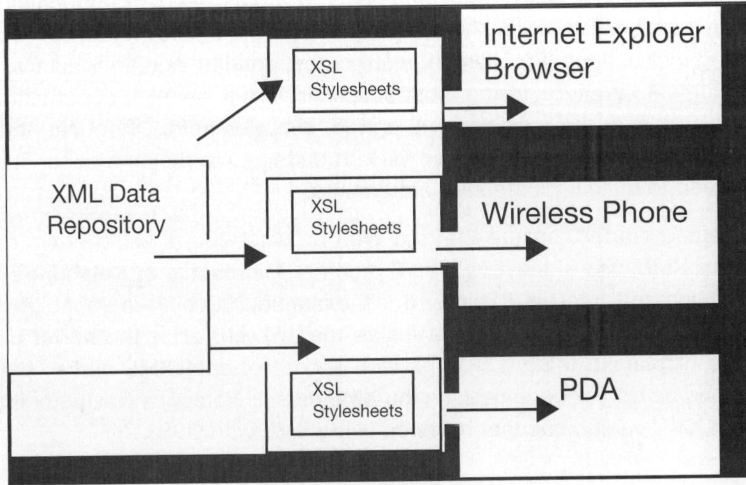

FIGURE 3.1 Information Sent Out to Different Devices

Basic Markup: EBNF Characters

EBNF stands for Extended Backus-Naur Form Notation and is a syntactic meta-language that defines all the components of an XML document. Specific **EBNF characters** are critical to the formation of any XML statement. Throughout your time of creating XML, you will be using these, and other, EBNF characters:

< is the beginning of a tag.

> is the end of a tag.

/ shows that it is an end tag.

<? ?> starts and ends a processing statement (PI).

! alerts that a reserved word keyword will follow.

[ ] shows the start and end of a range.

[shows the beginning of an internal DTD.

]> shows the end of an internal DTD.

<![ ]]> shows the start and end of a CDATA section.

| is a choice and allows any order of entry.

, shows a specific order of entry.

 # is used in front of PCDATA to determine default attributes.

& starts a parsed general entity.

; ends an entity.

? shows a content piece can happen up to once.

+ shows a content piece must happen once or more.

** shows a content piece can happen for an unlimited number of times.*

Well-Formed and Valid XML

XML is both well formed and valid but what does that mean? We'll look at the differences below. Just remember that when you compose code in XML, there are very stringent rules.

Well Formed

An XML document is considered **well formed** in its syntax when

- Each opening tag has a corresponding closing tag and tags must nest correctly.
- All cases match. Remember, `<ingredients>`, `<Ingredients>`, and `<INGREDIENTS>` are three separate tags, and will be read that way by a processor.
- There has to be at least one element, though there can be more.

Advice

Most code is written in lowercase for consistency, but it does not have to be.

- There can only be one **root element** and all other elements must be contained within it.
- Elements and their associated tags, like attributes, must nest correctly.
- Element names must follow some simple rules:
    - They start with either a letter or an underscore.
    - They are allowed to have letters, digits, periods (.), underscores (_), or hyphens (-).
    - No **whitespace**.
    - They cannot begin with anything that says "xml" either with or without quotes and must adhere to all XML naming conventions.

It is very important to understand that XML will not allow even one error in its code. (See Figure 3.2.)

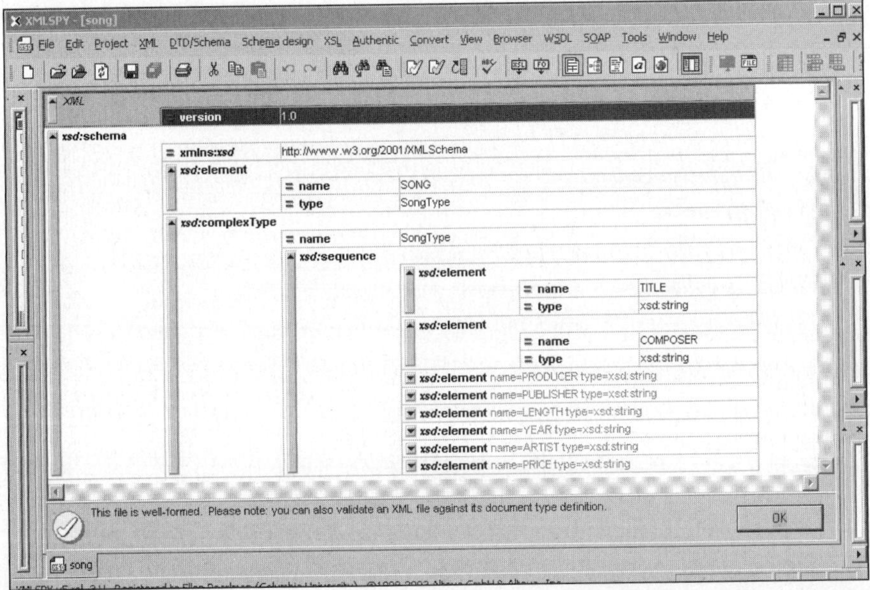

FIGURE 3.2 A Well-Formed XML Document That Uses a Schema
In this case, the document uses the three-letter extension .xsd file, not an .xml file.

Valid

> **Alert**
> An XML document must be well formed but does not have to be valid (though it usually should be).

A **valid** XML document, in addition to being well formed, *must* conform to rules defined in its **DTD (Document Type Definition)** or **XML Schema**. (See Figure 3.3.) DTDs were briefly mentioned in Chapter 2. We will look at DTDs in depth in Chapter 4 and at schemas in Chapter 5. For now just know that an XML document must conform to predefined rules in order to be considered valid. A DTD ensures that an XML document meets these standards by defining the grammar and vocabulary of the markup language. The DTD lists everything that a parser needs to know in order to display and process an XML document, as does the XML schema.

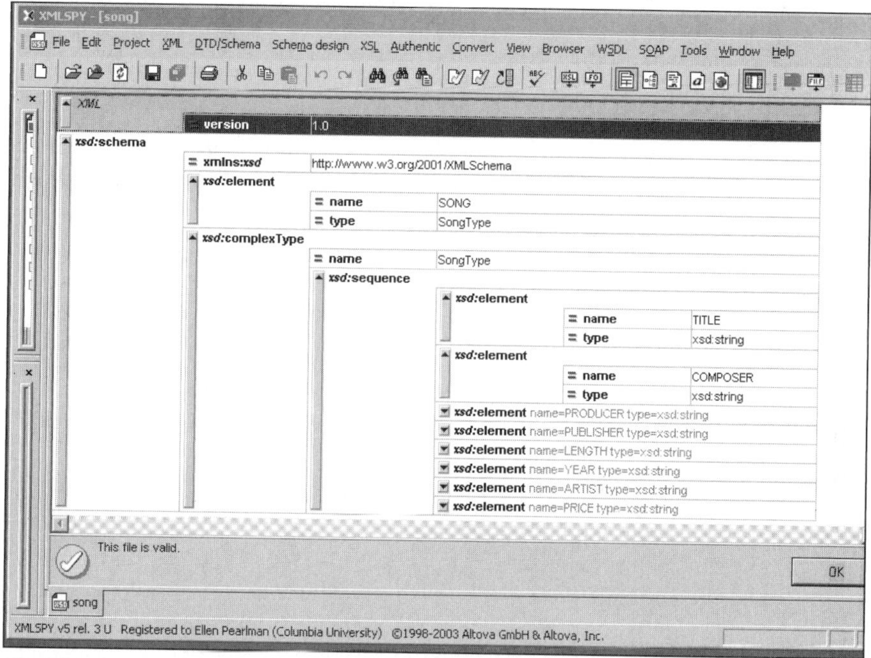

FIGURE 3.3 Valid File, in This Case, Using the Same One as Well-Formed

Downloading XML Spy

Go to http://www.xmlspy.com/ and click on download to download **XML Spy** to your computer. Set it up in the drive path specification of your choice. This will be one of the editors we will work with throughout this book. A free 30-day evaluation copy is available from the site.

> **Advice**
>
> For a good list of XML-compliant editors, look at http://www.perfectxml.com/soft.asp?cat=6. We will look at editors more in depth in Chapter 6.

Tagging an XML Document

Every XML document must begin with the **processing instruction (PI)** shown in Listing 3.1.

LISTING 3.1

```
<?xml version="1.0"?>
```

Without this PI, the software programs and processors are not aware that they are dealing with an XML document. It is called the **prologue** and contains the version number (as we saw in Chapter 2, either XML 1.0 or the newer XML

1.1) but also can have other information such as what character set it is using (see Chapter 6 on Unicode) and if it stands alone or references sources from an external document that might even reside on another server. The PI is not part of the actual XML text but just instructions that move from the processor to the application.

Very First Example

Type the text in Listing 3.2 into Notepad or the editor of your choice. Save it as `veryfirst.xml`. If you are using Notepad, you will need to save it as document type "all", not "txt", and encoding "UTF-8".

LISTING 3.2

```
<?xml version="1.0"?>
<!DOCTYPE veryfirst [
<!ELEMENT veryfirst (#PCDATA)>
]>
<veryfirst>
This is my very first XML document
</veryfirst>
```

Open `veryfirst.xml` up in XML Spy. To do this go to `File | Open` and find `veryfirst.xml` in your own drive path specification. It should resemble Figure 3.4.

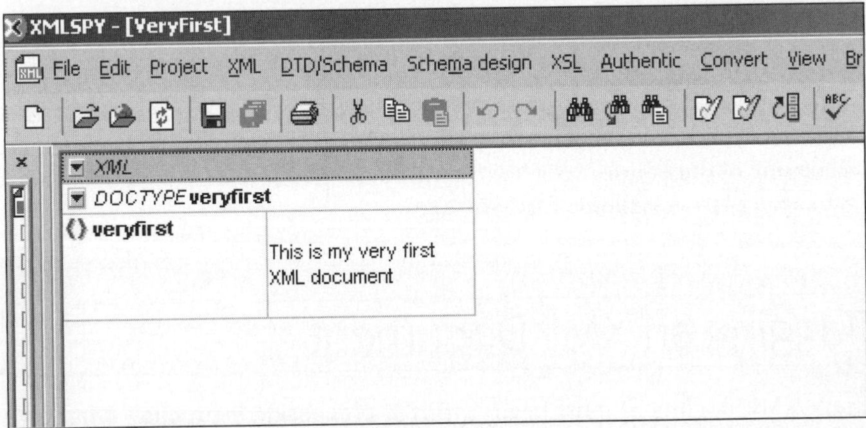

FIGURE 3.4 *veryfirst.xml* in XML Spy

You have now created your first XML document.

```
<?xml version="1.0"?>
```

This is the PI. It begins with an open tag < and then a question mark ? has the xml version number enclosed in quotes "1.0", and then ends with a question mark and a closing tag ?>.

```
<!DOCTYPE veryfirst [
```

This sets the name of the DOCTYPE, which is veryfirst, and starts the DTD with the open bracket [.

```
<!ELEMENT veryfirst (#PCDATA)>
```

This declares the veryfirst root element, which can contain parsed character data.

```
]>
```

This ends the DTD.

```
<veryfirst>
```

This starts the data that will be output using a start tag.

```
This is my very first XML document
```

This is parsed character data typed in after the start tag.

```
</veryfirst>
```

This closes the document with an end tag.

You also could open this file up in IE Explorer.

Alert

Opening up an XML document in IE5 or higher or Netscape 6 or higher already subjects it to a parser within the program.

Character References

Character references are used to insert special characters into an XML document. Character references come from the **ISO/IEC character set,** an international numbering system that references characters from all languages. They are used in case you want to actually insert a specific character into your code, and that character is reserved for use by the processor. Table 3.1 shows just a few of the more common ones used.

Tech Tip

To look up any character reference, go to http://www.zvon.org/other/charSearch/PHP/search.php.

Take a look at Figure 3.5 to see the search results for the < symbol.

TABLE 3.1 Some Typical Character References

Symbol	Explanation	Character Reference	Character Name
<	Less than	<	<
>	Greater than	>	>
&	Ampersand	&	&
"	Quote		"
'	Apostrophe		'

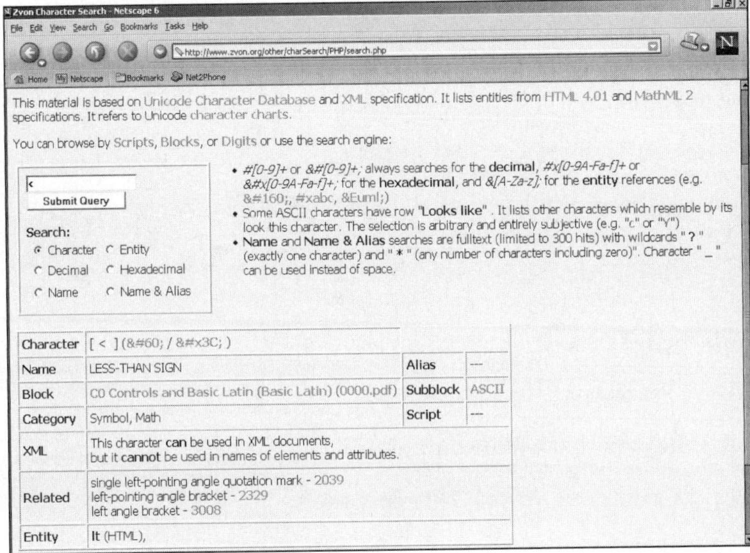

FIGURE 3.5 Character Reference Lookup

Thinking Through XML

Let's say Pasta Primavera, a spaghetti lover's site, has decided to go online and let everyone in the world know just how wonderful and delicious their products are. First, they must categorize their products. Here is one way they could do it:

Subdivision
Market
Product
Type
Packaging
Size
Ingredients

One example of content for these categories might be:

North America
Northeast
Spaghetti sauce
Alfredo
Glass
12 oz.
Spices or Seasonings

These descriptions show products for Pasta Primavera. The way we would set up these descriptions as an XML statement is shown in Table 3.2.

TABLE 3.2 Pasta Primavera XML Statement

Opening Tag	Information	Closing Tag
<Company>	(Name of Document Type Definition)	</Company>
<Subdivision>	North America	</Subdivision>
<Market>	Northeast	</Market>
<Product>	Spaghetti Sauce	</Product>
<Type>	Alfredo	</Type>
<Packaging>	Glass	</Packaging>
<Size>	12 oz.	</Size>
<Ingredients>	Spices or Seasonings	</Ingredients>

Understanding the Tree Structure of a Document

The descriptions are more or less on the same hierarchical level, in terms of a **tree structure.** Think of a tree as your family. There are great-grandparents, grandparents, parents, and children. Therefore, **parents** have one level above and one level below. The root of this is `Company`, because without the company, there would be no product. `Company` fits all the other levels under it, such as `Subdivision` and `Type`. `Ingredients` is an element under the root element `Company` and we have given it an either-or choice, that is, `Spices` or `Seasonings`.

PastaPrimavera DTD

Here we are going to supply the entire `PastaPrimavera` statement (see Listing 3.3) and then break it apart. Remember, we are going to go into DTDs in depth in the next chapter. This is just so we can get a look at the components and logic of an XML statement.

LISTING 3.3

```
<?xml version="1.0"?>
<!DOCTYPE Company [
<!ELEMENT Company (Subdivision,Market,Product,Type,
  Packaging,Size,Ingredients)>
<!ELEMENT Subdivision (#PCDATA)>
<!ELEMENT Market (#PCDATA)>
<!ELEMENT Product (#PCDATA)>
<!ELEMENT Type (#PCDATA)>
```

```
<!ELEMENT Packaging (#PCDATA)>
<!ELEMENT Size (#PCDATA)>
<!ELEMENT Ingredients (Spices|Seasonings)>
<!ELEMENT Spices (#PCDATA)>
<!ELEMENT Seasonings (#PCDATA)>
]>

<Company>
<Subdivision>North America </Subdivision>
<Market>Northeast</Market>
<Product>Spaghetti Sauce</Product>
<Type>Alfredo</Type>
<Packaging>Glass</Packaging>
<Size>12 oz.</Size>
<Ingredients>
<Spices>Pepper</Spices>
</Ingredients>
</Company>
```

The example in Listing 3.3, shown in Figures 3.6 and 3.7, says the following:

- The DTD (or `DOCTYPE`) is named `Company`.
- `Company` includes the root element `Company` as well as the `ELEMENT`s `Subdivision`, `Market`, `Product`, `Type`, `Packaging`, `Size`, and `Ingredients`.
- The `ELEMENT`s allow `(#PCDATA)`, or parsed character data.
- We have chosen one `ELEMENT`, `Ingredients`, to contain the **child** elements of either `Spices` or `Seasonings`.

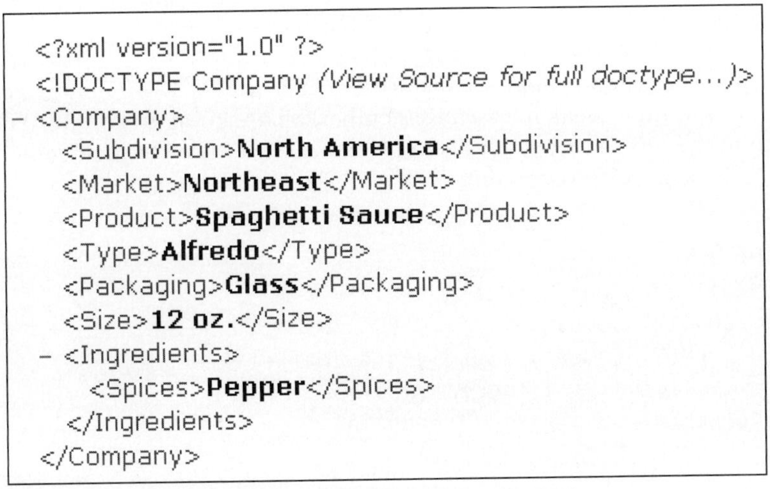

```
<?xml version="1.0" ?>
<!DOCTYPE Company (View Source for full doctype...)>
- <Company>
    <Subdivision>North America</Subdivision>
    <Market>Northeast</Market>
    <Product>Spaghetti Sauce</Product>
    <Type>Alfredo</Type>
    <Packaging>Glass</Packaging>
    <Size>12 oz.</Size>
  - <Ingredients>
      <Spices>Pepper</Spices>
    </Ingredients>
  </Company>
```

FIGURE 3.6 *PastaPrimavera* Shown in Internet Explorer

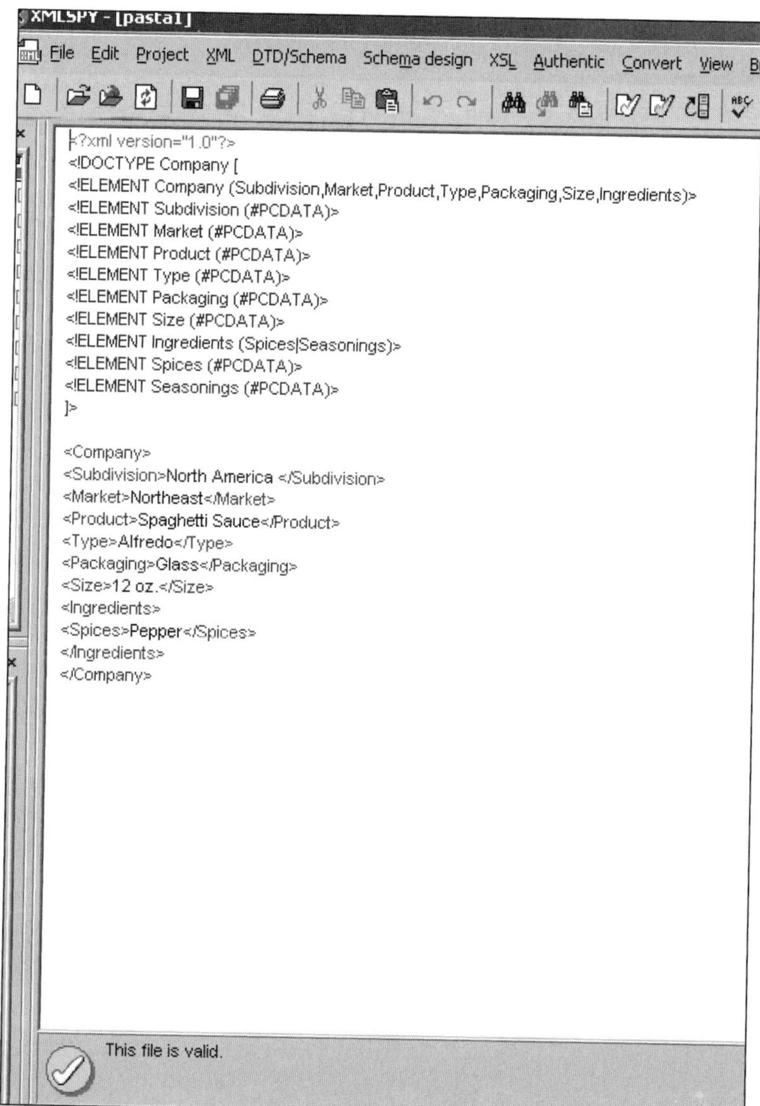

FIGURE 3.7 `PastaPrimavera` in XML Spy

Creating a Root Element

Every XML document must have one root element. The root element contains all the other elements and attributes inside of it. The root element is the most important in the document, and usually takes a name that describes its function. For this example, we will make `Company` the root element. Remember, we created this, and it did not come from any outside source.

> **Tech Tip**
> It is always a good idea to make the root element have the first name as the DTD.

So now do the following. Type this example into an editor such as Notepad. Save it as a **UTF-8 file** with an .xml extension. When we go into Unicode, in Chapter 5, we will explain UTF-8, but for now think of it as an expanded character set. Call the file `PastaPrimavera.xml`. You must save it with the **.xml extension** or it will not be read as an XML file.

There are many advantages to coding the information this way. The first is that you know what the code is referencing. The code is not written in some programming language. The next is you can edit it with a standard text editor. You don't need anything except a recent browser to view it.

Tech Tip

If you are using Windows 98, you might need to enclose the filename in quotes, such as "`PastaPrimavera.xml`", or the name might display as `PastaPrimavera.xml.xml`, depending on which version of Windows 98 is installed.

Comments

Insert **comments** when you want either to write notes about the code to guide you through revisions or to leave instructions for others. Although comments are contained within an XML statement, they do nothing in terms of its programming instructions. This is very helpful when you are coding large statements. Listing 3.4 demonstrates a basic comment.

LISTING 3.4

```
<!-I like spaghetti->
```

In your file after the first line of code, insert this comment, exactly as you see it, including the exclamation point and the two dashes. Then resave your file. It should resemble Figure 3.8.

Elements

An **element** is the basic building block of an XML document. The best way to think of elements is that they are like the nouns of an XML statement. The declaration begins with an opening bracket (<) and exclamation point (!) followed by the keyword `ELEMENT`. An element name must start with a letter or underscore (_) character. See Table 3.3.

There are specific naming conventions for elements:

- Element names cannot have whitespace.
- Element names cannot use any combination of the letters "xml".
- Element names can start with letter characters or "_" but cannot start with numbers or punctuation characters.

Some invalid and valid element names are given in Table 3.4.

Advice

There is no limit on how long an element name can be, but there are some restrictions on what characters are allowed. Element names must begin with a letter, an underscore character (_), or a colon (:). They may contain numbers and some punctuation marks. Case-sensitivity is important; an element named `child` is different from an element named `Child`.

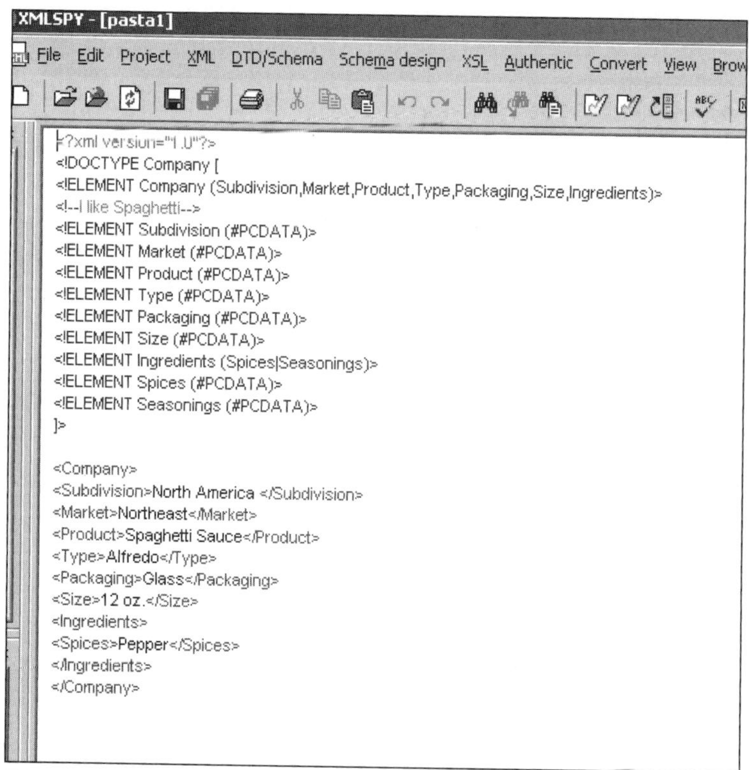

FIGURE 3.8 *I like spaghetti* Comment

TABLE 3.3

Symbol	Description
<	Start delimiter
</	End delimiter
!ELEMENT	Element declaration (all caps necessary)
>	Close delimiter
/>	Empty tag

Empty Element Tags

What is an empty element? Essentially, an **empty element** is a placeholder for content and doesn't add anything to the markup in terms of its semantics. It tells the parser that later on something is going to fill in the space. It is similar to your saving a seat for your friend at the movies. No one is there yet, but someone is on his or her way.

TABLE 3.4 Invalid and Valid Element Names

Invalid	Valid
<cool time>	<cool.time>
<xmlcode>	<codexml>
<903>	<September903>
<two+two>	<twoplustwo>

Alert

You can create elements that need not contain any data. A convention for empty elements shortens the opening and closing tags into a single tag. The tag would include an open bracket, the name of the element, a blank space, a slash mark, then the closing bracket. Here's what it looks like: instead of <pagebreak> . . . </pagebreak>, this tag would instead display as the following empty element: <pagebreak />.

Why use an empty element? One example might be if you were designing a logo for a company and it wasn't ready yet. You could reserve a place in your code for where the element is to be placed. Empty elements are also used for line breaks.

Here is an example of an empty element:

```
<image/>
```

Notice the forward slash (/) comes at the end of the word. That distinguishes it from an end tag (</image>). An <image> is a good example to use, because you might go back and fill it in with something like

```
<image src="PastaPrimavera.jpg"/>
```

#PCDATA

Parsed character data (#PCDATA) is data that has text. That text can be a string of characters that contains either markup, content, or both. If there were unparsed data, it would have a string of characters containing markup or content that could be other than XML. Parsed character data is sent through an XML processor and unparsed information involves itself with data that refers to an application other than XML. You must tell the processor what type of data is allowed in an element statement. It is always capitalized. Listing 3.5 shows an example of #PCDATA.

LISTING 3.5

```
<?xml version="1.0"?>
<!DOCTYPE myfirstpcdata [
<!ELEMENT myfirstpcdata (#PCDATA)>
```

```
]>
<myfirstpcdata> This is my first xml document
  </myfirstpcdata>
```

What this says, in terms of the element, is that the statement "This is my first xml document" is allowed to be written as `#PCDATA`. This has been defined by the parameters of `myfirstpcdata`. It is also saying, implicitly that something like an image or graphic is *not* allowed. If we would try and place an image, the statement would fail.

CDATA

CDATA is very important for putting large blocks of text into a special section that the XML processor looks at only as pure text. This is because the character reference for the < symbol is "<"; and other character symbols are equally as cumbersome. It would be extremely odd to have hundreds of lines of text looking like "<". A `CDATA` statement is shown in Listing 3.6.

LISTING 3.6

```
<![CDATA[
  Text Information (for example "<")
]]>
```

The only symbols you cannot use in this statement are `]]>` since all XML parsers think that this text string is the marker that terminates the `CDATA` statement. But it can contain the markup symbols <, >, and `&`, and they will be viewed by an XML parser as text and not markup. A `CDATA` statement can be situated in between opening and closing element tags, but it cannot be nested inside of another `CDATA` statement. Neither can a `CDATA` statement be empty.

What if you wanted to have a sidebar in the XML file for Pasta Primavera advertising this month's special. Without going into the styling of it, the `CDATA` statement part would appear as in Listing 3.7.

LISTING 3.7

```
<sidebar>
<![CDATA[
This month only, straight from Verona, Italy, is our
  special plum tomato and basil sauce
]]>
</sidebar>
```

Alert

The `CDATA` attribute type is *not* the same as a `CDATA` section in an XML document. Though it is true that they both mean character data, they exist for different reasons altogether. `CDATA` as an attribute never represents markup of any kind and is also known as a String type.

Attributes (#!ATTLIST)

Attributes give more information about an element and reside inside of the element's start tag, listed underneath the element with which it is affiliated. Attributes can further define the behavior of an element and also can allow it to have extended links through giving it an identifier. An element's color can be set, or the element can be formatted and aligned in a certain way, though this is usually taken care of by CSS (Cascading Style Sheets) or XSL (Extensible Style Sheets). Attributes follow the same naming rules as elements and each attribute has a name and a value. An element may have a great number of attributes, but having more than 10 makes it unmanageable. Interestingly enough, an empty XML element can have an attribute. The value of an attribute is enclosed in quote marks.

Attributes break into basic value types: `Tokenized`, `Enumerated`, `CDATA`, and `Default`. `Tokenized` breaks down into a simple unit, for example, a specific name. It imposes constraints on the values of the attribute.

`Tokenized` types are

- `Entity` or `Entities`
- `ID`
- `IDREF` or `IDREFS`
- `NMTOKEN` or `NMTOKENS`

`Enumerated` consists of one or more notations in which a choice of valid values is provided. `CDATA` means character data and the value is not constrained.

Attributes are looked at in great detail in Chapter 4, the chapter on DTDs.

Attributes have default declarations at the end of their attribute list declarations that sets an attribute's use. Attribute defaults are shown in Table 3.5.

The basic syntax for an attribute is shown in Listing 3.8 and an example is given in Listing 3.9.

Alert

One of the raging debates between XML users is when to describe something as an `!ELEMENT` or an attribute.

LISTING 3.8

```
<!ATTLIST ElementName AttributeName
Attribute TypeKeyword
"Possibledefaultvalue" #DEFAULTKeyword>
```

LISTING 3.9

```
<!ELEMENT squarebox (#PCDATA)>
<!ATTLIST squarebox color #IMPLIED>
```

In an XML document, it would look like

```
<squareboxcolor="green">Gift Box </squarebox>
```

TABLE 3.5 Attribute Defaults

Default Value	Description
#DEFAULT	This means if no value is provided in the XML data, the value specified in the DTD will be used.
#IMPLIED	This means the default value is optional. A developer can accept the default or let that processing application choose a default value that may or may not be the same default value as set in the DTD.
#FIXED	This means the default value is fixed and a different value cannot be entered. If no value is entered, the default value is taken.
#REQUIRED	This means the attribute value must be supplied.

Tech Tip

The pound sign (#) is used to differentiate these three keywords from valid XML names. That means you can use the words *implied, fixed,* and *required* inside of an XML DTD.

Entities

Entities are the basic storage units of any XML document. The actual data they store may be derived from a variety of sources, but the sources themselves are not entities. An entity can be declared once but used countless times and does not change the semantic markup of the actual document. Its real purpose is to streamline the code.

Listing 3.10 gives an example of an entity. This means that every time the parser finds the entity reference &PPV, it will replace it with the text "Pasta Primavera Superb". This example is referred to as a general parsed entity because the entity is parsed.

Alert

General entities and character references look similar. That is because a character reference is really a specific type of general entity called a *predefined entity*.

LISTING 3.10

```
<!ENTITY PPV "Pasta Primavera Superb">
<Announcement>This is the home of &PPV</Announcement>
```

Entities also can refer to a DTD, an element or attribute declaration, an external file that contains either character or binary data, and even a text string. Entities will be discussed more in Chapter 4.

How to Decide: Attribute versus !ELEMENT

The best way to decide in choosing an attribute instead of an element is to figure out their basic functions. Actual data about anything is usually an element. Anything that describes the data itself is probably an attribute. If the actual information needs to be displayed and read, then an element is best using child elements because it is more **extensible.** Attributes work best with identifiers or certain types of formatting. Things like external references, identification numbers, URLs, and information not critical to understanding an element are useful for an attribute. Attributes don't stand up to rigorous structure, as do elements. Attributes cannot have substructures, whereas elements can.

We used the example here of elements relating to our food company, Pasta Primavera. Everything that appears in either a valid or a well-formed XML document must be declared in a DTD that we have included above. Again, remember we will go into DTDs in much more depth in the next chapter.

What happens if we purposely make a mistake? Go back to `PastaPrimavera.xml`, and in the last tag, `</Company>`, delete the slash (/). Save it as `Mymistake.xml`. Open the file in your browser and see what happens. Both Netscape and IE will tell you what is wrong and where the problem is. Older versions of the browsers might at least tell you there is a problem. Now go back to `Mymistake.xml` and put the slash back in and save it again. Open it again in a browser. See the difference one keystroke can make!

Key Terms

attribute
BBEdit
CDATA
character references
child
comment
#DEFAULT
Document Type Definition (DTD)
EBNF characters
element
empty element
entities
extensible
#FIXED
IDREF
#IMPLIED
ISO/IEC character set
NMTOKEN
Notepad
parent
#PCDATA
processing instruction (PI)
prologue
#REQUIRED
root element
stylesheet
tree structure
UTF-8 file
valid
well formed
whitespace
XML-compliant browser
.xml extension
XML Schema
XML Spy

Code Summary

1. **Listing 3.1:**

```
<?xml version="1.0"?>
```

2. **Listing 3.2:**

```
<?xml version="1.0"?>
<!DOCTYPE veryfirst [
<!ELEMENT veryfirst (#PCDATA)>
]>
<veryfirst>
This is my very first XML document
</veryfirst>
```

3. **Listing 3.3:**

```
<?xml version="1.0"?>
<!DOCTYPE Company [
<!ELEMENT Company (Subdivision,Market,Product,Type,Packaging,Size,Ingredients)>
<!ELEMENT Subdivision (#PCDATA)>
<!ELEMENT Market (#PCDATA)>
<!ELEMENT Product (#PCDATA)>
<!ELEMENT Type (#PCDATA)>
<!ELEMENT Packaging (#PCDATA)>
<!ELEMENT Size (#PCDATA)>
<!ELEMENT Ingredients (Spices|Seasonings)>
<!ELEMENT Spices (#PCDATA)>
<!ELEMENT Seasonings (#PCDATA)>
]>

<Company>
<Subdivision>North America </Subdivision>
<Market>Northeast</Market>
<Product>Spaghetti Sauce</Product>
<Type>Alfredo</Type>
<Packaging>Glass</Packaging>
<Size>12 oz.</Size>
<Ingredients>
<Spices>Pepper</Spices>
</Ingredients>
</Company>
```

4. **Listing 3.4:**

```
<!-I like spaghetti->
```

5. **Listing 3.5:**

```
<?xml version="1.0"?>
<!DOCTYPE myfirstpcdata [
<!ELEMENT myfirstpcdata (#PCDATA)>
]>
<myfirstpcdata> This is my first xml document </myfirstpcdata>
```

6. **Listing 3.6:**

```
<![CDATA[
  Text Information
]]>
```

7. **Listing 3.7:**

```
<sidebar>
<![CDATA[
This month only, straight from Verona, Italy, is our special plum
  tomato and basil sauce
]]>
</sidebar>
```

8. **Listing 3.8:**

```
<!ATTLIST ElementName AttributeName
Attribute TypeKeyword
"Possibledefaultvalue" #DEFAULTKeyword>
```

9. **Listing 3.9:**
```
<!ELEMENT squarebox (#PCDATA)>
<!ATTLIST squarebox color #IMPLIED>
```

10. **Listing 3.10:**
```
<!ENTITY PPV "Pasta Primavera Superb">
<Announcement>This is the home of &PPV</Announcement>
```

Review Questions

1. What are the three steps to creating an XML document?
2. An XML document has to be valid. True or False?
3. How many root elements are there in a well-formed XML document?
4. XML allows three errors in its coding structure. True or False?
5. What is a PI?
6. XML is case-sensitive. True or False?
7. How many root elements are allowed?
8. XML documents do not have to be well formed. True or False?
9. An XML document must conform to the rules of its developer. True or False?
10. What is EBNF syntax?
11. What are character references used for?
12. A one-keystroke mistake is allowed in an XML document. True or False?
13. Element names can have whitespace. True or False?
14. Element names can be only seven characters long. True or False?
15. What is the difference between `(#PCDATA)` and `CDATA`?
16. What do attributes do?
17. What are the four different types of attributes?
18. What are the different default values of attributes?
19. Why is the # sign used?
20. How many times can an entity be used?
21. List three instances of when you should use an element instead of an attribute.

Case Study

The government in the United Kingdom has been especially vigilant in getting its documents up to speed in XML. Go to http://www.govtalk.gov.uk/default-content.asp and click under Schemas and Standards, the middle column, on Data Standards Catalogue. The next screen will say "UK Government Data Standards Catalogue" and asks you if you want frames or no frames. Choose frames and when the next page comes up, see the listings. Choose the "Person Birth Date". You will then see a UK Government Data Standards Catalogue on your right. Below you will see, under XML Schema, the schema displayed as either XML or HTML. To see the actual XML, choose Person Descriptive Types. Here you will see the information displayed as a schema, which we will go into in Chapter 5. However, notice how you can actually see what the information is showing. Now go to another category beside "Person Birth Date" and display that category's XML data link as well. As you can see, XML is currently being used by a major government to categorize the most important documents of its citizens.

Below is the code for a well-formed and valid file.

```
<?xml version="1.0"?>
<xsd:schema xmlns:xsd="http://www.w3.org/2001/XMLSchema">
  <xsd:element name="SONG" type="SongType"/>
  <xsd:complexType name="SongType">
    <xsd:sequence>
      <xsd:element name="TITLE" type="xsd:string"/>
      <xsd:element name="COMPOSER" type="xsd:string"/>
      <xsd:element name="PRODUCER" type="xsd:string"/>
      <xsd:element name="PUBLISHER" type="xsd:string"/>
      <xsd:element name="LENGTH" type="xsd:string"/>
      <xsd:element name="YEAR" type="xsd:string"/>
      <xsd:element name="ARTIST" type="xsd:string"/>
      <xsd:element name="PRICE" type="xsd:string"/>
    </xsd:sequence>
  </xsd:complexType>
</xsd:schema>
```

1. Using Notepad or the editing program of your choice, type this code into it and save it as `song.xsd` (an XML schema file) with a UTF-8 encoding into the drive path specification of your choice. Open it in XML Spy and test it for both well-formedness and validity by clicking both the yellow and green buttons on the tool bar. If you have typed it into Notepad correctly, the file should be both well formed and valid.

2. Now go and purposely change something in the file. For instance, make it xml version 2.0 instead of 1.0. Save this file as `songmistake.xsd`. Run it through XML Spy. Or misspell `compleType`. See if it is still valid and well formed.

3. Now try opening `song.xsd` in Internet Explorer. What happens? Can you figure out why? Try it in Netscape. What does this say about a browser's ability to handle schemas?

4. Next, using the Pasta Primavera categories, add some new ones and save the file as `mypastaprimavera.xml` in the editing tool of your choice. Add the elements `distributor`, `shipper`, and `inventory#`. Put them anywhere within the root element. Test the file in both XML Spy and Internet Explorer. See if it is well formed. Then test it to see if it is valid.

CHAPTER 4

Creating Document Type Definitions (DTDs)

LEARNING OBJECTIVES

1. To understand the function and syntax of a DTD.
2. To learn what distinguishes internal and external subsets of DTDs.
3. To define the order and frequency of elements.
4. To understand how to create attributes and apply them to elements.
5. To explore how entity declarations and notation elements work.

By now, you've learned that you can use XML to define your own tags in your own markup language. And as you've seen, an XML document must conform to predefined rules in order to be considered valid. You will set up these rules using a **schema,** which is a formal description of your language that can be read by a validator. The next two chapters will focus on how to formally define your own language.

There are two common schema languages used in XML. The first is the Document Type Definition (DTD), which defines the grammar and vocabulary of your markup language. The DTD lists everything that a parser needs to know in order to display and process your XML document. In this chapter, we will examine how a DTD works; you'll also learn how to create and edit a DTD to define the elements that appear in your documents. The second common schema language is **XML Schema,** which is well-suited for more complex XML documents; you'll learn about XML Schema in Chapter 5.

IMPORTANT

The World Wide Web Consortium (W3C) defines and oversees both the DTD and XML Schema specifications.

Introducing DTDs

What should a DTD contain? It can hold a simple listing of all of your language's components—the elements, tags, attributes, and entities—that your documents may contain. Or it could be more complex, defining the relationship between those elements; for example, a book element could contain a category element that tags it as fact or fiction, but never both at the same time.

Imposing Grammar and Structure

To help you gain a better sense of what a DTD does, consider the following statement:

need

love.

you all is

Every word and bit of punctuation in this statement is a well-formed part of the English language, but the statement holds little meaning in its current state. In order for it to be recognized as a valid sentence in the English language—and hold meaning for those reading and interpreting it—the words need to conform to a standard grammatical structure. The version below meets these requirements:

All you need is love.

In a similar way, a DTD uses grammar and structure to bring order to the elements of a markup language defined by XML. To stipulate grammatical rules, a DTD compares a set of expressions against predefined patterns in an XML document to figure out whether that document is valid or not. The matching is very nitpicky; for example, pressing the space bar twice when the processor is looking for a single blank space is a mismatch. This is designed to rule out anything that is not specifically allowed by the DTD.

Checking for Validation

As you gain experience writing XML documents, consider using a validating parser—a parser that reads the DTD and refers to it in scanning your documents for errors.

An **interactive validation** process pops up warnings and error messages as you're constructing an XML document, alerting you immediately if something is amiss. If your word processing program spell-checks what you're typing on the fly, you've seen how this type of functionality works.

With a parser that performs **batch validation,** you submit a complete XML document for error checking and then see a complete report listing all errors and warnings that may apply. If you've created Web pages in the past, you may already be familiar with validating HTML documents through an HTML authoring program like Homesite or Dreamweaver. Figure 4.1 shows how the document management view within an XML development environment called TIBCO TurboXML tracks which files in a directory have already been validated.

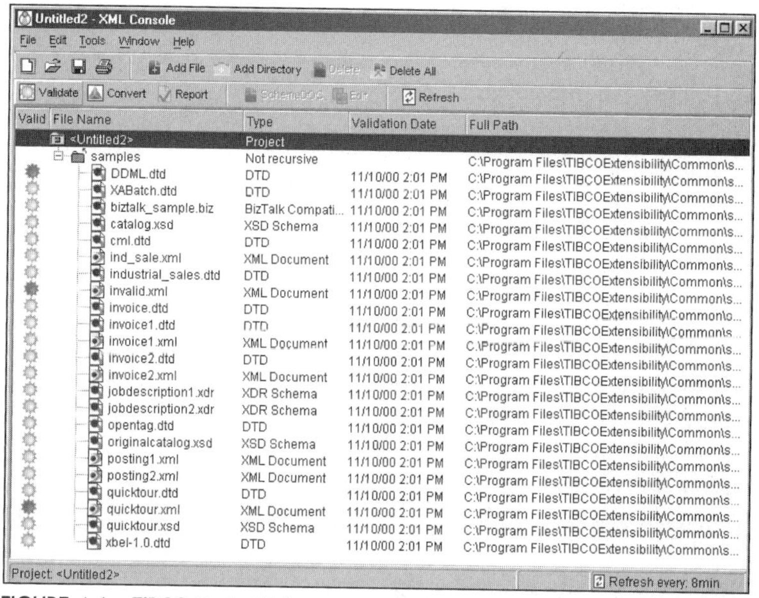

FIGURE 4.1 TIBCO TurboXML

TIBCO TurboXML is an integrated development environment for XML that provides an overview of which XML documents in a directory have been validated.

There are even online validators that you can use to validate your XML for you after you enter a URL or copy and paste the code. The Scholarly Technology Group at Brown University, for example, offers such an interactive tool at http://www.stg.brown.edu/service/xmlvalid/xmlvalid.var, as shown in Figure 4.2.

While using a validating parser is a good way to catch mistakes, it's not a substitute for your own careful review of your code. For example, your parser will

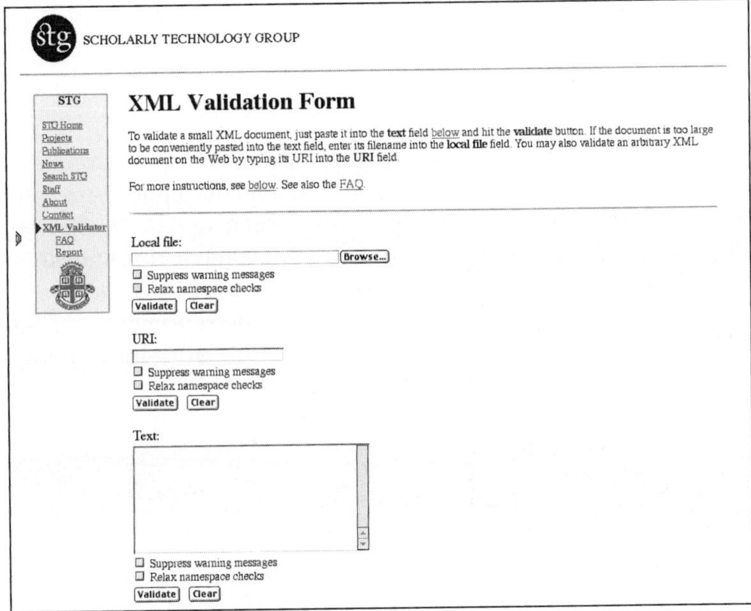

FIGURE 4.2 XML Validation Form
The Scholarly Technology Group at Brown University provides an online XML validator.

note if a song title is missing from an XML document containing lyrics if the songbook DTD states that every song must have a title. If, however, an entire verse is omitted, the parser will not complain as long as the DTD contains no rules governing how many verses are in a song.

To demonstrate this, let's look at a sentence that a spell-checker would find no errors with:

> I want to see the mall.

What's the problem? The intended sentence separates the last two words a little differently:

> I want to see them all.

A spell-checker doesn't catch the error because both words in the phrase "them all" as well as in "the mall" are valid in the English language. In order for the mistake to be caught, sentences like this need to be reviewed by a human editor as well. Similarly, an XML parser on your computer can only flag errors based on what's been excluded from the DTD; it has no way of determining context.

Using DTD Syntax

A DTD consists of a number of **declarations.** Each declaration is assigned to one of the following categories:

- `ELEMENT`, for defining tags.
- `ATTLIST`, for specifying attributes in your tags.
- `ENTITY`, for identifying sources of data.
- `NOTATION`, for defining data types for non-XML data.

The declarations that make up a DTD can be stored either at the beginning of an XML document or in an external file. Each method has its own advantages. When the declarations in a DTD are stored with the document it describes, you can easily move the file to a new location and have the DTD travel with it. On the other hand, the effort involved in creating a DTD usually only makes sense if it will apply to multiple documents. If you define a new DTD for each of your documents and then modify an element, you'd have to make the same modification in multiple files. For this reason, it's often most efficient to create an **external DTD** that you can reference from many different files.

Sometimes you may want to be very flexible and use an external DTD for a whole set of documents, but still have the ability to make exceptions—say, use an element declaration to create a special tag—in just a single document. In that case, you can use an **internal subset** of declarations defined right in your document to make sure those exceptions are recognized, while still referencing an **external subset** in a separate document that includes all the standard definitions you're using. We'll look at the details of both internal and external subsets of DTDs later in this chapter.

Writing Element Declarations

An element declaration is used to define a new tag and specify what kind of content it can contain. The declaration begins with an opening bracket (<) and exclamation point (!) followed by the keyword `ELEMENT`. The name of the element you're declaring follows next; it's often called a **generic identifier.** The rest of the tag states what content is allowed in the element, also known as the **content specification.** Table 4.1 shows examples of what a variety of element declarations might look like.

TABLE 4.1 Sample Element Declarations in a DTD

Example	What It Means	How It's Used in an XML Document
`<!ELEMENT image EMPTY>`	This defines an <image> tag. It may not contain any elements or free text within it.	<image src="newlogo.gif"></image> or <image />
`<!ELEMENT p ANY>`	This defines a <p> tag. This tag can contain all of the other elements included in the DTD. (As a result, in practice few elements contain the keyword ANY.)	<p> <!--other tags and free text appear here --> </p>
`<!ELEMENT zipcode (#CDATA)>`	This creates a tag called <zipcode>. It registers the literal value of any content surrounded by opening and closing <zipcode> tags.	<zipcode>90210</zipcode>
`<!ELEMENT songtitle (#PCDATA)>`	This defines a <songtitle> tag. It allows parsing, or interpreting, of tags contained within its content.	<songtitle>Frère Jacques</songtitle> (This would display in a browser as Frère Jacques.)
`<!ELEMENT author (firstname, lastname)>`	This creates a tag called <author> that contains a tag called <firstname> and one called <lastname>. In addition, there can only be one <firstname> and <lastname> element in this document.	<author> <firstname>Marge</firstname> <lastname>Piercy</lastname> </author>

IMPORTANT

Apart from a few exemptions, you may choose any name you like for your element name. One exception: element names cannot begin with the letters XML, xml, or any other mixed-case variation of these letters.

IMPORTANT

In order to display certain typographical characters correctly in your XML (or HTML) documents, you'll need a way to tell the parser how to interpret them. **Character entity codes** are sets of characters that you can use to represent the special characters or accents you want.

Entity	Special Character
<	<
>	>
&	&
"	“
'	‘
è	è
é	é

An element must be allowed to contain **parsed character data** (shown in your DTD as `#PCDATA`) in order for it to properly display these kinds of character entity codes. There are many online listings of character entity references supported in XHTML; one we refer to is at http://www.evolt.org/article/A_Simple_Character_Entity_Chart/17/21234/.

Model Groups

The final example in Table 4.1 shows an example of a **model group.** A model group defines an element that may contain other elements (called **child elements**) or an element that contains a combination of both document text and child elements:

```
<author>
<firstname>Marge</firstname>
<lastname>Piercy</lastname>
</author>
```

In this example, an `<author>` tag requires that both first name and last name elements be entered so that this entry can be located appropriately in subsequent searches.

A model group always appears within parentheses—the symbols (and)—and contains at least one **token,** which may be the name of a child element. The model group for the `<author>` tag contains two tokens: `firstname` and `lastname`.

Controlling Quantity

You can impose requirements about how often each element can be used. For example, some books—like this one!—may have more than one author. Accordingly, you could add a requirement that while an element called book must have at least one author, it could have more. To do so, place a plus sign (+) after the token name author in the overall element declaration for book. Here's what that would look like in your DTD:

```
<!ELEMENT book (title, author+, publisher)>
```

Table 4.2 shows all the different ways you can specify how many times an element should occur in a document.

TABLE 4.2 Defining Element Instances in a DTD with an Occurrence Indicator

Symbol	What It Means	How It's Used in a DTD
None	This element must occur exactly one time.	`<!ELEMENT birthdate (month, day, year)>`
+	This element should appear one or more times.	`<!ELEMENT scientist (name, expertise+)>`
*	This element can appear zero or more times.	`<!ELEMENT chapter (paragraph+, illustration*)>`
?	This element is optional, but if it appears, it must appear only once.	`<!ELEMENT fullname (firstname, initial?, lastname)>`

Controlling Order

When you define two or more tokens in an element, you also can control the order in which the child elements should appear, as well as any conditions about when they can be used.

IMPORTANT

You also can indicate how often a model group as a whole should occur. The entire group can be required, optional, or repeatable. For example, the pubinfo element in the following declaration states that the sequence listing a publisher and publication date must either occur together in sequence or be omitted altogether:

```
<!ELEMENT pubinfo ((publisher, pubdate)?)>
```

All of the examples you've seen so far use commas to separate the tokens in an element declaration. This is called a **sequence connector** and dictates that the child elements must appear in the order shown. The declaration for an element called `flight` might appear as follows:

```
<!ELEMENT flight (airline, number, from, to, depdate)>
```

and could be used to generate the following code fragment:

```
<flight>
<airline>United</airline>
<number>21</number>
<from>LGA</from>
<to>SFO</to>
<depdate>July 27</depate>
</flight>
```

Another way you can control which elements appear is through a **choice connector,** which indicates that only one of a selection of elements can be used. Instead of commas, the tokens are separated by a pipe character (|) in an element declaration:

```
<!ELEMENT season (winter | spring | summer | fall)>
```

This tagging might be put to use in a clothes catalog, for instance:

```
<season>
<winter> . . . </winter>
</season>
```

or

```
<season>
<summer> . . . </summer>
</season>
```

Figure 4.3 depicts how the logic employed by a sequence connector and a choice connector works in a workflow diagram.

Avoiding Ambiguity

If there is any danger of ambiguity in an element declaration about which elements have an either-or relationship, you should use additional sets of parentheses to enclose the choice pairs. In the following example, it may not be clear that the title is required no matter whether the CD is an audio CD (for playing on a stereo) or a data CD (for use in a computer's CD-ROM drive):

```
<!ELEMENT cd (title, audio | data)>
```

Enclose the audio-or-data elements in parentheses to clear things up:

```
<!ELEMENT cd (title, (audio | data))>
```

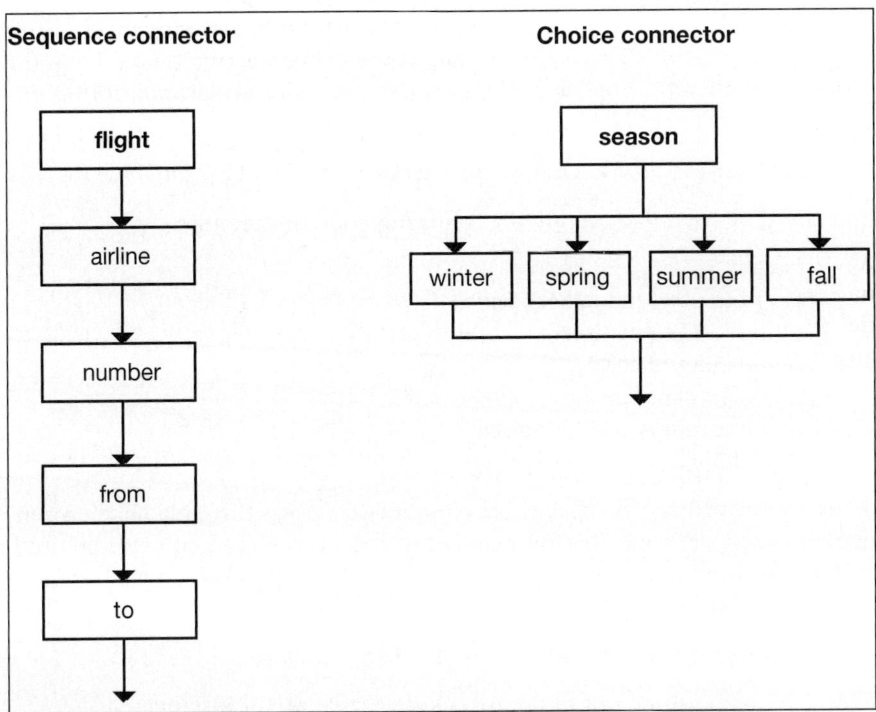

FIGURE 4.3 Ordering Elements Using a Sequence Connector and a Choice Connector

Free Text

As you've seen in previous chapters, any elements that may contain freeform document text are indicated by the keyword PCDATA preceded by a hash mark (#) in the element declaration. Some examples include

```
<!ELEMENT question (#PCDATA)>
<!ELEMENT response (#PCDATA)>
```

It's also possible to define elements that contain free text as well as child elements. Here's what such an element declaration might look like:

```
<!ELEMENT scrapbook (#PCDATA | caption | quote)*>
```

In this case, either PCDATA or one of the child elements (a caption or a quote) can appear within a <scrapbook> . . . </scrapbook> set of tags. The asterisk at the end means that any of these can occur zero or more times in succession. This is an example of what's known as a **mixed-content model,** in which any number of caption or quote elements can be interspersed with the text. Mixed-content models must always be defined with #PCDATA appearing first, followed by one or more alternative items divided by a pipe character (|), and an asterisk (*) at the end.

Writing Attribute List Declarations

You define attributes separately from elements in what's called an **attribute list declaration.** All of the attributes that apply to a single element are usually grouped in the same attribute list declaration. The declaration begins with an opening bracket (<) and exclamation point (!) followed by the keyword ATTLIST. The name of the associated element appears next, followed by the name of the attribute itself. The rest of the tag states its type and possibly its default value. Figure 4.4 shows several examples of attribute list declarations and breaks down their various parts.

```
          Element Attribute Attribute  Required and
           name     name      type     default values

<!ATTLIST address country   CDATA    #FIXED  "USA">
<!ATTLIST price   shipping  CDATA    #IMPLIED>
<!ATTLIST img     alt       CDATA    #REQUIRED
                  src       CDATA    #REQUIRED
                  width     CDATA    #IMPLIED
                  height    CDATA    #IMPLIED>
<!ATTLIST file    format    NOTATION (ps | pdf)>
<!ATTLIST salad   dressing  (french | bluecheese | italian) #REQUIRED>
```

FIGURE 4.4 Attribute List Declarations
An attribute list declaration defines the name of an attribute, specifies its attribute type, and includes any required or default value.

Let's examine what each of these components means in detail below.

Attribute Name

The name of your new attribute is subject to the same restrictions as element names. For example, an **attribute name** can't begin with a number or the letters XML (or any uppercase or lowercase variation thereof). It's always a good idea to choose names that are as descriptive as possible for your attributes.

Attribute Type

An attribute's type can restrict the range of values that the attribute can hold. It also can identify special attributes that may be of importance to the parser. Table 4.3 shows the different kinds of **attribute types** that can be used.

TABLE 4.3 Examples of Attribute Types in an Attribute List Declaration

Type	Description
CDATA	**Character data.** This recognizes the literal value of any string of characters entered for this attribute. See Figure 4.4 for several examples of the CDATA attribute type: <!ATTLIST price shipping CDATA #IMPLIED>
ENTITY	This attribute type is a special case, indicating that the attribute value is really an entity reference.
ENTITIES	The plural form of the ENTITY attribute type, this indicates a list of entities data.
ID	Unique ID data. It's used when hyperlinking among documents.
IDREF	ID of another element. It's used when hyperlinking among documents.
IDREFS	The plural form of the IDREF attribute type, this indicates a list of IDs of other elements.
NMTOKEN	XML name data. This type indicates a word, or token. It follows the same naming convention rules as attributes, except that a **name token** can begin with a number.
NMTOKENS	The plural form of the NMTOKEN attribute type, this indicates a list of XML names.
NOTATION	Name of a notation. As shown in Figure 4.4, here is an example of the NOTATION attribute type: <!ATTLIST file format NOTATION (ps | pdf)>
(*value1* | *value2* | . . .)	Here, the values assigned to this attribute can only come from this predefined, finite set. The following attribute list declaration: <!ATTLIST options finish (metal | polished | matte) #REQUIRED> indicates that the value of the finish attribute must be either metal, polished, or matte.
xml:	There are several names beginning with xml: for **reserved attributes.** These include xml:lang and xml:space. <!ATTLIST french xml:lang NMTOKEN "fr"> <!ATTLIST english xml:lang NMTOKEN "en">

Required or Default Values

The last parameter that appears in an attribute list declaration is the **default value.** The attribute is set to any value entered here if and when the document author fails to supply another. Table 4.4 shows what values may be used here.

Refer back to Figure 4.4 to see more examples of required and default values for attribute list declarations.

IMPORTANT

All attribute values are normalized before being sent on to an application, which means that extra whitespace in your document is reduced to a minimum and any parsing is carried out. If you have an `ATTLIST` declaration that you created to span several lines in order to define multiple attributes for an element declaration, the end-of-line codes will be replaced by whitespace. Any `ENTITY` types are replaced by the entity content.

TABLE 4.4 Sample Required and Default Values for Attribute List Declarations

Example	Description
`#DEFAULT` *value*	If no value is provided in the XML data, the value specified in the DTD will be used.
`#FIXED` *value*	This ensures that this attribute holds the value specified in the DTD, a **fixed value.** If another value appears in the XML data, an error will occur.
`#IMPLIED`	The value doesn't necessarily have to be supplied in the XML data.
`#REQUIRED`	Since this attribute is required to have a value, an error will occur if one is not defined in the XML data.

Now let's consider what your attributes will ultimately be used for. When it's used in an XML or XHTML document, an attribute modifies or provides more information about a particular tag. It appears inside a tag as a name-value pair separated by an equal sign (=). Attribute values must always be quoted. Table 4.5 shows several sample attribute list declarations and what some tags based on a DTD containing these attribute declarations might look like.

As the examples in Table 4.5 show, attribute declarations specify which elements may have attributes, what types of attributes these are, what values the attributes can hold, and what default value each attribute has.

The declarations in attribute lists identify the name, data type, and default value (if there is one) of each attribute associated with a given element type:

- **Name.** This defines the full set of attributes that pertain to a given element type.
- **Type.** This establishes the type constraints for the attribute.
- **Default value.** This provides a value to be used for that attribute unless it is changed.

There are three kinds of XML attribute types: a string type, a set of tokenized types, and enumerated types.

TABLE 4.5 Sample Attribute List Declarations in a DTD

<table>
<tr><th>Example</th><th>What It Means</th><th>How It's Used in an XML Document</th></tr>
<tr><td><!ATTLIST person gender (male | female) "male"></td><td>This defines the allowable values for the attribute gender for an element called person. If the gender were not specified, it would not be an acceptable value according to the rules of this DTD.</td><td><person gender="male"></td></tr>
<tr><td><!ATTLIST essay author CDATA #REQUIRED></td><td>This defines an author attribute for an element called essay. A value is required, but no default is assigned. The CDATA type indicates you can use a simple string of characters.</td><td><essay author="Thomas Merton"></td></tr>
<tr><td><!ATTLIST creditpay transid CDATA #REQUIRED creditpay cardid CDATA #REQUIRED creditpay creditnum CDATA #REQUIRED creditpay expdate CDATA #IMPLIED></td><td>This defines a series of attributes or an element describing credit card payments.</td><td><creditpay transid= "00001" cardid="00027" creditnum="797887530" expdate="2004/09/30" /></td></tr>
</table>

Writing Parameter Entity Declarations

The purpose of an entity is really to act as a placeholder for content; it's a variable that represents other values. Entities fall into one of two groups: general and parameter entities. In Chapter 2, we looked at how **general entities** can be used broadly to substitute the longer, wordier value of an entity for the entity name when the XML document is parsed. A second kind of entity, called a **parameter entity,** works a little differently. Parameter entities are used exclusively for assisting with constructing a DTD.

For example, you can use a parameter entity to assign a short name for a model group that's in common use throughout your documents. You identify a parameter entity by preceding its name in the declaration with a percentage sign (%) and a blank space. Here's what this looks like in practice:

```
<!ENTITY % tablecell "(p | ul | ol)*" >
```

You can then refer to the parameter entity (and, indirectly, to the model group it contains) as you define other elements or entities:

```
<!ENTITY % tablecell "(p | ul | ol)*" >
<!ENTITY % lists "DL | %tablecell;" >
<!ELEMENT tablecell (%tablecell;) >
```

This can help reduce authoring errors—especially as your DTDs grow more and more complex. Spelling out fewer model groups hopefully means you'll have fewer pipe characters and parentheses to type—and fewer chances you'll omit a parenthesis mark or delimiter by accident.

One thing to watch out for is to make sure you don't create recursive parameter entities—that is, two parameter entities that refer endlessly to each other. Here's an example:

```
<!ENTITY % lists "OL | UL | DL | %myLists;" >
<!ENTITY % myLists "PhoneList | CodeList | %lists;" >
```

To avoid this, keep an eye out when you proofread your code to trace where each parameter entity is defined, especially if you have a parameter entity that refers to another.

```
<!ENTITY % section (%tablecell;)*>
```

Writing Notation Declarations

In an XML document, an entity or element is permitted to contain non-XML format data. When this happens, the element declaration has to specify which formats may be embedded. The entity declaration must detail exactly which format is embedded. In both cases, this is done by referring to a notation name, which is defined in a **notation declaration.**

Let's look at how this might work in a real-world situation. If you were updating an XML-based photo catalog, you might deal with some graphics file formats (like PNG or TIF) that your processor doesn't recognize. When that happens, you must define the **notation.** Here's what it looks like:

```
<!NOTATION PNG SYSTEM "photoshop.exe">
```

A notation declaration begins with an opening delimiter, followed by an exclamation mark and the keyword `NOTATION`. The notation name follows next; you should use an obvious name for the format. Here, the notation name `png` matches the filename extension. Next, an external notation identifier indicates whether a public or system indicator can provide information about the

IMPORTANT

When you indicate in an element declaration how often a parameter entity (representing a model group) appears, you have the option of using parentheses to enclose the parameter entity before adding the +, *, or ? symbol.

data format. Here, SYSTEM is used because the application that can open PNG files is on a local system. Finally, the application in question (photoshop.exe) that will process and define PNG file types for the XML processor is listed. If a public identifier were used, the path to the filename would have appeared here instead, as in the following example:

```
<!NOTATION gif_pix PUBLIC "-//ISBN 0-7923-9432-1::Graphic
  Notation//NOTATION CompuServe Graphic Interchange
  Format//EN">
```

Now that a notation declaration is defined, an entity or element declaration can safely refer to the PNG format. When the XML processor runs across an entity called logo_graphic, it turns to the DTD for the full definition:

```
<!ENTITY logo_graphic SYSTEM "baselinelogo.png" NDATA PNG>
```

Here, NDATA (short for **notational data**) is the indicator that a non-XML data format is embedded in this entity declaration. The data type for the file called baselinelogo.png, according to this declaration, is PNG. Although the parser has no use for a PNG file, it now knows to pass it on to an application that should be able to work with it (photoshop.exe).

Attribute declarations also can refer to a declared notation in this way. The DTD for this example could include the following declarations:

```
<!NOTATION PNG SYSTEM "photoshop.exe">
<!ELEMENT image (#PCDATA)>
<!ATTLIST image format NOTATION (EPS | TIF | PNG) "TIF">
```

The XML document could then include a tag for <image format="PNG"> . . . </image> that would be sent to Photoshop to process. The image format defaults to TIF if no other is asked for.

Referencing DTDs

As mentioned earlier in this chapter, the declarations that make up a DTD can be stored in one of two locations. For starters, they can appear at the top of each of your XML documents. Most of the time, though, they're stored in a separate data file that's simply referenced from the XML document.

IMPORTANT

The minimal form for a notation declaration includes a system identifier with no value, just an empty set of quotation marks. The example shown below refers to TADS, a software environment for developing and running computing games:

```
<!NOTATION TADS SYSTEM "">
```

A `DOCTYPE` declaration is used in both cases. When the DTD declarations are enclosed internally within an XML document, the `DOCTYPE` declaration list encloses the list of declarations within a set of square brackets (`[]`) as shown in Listing 4.1.

LISTING 4.1 Referencing an Internal DTD

```
<?xml version="1.0"?>
<!DOCTYPE message [
  <!ELEMENT message (to,from,date,time,subject,body)>
  <!ELEMENT to (#PCDATA)>
  <!ELEMENT from (#PCDATA)>
  <!ELEMENT date (#PCDATA)>
  <!ELEMENT time (#PCDATA)>
  <!ELEMENT subject (#PCDATA)>
  <!ELEMENT body (#PCDATA)>
]>
<message>
  <to>Ross</to>
  <from>Bunny</from>
  <date>July 25</ date >
  <time>11:15 a.m.</time>
  <subject>Reminder</ subject >
  <body>Please don't forget to tape Survivor tonight!
    </body>
</message>
```

When the DTD declarations appear in a separate document, the `DOCTYPE` declaration includes the path to the DTD file, as the line of code appearing in italic in Listing 4.2 demonstrates.

LISTING 4.2 Referencing an External DTD

```
<?xml version="1.0"?>
<!DOCTYPE message SYSTEM "message.dtd"><message>
  <to>Ross</to>
  <from>Bunny</from>
  <date>July 25</ date>
  <time>11:15 a.m.</time>
  <subject>Reminder</ subject>
  <body>Please don't forget to tape Survivor tonight!
    </body>
</message>
```

The `message.dtd` file, in turn, contains a listing of the elements used in the XML document in Listing 4.2:

```
<!ELEMENT message (to,from,date,time,subject,body)>
<!ELEMENT to (#PCDATA)>
<!ELEMENT from (#PCDATA)>
<!ELEMENT date (#PCDATA)>
```

```
<!ELEMENT time (#PCDATA)>
<!ELEMENT subject (#PCDATA)>
<!ELEMENT body (#PCDATA)>
```

Figure 4.5 shows how the `message.dtd` file is truly external to the XML document that references it.

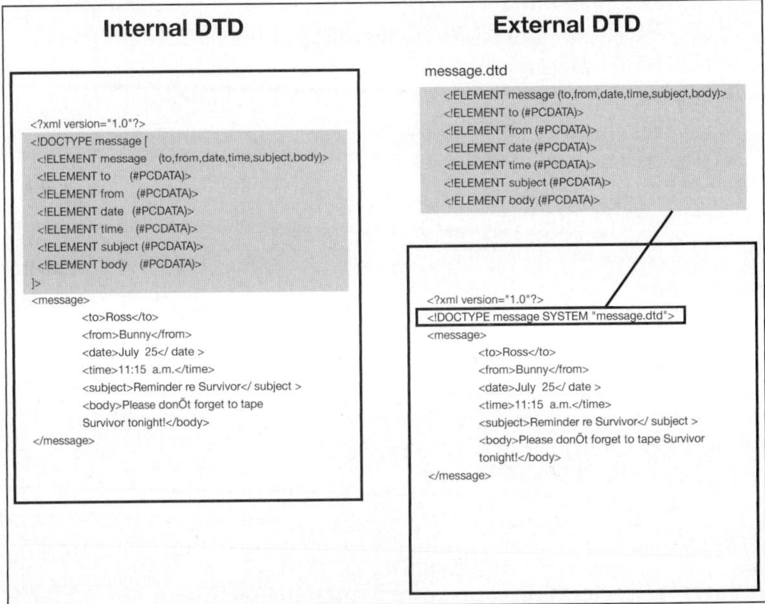

FIGURE 4.5 Internal versus External DTD

An XML document containing an internal DTD is compared with one that references its DTD via a separate data file.

If any element shown in the `message.dtd` file is changed, it affects not just this document but any document that points to the `message.dtd` file. This raises an interesting question: what if you want to declare a certain number of elements across multiple XML documents but also want to allow for exceptions in particular documents? You can do that with internal subsets (the exceptions, which are parsed first) and external subsets (which make it easy to declare the same elements across many documents). An XML parser first processes an internal subset of declarations before referring to an external subset; this processing patch is shown in Figure 4.6. This is useful to know because it can give you control over how your external subset is used in any particular document.

Another way you can control whether or not certain declarations are accessible to any given document is by including instructions that say whether or not a particular set of declarations within an external subset are available. This is called a **conditional section** because the declarations contained within such a section are only available if all conditions are met. If the conditions aren't

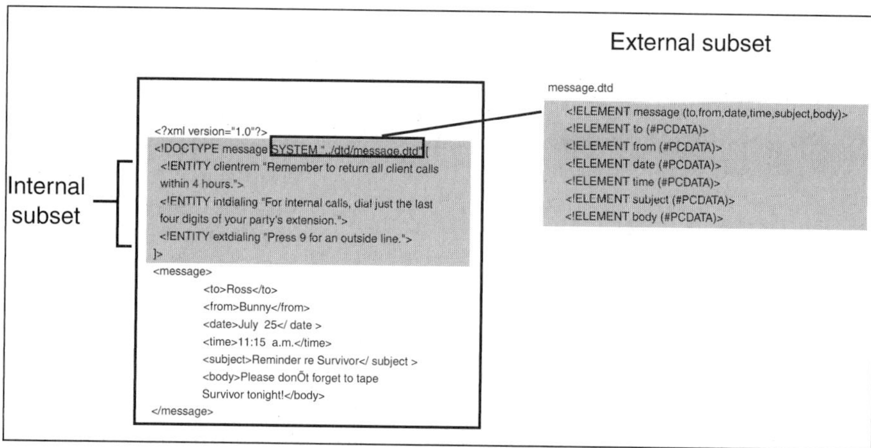

FIGURE 4.6 Internal versus External Subsets
An XML parser processes an internal subset of declarations before an external subset.

met, this subset of declarations is rendered invisible to the XML parser or processor.

Creating External DTD Subsets

Although you can embed a DTD entirely within an XML document, it's not efficient to maintain dozens or hundreds of XML documents this way. In order to design and maintain a consistent look across a large body of documents, you need a way to manage your DTD's declarations centrally. To handle this, you can store some or all of your declarations in a separate file that's named with a .dtd extension (such as `termpaper.dtd`). This kind of file is known as an external subset; you can refer to it from multiple documents by placing a URL pointing to the file's path after the `SYSTEM` keyword in your `DOCTYPE` declaration. An example is shown in italic below:

```
<!DOCTYPE termpaper SYSTEM "http://www.genuineclass.com/
   xml/dtd/termpaper.dtd" [
<!-- the rest of the termpaper DTD local to this document
   appears here, if needed-->
<! . . . .>
]>
```

Using Internal DTD Subsets

After you define an external DTD, you may not have many declarations left to include in an internal subset. These leftover declarations typically include entity declarations for important phrases or images that appear frequently within this particular document but not others. An internal subset is also a good place to define special characters used here that aren't needed in the majority of your documents.

IMPORTANT

Entity declarations and attributes defined in a declaration that appear in an internal subset will override those with the same name in an external subset. This allows you to make any document-specific changes you want while still applying the same DTD external subset to a large number of documents.

Using Conditional Sections with Entities

You can control whether to include or omit declarations by using what's known as a conditional section in a DTD. The keyword `INCLUDE` specifies when a certain declaration should be included, while the keyword `IGNORE` dictates when a declaration is excluded. Here, for example, the parser is directed to include an element declaration called `suggestion`:

```
<![INCLUDE [ <!ELEMENT suggestion ( #PCDATA )> ]]>
```

Similarly, the following conditional section tells the parser to exclude the declaration of an element called `graffiti`:

```
<![IGNORE [ <!ELEMENT graffiti ( #PCDATA )> ]]>
```

Conditional sections are often used with entities, as demonstrated in Listing 4.3.

LISTING 4.3 Conditional Sections Used with Entities in a DTD

```
<!ENTITY % reject "IGNORE">
<!ENTITY % accept "INCLUDE">
<![ %accept; [
<!ELEMENT order ( approved, signoff )>
]]>
<![ %reject; [
<!ELEMENT order ( approved, reason, signoff )>
]]>
<!ELEMENT approved EMPTY>
<!ATTLIST approved flag ( true I false ) "false">
```

IMPORTANT

Conditional sections can only be used with external subsets of DTDs, not internal ones.

```
<!ELEMENT reason ( #PCDATA )>
<!ELEMENT signoff ( #PCDATA )>
```

As Listing 4.3 shows, you can declare parameter entities to represent the keywords `IGNORE` and `INCLUDE`. Here, the parameter entities `accept` and `reject` are used to represent the strings `INCLUDE` and `IGNORE`. When an order is accepted, the `flag` attribute in the approved entity is switched to `true`, and the CEO's signoff displays. Listing 4.4 shows an XML document that conforms to the DTD containing the conditional section shown in Listing 4.3.

LISTING 4.4 An XML Document That Utilizes Conditional Queries

```
<?xml version = "1.0" standalone = "no"?>
<!DOCTYPE order SYSTEM "conditional.dtd">
<message>
<approved flag = "true" />
<signoff>Chief Executive Officer</signoff>
</order>
```

In the next chapter, you'll learn how XML implements the display and encoding of characters in languages other than English through its support for Unicode.

Key Terms

attribute list declaration
attribute name
attribute type
batch validation
character data
character entity codes
child elements
choice connector
conditional section
content specification
declaration
default value
external DTD
external subset
fixed value
general entities
generic identifier
interactive validation
internal subset
mixed-content model
model group
name group
name token
notation
notation declaration
notational data (`NDATA`)
parameter entities
parsed character data
reserved attributes
schema
sequence connector
token
XML Schema

Code Summary

1. **Model groups:**

```
<author>
<firstname>Marge</firstname>
<lastname>Piercy</lastname>
</author>
```

2. **Occurrence indicators in element declarations:**

```
<!ELEMENT birthdate (month, day, year)>
<!ELEMENT scientist (name, expertise+)>
<!ELEMENT chapter (paragraph+, illustration*)>
<!ELEMENT fullname (firstname, initial?, lastname)>
```

3. **Controlling how frequently an element can be used:**

```
<!ELEMENT book (title, author+, publisher)>
```

4. **Using** PCDATA **to indicate elements that contain freeform text:**

```
<!ELEMENT question (#PCDATA)>
```

5. **Sample attribute declarations in a DTD:**

```
<!ATTLIST person gender (male | female) "male">

<!ATTLIST essay author CDATA #REQUIRED>

<!ATTLIST creditpay transid CDATA #REQUIRED
  creditpay cardid CDATA #REQUIRED
  reditpay creditnum CDATA #REQUIRED
  creditpay expdate CDATA #IMPLIED>
```

6. **Writing parameter entity declarations:**

```
<!ENTITY % tablecell "(p | ul | ol)*" >
<!ENTITY % lists "DL | %tablecell;" >
<!ELEMENT tablecell (%tablecell; >
```

7. **Writing notation declarations:**

```
<!NOTATION PNG SYSTEM "photoshop.exe">
```

8. **Referencing an internal declaration:**

```
<?xml version="1.0"?>
<!DOCTYPE message [
   <!ELEMENT message (to,from,date,time,subject,body)>
   <!ELEMENT to (#PCDATA)>
   <!ELEMENT from (#PCDATA)>
   <!ELEMENT date (#PCDATA)>
   <!ELEMENT time (#PCDATA)>
   <!ELEMENT subject (#PCDATA)>
   <!ELEMENT body (#PCDATA)>
]>
<message>
   <to>Ross</to>
   <from>Bunny</from>
   <date>July 25</date >
   <time>11:15 a.m.</time>
   <subject>Reminder</subject >
   <body>Please don't forget to tape Survivor tonight!</body>
</message>
```

9. **Referencing an external declaration:**

```
<?xml version="1.0"?>
<!DOCTYPE message SYSTEM "message.dtd">

<message>
   <to>Ross</to>
   <from>Bunny</from>
   <date>July 25</date>
   <time>11:15 a.m.</time>
   <subject>Reminder</subject>
   <body>Please don't forget to tape Survivor tonight!</body>
</message>
```

Review Questions

1. What are the two major schema languages used by XML?
2. What is the purpose of a DTD?
3. Describe what each of the following categories of DTD declarations does:
   a. `ELEMENT`
   b. `ATTLIST`
   c. `ENTITY`
   d. `NOTATION`
4. Briefly describe what model groups are and how occurrence indicators work.
5. When might you use elements instead of attributes, and vice versa?
6. What does a conditional section within a DTD do?

Case Study

In this chapter, you learned about how you could use an XML validator to check for errors in your XML documents. For this case study, point your browser to one of the following interactive XML validation tools, which were all operational as this book went to press. Try running the code from Listings 4.1 through 4.4 through the validator and see what results you get.

1. XML.com's validator:http://www.xml.com/pub/a/tools/ruwf/check.html This site includes several sample files you can try out as well.
2. Language Technology Group at the University of Edinburgh's validator: http://www.ltg.ed.ac.uk/~richard/xml-check.html
3. Scholarly Technology Group at Brown University's validator: http://www.stg.brown.edu/service/xmlvalid/xmlvalid.var
4. Userland Frontier's XML Syntax Checker: http://frontier.userland.com/stories/storyReader$1092

This site includes URLs you can enter to test a number of XML-based sites.

Note the name of the parser that each of these tools says it is based on. What differences do you see based on what parser is used?

Hands On Project

In this two-part project, you'll create a DTD that's appropriate for marking up a newspaper article. Afterward, you'll mark up a sample news story using the new newspaper markup you just created.

Part I

1. Make a list of the major components that comprise a typical news story. Your list might include some or all of the following: headline, subhead, byline, and article body (including paragraphs and pull quotes).

2. Open Notepad (or whichever plain text processor or Web authoring tool you're using instead) and create a new untitled document.

3. Type in the following element declaration to define an element called `article`:

   ```
   <!ELEMENT article (headline, subhead, byline, body)>
   ```

   Note that this element specifies that an article can contain exactly one headline, one subhead, one byline, and one body element.

4. Type in the following element declarations to specify additional elements:

```
<!ELEMENT headline (#PCDATA)>
<!ELEMENT subhead (#PCDATA)>
<!ELEMENT byline (#PCDATA)>
```

Notice that these three elements create tags that can enclose freeform document text.

5. Type in the following element declaration to define the element called `body`:

```
<!ELEMENT body (paragraph+, pullquote*)>
```

Be prepared to explain how many paragraphs and pull quotes, respectively, the article body should or can contain.

6. Type in an additional element declaration and a related attribute declaration:

```
<!ELEMENT paragraph (#PCDATA)>
<!ATTLIST paragraph align ( left | right | justified | forced ) "justified">
```

Make sure you can explain what the paragraph element can contain and what values can appear for the `align` attribute. If no `align` value has been specified, what default value will be used?

7. Add one more element declaration and a related attribute declaration:

```
<!ELEMENT pullquote (#PCDATA)>
<!ATTLIST pullquote align ( left | right | justified | forced ) "left">
```

As above, make sure you can explain what the `pullquote` element can contain. Review what values are permitted for the `align` attribute, and how a `pullquote` will be aligned by default if no value is specified.

8. Save your file using the filename `article.dtd`.

Part II

1. Open a new document in Notepad (or other plain text processor or XML authoring tool) and create a new untitled document. Save this file under the filename `test_article.xml`.

2. Add the following lines of code to your new XML document. If you post these files online, you'll want to include the full path to the `article.dtd` file. For now, just use the local system path, or make sure that the article DTD and XML file are in the same directory.

```
<?xml version="1.0"?>
<!DOCTYPE article SYSTEM "article.dtd">
```

3. Next, you'll need to copy and paste in a sample newspaper article from your campus paper's Web site or another news source. Paste the article right after the `<DOCTYPE>` declaration. Remember, you're using these works for your own study of XML; don't post the copyrighted works of others online!

4. Place an opening `<article>` tag after the `DOCTYPE` declaration. Scroll down to the bottom of the article and add the closing `</article>` tag at the very end. All of the new tags you add after this will enclose parts of the article's text.

5. Locate the article's headline in the cut-and-pasted text and surround it with opening and closing `<headline>` tags. Since you defined a headline element as subordinate to the root element (article), make sure that the `<headline>` tag appears after the opening `<article>` tag.

6. Locate the article's subhead in the cut-and-pasted text and surround it with opening and closing `<subhead>` tags. If the article doesn't have a subhead, how will you modify the DTD to say that a subhead is not required?
7. Find the reporter's byline and surround it with opening and closing `<byline>` tags. If two reporters wrote the story instead of one, will you need to modify the `<byline>` tag?
8. Next, enter the `<body>` tag after the closing `</byline>` tag. Scroll down to the closing `</article>` tag and place the closing `</body>` tag immediately preceding it.
9. Now let's looks at the individual paragraphs and pull quotes in more detail. Within the opening and closing `<body>` tags, find each individual paragraph and surround it with opening and closing paragraph tags. Keep an eye out for any pull quotes. If the article contains a pull quote, enclose it within opening and closing `<pullquote>` tags.
10. Save your `article.xml` file. You can view your finished XML code by opening the `article.xml` file within your XML-compliant browser.

CHAPTER 5

Schemas

LEARNING OBJECTIVES

1. To understand the difference between a DTD and an XML Schema.
2. To learn about schema namespaces.
3. To differentiate between simpleType schema data.
4. To manipulate complexType schema data.
5. To work with child elements.
6. To set MinOccur and MaxOccur instances.
7. To work with choices in schemas.

DTDs were the original way to describe the structure of information within an XML document and language, and they derived from the structure of SGML. But W3C had already realized that there were a variety of limitations inherent in DTDs when the XML 1.0 was accepted in February 1998. W3C was already creating a Schema Recommendation to set the framework of a new modeling definition, called the XML **Schema Definition Language (XSD)**, as part of their XML Activity Group. It very specifically defines how to describe elements in an XML document so each piece of information within a document conforms to the actual description of the element in which the piece of information is to be placed. Overall, it is a representation of the multirelationships between elements and attributes in an XML document. In order to do this, structure must be analyzed and each element also must be analyzed. Plus it is more straightforward and is actually written in XML so it doesn't need a secondary processing by a parser. However, for some it could be rather difficult to write such exacting statements. The first working draft was released in April 2000, and a Candidate Recommendation followed in October 2000 divided into schema structures and data types. In May 2001, the W3C's

XML Schema Part 1: Structures and XML Schema Part 2: Datatypes became official W3C recommendations. Now W3C is working to update Schema 1.0 with a new version, 1.1, that will include a number of fixes and patches.

Advice

You can find part one of the W3C spec on schema structures at http://www.w3.org/TR/xmlschema-1/ and part two on **schema data types** at http://www.w3.org/TR/xmlschema-2/.

DTDs versus Schemas

The problem with DTDs is that their syntax is not particularly flexible. Documents follow one syntax and DTDs follow another. It's hard to read attribute list declarations and it is very difficult for many organizations that use precise pattern data to share that data because oftentimes it cannot be defined in exactly the same way. One organization might write "dateofhire" and another "hiredate". This small difference can make a DTD unworkable. XML Schema (also called **Xschema**) is already constructed as well-formed XML and edits correctly with most XML tools providing consistent validation models through sets of XML instances. It is especially handy in defining datatypes and patterns. It allows much more sophisticated descriptions and, more importantly, shared markup vocabularies. It does this by creating a structure that will either accept or reject specific XML data before it performs a function on it. It also has the ability to define hierarchical, nested elements and various options and constraints on those elements, as well as define a range for either an element or an attribute.

Interestingly enough, the actual term **schema** derives from database terminology, and within that context describes the actual structure of data in relational tables throughout a relational database. The word *schema* in database technology derives from the Greek word that means form or shape. Within the context of XML, a schema refers to a model that describes how elements, attributes, and text can be arranged. These models are described by their **constraints.** There are two types of constraints: those for content models and those for datatypes. The content model defines the actual elements that can be used, setting down the basic language of that particular schema. It describes the patterning of the language, such as how many and what type of units are used, in what order they can be displayed, and whether they are required or optional. Datatype constraints are much simpler. They only define the type of units of data that the schema will allow and consider valid. Both DTDs and schemas perform validation against data, but DTDs are not capable of complying with C++ and Java classes, which employ object-oriented technology, also referred to as instance documents. Schemas can comply.

Advice

XML Schemas are actually validated in two processes. First the schema has to be constructed against the overall XML Schema structure. Then, documents created under the schema itself must be parsed and validated.

Many businesses still use one type of XML category DTD to describe their goods and services. Schemas allow all variations of a DTD to be incorporated for reuse and sharing between common standards. Think of it this way. In the United States, dates are written 05-22-2004, but in Europe the same date is written 22-05-2004. An XML schema could easily interpret a date in both ways. However, XML Schemas are not easy to write and tend to contain enormous amounts of information that is difficult to track and follow.

Some Problems with DTDs

The most difficult aspect of a DTD is that it employs its own syntax, which is not the same as XML syntax. DTDs can't describe the actual data contained in elements. They can designate that it is indeed character data, or parsed character data, but they can't say if it should be formatted or structured in a specific format such as a date, restricted social security number, or different monetary systems. This leads into the next drawback of a DTD: its limited ability to deal with namespaces. DTDs are not context sensitive and cannot filter information based on what is inside of it. They only look for three things: a basic text string, the basic text string mixed in with other child elements, and a set of child elements.

Think of it this way. Your school alumni association lists your name, where you live, and what year you graduated, but may not list your major or what clubs and organizations you belonged to. Maybe you took a year abroad and would like people to know that in a special list, if others went to the same country within a few years of when you did. Within the structure of the DTD, you could say that you have a first and last name element, an address element, and the year you graduated element. But is there any space to list what year you went abroad? You already have a year element for your graduation. So you have to make up `yearAbroad` as another element. Since a DTD is strictly hierarchal, it does not allow for variations on a `year` element, but instead requires a whole new definition of the `year` element altogether to define `yearAbroad`.

However, it must be said in a DTD's favor that all SGML tools and a significant number of XML tools do work with DTDs. Some of the most common Web standards, including XHTML, work off a standardized DTD, and work is ongoing with different standards bodies to bring DTDs more into compliance with other standards. So DTDs are certainly not irrelevant yet, and, in terms of validation, they always take precedence over a schema.

Thinking of Speed

Below is an example of a few ways to measure motion according to a **schema structure.** Instead of just thinking of speed as miles per hour, the element `motionMeasures` would allow all the following variations. This would not be possible in a DTD, where you would have to write a definition for every variation of motion separately. Take a look at the example in Listing 5.1 to see definitions of types of speed.

LISTING 5.1

```
<xsd:simpleType name="motionMeasures">
  <xsd:restriction base="xsd:string">
    <xsd:numeric value="miles per hour"/>
    <xsd:numeric value="mph"/>
    <xsd:numeric value="meters per second"/>
    <xsd:numeric value="m/sec"/>
    <xsd:numeric value="kilometers per hour"/>
```

```
        <xsd:numeric value="km/hr"/>
        <xsd:numeric value="knots"/>
        <xsd:numeric value="kn"/>
        <xsd:numeric value="kt"/>
        <xsd:numeric value="nautical miles per hour"/>
        <xsd:numeric value="mach"/>
        <xsd:numeric value="M"/>
        <xsd:numeric value="Ma"/>
      </xsd:restriction>
    </xsd:simpleType>
```

Here is a `simpleType` schema (more on that below) we have called `motionMeasures`, written as a simple string. Here we are making a variety of definitions for types of speed such as "miles per hour" or its variation "mph". That way, if a sports site is inputting information into its racing reports, it's not just limited to one type of definition of motion. This is just a basic example to give you an idea. In this simple example, you can see what is allowable content; what content could conceivably be taken from a database (speed is usually a standardized measure); what, if any, restrictions there are on the data; and what, if any, patterns of data are allowed. Now let's take a further look at schemas

Developing Schemas

Namespaces

One of the first things a schema has is a namespace. Namespaces uniquely identify attribute and element names. Schemas actually employ not one, but two namespaces. The first is the **XML Schema namespace** itself and the second is a target namespace for the tags that are created in any instance of a particular schema.

An example of this might be as follows:

```
xmlns:xs="http://www.w3.org/2001/XMLSchema"
```

The first part, the *xmlns*, tells the processor that it is about to invoke a namespace. `xs` is a specific abbreviation that will connect the elements and all other types of data to the namespace specified. Here it identifies elements what are W3C instructions, but goes even further. It will prefix those **data types** with `xs`. It could also be `xsd`, or a variation of other allowable terms. The `w3` address mentioned is the URI (Uniform Resource Identifier), and here it is the more commonly known URL (Uniform Resource Locator) on the W3C site defining the `XMLSchema`.

Namespaces are particularly important in schemas because they are set up to process data and documents from different sources. One element, for example, might have three different names, and if the schema document was set up to encompass all three names, then there would be no problem validating it.

The names that a schema defines are commonly called the "target" namespace. However, the syntax of a namespace can be confusing. Even if it starts with `http://`, it actually does not reference a file at the URL that contains the schema. If a definition in a schema refers to other namespaces, they are called **source namespaces.** Every schema has one target and potentially numerous source namespaces. This potentially allows previously unknown elements and attributes to penetrate a schema definition structure, which is a good thing. It allows the schema to grow and be redefined without damaging its inherent structure.

Let's now build a schema for a mythical McGraw-Hill techbook site (see Listing 5.2).

LISTING 5.2

```
<xs:schema targetNamespace="http://mcgrawhill.com/ns/
  xmltechbook/"
  xmlns:xs="http://www.w3.org/2001/XMLSchema"
  xmlns:bk="http://mcgrawhill.com/ns/xmltechbook/"
  elementFormDefault="qualified"
  attributeFormDefault="unqualified">
  . . . / . . .
</xs:schema>
```

Here is an example with an

```
xmlns:bk="http://mcgrawhill.com/ns/xmltechbook/"
```

namespace we made up having its own unique `bk`, or book, prefix. This means that any reference to elements, attributes, or datatypes that begin with the namespace `bk` are defined in this theoretical instance. In fact, `bk` could have been the default namespace if we so chose. That way you could even nest more namespace declarations, commonly referred to as the **Russian doll** approach.

An XML statement can point to a schema that applies to non–namespace qualified elements using `xsi:noNamespaceSchemaLocation`, an attribute usually placed within the root element. Conversely, a schema can point to a namespace qualified element using the `xsi:schemaLocation` attribute, also placed within the root element.

Elements and Attributes

Simple and Complex

There are two element types in a schema. The first is the **simple type.** A simple element is precisely that, it has absolutely no attributes or elements for content. The second kind is the **complex type.** A complex type contains element and attribute declarations. This differs from a DTD in that a DTD has content that is a string within the element declaration and has attributes declared separately in a list of attributes.

A Little Schema

Let's make a really simple XML file (see Listing 5.3).

LISTING 5.3

```
<?xml version="1.0"?>
<FIRSTWORDS>
My First XML Schema!
</FIRSTWORDS>
```

Save Listing 5.3 as `FIRSTWORDS.xml`. The only element here is `FIRSTWORDS`, which just by its content would traditionally contain parsed character data (`#PCDATA`). Therefore, a schema for the statement has to declare `FIRSTWORDS` (see Listing 5.4).

LISTING 5.4

```
<?xml version="1.0"?>
<xsd:schema xmlns:xsd="http://www.w3.org/2001/xmlSchema">
<xsd: element name="FIRSTWORDS" type="xsd:string" />
</xsd:schema>
```

Save Listing 5.4 as `FirstSchema.xsd`. Because this is, in its essence, an XML document, it has a basic XML declaration. The root element of this schema is the namespace of `http://www.w3.org/2001/xmlSchema`. Elements are declared using `xsd:element`. The `name` attribute will target which element will be declared. In this example, it is `FIRSTWORDS`. In addition, this particular `xsd:element` uses a standard `type` attribute that has a value of the data type of the element. Here it is `xsd:string`, which means that the element is allowed to have any amount of text in any form, but it cannot contain any child elements. `xsd:string` is equivalent to `#PCDATA` in a DTD.

Thinking About Validation

When you use your own DTD, or even an industry standard DTD, the document has to declare a DTD declarative statement that points to the DTD and where it resides. It does this so the statement can be validated against the DTD. This makes it difficult to validate a DTD from a third party because you have to go and locate their DTD, wherever it might reside, to validate it. Sometimes you can't locate it. This becomes a really big issue when e-commerce transactions are involved. Also, it's important to be careful about whose DTD you choose to validate against, because a hacker could write a corrupt script to base a validated statement against, so you need to make sure that its sources are secure. With the schema specification, there is a lot more room to maneuver. Different documents can be affiliated with different schemas. The instance document has to point to the schema. The way to do this is to attach the schema to a particular document, which can be done by applying the attribute

```
xsi:noNamespaceSchemaLocation
```

and attaching it to the root element of the document (see Listing 5.5).

Advice

The `xsi` prefix in this example maps to http://www.w3.org/2001/XMLSchema-instance URI.

LISTING 5.5

```
<?xml version="1.0"?>
<FIRSTWORDS xsi:noNamespaceSchemaLocation="FIRSTWORDS.xsd"
  xmlns:xsi="http://www.w3.org/2001/XMLSchema-instance">
</FIRSTWORDS>
```

Listing 5.5 is an example of a simple type element. It has only text and does not have either attributes or child elements. However, the text could be limited, and a range could be specified, which makes it good for instances where limited input is desired, such as when using a date, an integer, or a decimal value. Limiting the data type is done by adding **facets,** or restrictions, which requires it to match a defined pattern.

There are 44 **built-in** simple types in the W3C XML Schema language. They are divided into seven basic groups:

- Binary
- Boolean
- Numeric
- String
- Time
- URI reference
- XML

Numeric data types are divided into three basic categories:

- Integer and floating point.
- Finite size numbers (like those in Java and C).
- Signed and unsigned numbers.

Table 5.1 shows the Schema numeric types.

Most **numeric types** are already well known to programmers, and the XML Schema definition has had a lot of input from programmers to make all of these specific definitions. They are very useful in making high-end scientific calculations and financial calculations.

Table 5.2 shows Schema **time types.**

The way the dates are formatted is year, month, day, hour, and so forth. The largest unit of time reads from left to right and this is shown in Table 5.3.

TABLE 5.1 Schema Numeric Types

Schema	Type	Example
xsd:byte	Integer with one-byte two's complement	1, 123, -1, -123
xsd:decimal	Arbitrary decimal number	5.2
xsd:double	64-bit floating point number	24, -2AB, 15.73F
xsd:float	32-bit floating point number	24, -2AB, 15.73F
xsd:int	Integer represented by same as Java int, four-byte	1, -1, -1234567890, 1234567890
xsd:integer	Arbitrary large or small integer	1, -1, -1234567890, 1234567890
xsd:long	Eight-byte two's complement	1, -1, -1234567890123456789
xsd:nonPositive Integer	Integer less than or equal to zero	0, -1, -2
xsd:negativeInteger	Integer less than zero	-1, -2, -3
xsd:positiveInteger	Integer greater than zero	1, 2, 3
xsd:short	Integer represented by two-byte two's complement number	1, 2, 0, -1, -2, 12345, -12345
xsd:unsignedByte	One-byte unsigned integer	0, 1, 2, 12345
xsd:unsignedInt	Four-byte unsigned integer	0, 1, 2, 1234567890
xsd:unsignedLong	Eight-byte unsigned integer	0, 1, 2, 1234568901234567890
xsd:unsignedShort	Two-byte unsigned integer	0, 1, 2, 12345

TABLE 5.2 Schema Time Types (Greenwich Mean Time)

Schema	Type	Example
xsd:date	An actual day	2004-03-15, -0003-03-15
xsd:datetime	Moment up to arbitrary fraction	2004-08-21T16:33.00.00-09:00.442
xsd:duration	Length of time with no fixed endpoint, including fraction of a second	P2004Y03M15DT07H21M4.6322S
xsd:gDay	Random day in any month	--01, --02, --28
xsd:gMonth	Random month in any year	--01, --12
xsd:gMonthDay	Date in any year	2004-08
xsd:gYear	Random year	-0001, 2001
xsd:gYearMonth	Actual month in actual year	2004-10

TABLE 5.3 Schema XML Data Types (XML 1.0)

Schema	Type	Example
`xsd:ENTITY`	Unparsed entity attribute in a DTD	`AB12, Bart_Simpson`
`xsd:ENTITIES`	White-space-separated `ENTITY` names	`AB12 AB!#`
`xsd:ID`	XML ID	`A1, ss123-45-6789, purple, sweetsixteen`
`xsd:IDREFS`	White-space-separated attribute XML names used as values of `ID` type	`A1, ss123-45-6789, purple, sweet sixteen`
`xsd:language`	Values for `xml:lang`	`En, en-GB, en-US`
`xsd:Name`	XML name with or without colons	`smil, svg, xml:lang`
`xsd:NCName`	Local name without colons	`href, title`
`xsd:NMTOKEN`	XML `NMTOKEN` attribute	`14 go cat go`
`xsd:NMTOKENS`	White-space-separated list of name tokens	`AL MI UT`
`xsd:NOTATION`	XML name declared as `NOTATION`	`GIF, jpeg, TIF, pdf`
`xsd:QName`	Prefixed name	`book:title`

The **string type** is quite common and takes a sequence of Unicode characters, indiscriminate of length, which is the same as XML elements and attributes and is enumerated in Table 5.4.

TABLE 5.4 Schema String Types

Schema	Type	Example
`xsd:normalizedString`	String that does not have tabs, carriage returns, or linefeeds	A world without SMIL
`xsd:string`	Zero or more Unicode characters	Ch1, 23, %#*^, first
`xsd:token`	String without leading or trailing whitespace, tabs, linefeeds, or more than one consecutive space	A1, ss123-45-6789, purple, sweetsixteen

Binary types can be included for certain types of data and are supported with just two encodings, usually used for digital signatures:

```
xsd:base64Binary
xsd:hexBinary
```

The final two are

```
xsd:Boolean
xsd:anyURI
```

The first, **Boolean,** is similar to C++'s `bool` data type. The second is used quite often as it includes a relative or absolute URI or URL, such as http://www.w3.org/TR/20002/schema. You also can create new simple types by using `xsd:simpleType` *`new elements`*, something very useful for object-oriented programming.

Default or Fixed Value

Simple elements are allowed either to be fixed or to revert to the default value. The default value is automatically assigned to an element when nothing else is indicated. In this example, it would revert to fast:

```
<xs:element name="speed" type="xs:string" default="fast"/>
```

But if you use a fixed value, you cannot use any other value such as slow:

```
<xs:element name="speed" type="xs:string" fixed="fast"/>
```

A Word About Facets

There are two types of facets (see http://www.w3.org/TR/xmlschema-2/#facets): a fundamental facet that defines a value space and a nonfundamental, or constraining, facet that puts a constraint on the allowed value. Table 5.5 shows a list of facets and their restrictions.

TABLE 5.5 Facets and Their Allowable Data Types

Facet	Restrictions
`enumeration`	A list of acceptable values
`fractionDigits`	Maximum number of decimal places equal to or greater than zero
`length`	Exact number of either characters or list items, equal to or greater than zero
`maxExclusive`	Tells the upper limit of one value compared to another and it must be less
`maxInclusive`	Tells the upper limit of one value compared to another and it must be less or equal to
`maxLength`	Maximum number of characters or list items allowed, equal to or greater than zero
`minExclusive`	Specifies the lower range for numeric values and must be less than the one stated
`minInclusive`	Specifies the lower range for numeric values and must be greater than or equal to zero
`minLength`	Minimum number of characters or list items acceptable, equal to or greater than zero
`pattern`	Exact sequence of characters
`totalDigits`	Exact number of digits allowed, greater than zero
`whiteSpace`	Defines how whitespace such as carriage returns, linefeeds, spaces, and tabs are dealt with

Making Your Own Simple Type

It is possible to make up your own simple type. You do it by restricting the type that exists already (for example, `xsd:string`) with an `xsd:restriction` element. The child element of `xsd:restriction` has an attribute that specifies what type it comes from. Furthermore, each `xsd:restriction` element has one or, oftentimes, more child elements that represent facets. Then the `xsd:simpleType` element can combine each existing type using an `xsd:union` child element. It is important to know this is possible to do, but we will not be using any new `simpleTypes` in this chapter.

Complex Types

Complex schemas can contain both attributes and child elements. Most, but not all, schemas will be a mix of both complex and simple and will contain mixed content. In Listing 5.6 we use an example of a book catalog to show how a document can become a complex schema.

LISTING 5.6

```
<?xml version="1.0"?>
<BOOK xmlns:xsi="http://www.w3.org/2001/XMLSchema-instance"
  xsi:noNamespaceSchemaLocation="book.xsd">
<TITLE>XML</TITLE>
<AUTHOR>Bart Simpson</AUTHOR>
<TECHEDITOR>Lisa Simpson</TECHEDITOR>
<PUBLISHER>McGrawHill</PUBLISHER>
<LENGTH>300</LENGTH>
<YEAR>2003</YEAR>
<ILLUSTRATOR>Marge Simpson</ILLUSTRATOR>
<PRICE>$50.00</PRICE>
</BOOK>
```

This basic XML statement says that there is a book that takes its schema instance from `book.xsd`, which has no namespace handy, so the schema will locate one, **noNamespaceSchemaLocation**, which usually means it is local and does not have a strict URL. Listing 5.7 is the actual schema, which is diagrammed in Figure 5.1.

LISTING 5.7

```
<?xml version="1.0"?>
<xsd:schema xmlns:xsd="http://www.w3.org/2001/XMLSchema">
<xsd:element name="BOOK" type="BOOKTYPE"/>
<xsd:complexType name="BOOKTYPE">
<xsd:sequence>
<xsd:element name="TITLE" type="xsd:string"/>
<xsd:element name="AUTHOR" type="xsd:string"/>
```

```
<xsd:element name="TECHEDITOR" type="xsd:string"/>
<xsd:element name="PUBLISHER" type="xsd:string"/>
<xsd:element name="LENGTH" type="xsd:string"/>
<xsd:element name="YEAR" type="xsd:string"/>
<xsd:element name="ILLUSTRATOR" type="xsd:string"/>
<xsd:element name="PRICE" type="xsd:string"/>
</xsd:sequence>
</xsd:complexType>
</xsd:schema>
```

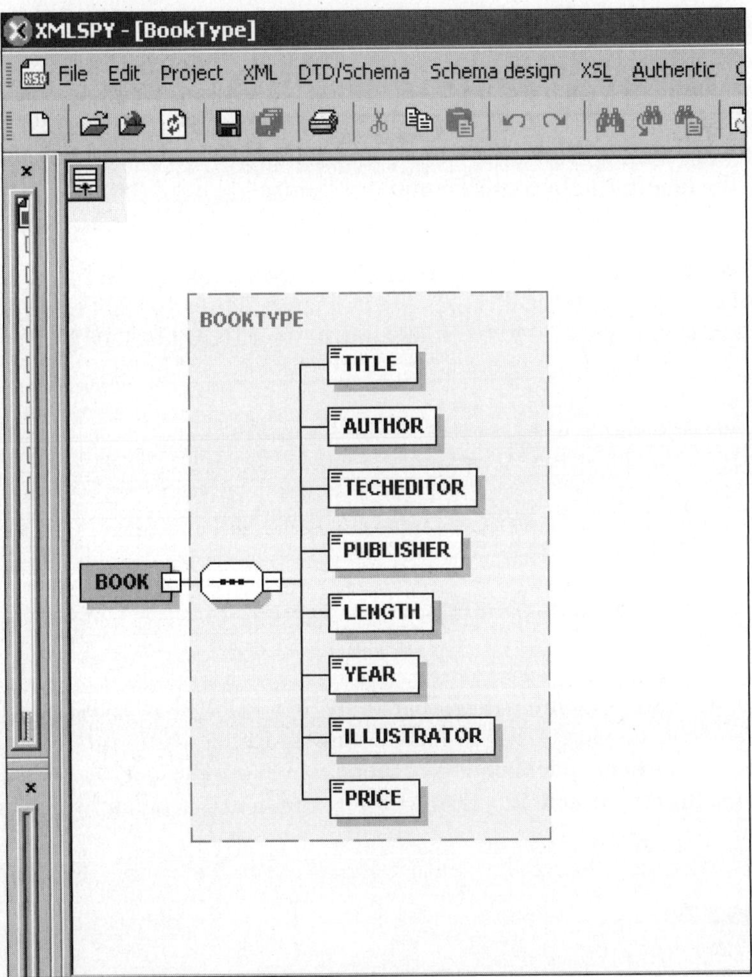

FIGURE 5.1 *BOOKTYPE* Schema Diagram in XML Spy

This statement begins with an XML declaration and then the root element, `xsd:schema`. The namespace and prefix `xsd` are mapped to the URI, the w3 XML Schema. There is only one top-level element, a child element of the root element `xsd:schema`, and that is `BOOKTYPE`. The `name` attribute of the element `complexType` allows for the `name` type `BOOKTYPE`, or any other type for that matter.

`BOOKTYPE` is a made-up element, and thus is known as a user-defined type. The way to know that it is not a built-in `name` type is that it does not start with an `xsd` prefix.

The statement `xsd:complexType` is an element that defines what kind of content `BOOKTYPE` will contain. Here it says, instead of the `#PCDATA` and other statements we are used to seeing in XML DTDs, it contains a sequence of eight different child elements and lists them as `xsd:sequence`—`TITLE`, `AUTHOR`, `TECHEDITOR`, `PUBLISHER`, `LENGTH`, `YEAR`, `ILLUSTRATOR`, `PRICE`—and each has the built-in type `xsd:string`.

Now the example in Listing 5.7 is fine for a first glance, but what if there was a joint author, three tech editors, and two illustrators? What if there were softcover and hardcover editions and two different prices? How would a schema deal with that? Fortunately, the designers of schemas thought this out well in advance and created the ever useful attributes that set how many times and how many variations of an element can exist. It is done through the **minOccurs** and **maxOccurs** attributes. So now this statement can be written as shown in Listing 5.8, which is diagrammed in Figures 5.2 and 5.3.

Tech Tip

Built-in `name` types are defined at http://www.w3.org/2001/XMLSchema#xmlschemap1.

Alert

The `BOOKTYPE` element must contain exactly one of each element stated, and in exactly the order they are stated. The only exception is whitespace between the tags.

LISTING 5.8

```
<?xml version="1.0"?>
<xsd:schema xmlns:xsd="http://www.w3.org/2001/XMLSchema">
<xsd:element name="BOOK" type="BOOKTYPE"/>
<xsd:complexType name="BOOKTYPE">
<xsd:sequence>
<xsd:element name="TITLE" type="xsd:string"
  minOccurs="1" maxOccurs="1"/>
<xsd:element name="AUTHOR" type="xsd:string"
  minOccurs="1" maxOccurs="unbounded"/>
<xsd:element name="TECHEDITOR" type="xsd:string"
  minOccurs="0" maxOccurs="unbounded"/>
<xsd:element name="PUBLISHER" type="xsd:string"
  minOccurs="1" maxOccurs="1"/>
<xsd:element name="LENGTH" type="xsd:string"
  minOccurs="1" maxOccurs="1"/>
<xsd:element name="YEAR" type="xsd:string"
  minOccurs="1" maxOccurs="1"/>
<xsd:element name="ILLUSTRATOR" type="xsd:string"
  minOccurs="1" maxOccurs="unbounded"/>
<xsd:element name="PRICE" type="xsd:string"
  minOccurs="0" maxOccurs="unbounded"/>
</xsd:sequence>
```

```
</xsd:complexType>
</xsd:schema>
```

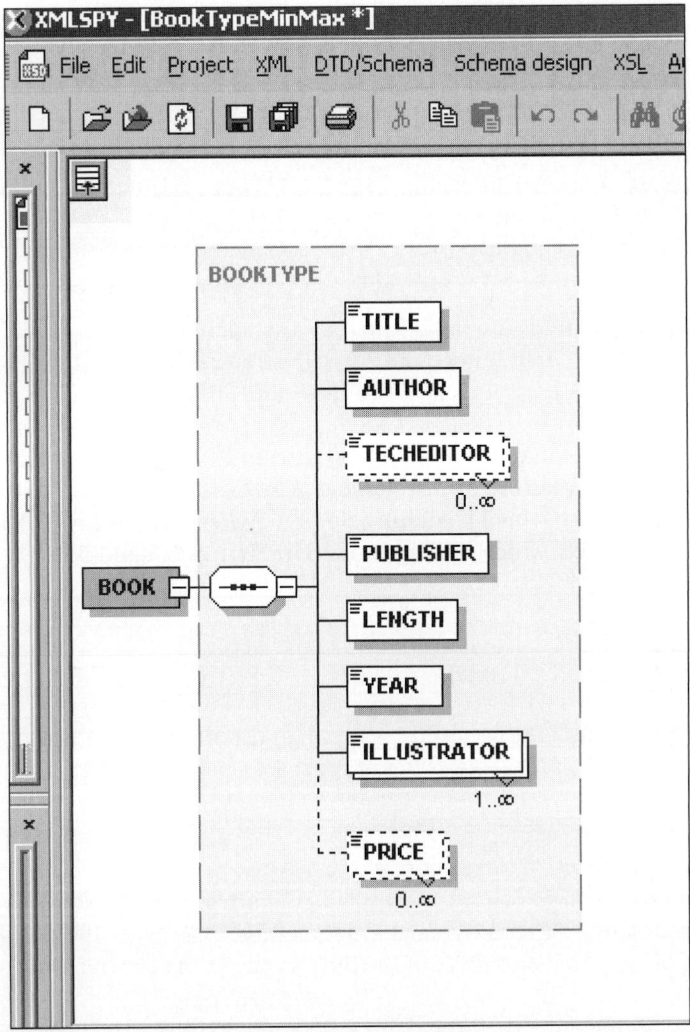

FIGURE 5.2 Schema Diagram Shown in XML Spy
Note: TECHEDITOR and PRICE are "0" and ILLUSTRATOR is "1".

Now we have a more flexible and more realistic schema to work with. It allows for one TITLE,

```
minOccurs="1" maxOccurs="1"/>
```

at least one and presumably an infinite (**unbounded**) number of AUTHORs,

```
minOccurs="1" maxOccurs="unbounded"/>
```

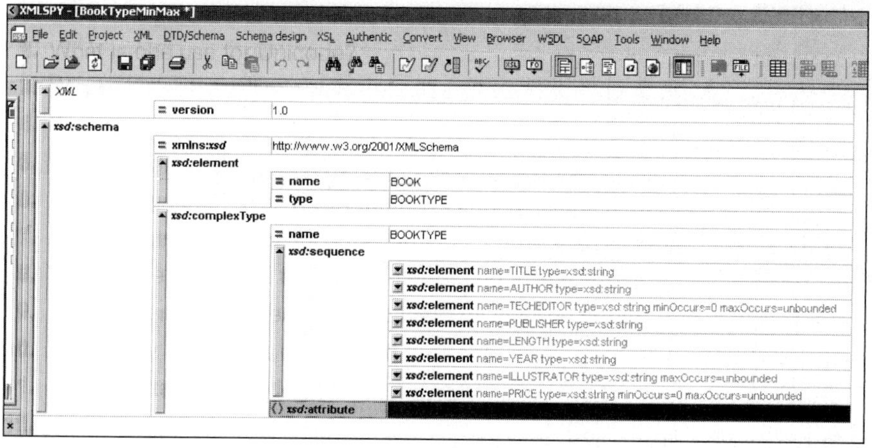

FIGURE 5.3 Enhanced Grid View in XML Spy of Min/Max Occurrences for `BOOKTYPE`

anywhere from none to an infinite number of `TECHEDITOR`s,

```
minOccurs="0" maxOccurs="unbounded"/>
```

only one publisher,

```
minOccurs="1" maxOccurs="1"/>
```

a set amount of pages, or `LENGTH`,

```
minOccurs="1" maxOccurs="1"/>
```

one `YEAR` of publication,

```
minOccurs="1" maxOccurs="1"/>
```

at least one `ILLUSTRATOR`,

```
minOccurs="1" maxOccurs="unbounded"/>
```

and no `PRICE` type to an infinite number for test copies to foreign markets

```
minOccurs="0" maxOccurs="unbounded"/>
```

When you attempt to write this kind of restriction in a DTD, first of all you are confined to using `*`, `?`, or `+`, which makes it very complex. You could never include a range, say of between 5 and 15, but with `minOccurs="5"` and `maxOccurs="15"` you easily could.

Deep Schema

So far we have started with a root element with simple data, and elements off the root element. None of the elements have had their own child elements. What if `AUTHOR` and `TECHEDITOR` had child elements called `NAME` (see Figure 5.4 and Listing 5.9)?

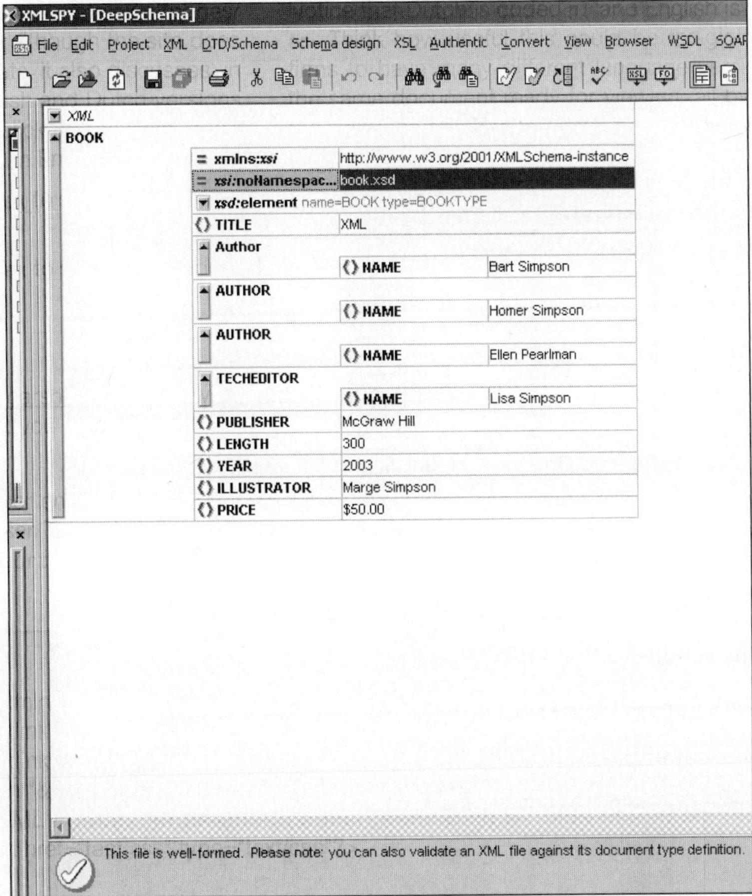

FIGURE 5.4 *Name* Child Elements in XML Spy

LISTING 5.9

```
<?xml version="1.0"?>
<BOOK xmlns:xsi="http://www.w3.org/2001/XMLSchema-instance"
  xsi:noNamespaceSchemaLocation="book.xsd">
<TITLE>XML</TITLE>
<AUTHOR>
<NAME>Bart Simpson</NAME>
</AUTHOR>
<AUTHOR>
<NAME>Homer Simpson</NAME>
</AUTHOR>
<AUTHOR>
<NAME>Ellen Pearlman</NAME>
</AUTHOR>
<TECHEDITOR>
```

```
<NAME>Lisa Simpson</NAME>
</TECHEDITOR>
<PUBLISHER>McGraw Hill</PUBLISHER>
<LENGTH>300</LENGTH>
<YEAR>2003</YEAR>
<ILLUSTRATOR>Marge Simpson</ILLUSTRATOR>
<PRICE>$50.00</PRICE>
</BOOK>
```

However, even though this is a valid XML file, there are problems with the schema structure. Since `AUTHOR` and `TECHEDITOR` have complex content, `type=xsd:string` is not correct in a declaration because it is a built-in type, and `NAME` is something that we created and, therefore, is not built in. This is done in the Listing 5.10 and diagrammed in Figure 5.5.

LISTING 5.10

```
<?xml version="1.0"?>
<xsd:schema xmlns:xsd="http://www.w3.org/2001/XMLSchema">
  <xsd:element name="BOOK" type="BOOKTYPE"/>
  <xsd:complexType name="AUTHORTYPE">
    <xsd:sequence>
      <xsd:element name="NAME" type="xsd:string"/>
    </xsd:sequence>
  </xsd:complexType>
  <xsd:complexType name="TECHEDITORTYPE">
    <xsd:sequence>
      <xsd:element name="NAME" type="xsd:string"/>
    </xsd:sequence>
  </xsd:complexType>
  <xsd:complexType name="BOOKTYPE">
    <xsd:sequence>
      <xsd:element name="TITLE" type="xsd:string"/>
      <xsd:element name="AUTHOR" type="AUTHORTYPE"
        maxOccurs="unbounded"/>
      <xsd:element name="TECHEDITOR" type="TECHEDITORTYPE"
        minOccurs="0" maxOccurs="unbounded"/>
      <xsd:element name="PUBLISHER" type="xsd:string"
        minOccurs="0"/>
      <xsd:element name="LENGTH" type="xsd:string"/>
      <xsd:element name="YEAR" type="xsd:string"/>
      <xsd:element name="ILLUSTRATOR" type="xsd:string"
        maxOccurs="unbounded"/>
      <xsd:element name="PRICE" type="xsd:string"
        minOccurs="0"/>
    </xsd:sequence>
  </xsd:complexType>
</xsd:schema>
```

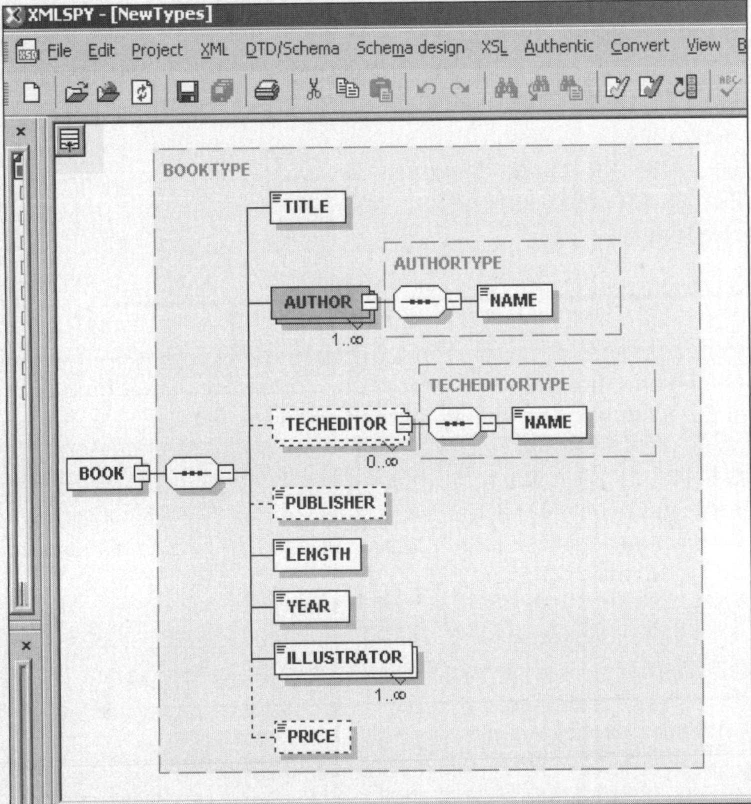

FIGURE 5.5 Complex Types Defined in XML SPY Hierarchy View

Here we have defined two new complexType(s) named AUTHORTYPE and TECHEDITORTYPE. Within the new complexType(s) there is a new element named NAME, which is declared as a type xsd:string. We've also decided that AUTHORTYPE has no minOccurs, just unbounded maxOccurs, something we are allowed to do. However, TECHEDITOR has a set minOccurs and unbounded maxOccurs. We've changed a few others as well, which is not essential but streamlines the code.

Grouping

So far the order in which elements and their attributes have appeared has been critical. If an element is out of order, the entire schema won't function properly. But in something that is data centric, such as e-commerce transactions, element order may not be as critical. When a machine exchanges data with another machine, if all the elements match up, does it really matter which order they arrive? If a person is going to see the document, it will most likely be transformed with an XSLT style sheet (see Listing 5.11).

LISTING 5.11

```
<?xml version="1.0"?>
<BOOK xmlns:xsi="http://www.w3.org/2001/XMLSchema-instance"
    xsi:noNamespaceSchemaLocation="BOOK.xsd">
  <ILLUSTRATOR>Marge Simpson</ILLUSTRATOR>
  <TITLE>Homer's XML</TITLE>
  <AUTHOR>
    <NAME>Bart Simpson</NAME>
  </AUTHOR>
  <PUBLISHER>McGraw Hill</PUBLISHER>
  <AUTHOR>
    <NAME>Ellen Pearlman</NAME>
  </AUTHOR>
  <YEAR>2003</YEAR>
  <AUTHOR>
    <NAME>Matt Groening</NAME>
  </AUTHOR>
  <TECHEDITOR>
    <NAME>Lisa Simpson</NAME>
  </TECHEDITOR>
  <PRICE>$30.00</PRICE>
</BOOK>
```

There are three **grouping** designations within the W3C XML Schema language that tell if and how the order of individual elements should be handled:

- `xsd:all`. Each element in the group must occur at most once, but the order is not important.
- `xsdxsd:choice`. Any one or more element from the group should appear, and a certain subsection of group elements should appear in a certain order.
- `xsd:sequence`. Each element in the group should appear only once in the exact specified order.

However, even though it may look like this adds flexibility, it is not all encompassing. It does not allow a book to have one or more authors or one or more illustrators. Listing 5.12 gives an example of an `xsd:all` group setting.

LISTING 5.12

```
<xsd:complexType name="BOOKTYPE">
  <xsd:all>
    <xsd:element name="TITLE" type="xsd:string"
      minOccurs="1" maxOccurs="1"/>
    <xsd:element name="AUTHOR" type="PersonType"
```

```
        minOccurs="1" maxOccurs="unbounded"/>
      <xsd:element name="TECHEDITOR" type="PersonType"
        minOccurs="0" maxOccurs="unbounded"/>
      <xsd:element name="PUBLISHER" type="xsd:string"
        minOccurs="0" maxOccurs="1"/>
      <xsd:element name="LENGTH" type="xsd:string"
        minOccurs="1" maxOccurs="1"/>
      <xsd:element name="YEAR" type="xsd:string"
        minOccurs="1" maxOccurs="1"/>
      <xsd:element name="ILLUSTRATOR" type="xsd:string"
        minOccurs="1" maxOccurs="unbounded"/>
      <xsd:element name="PRICE" type="xsd:string"
        minOccurs="0"/>
    </xsd:all>
  </xsd:complexType>
```

The usage of `minOccurs` and `maxOccurs` uniquely changes within the `xsd:all` element designation. Each value must be "0" or "1". It cannot be set to "5" or "3" or unbounded. Therefore, much of the example in Listing 5.12 would be incorrect because, for instance, it uses `unbounded`. As you can see, `xsd:all` is quite restricted and should be used wisely.

Making a Choice

DTDs allow one to choose an element by using the pipe (|) symbol. Schemas use the term `xsd:choice`. When `xsd:choice` is used, then only one of the referenced elements must appear in the document. For example, in Listing 5.13, `xsd:complexType` means there must be either an author or a techeditor, but not both! And for good measure, we created a new type; instead of `name`, we have expanded it to `personType`.

LISTING 5.13

```
  <xsd:complexType name="BOOKTYPE">
    <xsd:sequence>
      <xsd:element name="TITLE" type="xsd:string"/>
      <xsd:choice>
        <xsd:element name="AUTHOR" type="PersonType"/>
        <xsd:element name="TECHEDITOR" type="PersonType"/>
      </xsd:choice>
      <xsd:element name="PUBLISHER" type="xsd:string"
        minOccurs="0"/>
      <xsd:element name="LENGTH" type="xsd:string"/>
      <xsd:element name="YEAR" type="xsd:string"/>
      <xsd:element name="ILLUSTRATOR" type="xsd:string"
        maxOccurs="unbounded"/>
      <xsd:element name="PRICE" type="xsd:string"
        minOccurs="0"/>
```

```
    </xsd:sequence>
  </xsd:complexType>
```

Here we can have either AUTHOR or TECHEDITOR but not both. That is because they are placed between the <xsd:choice> . . . </xsd:choice> element. Unlike xsd:all, the xsd:choice element is allowed minOccurs and maxOccurs attributes that let the user define just how many selections can be made from a **choice** (see Listing 5.14). For instance, if you had 10 different elements, you could choose all, one, some, or a combination therein.

LISTING 5.14

```
<xsd:complexType name="BOOKTYPE">
  <xsd:sequence>
    <xsd:element name="TITLE" type="xsd:string"/>
    <xsd:element name="AUTHOR" type="PersonType"/>
    <xsd:choice minOccurs="0" maxOccurs="unbounded">
      <xsd:element name="TECHEDITOR" type="PersonType"/>
      <xsd:element name="AUTHOR" type="PersonType"/>
      <xsd:element name="ILLUSTRATOR" type="xsd:string"/>
    </xsd:choice>
    <xsd:element name="ILLUSTRATOR" type="xsd:string"/>
    <xsd:element name="PUBLISHER" type="xsd:string"
        minOccurs="0"/>
    <xsd:element name="LENGTH" type="xsd:string"/>
    <xsd:element name="YEAR" type="xsd:string"/>
    <xsd:element name="PRICE" type="xsd:string"
      minOccurs= "0"/>
  </xsd:sequence>
</xsd:complexType>
```

The xsd:choice element is allowed to have minOccurs and maxOccurs attributes that define just how many selections can be made. But in this example, since we are saying there should be at least one ILLUSTRATOR and one AUTHOR element, so all of them can't be filled by TECHEDITOR, it is important to put the xsd:element declarations for these two elements outside of the xsd:choice statement.

Importing Elements

Schemas, unlike DTDs, allow the importing of elements with the xsd:import element, by attaching to a different namespace derived from a different schema document; they also work with xlink. This is done through the xsd:import's schemaLocation attribute. That attribute informs the XML processor where to find the correct schema to import. The namespace attribute in such a statement tells which elements and attributes the schema declares. When the schema gets imported, its attributes can be added to an xsd:complexType by assigning it an xsd:attribute child that has a ref attribute pointing to the attribute to be attached.

Key Terms

binary types
Boolean
built-in
choice
complex type
constraint
data types
facets
grouping
`maxOccurs`
`minOccurs`
`noNamespaceSchemaLocation`
numeric types
Russian doll
schema
(schema) data type
Schema Definition Language (XSD)
schema structure
simple type
source namespace
string types
time types
unbounded
XML Schema namespace
`xmlns`
Xschema
XSD
`xsd:string`

Code Summary

1. **Listing 5.1:**

```
<xsd:simpleType name="motionMeasures">
   <xsd:restriction base="xsd:string">
      <xsd:numeric value="miles per hour"/>
      <xsd:numeric value="mph"/>
      <xsd:numeric value="meters per second"/>
      <xsd:numeric value="m/sec"/>
      <xsd:numeric value="kilometers per hour"/>
      <xsd:numeric value="km/hr"/>
      <xsd:numeric value="knots"/>
      <xsd:numeric value="kn"/>
      <xsd:numeric value="kt"/>
      <xsd:numeric value="nautical miles per hour"/>
      <xsd:numeric value="mach"/>
      <xsd:numeric value="M"/>
      <xsd:numeric value="Ma"/>
   </xsd:restriction>
</xsd:simpleType>
```

2. **Listing 5.2:**

```
<xs:schema targetNamespace="http://mcgrawhill.com/ns/xmltechbook/"
   xmlns:xs="http://www.w3.org/2001/XMLSchema"
   xmlns:bk="http://mcgrawhill.com/ns/xmltechbook/"
   elementFormDefault="qualified"
   attributeFormDefault="unqualified">
   . . . / . . .
</xs:schema>
```

3. **Listing 5.3:**

```
<?xml version="1.0"?>
<FIRSTWORDS>
My First XML Schema!
</FIRSTWORDS>
```

4. **Listing 5.4:**

```
<?xml version="1.0"?>
<xsd:schema xmlns:xsd="http://www.w3.org/2001/xmlSchema">
<xsd: element name="FIRSTWORDS" type="xsd:string" />
</xsd:schema>
```

5. **Listing 5.5:**

```
<?xml version="1.0"?>
<FIRSTWORDS xsi:noNamespaceSchemaLocation="FIRSTWORDS.xsd"
   xmlns: xsi="http://www.w3.org/2001/XMLSchema-instance">
</FIRSTWORDS>
```

6. **Listing 5.6:**

```
<?xml version="1.0"?>
<BOOK xmlns:xsi="http://www.w3.org/2001/XMLSchema-instance"
  xsi:noNamespaceSchemaLocation="book.xsd">
<TITLE>XML</TITLE>
<AUTHOR>Bart Simpson</AUTHOR>
<TECHEDITOR>Lisa Simpson</TECHEDITOR>
<PUBLISHER>McGrawHill</PUBLISHER>
<LENGTH>300</LENGTH>
<YEAR>2003</YEAR>
<ILLUSTRATOR>Marge Simpson</ILLUSTRATOR>
<PRICE>$50.00</PRICE>
</BOOK>
```

7. **Listing 5.7:**

```
<?xml version="1.0"?>
<xsd:schema xmlns:xsd="http://www.w3.org/2001/XMLSchema">
<xsd:element name="BOOK" type="BOOKTYPE"/>
<xsd:complexType name="BOOKTYPE">
<xsd:sequence>
<xsd:element name="TITLE" type="xsd:string"/>
<xsd:element name="AUTHOR" type="xsd:string"/>
<xsd:element name="TECHEDITOR" type="xsd:string"/>
<xsd:element name="PUBLISHER" type="xsd:string"/>
<xsd:element name="LENGTH" type="xsd:string"/>
<xsd:element name="YEAR" type="xsd:string"/>
<xsd:element name="ILLUSTRATOR" type="xsd:string"/>
<xsd:element name="PRICE" type="xsd:string"/>
</xsd:sequence>
</xsd:complexType>
</xsd:schema>
```

8. **Listing 5.8:**

```
<?xml version="1.0"?>
<xsd:schema xmlns:xsd="http://www.w3.org/2001/XMLSchema">
<xsd:element name="BOOK" type="BOOKTYPE"/>
<xsd:complexType name="BOOKTYPE">
<xsd:sequence>
<xsd:element name="TITLE" type="xsd:string"
  minOccurs="1" maxOccurs="1"/>
<xsd:element name="AUTHOR" type="xsd:string"
  minOccurs="1" maxOccurs="1"/>
<xsd:element name="TECHEDITOR" type="xsd:string"
  minOccurs="0" maxOccurs="unbounded"/>
<xsd:element name="PUBLISHER" type="xsd:string"
  minOccurs="1" maxOccurs="1"/>
<xsd:element name="LENGTH" type="xsd:string"
  minOccurs="1" maxOccurs="1"/>
<xsd:element name="YEAR" type="xsd:string"
```

```
  minOccurs="1" maxOccurs="1"/>
<xsd:element name="ILLUSTRATOR" type="xsd:string"
  minOccurs="1" maxOccurs="unbounded"/>
<xsd:element name="PRICE" type="xsd:string"
  minOccurs="0" maxOccurs="unbounded"/>
</xsd:sequence>
</xsd:complexType>
</xsd:schema>
```

9. **Listing 5.9:**

```
<?xml version="1.0"?>
<BOOK xmlns:xsi="http://www.w3.org/2001/XMLSchema-instance"
  xsi:noNamespaceSchemaLocation="book.xsd">
<TITLE>XML</TITLE>
<AUTHOR>
<NAME>Bart Simpson</NAME>
</AUTHOR>
<AUTHOR>
<NAME>Homer Simpson</NAME>
</AUTHOR>
<AUTHOR>
<NAME>Ellen Pearlman</NAME>
</AUTHOR>
<TECHEDITOR>
<NAME>Lisa Simpson</NAME>
</TECHEDITOR>
<PUBLISHER>McGraw Hill</PUBLISHER>
<LENGTH>300</LENGTH>
<YEAR>2003</YEAR>
<ILLUSTRATOR>Marge Simpson</ILLUSTRATOR>
<PRICE>$50.00</PRICE>
</BOOK>
```

10. **Listing 5.10:**

```
<?xml version="1.0"?>
<xsd:schema xmlns:xsd="http://www.w3.org/2001/XMLSchema">
  <xsd:element name="BOOK" type="BOOKTYPE"/>
  <xsd:complexType name="AUTHORTYPE">
    <xsd:sequence>
      <xsd:element name="NAME" type="xsd:string"/>
    </xsd:sequence>
  </xsd:complexType>
  <xsd:complexType name="TECHEDITORTYPE">
    <xsd:sequence>
      <xsd:element name="NAME" type="xsd:string"/>
   </xsd:sequence>
  </xsd:complexType>
  <xsd:complexType name="BOOKTYPE">
    <xsd:sequence>
      <xsd:element name="TITLE" type="xsd:string"/>
      <xsd:element name="AUTHOR" type="AUTHORTYPE"
        maxOccurs="unbounded"/>
      <xsd:element name="TECHEDITOR" type="TECHEDITORTYPE"
        minOccurs="0" maxOccurs="unbounded"/>
      <xsd:element name="PUBLISHER" type="xsd:string"
```

```
      minOccurs="0"/>
    <xsd:element name="LENGTH" type="xsd:string"/>
    <xsd:element name="YEAR" type="xsd:string"/>
    <xsd:element name="ILLUSTRATOR" type="xsd:string"
      maxOccurs="unbounded"/>
    <xsd:element name="PRICE" type="xsd:string"
      minOccurs="0"/>
  </xsd:sequence>
 </xsd:complexType>
</xsd:schema>
```

11. Listing 5.11:

```
<?xml version="1.0"?>
<BOOK xmlns:xsi="http://www.w3.org/2001/XMLSchema-instance"
  xsi:noNamespaceSchemaLocation="BOOK.xsd">
  <ILLUSTRATOR>Marge Simpson</ILLUSTRATOR>
  <TITLE>Homer's XML</TITLE>
  <AUTHOR>
    <NAME>Bart Simpson</NAME>
  </AUTHOR>
  <PUBLISHER>McGraw Hill</PUBLISHER>
  <AUTHOR>
    <NAME>Ellen Pearlman</NAME>
  </AUTHOR>
  <YEAR>2003</YEAR>
  <AUTHOR>
    <NAME>Matt Groening</NAME>
  </AUTHOR>
  <TECHEDITOR>
    <NAME>Lisa Simpson</NAME>
  </TECHEDITOR>
  <PRICE>$30.00</PRICE>
</BOOK>
```

12. Listing 5.12:

```
<xsd:complexType name="BOOKTYPE">
  <xsd:all>
    <xsd:element name="TITLE" type="xsd:string"
      minOccurs="1" maxOccurs="1"/>
    <xsd:element name="AUTHOR" type="PersonType"
      minOccurs="1" maxOccurs="unbounded"/>
    <xsd:element name="TECHEDITOR" type="PersonType"
      minOccurs="0" maxOccurs="unbounded"/>
    <xsd:element name="PUBLISHER" type="xsd:string"
      minOccurs="0" maxOccurs="1"/>
    <xsd:element name="LENGTH" type="xsd:string"
      minOccurs="1" maxOccurs="1"/>
    <xsd:element name="YEAR" type="xsd:string"
      minOccurs="1" maxOccurs="1"/>
    <xsd:element name="ILLUSTRATOR" type="xsd:string"
      minOccurs="1" maxOccurs="unbounded"/>
    <xsd:element name="PRICE" type="xsd:string" minOccurs="0"/>
  </xsd:all>
</xsd:complexType>
```

13. **Listing 5.13:**

```
<xsd:complexType name="BOOKTYPE">
  <xsd:sequence>
    <xsd:element name="TITLE" type="xsd:string"/>
    <xsd:choice>
      <xsd:element name="AUTHOR" type="PersonType"/>
      <xsd:element name="TECHEDITOR" type="PersonType"/>
    </xsd:choice>
    <xsd:element name="PUBLISHER" type="xsd:string"
        minOccurs="0"/>
    <xsd:element name="LENGTH" type="xsd:string"/>
    <xsd:element name="YEAR" type="xsd:string"/>
    <xsd:element name="ILLUSTRATOR" type="xsd:string"
        maxOccurs="unbounded"/>
    <xsd:element name="PRICE" type="xsd:string" minOccurs="0"/>
  </xsd:sequence>
</xsd:complexType>
```

14. **Listing 5.14:**

```
<xsd:complexType name="BOOKTYPE">
  <xsd:sequence>
    <xsd:element name="TITLE" type="xsd:string"/>
    <xsd:element name="AUTHOR" type="PersonType"/>
    <xsd:choice minOccurs="0" maxOccurs="unbounded">
      <xsd:element name="TECHEDITOR" type="PersonType"/>
      <xsd:element name="AUTHOR" type="PersonType"/>
      <xsd:element name="ILLUSTRATOR" type="xsd:string"/>
    </xsd:choice>
    <xsd:element name="ILLUSTRATOR" type="xsd:string"/>
    <xsd:element name="PUBLISHER" type="xsd:string"
        minOccurs="0"/>
    <xsd:element name="LENGTH" type="xsd:string"/>
    <xsd:element name="YEAR" type="xsd:string"/>
    <xsd:element name="PRICE" type="xsd:string" minOccurs="0"/>
  </xsd:sequence>
</xsd:complexType>
```

Review Questions

1. DTD and XML syntax are the same. True or False?
2. What are the three basic types of information DTDs look for when processing a statement? What do namespaces do?
3. What role do namespaces play in schemas that they do not perform in most other XML definitions?
4. What is the difference between a target and a source namespace for an XML schema?
5. A DTD can validate against a Java class. True or False?
6. Where does the word "schema" come from?
7. What are the two schema model types? How do they differ?
8. A DTD can describe the data contained in its elements. True or False?
9. What is the difference between `xs` and `xsd` in a namespace?
10. What does the "Russian doll" approach mean?

11. What are the two types of basic elements allowed in a schema? What are their differences?
12. What does an `xsd:string` statement do?
13. What does `noNamespaceSchemaLocation` do?
14. What are the seven simple types of groups in W3C XML Schema language?
15. What can `complexType` schemas contain?
16. How can you tell if a `complexType` element is user defined or built in?
17. What is the only exception allowed in the ordering of elements?
18. What does `minOccurs` do? What does `maxOccurs` do?
19. Child elements are allowed in a `simpleType` schema. True or False?
20. When is the order of elements and attributes critical. When is it not?
21. What are the three designations that define the order of individual elements?
22. What changes in the `xsd:all` element designation?
23. When `xsd:choice` is used, how many elements are allowed to appear?
24. It is possible to import elements into a schema. True or False?

Case Study

Go to http://www.deepthought.com.au/it/archetypes/output/gehr_example.html, a site that maintains electronic health records. What is particularly helpful about this example is the diagrams on the site and how they illustrate the relationship between the GOM extracted schema into XML and the XML Archetype Schemas within the context of the entire database records system. Since this project uses OOP (object-oriented programming), take a look at the illustration from the DSTC GEGH Archetype Editor PROTOTYPE. It uses an XML schema, which is parsed with a Java XML parser and stored in an object database. If you look under the Archetype Object Browser, you will see terms that we have already gone over such as "string", Minimum and Maximum occurrence, constraints, and so forth.

Hands On Project

An Exercise in Simple Types

Write a one- or two-element XML file. Name it `simple.xml`. Take that file and now write it as a schema document, calling it `simple.xsd`. Make sure to include the W3C namespace declaration. Think about how and where you would put the root element. Open it in XML Spy and check your mistakes.

Writing a DTD for `simple.xml`

Using the `ConvertDTD/Schema` tool in XML Spy, see how your *`simple.xml`* file converts to a schema using the commands under the `DTD/Schema` pull-down menu. Note: You must have a document open and active in XML Spy in order to use this menu.

An Exercise in Complex Types

Using Listing 5.6 as an example, make up a simple file that shows a CD music company catalog.

1. Write the file and call it `MusicCD.xml`.

2. Then make a schema for it you call `MusicCD.xsd`. This catalog should have its own made-up `NamespaceSchemaLocation` and contain elements that might show up in a real music CD. Assign it a root element and assign each element a type. If necessary, check the W3C address discussed in the Tech Tip reference for schema name types. Run this example through XML Spy and check your mistakes.

3. Next, assign each element an attribute of `minOccurs` and `maxOccurs` that would correspond to the real world. Again, run this through XML Spy and check your mistakes.

4. Finally, assign multiple musicians and multiple song titles to your CD and make your complex type schema reflect the new coding for these multiple listings. Run your example through XML Spy to check your mistakes.

CHAPTER 6

Using XML Parsers and Unicode

LEARNING OBJECTIVES

1. To understand what an XML parser does.
2. To work with the basic Microsoft parser.
3. To differentiate between valid documents in different parsers and the way they define error statements.
4. To learn about Unicode and **UTF-8**, **UTF-16**, and **UTF-32.**
5. To investigate different character sets and typefaces for Unicode.

A **parser** is a grammar and syntax checker for markup and other programming languages. A parser compares an XML document against the grammar in its DTD. This process, called **validation**, ensures there are no mistakes that could potentially confuse the XML applications that access your content. If a document follows the rules listed in its DTD, then it is said to be **valid**. If the document has markup errors that contradict the rules of the DTD, then it would be labeled **invalid.**

XML parsers are also referred to as editors. They are like spell checkers, and then they are also like passwords. The way they resemble spell checkers is they check your syntax and grammar. The way they are like passwords is that if so much as one **whitespace** or character is incorrect, the whole statement will fail! And to make things more complex, not all parsers in XML return the same conclusions or results. As we have stated previously, an XML statement must be **well formed** and valid. But what constitutes well formed and valid, as we shall see, depends on the parser that is being used. Internet Explorer, starting at version 5.5, and Netscape, starting at version 6, contain their own built-in versions of XML parsers. There are also both commercial and free parsers available on the market, as well as parsers that are derived from the SGML, like GNU, Emacs, and

Framemaker. In this chapter we will take a look at some of the good points and some of the pitfalls of the most popular ones.

In order for XML to be more universally accepted and recognized, it must allow and enable multilingual functions. This means that if you are an oil executive, and you need to read a document in English, your assistants and co-workers may need to read the same document in Arabic, Spanish, or Cyrillic. How could the same document be displayed to three people at the same time in three different languages? By using **Unicode** and the *xml:lang* attribute, it is possible.

The Unicode Consortium was founded with the goal to foster a character **encoding scheme** that encompasses all major scripts in the world. Currently it has a little less than 50,000 different characters encoded in 16 bits for a total of up to 65,536 possible characters. Already almost a third of the encoded characters are in Han Chinese ideographs. More languages are on the way, and so Unicode will jump to 32 bits per character, eventually encompassing two billion different characters. Because XML uses Unicode as its character set, all character sets are compatible.

Parsers

When XML parsers first became commonly used, they consisted of basic text editors like Microsoft's NotePad, Wordpad, and Apple SimpleText, and not much else. These basic text editors could not support Unicode. Now the parsers are divided into three categories: basic text editors, graphical text editors, and integrated development environments. Professional packs are available that are robust development environments that aid in creating not only DTDs, but XSL statements, **Web services** (services that use a combination of XML and related technologies to deliver services over the Web; see Chapter 14), and other higher-end database interfaces as well. There are **Java**-based editors like Morphon and <oXygen/> for robust development environments and XMLWriter for **C++** environments. Then there are the more common **Win32** (meaning a Windows-based 32-bit processing environment) such as XML Spy, XML Writer, EditML Pro, and Xmetal. The basic Microsoft Notepad is a Win32-only editor. Different editors exist for different uses. Since XML is derived from SGML, an editor like DocBook is designed mostly for actual text. And for those who use Mac computers, there is Elfdata or Emile.

Frequently, XML documents consist of nested table structures. This is especially true for XML documents that are oriented towards databases. Therefore, the need for professional editors becomes necessary to track these deep structures. Most XML editors can handle basic DTDs. But as Web services become more common, or DTDs become more specialized, for instance, **LegalXML,** these editors are indispensable.

In general, a parser looks for certain specifics, such as the beginning of an XML statement `<?xml version=` or even parentheses `()`, a percent sign `%`, and so on. Just like we look for a period "." to end a sentence, a parser looks for certain pre-established XML grammatical conventions to know that a statement is correctly formed.

Difference between an XML Parser and an HTML Parser

If you have ever dealt with HTML code, you have seen how the editor or parser actually has a wide body of knowledge of predefined elements and attributes. This is because there is already a preset standard for all of this code that already tells the software application how to rend the information visually. A Web browser usually takes the HTML code and, in a single swoop, silently funnels it to a specialized rendering engine, which you, the coder or designer, never see, and is all handled deep within the browser.

An XML editor or parser does not have any idea of preset code, which means element and attribute names; it only knows basic valid and invalid rules. It never recognizes words or names. It only knows how to look at pure character strings.

The Basic Microsoft Parser

As of this writing, Microsoft's basic XML parser, called Msxml, that comes with Internet Explorer is a good, free parser that is embedded into the browser and can be referred to as a graphical text editor. To begin with, this is the parser we will use. However, there are different versions of the parser available in different versions or upgrades of the browser, such as version 6.0 or 6.0SP1. To determine what version you have, go to http://support.microsoftcom/default.aspx?scid=kb;en-us;q269238 and scroll down to "XML versions that are included with Microsoft Internet Explorer." For discussion in this chapter, we are using IE 6.0.2600, which uses version 3.0 of the XML parser. It is a **WYSIWYG** (What You See Is What You Get) editor. That means that there are no implied statements, and everything is displayed on the screen. It also requires no additional tools or downloads other than the correct version.

Jon Bosak, one of the XML gurus, converted all of Shakespeare's text into simple XML statements. Figure 6.1 shows an example of the play *Titus Andronicus.* We will use this XML marked-up play to run a validation program against it.

```
<?xml version="1.0" ?>
<!DOCTYPE PLAY (View Source for full doctype...)>
- <PLAY>
   <TITLE>The Tragedy of Titus Andronicus</TITLE>
 - <FM>
     <P>ASCII text placed in the public domain by Moby Lexical Tools, 1992.</P>
     <P>SGML markup by Jon Bosak, 1992-1994.</P>
     <P>XML version by Jon Bosak, 1996-1999.</P>
     <P>The XML markup in this version is Copyright © 1999 Jon Bosak. This work may freely be distributed on condition that it
       not be modified or altered in any way.</P>
   </FM>
 - <PERSONAE>
     <TITLE>Dramatis Personae</TITLE>
     <PERSONA>SATURNINUS, son to the late Emperor of Rome, and afterwards declared Emperor.</PERSONA>
     <PERSONA>BASSIANUS, brother to Saturninus; in love with Lavinia.</PERSONA>
     <PERSONA>TITUS ANDRONICUS, a noble Roman, general against the Goths.</PERSONA>
     <PERSONA>MARCUS ANDRONICUS, tribune of the people, and brother to Titus.</PERSONA>
   - <PGROUP>
       <PERSONA>LUCIUS</PERSONA>
       <PERSONA>QUINTUS</PERSONA>
       <PERSONA>MARTIUS</PERSONA>
       <PERSONA>MUTIUS</PERSONA>
       <GRPDESCR>sons to Titus Andronicus</GRPDESCR>
     <PGROUP>
     <PERSONA>Young LUCIUS, a boy, son to Lucius.</PERSONA>
     <PERSONA>PUBLIUS, son to Marcus the Tribune.</PERSONA>
   - <PGROUP>
       <PERSONA>SEMPRONIUS</PERSONA>
       <PERSONA>CAIUS</PERSONA>
       <PERSONA>VALENTINE</PERSONA>
       <GRPDESCR>kinsmen to Titus.</GRPDESCR>
     </PGROUP>
     <PERSONA>AEMILIUS, a noble Roman.</PERSONA>
   - <PGROUP>
       <PERSONA>ALARBUS</PERSONA>
       <PERSONA>DEMETRIUS</PERSONA>
```

FIGURE 6.1 Titus Andronicus Coded in XML

Figure 6.2 shows part of the DTD for *Titus Andronicus*, called `play.dtd`. We obtained this by going to `View | Source` in IE.

This example displays perfectly in the browser. Having all the tags correctly coded and all the information in those tags sets the play up for a variety of uses. In the future, aspiring actors and actresses can pull just their lines of text onto, for example, a Palm Pilot to memorize their own particular dialogue. However, let's see what happens when we make just one mistake with the DTD. Let's take out the end title tag `</TITLE>` (see Figure 6.3).

Now we will run the DTD through the IE browser, which submits it to the parsing rules of the MS Version 3.0 parser.

The error messages (see Figure 6.4) tell us a few things. It says:

```
End tag 'PLAY' does not match the start tag 'TITLE'. Error
  processing resource
It gives us
Line 5224, Position 3
```

```
<?xml version="1.0" ?>
<!DOCTYPE PLAY SYSTEM "play.dtd">

<PLAY>
<TITLE>The Tragedy of Titus Andronicus</TITLE>

<FM>
<P>ASCII text placed in the public domain by Moby Lexical Tools, 1992.</P>
<P>SGML markup by Jon Bosak, 1992-1994.</P>
<P>XML version by Jon Bosak, 1996-1999.</P>
<P>The XML markup in this version is Copyright &#169; 1999 Jon Bosak.
This work may freely be distributed on condition that it not be
modified or altered in any way.</P>
</FM>

<PERSONAE>
<TITLE>Dramatis Personae</TITLE>

<PERSONA>SATURNINUS, son to the late Emperor of Rome, and afterwards declared Emperor.</PERSONA>
<PERSONA>BASSIANUS, brother to Saturninus; in love with Lavinia.</PERSONA>
<PERSONA>TITUS ANDRONICUS, a noble Roman, general against the Goths.</PERSONA>
<PERSONA>MARCUS ANDRONICUS, tribune of the people, and brother to Titus.</PERSONA>

<PGROUP>
<PERSONA>LUCIUS</PERSONA>
<PERSONA>QUINTUS</PERSONA>
<PERSONA>MARTIUS</PERSONA>
<PERSONA>MUTIUS</PERSONA>
<GRPDESCR>sons to Titus Andronicus</GRPDESCR>
<PGROUP>

<PERSONA>Young LUCIUS, a boy, son to Lucius.</PERSONA>
<PERSONA>PUBLIUS, son to Marcus the Tribune.</PERSONA>

<PGROUP>
<PERSONA>SEMPRONIUS</PERSONA>
<PERSONA>CAIUS</PERSONA>
<PERSONA>VALENTINE</PERSONA>
<GRPDESCR>kinsmen to Titus.</GRPDESCR>
</PGROUP>

<PERSONA>AEMILIUS, a noble Roman.</PERSONA>

<PGROUP>
<PERSONA>ALARBUS</PERSONA>
<PERSONA>DEMETRIUS</PERSONA>
<PERSONA>CHIRON</PERSONA>
<GRPDESCR>sons to Tamora.</GRPDESCR>
</PGROUP>

<PERSONA>AARON, a Moor, beloved by Tamora.</PERSONA>
<PERSONA>A Captain, Tribune, Messenger, and Clown; Romans.</PERSONA>
```

FIGURE 6.2 *play.dtd*

and even spells out the end tag </PLAY> but does not show it on the page:

```
</PLAY>
  --^
```

But what is really interesting is the fact that the only thing we really took out was </TITLE>. So the real mistake actually looks like this:

```
<PLAY>
  <TITLE>The Tragedy of Titus Andronicus <Missing Tag/
    TITLE>
```

```
<?xml version="1.0" ?>
<!DOCTYPE PLAY SYSTEM "play.dtd">

<PLAY>
<TITLE>The Tragedy of Titus Andronicus</TITLE>

<FM>
<P>ASCII text placed in the public domain by Moby Lexical Tools, 1992.</P>
<P>SGML markup by Jon Bosak, 1992-1994.</P>
<P>XML version by Jon Bosak, 1996-1999.</P>
<P>The XML markup in this version is Copyright &#169; 1999 Jon Bosak.
This work may freely be distributed on condition that it not be
modified or altered in any way.</P>
</FM>

<PERSONAE>
<TITLE>Dramatis Personae</TITLE>

<PERSONA>SATURNINUS, son to the late Emperor of Rome, and afterwards declared Emperor.</PERSONA>
<PERSONA>BASSIANUS, brother to Saturninus; in love with Lavinia.</PERSONA>
<PERSONA>TITUS ANDRONICUS, a noble Roman, general against the Goths.</PERSONA>
<PERSONA>MARCUS ANDRONICUS, tribune of the people, and brother to Titus.</PERSONA>

<PGROUP>
<PERSONA>LUCIUS</PERSONA>
<PERSONA>QUINTUS</PERSONA>
<PERSONA>MARTIUS</PERSONA>
<PERSONA>MUTIUS</PERSONA>
<GRPDESCR>sons to Titus Andronicus</GRPDESCR>
<PGROUP>

<PERSONA>Young LUCIUS, a boy, son to Lucius.</PERSONA>
<PERSONA>PUBLIUS, son to Marcus the Tribune.</PERSONA>

<PGROUP>
<PERSONA>SEMPRONIUS</PERSONA>
<PERSONA>CAIUS</PERSONA>
<PERSONA>VALENTINE</PERSONA>
<GRPDESCR>kinsmen to Titus.</GRPDESCR>
</PGROUP>

<PERSONA>AEMILIUS, a noble Roman.</PERSONA>

<PGROUP>
<PERSONA>ALARBUS</PERSONA>
<PERSONA>DEMETRIUS</PERSONA>
<PERSONA>CHIRON</PERSONA>
<GRPDESCR>sons to Tamora.</GRPDESCR>
</PGROUP>

<PERSONA>AARON, a Moor, beloved by Tamora.</PERSONA>
<PERSONA>A Captain, Tribune, Messenger, and Clown; Romans.</PERSONA>
```

FIGURE 6.3 `play.dtd` with `</TITLE>` End Tag Missing

The parser tells us, in the browser, that the mistake is at Line 5223, Position 3. Going back to `play.dtd`, in Figure 6.5 we see Line 5223 (yes, there are that many lines in the text).

But wait, isn't the real error in Line 4, `</TITLE>`? This shows how tricky editing in a parser can be. You need deductive logic here, and you need to go all the way back to the first `<PLAY>` tag on Line 3 and see that it is above the opening `<TITLE>` on Line 4. Then you need to understand tag structure to realize that `<PLAY>` is looking to actually close `<TITLE>`, which never properly closed.

```
  <LINE>Will, hand in hand, all heading cast us down.</LINE>
  <LINE>And on the ragged stones beat forth our brains,</LINE>
  <LINE>And make a mutual closure of our house.</LINE>
  <LINE>Speak, Romans, speak; and if you say we shall,</LINE>
  <LINE>Lo, hand in hand, Lucius and I will fall.</LINE>
</SPEECH>
The XML page cannot be displayed

Cannot view XML input using XSL style sheet. Please correct the error and then click the Refresh button, or try again later.

End tag "PLAY" does not match the start tag "TITLE". Error processing resource
  "file:///c:/XMLbk/NewXMLBook/shakespeare.2.00.xml/titusmistake.xml". Line 5224, Position 3

</PLAY>
  --^
```

FIGURE 6.4 The Error Messages for *play.dtd* with the *</TITLE>* End Tag Missing

```
<LINE>But throw her forth to beasts and
<LINE>Her life was beast-like, and dev
<LINE>And, being so, shall have like with
<LINE>See justice done on Aaron, that
<LINE>By whom our heavy haps had their
<LINE>Then, afterwards, to order well
<LINE>That like events may ne'er it ru
</SPEECH>

<STAGEDIR>Exeunt</STAGEDIR>
</SCENE>
</ACT>
</PLAY>
```

FIGURE 6.5 Line 5223 of *play.dtd*

Now let's put back in `</TITLE>` and parse the statement again. (See Figure 6.6.) The closing `</PLAY>` tag finally displays in its proper order, at the very last line. But the true error was actually on Line 4.

Alert

There is no substitute for understanding proper tag structure rules. Even though a parser can indicate errors, it cannot explain the logic behind the errors. This is why even though editing programs and parsers may become more sophisticated, they cannot point out certain coding errors in their entirety.

Creating Your Own Valid Document

It's a good idea to use a really simple document as our first document to test out a parser. Copy the code in Figure 6.7 into Notepad or the text editor of your choice. Save it as a UTF-8 file under `all files` and call it `validatortest.xml`, with your own drive path specification. Now let's open it up in IE (see Figure 6.8). For a second test at validation, try opening it up in Netscape as well (see Figure 6.9).

```
        <LINE>And give him burial in his father's grave:</LINE>
        <LINE>My father and Lavinia shall forthwith</LINE>
        <LINE>Be closed in our household's monument</LINE>
        <LINE>As for that heinous tiger, Tamora,</LINE>
        <LINE>No funeral rite, nor man m mourning weeds,</LINE>
        <LINE>No mournful bell shall ring her burial;</LINE>
        <LINE>But throw her forth to beasts and birds of prey:</LINE
        <LINE>Her life was beast-like, and devoid of pity;</LINE>
        <LINE>And, being so, shall have like want of pity.</LINE>
        <LINE>See justice done on Aaron, that damn'd Moor,</LINE
        <LINE>By whom our heavy haps had their begining:</LINE>
        <LINE>Then, afterwards, to order well the state,</LINE>
        <LINE>That like events may ne'er it ruinate.</LINE>
      </SPEECH>
      <STAGEDIR>Exeunt</STAGEDIR>
    </SCENE>
  </ACT>
</PLAY>
```

FIGURE 6.6 Showing *play.dtd* with Line 5223 Now Complete

```
validatortest - Notepad
File  Edit  Format  Help
<?xml version="1.0" encoding="UTF-8"?>
<!-- This is good to use as a test -->
<!DOCTYPE scribble [
        <!ELEMENT scribble (first, second, third, fourth)>
        <!ELEMENT first (#PCDATA)>
        <!ELEMENT second (#PCDATA)>
        <!ELEMENT third (#PCDATA)>
        <!ELEMENT forth (#PCDATA)>
]>
<scribble>
        <first>Our first line</first>
        <second>Our second line</second>
        <third>Our third line</third>
        <fourth>Our fourth line</fourth>
</scribble>
```

FIGURE 6.7 *validatortest.xml* Document

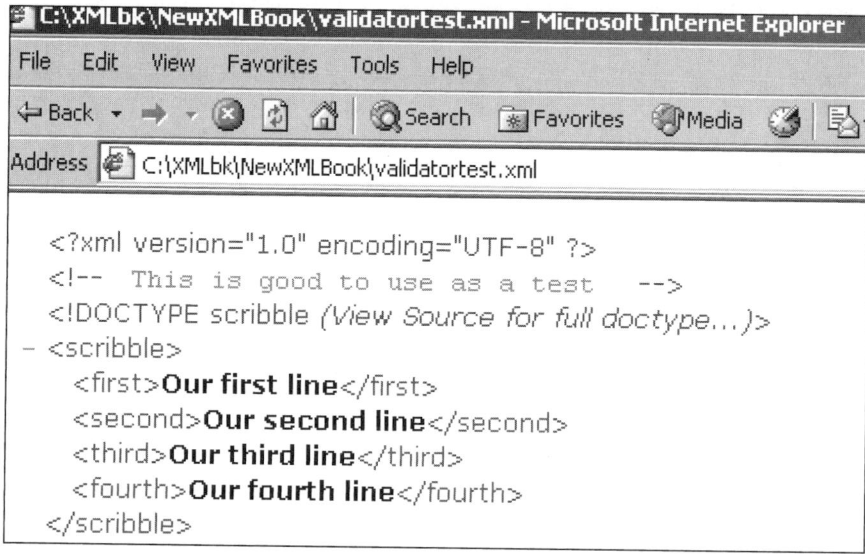

FIGURE 6.8 `validatortest.xml` Document in IE

FIGURE 6.9 `validatortest.xml` Document in Netscape

Now we are ready to examine other parsers since we now know our file is both valid and well formed, in both Netscape and IE.

A Word about Errors

Most parsers deal with errors in XML in one of two ways. There are errors and then there are fatal errors. A basic error is a violation of the rules in whatever specification it is checking the code against (i.e., XSLT, plain XML). The parser points out the error and continues processing. A **fatal error** stops the parser from checking the code. It also stops the XML document from being well

Tech Tip

Many parsers hang when it comes to parsing attributes. That is why it is always important to have a basic XML statement that you know is correct to use as a test in determining just how accurate the parser is. This also emphasizes how important it is to plan your code in advance and decide what should and should not be an element or an attribute.

formed. HTML does not insist that documents be well formed, although if HTML is not well formed, it will invariably cause problems with display or could even cause a browser to hang. XML does insist that a statement be well formed. These errors must be taken care of immediately or parsing will not continue.

Using XML Spy

Now let's look at a commercially available product, Altova's XML Spy. Go to http://www.altova.com/ (see Figure 6.10) and download a free, 30-day evaluation copy. As of this writing, Version 5 is the one we will be using; however, that could change to a newer version in the future. XML Spy can be thought of as an IDE because it not only has a text and code editor, but also a compiler, debugger, and GUI intuitive interface. With XML Spy, a developer could actually build a sophisticated project.

Advice

Learning to use XML Spy requires reading through their tutorial, and learning to work with schema templates, and other methods templates supplied by the program. It is aimed at a more specific development environment and after 30 days requires purchasing the program, which is rather costly. However, as a free learning tool for a month, it is a great program to play around with and their tutorial, which comes with the package, is worth going over, especially with a small group of students.

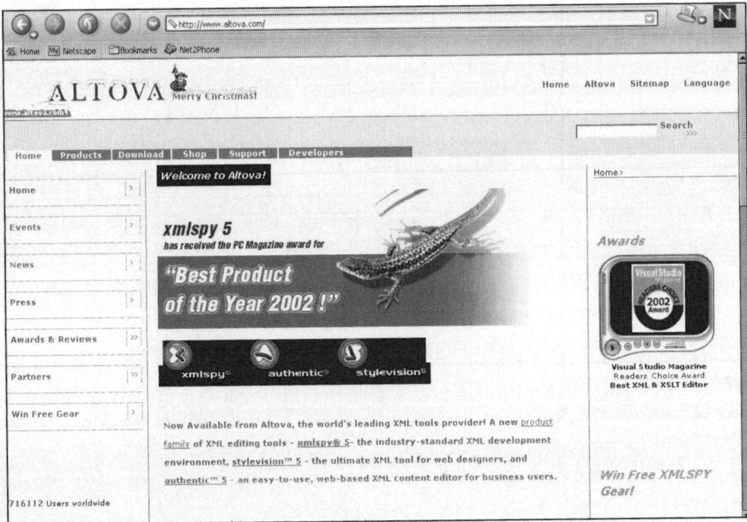

FIGURE 6.10 Altova XML Spy Home Page

Follow the instructions for installing the program, and for obtaining the license code to use it free for a month. There are two basic views: the Text view, which resembles any text editor, and the Enhanced Grid View, which shows more of the schema of the document.

The code for `validatortest.xml` is shown in Listing 6.1. Type it into the text editor of your choice and save it.

LISTING 6.1

```
<?xml version="1.0" encoding="UTF-8"?>
<!- This is good to use as a test ->
<!DOCTYPE scribble [
  <!ELEMENT scribble (first, second, third, fourth)>
  <!ELEMENT first (#PCDATA)>
  <!ELEMENT second (#PCDATA)>
  <!ELEMENT third (#PCDATA)>
  <!ELEMENT forth (#PCDATA)>
]>
<scribble>
  <first>Our first line</first>
  <second>Our second line</second>
  <third>Our third line</third>
  <fourth>Our fourth line</fourth>
</scribble>
```

Open up `validatortest.xml` in the XML Spy program. XML Spy has determined that the file is *not* valid (see Figure 6.11). Let's try and figure out what has happened!

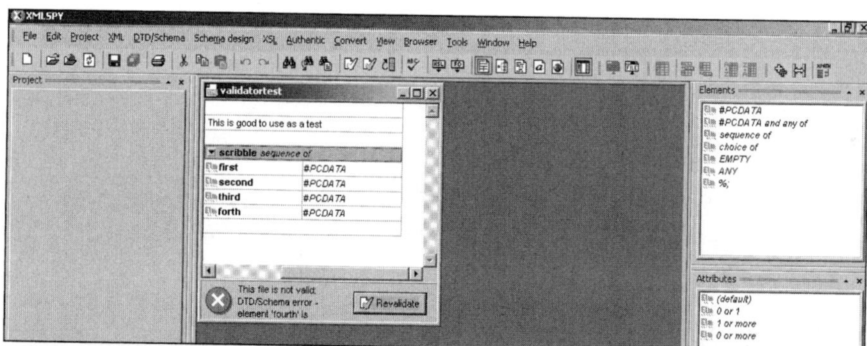

FIGURE 6.11 Invalid *validatortest.xml* In XML Spy program

The program gives the following error message:

```
This file is not valid
DTD/Schema error -
element 'fourth' is
```

Figure 6.12 displays the DTD in IE.

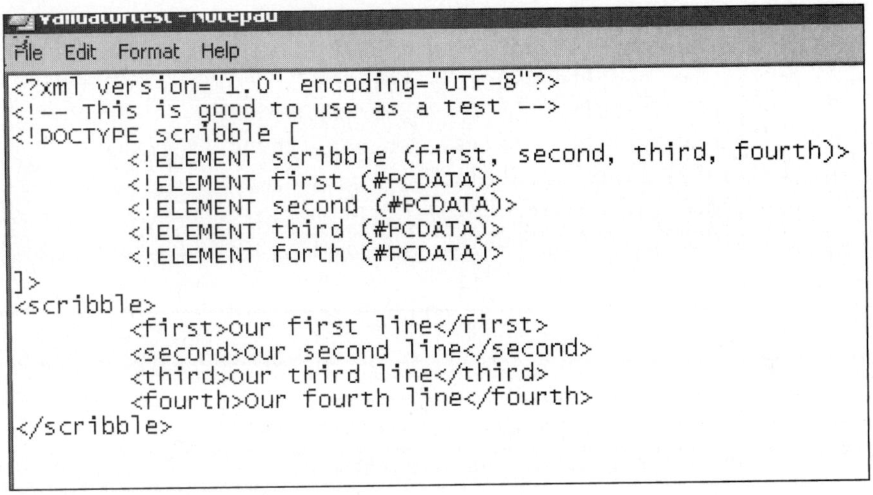

validatortest - Notepad

File Edit Format Help

```
<?xml version="1.0" encoding="UTF-8"?>
<!-- This is good to use as a test -->
<!DOCTYPE scribble [
        <!ELEMENT scribble (first, second, third, fourth)>
        <!ELEMENT first (#PCDATA)>
        <!ELEMENT second (#PCDATA)>
        <!ELEMENT third (#PCDATA)>
        <!ELEMENT forth (#PCDATA)>
]>
<scribble>
        <first>Our first line</first>
        <second>Our second line</second>
        <third>Our third line</third>
        <fourth>Our fourth line</fourth>
</scribble>
```

FIGURE 6.12 Viewing *validatortest.xml* in IE

Look closely at the very last element, !element forth. It is spelled "forth." Our tags for that line read <fourth> . . . </fourth>. Both spellings are correct, in that they are real words. Yet, in the logic of the statement "fourth" is the correct spelling, next to third, and so forth. Both IE and Netscape did not catch the error. XML Spy did. That is how sensitive XML coding can become with a professional tool at your disposal, instead of a freely available one.

This chapter is not designed to teach any particular program like XML Spy, but is designed to alert you to the advantages and disadvantages of just a few of the both free and commercially available editors.

Listing 6.2 gives the corrected version of validatortest.xml.

LISTING 6.2_Corrected Version

```
<!- This is good to use as a test ->
<!DOCTYPE scribble [
  <!ELEMENT scribble (first, second, third, fourth)>
  <!ELEMENT first (#PCDATA)>
  <!ELEMENT second (#PCDATA)>
  <!ELEMENT third (#PCDATA)>
  <!ELEMENT fourth (#PCDATA)>
]>
<scribble>
  <first>Our first line</first>
  <second>Our second line</second>
```

```
    <third>Our third line</third>
    <fourth>Our fourth line</fourth>
</scribble>
```

Other XML Editors

There are a number of other freeware xml editors. Let's take a brief look at a few of them. Go to http://www.webattack.com/Freeware/webpublish/fwxml.shtml. Select XML Edit Pro and download it to the directory of your choice. Set up and install the program. Then go and open `validatortest.xml` in XML Edit Pro's window. In the browse view tab, it should resemble the program in Figure 6.13.

Advice

A good place to look at a variety of specialized XML parsers is at http://www.topxml.com/parsers/other_parsers.asp or http://www.alphaworks.ibm.com/nav/XML?open&c=XML+-+Parsers.

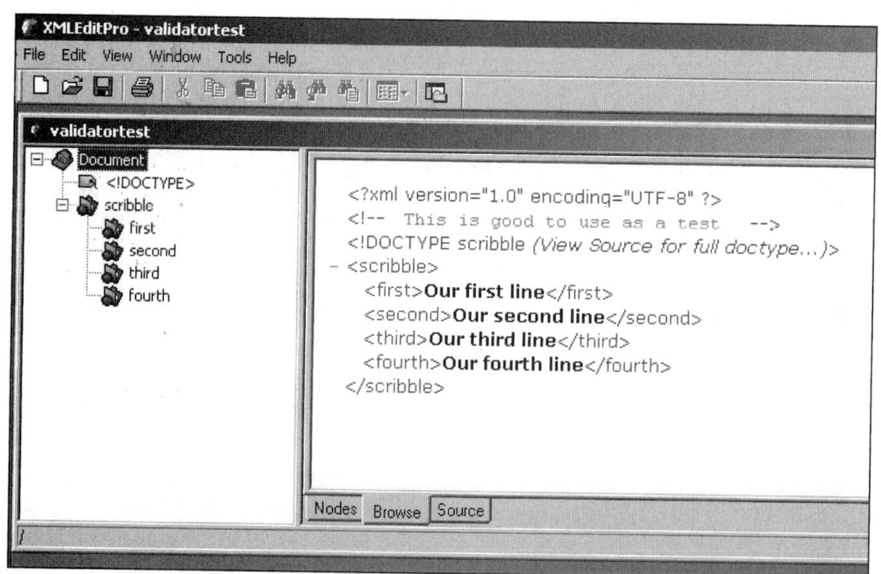

FIGURE 6.13 Viewing *validatortest.xml* in XML Edit Pro

Again, this is another program, and another view of the same XML code. Different programs can display the information in different structural forms. There is a tree structure, which we are already familiar with, and a more complex DTD schema structure. Some parsers will not parse attributes very well, which is why we did not use any in this example because then different code examples would and would not work. However, there is an exercise below to encourage you to use XML with an attribute statement.

Tech Tip

It's a good idea to start by using the standard parsers affiliated with IE and Netscape. The more professional a parser you can use, the more fine-tuned it will be to handle attributes correctly. It's also a good idea to read articles on commercially available parsers at Zdnet, Cnet, and other software information sites.

What Is Unicode: The Development of a Global Standard

In the beginning of the common use of computers, there were hundreds of different encoding systems giving individual character, and **character sets** numbers. The one most readers of this book with be familiar with using is **ASCII** (again, you see it in files that you give the .txt three character ending to, or you may have used it on your word processor by assigning a number coupled with the Alt key). ASCII defines 128 characters, 0 to 127 decimal (and 0 to FF hexadecimal for those of you who work in hexadecimal). ASCII is actually a subset of other character sets that contain 256 characters such as the ANSI character set of MS Windows, the Roman-8 character set of HP systems, the IBM PC Extended Character Set of DOS, and finally the ISO Latin-1 character set used by Web browsers. To see a list of these characters, look in Appendix A. ASCII was a **7-bit** coding system with a limited range and in order to increase its range, an **8-bit** coding system was developed, **Latin-1 (ISO 646),** which coded 256 characters. It became the language character set of choice for the Internet, email, gopher, and ftp sites. However, this did not cover all characters that existed in all other non-Latin-based languages. It certainly could not deal with, for instance, Chinese characters that are represented by what our browsers would interpret as pictures and usually renders as unreadable code, unless a specific language patch is downloaded from either Microsoft or Netscape. Plus, many of these encoding systems in the past actually conflicted with one another by assigning the same number to different characters. So, if the letter "A" was number one in one system, and number 22 in another, it became a real problem. When a computer tried to read all those different codes, it couldn't and the result was confusing and frustrating for most people, except those who could keep all these disparate systems in their mind at the same time.

In order to read typeface, or different scripts, it is necessary to have a unique character set for the script, special and common fonts for the character sets, and operating systems and application software that can understand all of these variations. In order to expand the range of permissible characters in 1983, **ISO 10646** was developed that used **32 bits** and could code four billion different characters. However, the code string became too big, and actually clogged up the bandwidth pipes it flowed through. Unicode, developed in 1987 by the **International Organization for Standardization** (ISO/IEC) and maintained since 1991 by the Unicode Consortium, halved the code to

16 bits, making it a workable solution because now it could handle more characters using less bandwidth. If your browser has difficulties displaying characters outside of the common character sets, you might need to download a language patch from either Microsoft or Netscape.

Unicode provides a unique number for each and every character in the world, no matter what platform, program, or language they are viewed on. Every major vendor and standards body, operating system, browser, and host of other products has adopted the standard. This is not to say it works perfectly yet, but there is a consensus on how to make it all fit together starting with W3C, the World Wide Web Consortium. Also, another standard, ISO 10646-1:1993, is being used on the Web and, for all purposes, Unicode has become a subset of that ISO standard. So far it allows for 65,535 different characters and that number is constantly expanding; recently the Unicode Consortium has released Unicode 4.0.

Unicode-Enabled Operating Systems

Below is a list of operating systems that are Unicode-enabled:

Apple Mac OS 9.2, Mac OS X 10.1, Mac OS X Server, ATSUI
Bell Labs Plan 9
Compaq's Tru64 UNIX, Open VMS
GNU/Linux with glibc 2.2.2 or newer—FAQ support
IBM AIX, AS/400, OS/2
Inferno by Vita Nuova
Java
Microsoft Windows CE, Windows NT, Windows 2000, and Windows XP
SCO UnixWare 7.1.0
Sun Solaris
Symbian Platform

`xml:lang` Attribute

One of the most important attributes used in combination with XML and Unicode is the `xml:lang` attribute. It is the only attribute to use a language code. This attribute asks the XML software to call upon the server to process the current document with the specified language.

An example of this would be as follows, coded in an XML statement:

```
<spanishtext xml:lang=ES>
Hola amigo
</spanishtext>
```

ES means that the enclosed text should be in Spanish and, more specifically, Spanish from Spain. The dialect of Spanish spoken in Argentina, for example would be coded as AR and from Ecuador EC, El Salvador SV, and Mexico MX. The language cited in the xml:lang attribute stays in effect until it is changed by the same code. See Appendix B for a listing of 239 country names using ISO 3166-1, taken courtesy of the ISO, the International Organization for Standardization, http://www.iso.ch/iso/en/prods-services/iso3166ma/02iso-3166-code-lists/list-en1.html.

Figure 6.14 is an example of Unicode for the Native American Cherokee language, one of the many languages encoded by the Unicode Consortium. As you can see, each character is assigned a number.

13A0 **Cherokee** **13FF**

	13A	13B	13C	13D	13E	13F
0	Ꭰ 13A0	Ꮀ 13B0	Ꮐ 13C0	Ꮠ 13D0	Ꮰ 13E0	Ᏸ 13F0
1	Ꭱ 13A1	Ꮁ 13B1	Ꮑ 13C1	Ꮡ 13D1	Ꮱ 13E1	Ᏹ 13F1
2	Ꭲ 13A2	Ꮂ 13B2	Ꮒ 13C2	Ꮢ 13D2	Ꮲ 13E2	Ᏺ 13F2
3	Ꭳ 13A3	Ꮃ 13B3	Ꮓ 13C3	Ꮣ 13D3	Ꮳ 13E3	Ᏻ 13F3
4	Ꭴ 13A4	Ꮄ 13B4	Ꮔ 13C4	Ꮤ 13D4	Ꮴ 13E4	Ᏼ 13F4
5	Ꭵ 13A5	Ꮅ 13B5	Ꮕ 13C5	Ꮥ 13D5	Ꮵ 13E5	
6	Ꭶ 13A6	Ꮆ 13B6	Ꮖ 13C6	Ꮦ 13D6	Ꮶ 13E6	
7	Ꭷ	Ꮇ	Ꮗ	Ꮧ	Ꮷ	

FIGURE 6.14 Unicode for Cherokee Language

UTF-8 and Beyond

UTF, which stands for Universal Character Set Transformation Format, allows Unicode to be broken into 8-, 16-, or even 32-bit values that are used in email and on the Internet. **UTF-8** at present is best known on the Web. You can see this in a typical XML statement when it says <?XML version ="1.0" encoding= "UTF-8">. Unicode encodes all text by the type of script (i.e., English language, Cyrillic, etc.) used, not the language used, an important distinction that avoids unnecessary duplication of letters. What that means is the letter

"E" is really the same in many different languages and does not need to be duplicated in British English, French, German, or Spanish.

Most of us use English or equivalent keyboards, and typing in other languages such as Chinese, Korean, or Japanese is impossible, but all of these different languages are represented by the ISO/IEC 10646 standard that we have already mentioned. A list of all of the **language codes** in use, referred to specifically as ISO 639, can be found at http://www.oasis-open.org/cover/iso639a.html. It contains the language as well as the language code; for example, "Burmese" is the name of the language, "MY" is the code used to refer to the language, and "Asian" is the language family. One other thing to note about UTF-8 is that is it is actually a compressed version of Unicode. It uses only a single byte for the most common ASCII characters between 0 and 127, and then uses three bytes for more uncommon characters, such as Chinese Han ideographs.

Tech Tip

UTF-8 can be converted to **UTF-16** and vice versa, although knowledge of Java Script is necessary.

Alert

XML's default on text is UTF-8 unless another UTF value is specified.

Character Sets and Typeface

Character sets do not refer to display formats, colors, or typefaces. Unicode characters become visible to the user through a special rendering process that maps characters into glyphs. **Glyphs** are the specific shape of any given character as it is displayed. The actual character "A" is really a generic "A" that might look like the plain letter "A". Through the use of glyphs (fonts), it can appear as something as beautifully scripted as "A". So this rendering process is basically the interaction of hardware and software that translates character codes into glyphs. Many things affect this rendering process such as operating systems, language settings, keyboard and display software, word processing software, type rasterizer, and input and output hardware.

In ASCII there is a one-to-one correlation between the character, the glyph, and the character set. That means that ASCII strips a character raw and renders it in basic text that resembles to most of us plain Courier. This is not true for Unicode. It can render beautiful scripts. Different standards bodies have been set up to make sure languages and scripts coordinate. In fact, this is such a substantial issue, that Agfa Monotype Corporation (http://www.agfamonotype.com/software), a company that specializes in font technologies and character and glyph conversion, has written a very helpful white paper on the subject. Visit http://www.agfamonotype.com/software/uni whitepaper.asp to read more about it, especially if you are in the graphics, publishing, or multimedia fields.

Advice

For a special look at fonts and font-related issues for the design professional, point your browser to http://www.fonts.com/usefullinks/usefullinks home.asp?nCo=AFMT.

This is just a basic introduction to Unicode, as Unicode is becoming an important element of any XML multilingual world. If this is a subject that you want to pursue, take a look at http://www.unicode.org/unicode/conference/about-conf.html to find out about international conferences on Unicode.

Key Terms

7 bits
8 bits
16 bits
32 bits
ASCII
C++
character set
encoding scheme
fatal error
glyphs
International Organization for Standardization
invalid
ISO 8859
ISO 10646
Java
language codes
Latin-1 (ISO 646)
LegalXML
parser
Unicode
UTF-8
UTF-16
UTF-32
valid
validation
Web services
well formed
whitespace
Win32
WYSIWYG
xml:lang

Code Summary

1. **Listing 6.1:**

```
<?xml version="1.0" encoding="UTF-8"?>
<!- This is good to use as a test ->
<!DOCTYPE scribble [
   <!ELEMENT scribble (first, second, third, fourth)>
   <!ELEMENT first (#PCDATA)>
   <!ELEMENT second (#PCDATA)>
   <!ELEMENT third (#PCDATA)>
   <!ELEMENT forth (#PCDATA)>
]>
<scribble>
   <first>Our first line</first>
   <second>Our second line</second>
   <third>Our third line</third>
   <fourth>Our fourth line</fourth>
</scribble>
```

2. **Listing 6.2, the corrected version:**

```
<!- This is good to use as a test ->
<!DOCTYPE scribble [
   <!ELEMENT scribble (first, second, third, fourth)>
   <!ELEMENT first (#PCDATA)>
   <!ELEMENT second (#PCDATA)>
   <!ELEMENT third (#PCDATA)>
   <!ELEMENT fourth (#PCDATA)>
]>
<scribble>
   <first>Our first line</first>
   <second>Our second line</second>
   <third>Our third line</third>
   <fourth>Our fourth line</fourth>
</scribble>
```

Review Questions

1. What is a parser and what does it do?
2. What is one use for Unicode?
3. What are the three basic types of editors?
4. Basic text editors can support Unicode. True or False?
5. An XML editor understands preset code. True or False?
6. What will happen to an XML statement if there is one error? Two errors?
7. An XML parser understands tag structure better than a person. True or False?
8. What is the difference between an error and a fatal error?
9. XML parsers can understand and interpret spelling errors. True or False?
10. How many characters does ASCII define?
11. Who maintains Unicode?
12. How many bits are used in Unicode?
13. Unicode provides a unique ______ for every character.
14. What is the XML attribute used with Unicode?
15. UTF-8 is a compressed version of Unicode. True or False?
16. What is a glyph?
17. Unicode has a one-to-one correlation between character, glyph, and character set. True or False?
18. What is the difference between the way IE and Netscape handle Unicode?

Case Study

Go to http://www.amzi.com/articles/youbet.htm and take a look at how a betting site for horseracing was constructed using XML and other technologies. Go to the section called "Implementation". Read how it takes a Java server message and translates it into XML. Now go to the section called "Parsing". See how it shows an XML statement, and how it can be changed into a higher statement, called a Prologue statement. Then go to the section called "Message Translation" and read what it says about XML and how there is a need for a vendor-neutral DTD. Of course, this is a higher-level program, but it shows the logic of parsers checking statements from Java to XML to Prologue. This is because XML parsers can actually be built on top of other parsers in terms of layering the middleware stack. Finally go to http://www.youbet.com/ and take a look at how a live feed of information is used. Going to the site does not endorse any kind of gambling, but is used for educational purposes only to see a real-world example of technical code.

Use of an Apache server-side XML parser is something that is useful for Webmasters, but only if your site is hosted on an Apache server. However, if you are headed in that direction, or are just curious about some other ways to use these higher-end parsers, take a look at http://techupdate.zdnet.com/techupdate/stories/main/0,14179,2850268,00.html to see how the WeddingChannel.com worked with different store gift registries and XML Apache server parsers. Though the raw information resides in an Oracle 8i database, it is served up to the client (customer) via XML with real-time updates. Without XML, real-time updates are not possible, and the wedding registry must rely on more standardized "batch" transfers, or transfers that occur at set times only. Now go to http://www.weddingchannel.com and go into the registries. See that there are many major department stores that participate. This means that these stores must be XML-enabled in their databases and that all of this information has been parsed not on the creation side, but on the server side, an advanced topic for server administrators.

Go to the site http://www.metalex.nl/pages/examples.html. Notice that, although the site does discuss the use of stylesheets, it also discusses, in depth, the use of both English and Dutch versions of legal documents. If you click on the links, it will display the same document in English and Dutch.

1. Click on `nl/rome-xml_ex` to see the legal document in Dutch.
2. Click on `en/rome-xml_ex` to see the legal document in English.

Notice that Dutch is coded `nl` and English is coded `en`. Think how useful this could be for global law firms to have many different language versions of the same document ready for viewing, all by using the language attribute available because of XML.

Then go further down the page and click on

1. `xml/xslfo/nl/WIB-CIR_1992` to see a legal document in Dutch.
2. `xml/xslfo/fr/WIB-CIR_1992` to see the same document in French.

Hands On Project

1. Go to http://www.garshol.priv.no/download/xmltools/cat_ix.html#SC_XMLBrowsers. Select one of the parsers that you are not familiar with, but which works on the platform you use, and try using it.
2. To test your browser and any other browser, go to http://www.ucc.ie/test.xml and open up the page in your browser. Then view the code source. See if it passes the tests named in the instructions. Use `validatortest.xml` as your test code.

BrowserTest

```
<!ATTLIST test xmlns:xlink CDATA #FIXED "http://www.w3.org/1999/xlink"
               xlink:type (simple) #FIXED "simple"
               xlink:href CDATA #IMPLIED>
<!ENTITY mdash "&#0151;">
<!DOCTYPE HTML PUBLIC "+//Silmaril//DTD Test Document//EN" "dtds/test.dtd">
<?xml-stylesheet href="test.css" type="text/css"?>
<test>
   <doctitle>This is an XML browser test</doctitle>
   <subtitle>(sometimes known as a <q>Hiya World!</q>)</subtitle>
   <para>This is a short test file which you can use to see how XML
          displays. It should show up in any browser which understands
          XML-currently these are:</para>
   <note>That should be an em rule between <q>XML</q> and
   <q>currently</q> in the previous line. </note>
   <para>Browsers supporting XML include:</para>
   <list>
     <item>the <product>DocZilla</product> browser based on
            <product>Netscape</product> and <product> MultiDoc
            Pro</product>; </item>
     <item><product>MultiDoc Pro</product> itself;</item>
     <item><product>Netscape 6</product> and
            <product>Mozilla</product>; and</item>
     <item><product>Opera</product>;</item>
     <item>Microsoft <product>Internet Explorer 5. and 6*</product>
            (partial).</item>
</list>
```

```
<para><product>Netscape 4</product> does not support XML at all.
        Be warned: browsers have bugs-not all of them
        support all of XML yet. But Nctscape 6 does, somewhat</para>
<para>This next bit is a <important>very important</important>
       [<code>&lt;test&gt;</code>]: between those square brackets you
       should see the world <q>test</q> in angle brackets using
       fixed-width type (<product>MSIE5 but not 6</product> has a weird problem
       here: check in View Source).</para>
```

3. Type `validatortest.xml` with the correct spelling of "fourth" (in Notepad or whatever other program you are using) and run it through XML Spy similar to Figure 6.11.

4. Using XML Spy, try to build `validatortest.xml` from the ground up as a DTD. Name it `Spytest.dtd`. Test it for being both well formed and valid. The best way to do this is to start with a new DTD in the selector box.

5. Using XML Edit Pro, look at `validatortest.xml` in different views like nodes and source. Then create a new document and start to build a DTD from the root element up. Play around with XML Edit Pro and remember to plan your DTD before you build it, not after.

6. Add one attribute to `validatortest.xml`. Run it through different editors. See what editor accepts the attribute and which ones do not. Then add a second attribute with coding that is different from the first. What do you notice?

7. Another free tool is an XML validator at http://www.stg.brown.edu/service/xmlvalid/. You can cut and paste your XML document into this site, or, if it is running on the Web, include the URL. To start with, use `validatortest.xml` and upload it from your computer to the site with the Browse button. Check the results with your fellow students. What worked? Why? What did not work? Why? How is this different from other parsers?

8. IBM maintains a useful website, http://www-124.ibm.com/icu/userguide/conversion.html. Although this site is aimed toward those with a C++ programming background, it is useful to explore. Of special note is the section that includes "conversion basics, converter, conversion Data, and compression.

9. Point your browser to http://www.unicode.org/. Click on code charts on the right-hand side of the page. Select Katakana, or any other non-English alphabetic script. You will need the Adobe Viewer to see the .pdf file with the Unicode. Look at 30D 1, which resembles two diagonal lines and a small circle. Katakana's code, therefore, is U+30A0 to U+30FF. Another useful page is http://www.unicode.org/unicode/onlinedat/languages-scripts.html to see what languages contain what scripts.

10. Take a look at http://www.basistech.com/products/index.html. Note the Sample Data Flow chart that discusses the Core Library for Unicode. Next take a look at the different language analyzers and script converters. If you want, go into the product demo page, though you will have to fill in personal information to view the demos.

11. Sun Systems, in conjunction with Reuters, has developed extensive use for Unicode to deliver information in many different languages to its different field offices. Read about it at http://www.sun.com/products-n-solutions/media-entertainment/docs/reuters.html.

CHAPTER 7

Applying Cascading Style Sheets

LEARNING OBJECTIVES

1. To access CSS stylesheets and associate them with XML documents.
2. To trace the evolution of the CSS format.
3. To differentiate CSS from the XSL format.
4. To understand the function and usage of CSS properties and values.
5. To examine emerging developments in applying CSS to XML.

Cascading Style Sheets, or **CSS** for short, provides a popular, straightforward way to format your XML documents. It was first developed to define how to display HTML elements within Web browsers, but later was applied to XML documents as well.

First introduced with the HTML 4.0 specifications, the main purpose of CSS was to give Web authors more control over the presentation of their Web pages. Although Web authors could not create new HTML tags, they could create and name new style definitions and then assign them at will to standard Web page components such as paragraphs, headings, or table cells. Web designers could save vast amounts of time by having all pages in a Web site—up to hundreds or thousands of pages—refer to a single set of styles (stored in an **external stylesheet**) for their formatting and display. In this way, a Web site redesign could be greatly simplified by tweaking the style definitions in a single stylesheet, instead of updating individual Web pages themselves. External stylesheets are stored in CSS files, which are text files with a .css file extension.

IMPORTANT

You can use any text editor software to create and edit a CSS file.

Developing XML Styles

If you have ever used a word processing program to update a resume or create a term paper, you've probably seen how applying styles to certain parts of your document—headings, bulleted lists, and the like—can save you a great deal of formatting time. And if you have ever created your own HTML documents before, you may have had some experience with using CSS to apply a consistent look and feel across a page or even all pages in a Web site. Similarly, applying styles to your XML documents can ensure your pages all conform to the same design, while making it easy to update multiple files any time a style changes.

When you apply CSS to HTML documents, there are several methods you can choose from. However—as you've come to see through many examples by now!—XML is more restrictive than HTML. Table 7.1 compares the ways in which CSS styles can be applied to HTML documents and XML documents, respectively.

TABLE 7.1 Applying CSS Styles to Both HTML and XML Documents

HTML method	Example	XML method	Example
Linked stylesheet	<head> <link rel="STYLESHEET" type="text/css" href= "mysite_stylesheet.css"> </head>	Linked stylesheet	<?xml version="1.0" encoding="UTF-8"?> <? xml-stylesheet href="mysite.css" type="text/css" ?>
Embedded stylesheet	<head><style type= "text/css">bodycopy {font-family: Verdana, Helvetica, Arial, sans-serif; font-size: 11px;}</style></head>		
Inline styles	<p style="color: green"> All text in this paragraph displays in green.</p>		

As Table 7.1 makes clear, there are several methods available within HTML to apply styles to a document. And this is really where the "cascading" nature of these styles comes in: You can override the global definitions defined in an external stylesheet with individual exceptions specified later. An external stylesheet dictates the styles used in a series of documents, but you can override a style's settings in a single HTML file by using an embedded stylesheet. This, in turn, can be overridden by an inline style for a particular instance.

XML documents, on the other hand, need a different approach. There is no counterpart to the <style> element in XML, for starters. To readily apply styles to an XML document, you utilize the linked stylesheet approach (as shown in Table 7.1) to access an external stylesheet.

But how do you actually associate a CSS stylesheet with an XML document? You link to an external stylesheet immediately after the opening line of your XML document. The standard uses the name `xml-stylesheet` and includes parameters for `href` and `type` that resemble XML attributes. Here, the `href` should point to the .css file in use, and the `type` should be set to `text/css`.

How CSS Has Evolved

The discussion in this chapter will distinguish between CSS1, which is widely used and supported by today's Web browsers, and CSS2, which is more robust and is intended to interact more fully with XML than its predecessor. We'll also cover the emerging CSS3 draft and its uses, most notably for mobile devices. Here's a quick timeline.

CSS1

CSS1 was first released as a W3C Recommendation—meaning that the specification is now officially considered a Web standard—in December 1996. The specification was updated again in 1999 at the same time that CSS2 was released. Netscape and Microsoft each began to include support for CSS1 in version 4 of their respective Web browsers.

Alert

Even browsers that claim to support CSS1 may have difficulty displaying certain properties. You'll want to bear that in mind to avoid adversely affecting the user experience for meaningful content.

CSS2

When CSS2 was first recognized by the W3C as a standard in 1999, it added several major style features that were lacking in CSS1. These include

- *Support for printers and aural devices.* The new print properties let you control how pages should be printed from the Web, including page orientation and where page breaks should occur. Aural stylesheets are designed to improve presentation of content via screen readers (often used by blind Internet users) that speak aloud the information that appears in your XML documents.

IMPORTANT

The CSS syntax that appears later will indicate which options are available only for CSS2 or later.

- *Element positioning.* This feature greatly increases your ability to control with exact precision where your content should appear on the screen. You can even control whether elements appear on top of one another.
- *Tables.* CSS2 adds a table-layout property that lets tables be rendered progressively on the screen, shortening the time necessary to display them.

By early 2002, newer browsers supported Web standards much better than their predecessors, including many CSS2 features. One notable subset of the CSS2 specification that has continued to steadily develop is the CSS Mobile standard, for formatting content on mobile devices.

CSS3

Still in the working draft stage, CSS3 is being published in modules—that is, in definitions of individual CSS properties—rather than in a single specification as CSS2 and CSS1 were. The purpose here was to have the W3C standards body continue to advance individual properties—for, say, defining backgrounds in CSS, as an example—on an ad hoc basis, without needing to wait for the rest of the specification to be ready first.

Introducing CSS Syntax

Take the time you need to absorb the structure and syntax of CSS statements. The more familiar you become with the syntax of styles defined with CSS, the easier you'll find it to control the display of your XML-generated content.

Properties and Values

The CSS syntax is comprised of three parts: a selector, a property, and a value. A sample style would look something like this:

```
selector {property: value}
```

The `selector` is usually the name of the element that you want to define. The `property` describes the attribute you wish to change; each property takes its own `value`. The selector name is followed by a pair of curly braces ({}) enclosing the property and value, which are separated by a colon:

```
body {color: black}
```

If the value contains more than one word, you should enclose it in quotation marks:

```
p {font-family: "sans serif"}
```

IMPORTANT

A number of CSS2 features, however, have yet to be widely implemented in current or popular browsers. As an example, although MS Internet Explorer began to include support for element positioning as early as version 4.0, other CSS2 features such as aural stylesheets are not yet supported. The W3C maintains a list of Web browsers that support CSS at http://www.w3.org/Style/CSS/#browsers.

If you want to specify more than one property, separate each property-value pair with a semicolon. The example below shows how to define a center-aligned paragraph with a red text color:

```
p { text-align: center; color: red }
```

Getting Literal: Display, List, and Whitespace Properties

When you create CSS styles for HTML tags, there's often some information about the tag's appearance that's assumed as a given and doesn't need to be made explicit. For example, if you add a style to make all boldface content within <b> tags appear colored in red, it's assumed that no line breaks should be generated before or after the <b> tags. Similarly, an ordered list (within <ol> tags) and unnumbered list (within <ul> tags) contain list items with numbers or bullets, respectively—hence the name! With CSS styles created for XML documents, nothing can be taken for granted. You need to be very explicit in these cases, for example, to say when line breaks should appear or when list markers need to be utilized.

IMPORTANT

You have the ability to add comments to your CSS styles, which can help remind you what a particular style is for or why you chose the display characteristics you did. The browser will ignore your comments when parsing the style definition to format your associated document's content. A CSS **comment** starts with a slash and an asterisk (/*) and ends with the reverse, an asterisk followed by a slash (*/). Here's a quick example:

```
/* This is a comment */
quote {
text-align: center;
/* You can even include comments in the middle of defining a style! */
color: green;
font-family: arial
}
```

Displaying Block and Inline Elements

The program presenting your XML needs to be able to differentiate two kinds of element content. Some elements appear within part of a larger block of text: Hypertext links, emphasized or boldface text, or superscript numbers (in a footnote, for example) are all good examples of this. By their nature, none of these would compel a line break in the text. These are all examples of **inline elements.**

In contrast, some kinds of content should be separated from their surrounding neighbors; headings and subheads, list items, or quoted passages are some examples that come to mind. Elements that fall into this category can be described as **block elements.** The code below shows an HTML example of a block element (the `<p>` or paragraph tags) containing several examples of inline elements (the emphasis and subscript tags, or `<em>` and `<sub>`, respectively):

```
<p>The chemical formula for water is H<sub>2</sub>O</p>
<p><em>Note:</em> The chemical formula for hydrogen
  peroxide is H<sub>2</sub>O<sub>2</sub></p>
```

Figure 7.1 shows how this displays in a Web browser.

CSS styles for XML documents use the `display` property to identify inline and block elements. If no `display` property is specified, the default value is `block`. For example:

```
blurb { font-size: 16pt }
```

is equivalent to

```
blurb { font-size: 16pt; display: block }
```

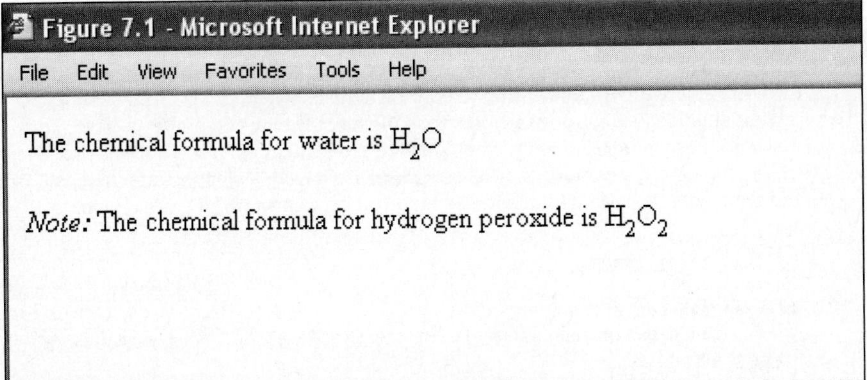

FIGURE 7.1 Example of Inline and Block Elements

Paragraphs are examples of block elements. Emphasized or italic text, for example, subscript characters, are formatted as inline elements with no extra line breaks preceding or following the formatting.

This `display` property can hold values of `inline` or `block` (indicating if text is run-in or separated by line breaks), `list-item` (for lists), or `none` (to hide the display altogether); CSS2 adds additional options, mostly for table markup. Take a look at the following elements defined in CSS with various `display` properties:

```
sidebar { display: block }
secret { display: none }
em { font-weight: bold; display: inline }
```

And here's how these styles might be applied within an XML document:

```
<sidebar>You will need to enter the registration code for
  your 30-day free trial when you first install the
  software.</sidebar>
<secret>The secret code for unlimited usage is XYZZY.
  </secret>
<sidebar>The registration code is located on the <em>back
  cover</em> of the CD packaging.</sidebar>
```

Figure 7.2 shows how this displays in a Web browser.

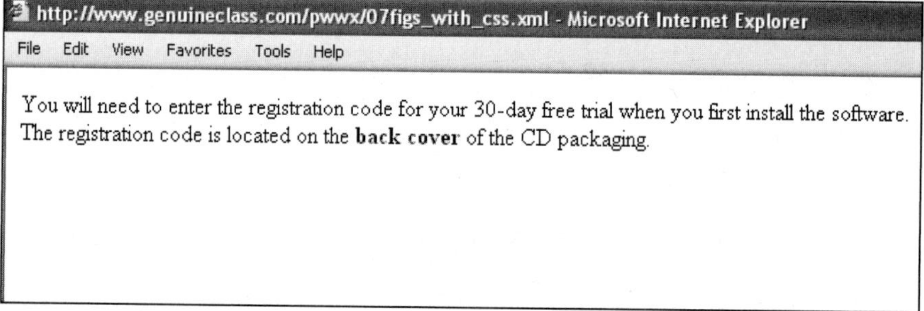

FIGURE 7.2 Displaying *`block`*, *`inline`*, and *`secret`* Elements from an XML Document

Lists

As you browse Web pages, you may see some lists numbered in ascending order and others displaying a number of bulleted items. The HTML tags `<ol>` and `<ul>` automatically generate these list item markers, and the `<li>` tag automatically demarcates where each new list item begins. In XML, though, you need to provide more specific instructions within the style definition in order for list formatting to kick in. You do this by setting the value of the `display` property to `list-item`, as in the following example:

```
bullet { display: list-item }
```

The list properties let you choose various `list-item` markers (numbers or bullets), set an image as a `list-item` marker (a very useful visual cue for readers), and set where to place a `list-item` marker (which affects indenting). Let's look at each of these in turn below:

The `list-style-type` Property This property sets the type of the `list-item` marker. You're probably most used to seeing lists on Web pages that appear as either ordered (numbered) lists or bulleted lists. The following code:

```
item {display: list-item; list-style-type: decimal}
```

when used in formatting a list

```
...
<item>This is the first item on my to-do list.</item>
<item>This is the second thing I have to do.</item>
<item>Remember what else I need to do.</item>
...
```

will display as shown in Figure 7.3.

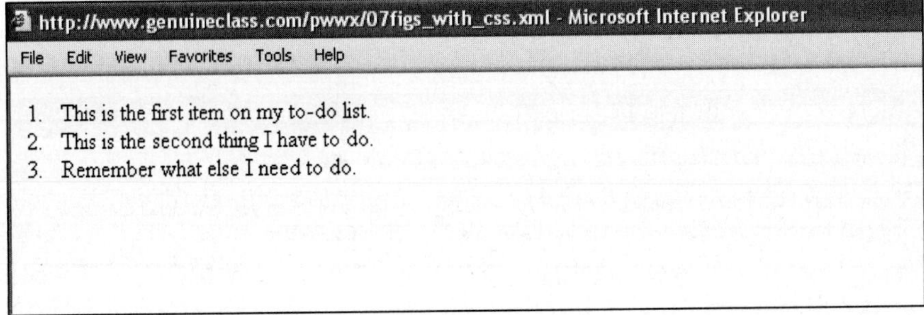

FIGURE 7.3 Putting the *list-style-type* Property to Work in Displaying a List Numbered 1, 2, 3, and so on

However, as Table 7.2 shows, the `list-style-type` property offers you many additional formatting choices.

In addition, alphabetic-ordered listings are also provided for use in global publishing purposes. Additional possible values for the `list-style-type` property include

- `lower-greek`
- `lower-latin`
- `upper-latin`
- `hebrew`
- `armenian`
- `georgian`
- `cjk-ideographic`
- `hiragana`

TABLE 7.2 Some Values for the *list-style-type* **Property**

Value	Sample Display
`disc`	Solid bullet
`circle`	Hollow bullet
`square`	Solid square
`decimal`	1, 2, 3, 4, 5, . . .
`decimal-leading-zero`	01, 02, 03, 04, 05, . . .
`lower-roman`	i, ii, iii, iv, v, . . .
`upper-roman`	I, II, III, IV, V, . . .
`lower-alpha`	a, b, c, d, e, . . .
`upper-alpha`	A, B, C, D, E, . . .

- `katakana`
- `hiragana-iroha`
- `katakana-iroha`

The `list-style-position` Property You can choose to have the number, bullet, or other `list-item` marker appear within the boundary of the text block (where the value would be `inside`) or outside in a hanging indent fashion (where the value would be `outside`). Within your CSS file, the styles would include these properties like this:

```
hanging-item {display: list-item; list-style-type: disc;
  list-style-position: outside}
noindent-item {display: list-item; list-style-type: disc;
  list-style-position: inside}
```

The styles are then applied in the XML document:

```
<hanging-item>This block of text utilizes what's known as
  a hanging indent. When a number of such pieces of
  information appear one after the other, the usefulness of
  visually separating them becomes clear.</hanging-item>
<noindent-item>In contrast, this second block of text
  begins with a bullet, which draws the reader's eye,
  but there is no hanging indent. Visually, this would
  run in with, say, a longer article in a less distracting
  way than a list of bullets with a hanging indent.
  </noindent-item>
```

Figure 7.4 shows how this displays in action.

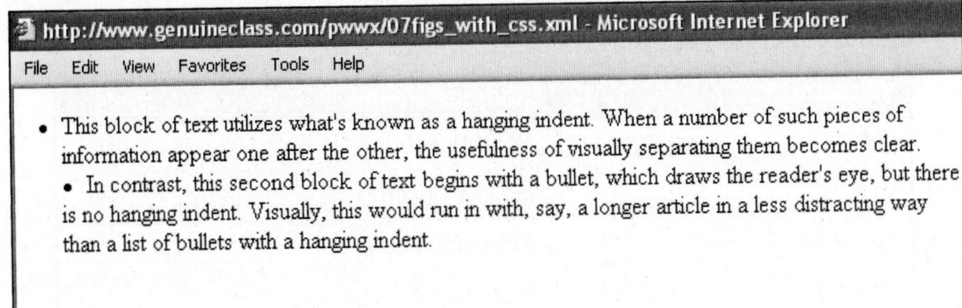
http://www.genuineclass.com/pwwx/07figs_with_css.xml - Microsoft Internet Explorer

File Edit View Favorites Tools Help

- This block of text utilizes what's known as a hanging indent. When a number of such pieces of information appear one after the other, the usefulness of visually separating them becomes clear.

• In contrast, this second block of text begins with a bullet, which draws the reader's eye, but there is no hanging indent. Visually, this would run in with, say, a longer article in a less distracting way than a list of bullets with a hanging indent.

FIGURE 7.4 Display Differences Seen When Changing the *`list-style-position`* Value

The `list-style-image` Property This property sets an image as the `list-item` marker. This is especially useful to draw the reader's eye to ratings or information next to a relevant icon—for example, a thumb's-up icon to accompany a numeric rating or score on a restaurant review site. Here's an example of how such images could appear with several features on a restaurant review site's roundup:

```
food { list-style-image: url(images/fork.gif) }
decor { list-style-image: url(images/window.gif) }
rating { list-style-image: url(images/thumb.gif) }
```

Within the XML document,

```
<food>Japanese</food>
<decor>Elegant</decor>
<rating>3.7</rating>
```

Figure 7.5 shows how this might appear online.

The Kitchen Sink: Combining List Properties in `list-style` This property is a catchall for setting all of the list properties—type, position, and/or image—in a single declaration. Some examples follow:

```
majorlist { list-style: lower-roman inside }
minorlist { list-style: decimal outside }
```

Whitespace

Most of the time, the extra spaces (**whitespace**) and carriage returns that you type when creating an HTML or XML file wind up getting ignored. If you type in two spaces in a row, for example, it will display on screen as just one. In HTML, if you want to preserve your spacing and line wraps just as they're typed in, you can do so using the `<pre>` (or preformatted) tag. To achieve this effect using CSS style sheets for XML documents, you need a slightly different approach. You'll need to set the value of the `white-space` property to `pre` (again, for preformatted) as shown below:

```
code { white-space: pre }
```

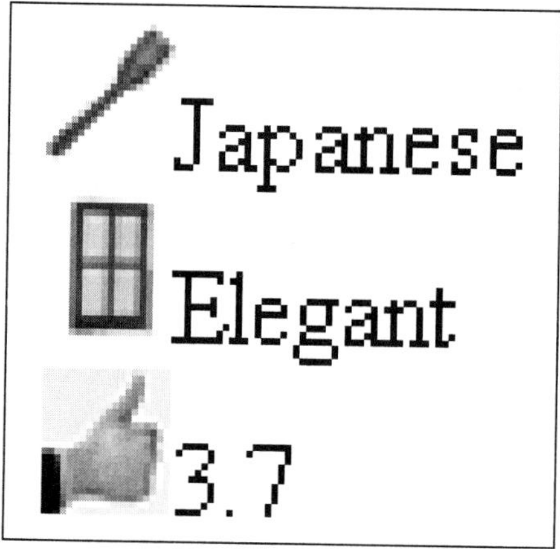

FIGURE 7.5 Utilizing the `list-style-image` Property

Table 7.3. shows all the possible values for the `white-space` property.

TABLE 7.3 Values Used by the `white-space` Property

Value	Purpose
`normal`	Collapses all extra spaces, as well as text wrapping imposed by text editing software.
`pre`	Maintains any extra typed-in spaces and carriage returns that have been added.
`nowrap`	Ensures that all content styled this way displays on a single line.

More Basic CSS Formatting

Next, let's look at more properties available in CSS1 that shape and format your XML content. We'll cover backgrounds, text, fonts, borders, margins, and padding.

Backgrounds

Using CSS's background properties, you can define the background effects of an element—including color or a background image, or details about the display of the background image.

Here's an example of putting CSS's background properties to work to affix a logo in the bottom right corner of the screen:

```
body {
background-attachment: fixed;
background-image:
url("http://www.genuineclass.com/images/pigtails.gif");
background-repeat: no-repeat;
background-position: 100% 100%
}
```

Figure 7.6 shows how this might appear onscreen. Even when you scroll down the page, the background image appears locked in place in the bottom right of the screen.

In this example, the **background-image** property indicates what graphic should display as the background image. The **background-attachment** property is set to **fixed**, meaning that the image appears fixed in place even as the reader scrolls down the page. Finally, the **background-position** property places the image at 100 percent across the screen and 100 percent of the way down; it's another way of saying the bottom right-hand corner of the screen.

Table 7.4 includes an extensive list of the background properties in CSS and their possible values.

Combining Settings: The Background Property Similar to the **list-style** property you saw earlier in this chapter, the **background-style** property is an all-in-one setting for defining background properties—attachment, color, image, position, and/or repeat—in a single declaration. Here's an example:

```
body { background: url(rainbow.gif) no-repeat 100% 100% }
```

Text

CSS's text properties let you control the appearance of text in your XML documents. Among other features, you can change text color, indent the first line in a block of text, transform upper- and lowercase, increase or decrease the space between characters, or set the text alignment.

In the past, Web designers struggled for years with inefficient workarounds in HTML for such simple formatting requests as indenting a line of text. CSS's capabilities in this area, then, are definitely worthy of appreciation!

Here's an example of styles that make use of CSS's text properties:

```
allcapshead { font-family: helvetica; text-transform:
  uppercase }
p { text-indent: 10 px }
```

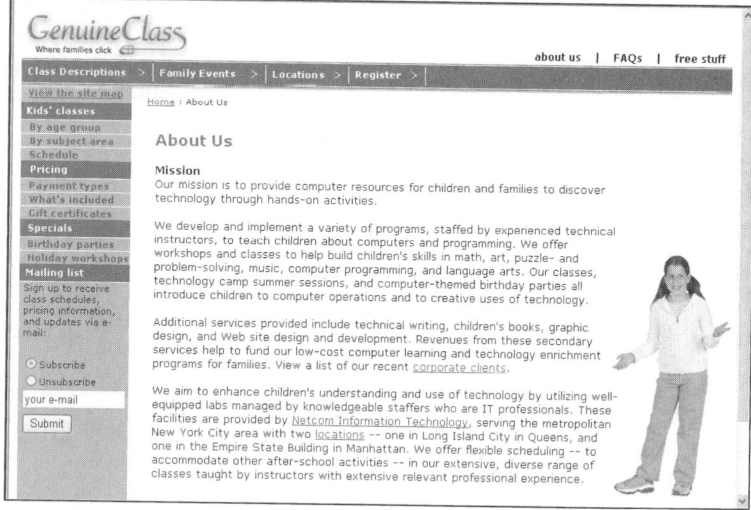

FIGURE 7.6

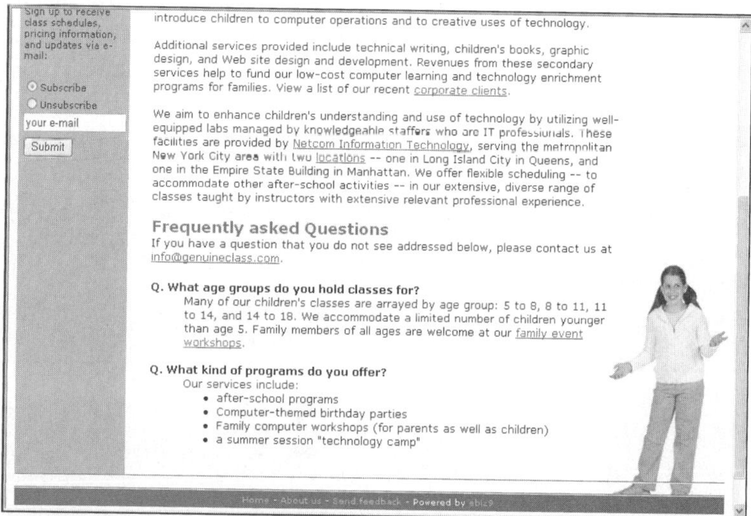

FIGURE 7.6 Making an Image Appear in the Bottom Right Corner of the Screen Display, Using CSS's Background Properties.

Applying these styles to the lines of text below will make the words "How to apply" appear entirely in uppercase. The following paragraph will have its first line indented 10 pixels from the left.

```
<allcapshead>How to apply</allcapshead>
<p>Enclose a current resume or background information
  illustrating your qualifications.</p>
```

TABLE 7.4 Background Properties and Their Values

Property	Description	Values	W3C Version
`background-attachment`	Indicates whether a background image should appear fixed in place or scroll as the reader scrolls down the page.	`scroll fixed`	CSS1

`background-color`	Sets the background color of an element.	`color-rgb`
		`color-hex`
		`color-name`
		`transparent`
			CSS1

`background-image`	Designates an image as the background image.	`url` `none`	CSS1

`background-position`	Determines where a background image should display.	`top left`
		`top center`
		`top right`
		`center left`
		`center center`
		`center right`
		`bottom left`
		`bottom center`
		`bottom right`
		`x-% y-%`
		`x-pos y-pos`
			CSS1

`background-repeat`	Indicates if and how a background image should tile (or repeat) across the screen.	`repeat`
		`repeat-x`
		`repeat-y`
		`no-repeat`
			CSS1

Figure 7.7 shows how this might appear onscreen.

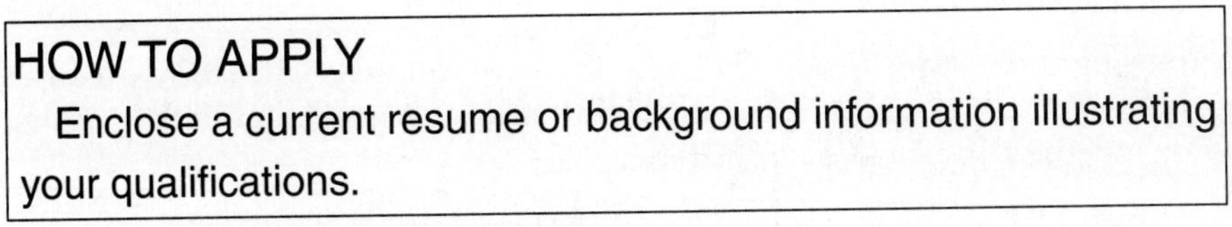

HOW TO APPLY

Enclose a current resume or background information illustrating your qualifications.

FIGURE 7.7 Example of CSS Text Properties

CSS's text properties let you change uppercase text to all lowercase with a single style change, or alter the size of an indent, much like in a word processing program.

IMPORTANT

One popular application is using the `text-decoration` property to remove the underlining that's generally seen with hyperlinked text:

```
a {text-decoration: none}
```

Table 7.5 includes more examples of how to leverage text properties.

TABLE 7.5 Text Properties and Their Values

Property	Description	Values	W3C Version
`color`	Indicates the text color	Color name or hex value	CSS1
`direction`	Sets the text direction (some languages, like Hebrew, are usually read right to left)	`ltr` (left-to-right) `rtl` (right-to-left)	CSS2
`letter-spacing`	Increase or decrease the space that appears between characters	`normal length` (in pixels)	CSS1

`text-align`	Aligns the text in an element	`left`
		`right`
		`center`
		`justify`
			CSS1

`text-decoration`	Adds decoration (such as underlining) to text	`none`
		`underline`
		`overline`
		`line-through`
		`blink`
			CSS1

`text-indent`	Indents the first line of text in an element	`length` (in pixels) `%`	CSS1
`text-transform`	Changes the case of the text in an element	`none` `capitalize`	CSS1
		`uppercase` `lowercase`	

`unicode-bidi`	Related to the direction property above, this affects the placement of text in bidirectional languages	`normal`
		`embed`
		`bidi-override`
			CSS2

`word-spacing`	Increase or decrease the space between words	`normal` `length` (in pixels)	CSS1

Fonts

The font properties enable you to change the font family, size, boldness, and style of a text. Here's a straightforward example:

```
caption { font-style: italic }
```

Table 7.6 includes an at-a-glance view of various font properties.

TABLE 7.6 Font Properties and Their Values

Property	Description	Values	W3C Version
`font-family`	A list, in order, of the preferred fonts to use if available for an element.	Any font name	CSS1

`font-size`	Indicates the size of a font.	`xx-small`
		`x-small`
		`small`
		`medium`
		`large`
		`x-large`
		`xx-large`
		`smaller`
		`larger`
		`length` (in pixels)
		`%`
			CSS1

`font-size-adjust`	Lets you preserve the height of lowercase letters even if your preferred `font-family` is not available (which can help increase readability)	Enter a decimal value	CSS2

`font-stretch`	Expands or condenses the current `font-family`	`normal`
		`wider`
		`narrower`
		`ultra-condensed`
		`extra-condensed`
		`condensed`
		`semi-condensed`
		`semi-expanded`
		`expanded`
		`extra-expanded`
		`ultra-expanded`
			CSS2

`font-style`	Sets the character formatting of the font	`normal`
		`italic`
		`oblique`
			CSS1

`font-variant`	Displays text in either a `small-caps` font or a `normal` one	`normal` `small-caps`	CSS1

Continued

TABLE 7.6 Font Properties and Their Values (continued)

Property	Description	Values	W3C Version

`font-weight`	Sets the weight of a font	`normal`
		`bold`
		`bolder`
		`lighter`
		`100`
		`200`
		`300`
		`400`
		`500`
		`600`
		`700`
		`800`
		`900`
			CSS1

Combining Settings: The Font Property Similar to the `list-style` and `background-style` properties, the font property lets you define multiple font properties—for typeface, size, weight, and so on—in a single declaration. Here's an example:

```
captioncopy: {oblique small-caps 900 10px/12px arial}
```

Borders

In the past, HTML designers would use tables to create a border effect. Now, though, you can use CSS's border properties to specify a border around any element, including style and color.

Here's an example that defines a callout with a thin border on all four sides. If you had the patience, you could set different-sized borders for all four sides:

```
callout {border-width: thin}
```

Table 7.7 includes the nitty-gritty on what values apply to the many individual border properties available to you. Be sure to read on after Table 7.7 to see how to combine multiple border properties into a single style definition.

Combining Settings: The Border Property The border property provides a shortcut to setting all of the properties for the four borders in a single declaration. With this property, though, you can't set varying margin or padding for individual sides of the border. Here's an example:

```
coupon { border: thin dotted #000000 }
```

Figure 7.8 shows the effect of adding this border to each of the styles first defined in Figure 7.7.

TABLE 7.7 Individual Border Properties and Their Values

Property	Description	Values	W3C Version

`border-style`	Denotes the style of the four borders. You can set from one to four styles.	`none`
		`hidden`
		`dotted`
		`dashed`
		`solid`
		`double`
		`groove`
		`ridge`
		`inset`
		`outset`
			CSS1

`border-bottom-color`	Denotes the color of the bottom border.	Enter a color value	CSS2
`border-bottom-style`	Sets the style of the bottom border.	Same as for `border-style` above	CSS2

`border-bottom-width`	Marks the width of the bottom border.	`thin`
		`medium`
		`thick`
		`length`
			CSS1

`border-color`	Denotes the color of the four borders. You can set from one to four colors.	Enter a color value	CSS1
`border-left-color`	Denotes the color of the bottom border.	Enter a color value	CSS2
`border-left-style`	Sets the style of the bottom border.	Same as for `border-style` above	CSS2
`border-left-width`	Marks the width of the bottom border.	Same as for `border-bottom-width` above	CSS1
`border-right-color`	Denotes the color of the bottom border.	Enter a color value	CSS2
`border-right-style`	Sets the style of the bottom border.	Same as for `border-style` above	CSS2
`border-right-width`	Marks the width of the bottom border.	Same as for `border-bottom-width` above	CSS1

Continued

TABLE 7.7 Individual Border Properties and Their Values (continued)

Property	Description	Values	W3C Version
`border-top-color`	Denotes the color of the bottom border.	Enter a color value	CSS2
`border-top-style`	Sets the style of the bottom border.	Same as for `border-style` above	CSS2
`border-top-width`	Marks the width of the bottom border.	Same as for `border-bottom-width` above	CSS1

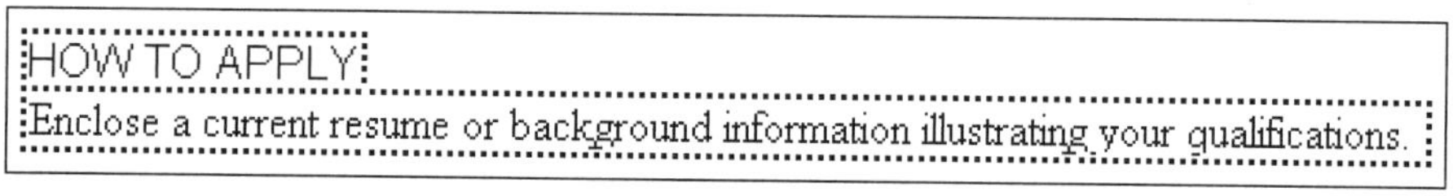

HOW TO APPLY

Enclose a current resume or background information illustrating your qualifications.

FIGURE 7.8 Boxing in Elements Using the CSS Border Properties

More Combined Border Settings You can set all the properties for any individual side of the border with the following properties:

- `border-bottom`
- `border-left`
- `border-right`
- `border-top`
- `border-width`

For example:

```
rulebeneath { border-bottom: solid #0000FF }
```

These combined properties are all CSS1-compatible.

Margins

The CSS margin properties define how much space should appear around elements. One interesting feature is that you can use negative values for margins, which will cause content to overlap. As with the border properties, you can change top, right, bottom, and left margins independently of one another using separate properties. You also can utilize a combined, shorthand margin property to change all of the margins at once. Here is an example of an element called `sidebar` that's styled to have different-sized margins on each side:

```
sidebar {margin: 2cm 4cm 3cm 4cm}
```

Here's how you might apply such a style within your XML document:

```
<bodytext>This is an example of the "bodytext" style.
  It displays without any special formatting for the
  margins.</bodytext>
<sidebar>Here, we've set up a block of text using the
  "sidebar" style.</sidebar>
<bodytext>And finally, let's return to the plain
  "bodytext" formatting.</bodytext>
```

Figure 7.9 demonstrates the onscreen effect of this code.

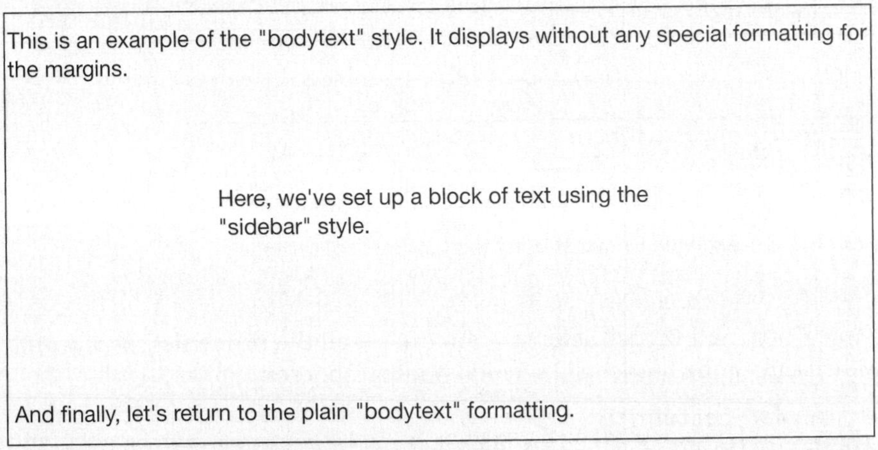

This is an example of the "bodytext" style. It displays without any special formatting for the margins.

Here, we've set up a block of text using the "sidebar" style.

And finally, let's return to the plain "bodytext" formatting.

FIGURE 7.9 Using the Margin Properties in CSS

As Table 7.8 shows, you also can set margins for individual sides by entering a margin in pixels or as a percentage.

TABLE 7.8 Individual Margin Properties and Their Values

Property	Description	Values	W3C Version
`margin-bottom`	Sizes the bottom margin	Length (in pixels) or percentage	CSS1
`margin-left`	Sizes the left margin	Same as above	CSS1
`margin-right`	Sizes the right margin	Same as above	CSS1
`margin-top`	Sizes the top margin	Same as above	CSS1

Padding

Use the padding properties to indicate how much space should appear between an element's border and the content contained therein. You can manipulate the padding on all four sides—top, right, bottom, and left—

individually. Or you can utilize a combined, shorthand padding property to change all of the padding at once. Here are two examples of elements that set different-sized padding on each side:

```
callout {padding: 7px}
rightindent {padding-left: 5px; padding-right: 50px}
```

Figure 7.10 shows the difference that varying the padding can make.

Select and apply padding when you want to ensure that a boxed area of text is fully readable.

This block of text, on the other hand, is heavily indented on the right. With the padding properties, you have a great deal of control over the display of tables when using CSS with XML.

FIGURE 7.10 Changing the Padding Properties Affects How Content Displays within Borders

As Table 7.9 shows, you also can indicate the padding for individual sides by entering a value for padding in pixels (or cm) or as a percentage.

TABLE 7.9 Individual Padding Properties and Their Values

Property	Description	Values	W3C version
`padding-bottom`	Sizes the bottom padding.	Length (in pixels or cm) or percentage	CSS1
`padding-left`	Sizes the left padding.	Same as above	CSS1
`padding-right`	Sizes the right padding.	Same as above	CSS1
`padding-top`	Sizes the top padding.	Same as above	CSS1

Advanced CSS Formatting

By now, you've seen how to apply CSS styling to manipulate the display and layout of your XML text in a great variety of ways. The next set of CSS proper-

IMPORTANT

Unlike the margin properties, the padding properties do not accept negative values.

ties covered here includes some additional content display capabilities that you might find useful. Overall, browser support for these features may be more limited to date; check the display thoroughly before relying on any of these features for delivering important content.

Dimension

CSS's dimension properties control the height and width of an element. You also can use it to increase the space between two lines.

As of this writing, only the CSS1-compatible properties are supported in current versions of Microsoft's and Netscape's browsers. These are listed in Table 7.10; the dimension properties added in CSS2 follow below.

TABLE 7.10 Selected Dimension Properties and Their Values

Property	Description	Values	W3C Version
`height`	Sets the height of an element	`auto` Enter a value for length	CSS1
`line-height`	Sets the distance between lines	`normal` Enter a value for number or length %	CSS1
`width`	Denotes an element's width	`auto` % Enter a value for length	CSS1

CSS2 adds properties for setting a maximum and minimum height and width:

- `max-height`
- `max-width`
- `min-height`
- `min-width`

Classification

This set of properties gives you control over how to display an element. You can determine where an image will appear in another element, position an element in absolute or relative terms, and manage the visibility of an element. You can even change how the cursor will appear when you drag it over a certain element—which, admittedly, is not terribly practical, but it's still an impressive visual trick! Table 7.11 provides an overview of the classification properties.

TABLE 7.11 Classification Properties and Their Values

Property	Description	Values	W3C Version

`Clear`	Determines which sides of an element prevent other floating elements from appearing.	`left`
		`right`
		`both`
		`none`
			CSS1

`Cursor`	Displays a certain type of cursor when the user drags with the mouse over this content.	`auto`
		`crosshair`
		`default`
		`pointer`
		`move`
		`e-resize`
		`ne-resize`
		`nw-resize`
		`n-resize`
		`se-resize`
		`sw-resize`
		`s-resize`
		`w-resize`
		`text`
		`wait`
		`help`
			CSS2

`Display`	Previewed earlier. This sets limits on how an element is displayed.	`none`
		`inline`
		`block`
		`list-item`
		`run-in`
		`compact`
		`marker`
		`table`
		`inline-table`
		`table-row-group`
		`table-header-group`
		`table-footer-group`
		`table-row`
		`table-column-group`
		`table-column`
		`table-cell`
		`table-caption`
			CSS1

`float`	Determines where an image or a text will appear in another element. Mostly used for images to stay on the left or right side, but is also useful for insets.	`Left`
		`Right`
		`None`
			CSS1

Continued

TABLE 7.11 Classification Properties and Their Values (continued)

Property	Description	Values	W3C Version

`position`	Puts an element in a static, relative, absolute or fixed position. Especially useful for superscripted or subscripted text.	`static`
		`relative`
		`absolute`
		`fixed`
			CSS2

`visibility`	Indicates whether an element should be visible or invisible.	`visible`
		`hidden`
		`collapse`
			CSS2

Positioning

Want to make sure your content displays just so? Then you'll want to leverage CSS's positioning properties. Both the Microsoft and Netscape browsers support these CSS2 properties. The positioning properties let you specify the left, right, top, and bottom position of an element. You also can set the shape of an element, place one element behind another, and determine what should happen if an element's content is too big to fit in a specified area. Figure 7.11 shows the positioning properties in action and Table 7.12 provides the rundown of the positioning properties.

The **heading** is placed 30px up from the bottom of the document, and 40px to the left from the right side of the document. The **paragraph** is placed 80px up from the bottom of the document, and 40px to the left from the right side of the document.

A heading

FIGURE 7.11 CSS's Positioning Properties at Work

TABLE 7.12 Positioning Properties and Their Values

Property	Description	Values	W3C Version

`bottom`	Indicates how far the bottom edge of an element appears above or below the bottom edge of the parent element.	`auto`
		`%`
		`length` (in pixels or cm)
			CSS2

`clip`	This sets the shape of an element. Your element is clipped and displayed according to the shape indicated.	`rect` (followed by four values for top, right, bottom, left) `auto`	CSS2

Continued

TABLE 7.12 Positioning Properties and Their Values (continued)

Property	Description	Values	W3C Version
`clip`	This sets the shape of an element. Your element is clipped and displayed according to the shape indicated.	`rect` (followed by four values for top, right, bottom, left) `auto`	CSS2

`left`	Marks how far the left edge of an element appears to the right or left of the left edge of the parent element.	`auto`
		`%`
		`length` (in pixels or cm)
			CSS2

`overflow`	Indicates the output if the content of an element overflows its area.	`visible`
		`hidden`
		`scroll`
		`auto`
			CSS2

`right`	Marks how far the right edge of an element appears to the right or left of the left edge of the parent element.	`auto`
		`%`
		`length` (in pixels or cm)
			CSS2

`top`	Indicates how far the top edge of an element appears above or below the top edge of the parent element.	`auto`
		`%`
		`length` (in pixels or cm)
			CSS2

`vertical-align`	Sets the vertical alignment of an element.	`baseline`
		`sub`
		`super`
		`top`
		`text-top`
		`middle`
		`bottom`
		`text-bottom`
		`length`
		`%`
			CSS1

`z-index`	Sets the stack order of an element—that is, which elements display atop others.	`auto` Enter a numeric value	CSS2

Comparing CSS to XSL

Up ahead in Chapter 8, we'll examine the **eXtensible Stylesheet Language (XSL),** another stylesheet standard for displaying Web pages. You may already be wondering why CSS and XSL are both offered as stylesheet standards. The short answer is that CSS is already widely supported by Web browsers, since it was introduced earlier than XSL. Additionally, as you'll find out quickly, CSS is easy to learn and its syntax is extremely readable. But more importantly, XSL has powerful capabilities for manipulating and displaying your data. With XSL, you can change the order of elements for display, or suppress elements in one place and have them appear in another. Table 7.13 shows an at-a-glance list of the relative advantages of CSS and XSL, respectively.

TABLE 7.13 Determining When to Apply CSS and When to Apply XSL to XML Documents

Advantages of CSS	Advantages of XSL
Relatively simple to implement. New application of an existing technology, which ensured broad support in current Web browsers.	Can convert XML into HTML, then sort and filter it based on the values in the data. Can process elements more than once. Can suppress elements in one place, then present them elsewhere. Adds generated text to the presentation (which CSS2 provides in only a limited way). Sorts and filters output into any language. Can produce more sophisticated page layouts and styles than CSS can.
Disadvantages of CSS	**Disadvantages of XSL**
Cannot transform or manipulate content.	Steeper learning curve than that for CSS.

In short, although CSS and XSL have similar goals—namely, in separating content from format—they really shouldn't be viewed as competing standards. Use CSS for straightforward formatting tasks that don't involve manipulating the order of your data. For more sophisticated transactions involving sorting or filtering your XML data, use an XSL implementation.

As an example, let's consider what would be involved in presenting a list of recording artists alphabetically by surname. Let's start with this source element:

```
<artist>
<firstname>Elvis</firstname>
<surname>Costello</surname>
</artist>
```

IMPORTANT

The W3C offers a detailed comparison of CSS and XSL, along with recommendations on their usage, at http://www.w3.org/Style/CSS-vs-XSL.

You'd need the powerful capabilities of XSL to accomplish this. CSS would provide a way to apply properties to both the `<firstname>` and `<surname>` elements, but would offer no mechanism for reordering them.

The syntax for associating CSS styles with an XML document is almost identical to the way you'd apply XSL styles to an XML document. As you've seen, linking a CSS stylesheet to an XML file might look something like this:

```
<?xml version="1.0" encoding="UTF-8"?>
<? xml-stylesheet href="mysite.css" type="text/css" ?>
```

Applying XSL to an XML document also uses `xml-stylesheet`. Here, though, the source file linked to the `href` parameter will end with .xsl extension. The `type` parameter changes as well, to `"text/xsl"`.

```
<?xml version="1.0" encoding="UTF-8"?>
<? xml-stylesheet href="mysite.xsl" type="text/xsl" ?>
```

Ensuring Your CSS Is Valid

The W3C provides an online CSS validation service at http://jigsaw.w3.org/css-validator/. You can provide your CSS data by uploading a .css file, copying and pasting the contents of the .css file, or just including the pathname to an online .css file. You also can specify which CSS version to validate against. Figure 7.12 shows how this interactive form appears online.

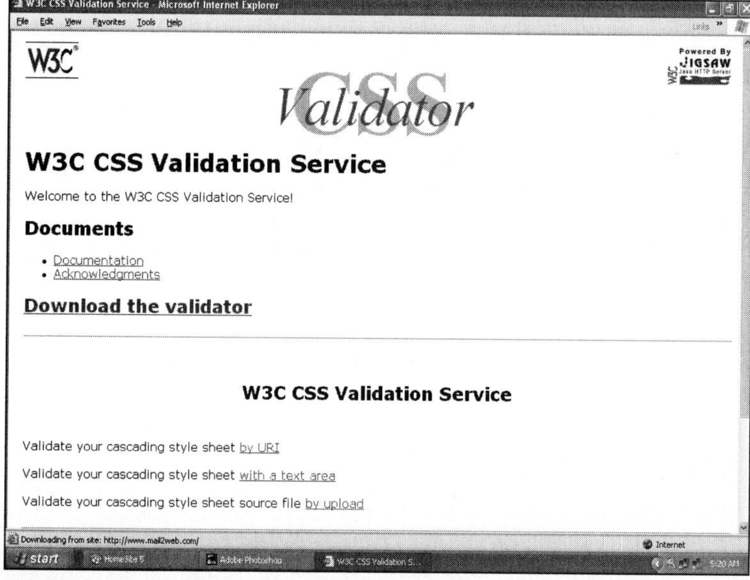

FIGURE 7.12 The W3C's Online CSS Validator

By now, you've seen that CSS offers dozens of property features for precisely defining the display of your XML data. Straight ahead in the next chapter, we'll go beyond formatting XML data to actually sorting, filtering, and transforming that data—even converting it into HTML—using XSL.

Key Terms

block elements
Cascading Style Sheets (CSS)
comments
eXtensible Stylesheet language (XSL)
external stylesheet
inline elements
whitespace

Code Summary

1. **Applying CSS styles to an XML document:**

```
<?xml version="1.0" encoding="UTF-8"?>
<? xml-stylesheet href="mysite.css" type="text/css" ?>
```

2. **Basic CSS syntax:**

```
selector {property: value}
```

3. **The `display` property in a CSS style:**

```
sidebar { display: block }
secret { display: none }
em { font-weight: bold; display: inline }
```

4. **The `list-item` marker in a CSS style:**

```
item {display: list-item; list-style-type: disc}
```

5. **Background properties in CSS:**

```
body {
background-attachment: fixed;
background-image:
url("http://www.genuineclass.com/images/pigtails.gif");
background-repeat: no-repeat;
background-position: bottom right
}
```

6. **Text properties in CSS:**

```
allcapshead { font-family: helvetica; text-transform: uppercase }
p { text-indent: 10 px }
```

7. **Font properties in CSS:**

```
caption { font-style: italic }
```

8. **Padding properties in CSS:**

```
callout {padding: 7px}
rightindent {padding-left: 5px; padding-right: 50px}
```

9. **Applying XSL to an XML document:**

```
<?xml version="1.0" encoding="UTF-8"?>
<? xml-stylesheet href="mysite.xsl" type="text/xsl" ?>
```

Review Questions

1. Describe the purpose of a stylesheet.
2. What are the differences between an internal and external stylesheet?
3. How would you override a stylesheet in an XML document?
4. Describe the differences between CSS1, CSS2, and CSS3.
5. Define each of the following parts of CSS syntax: selector, property, value.
6. What are block elements? What are inline elements?
7. When comparing CSS to XSL, what are the relative advantages and disadvantages of each approach?

Case Study

Let's examine the impact that a CSS stylesheet has on the display of an XML document, and manipulate its individual styles.

Locate an XML document that references an XML stylesheet. For an example file, visit http://www.w3.org/TR/xhtml1/, view the source code, and save the source code as an XML file.

Now open the XML stylesheet that was utilized by your sample document. (You may need to download this first if your sample document was one you found online. The link to the stylesheet within the document will help you identify its location.)

Next, remove the link to the XML stylesheet, save the file, and view the XML document again. What changes have taken place in the document's display?

Now add an XML stylesheet link to a new, empty stylesheet file. View the XML document and note its display. At this point, you should start building new styles for each of the ones used in your sample XML document. To speed up this process, you can refer to the original XML stylesheet used by your sample document; copy over each style one at a time, making slight changes (e.g., in fonts used, type size, colors, or background colors) to each style along the way. Refresh the display of the XML document frequently to see the immediate impact of your stylesheet changes.

Hands On Project

For this project, you'll retrieve the DTD that you created in Chapter 5 for marking up a newspaper article. Review the sample news story you marked up with the newspaper DTD you created. Consider how you can style the elements to replicate the look-and-feel of a printed newspaper in an online display.

1. Use the `background-image` property to position a logo that will not move as the reader scrolls through the page.
2. Add an indent to the first paragraph of news articles with the `text-indent` property. Experiment with different-sized indents.
3. Add callouts or pull quote elements to your news items to highlight interesting quotes. Use the text properties to color and align these special elements differently from the rest of the news item content.
4. Use the font properties to distinguish the headings and subheads for your news items.
5. Create boxed sidebars of content using the border, margin, and padding properties.
6. Use the positioning properties to precisely place an image with each news item. Next, try placing a caption underneath each image.

CHAPTER 8

Applying eXtensible Style Sheets (XSL)

LEARNING OBJECTIVES

1. To learn how XSL can transform XML documents into other formats such as HTML.
2. To examine how an XSL stylesheet consists of a set of rules called templates.
3. To discover the three components that comprise XSL: XSLT, XPath, and XSL Formatting Objects.
4. To use XSLT to output an XML source document into an XML result document.
5. To use XPath expressions in matching patterns to locate parts of an XML document.

As you saw in the previous chapter, applying stylesheets to the elements you create in XML makes it easier for you to manage the presentation and display of your documents. Both CSS and eXtensible Style Sheets (XSL) are stylesheet languages that can be used for this purpose. However, while CSS can be used to format HTML or XML documents, XSL is capable of much more than just document formatting. You can use XSL to transform documents—for example, to transform XML data into an HTML document with a CSS stylesheet on a Web server. In this way, XSL and CSS complement each other and can even be used together. You also can use XSL to format data based on its value—for example, to display negative numbers in a financial report in red.

Understanding XSL

XSL consists of three parts:

- **XSLT (XSL Transformations),** a language for transforming XML documents.
- **XPath,** a language that defines parts of an XML document.
- **XSL Formatting Objects,** a vocabulary for styling XML documents.

What does this mean? Table 8.1 provides an overview of what each of these parts does; we'll cover each of these functions in detail later in this chapter.

TABLE 8.1 Uses for the Components of XSL

XSL Component	What It Does
XSLT	Transforms XML data into another XML document or a document based on another language, like XHTML. You can grab content from other documents, create new elements and attributes, or apply a combination of these two.
XPath	Is used by XSLT to locate elements and/or attributes within an XML document.
XML Formatting Objects	Specifies the formatting properties for rendering the document.

In short, XSL can filter and sort XML data using the criteria you define, as well as format its display based on the value of the data itself. When the data is output, you can use XSL to send your XML data to various devices, including handhelds, print, or voice output. Figure 8.1 traces this process.

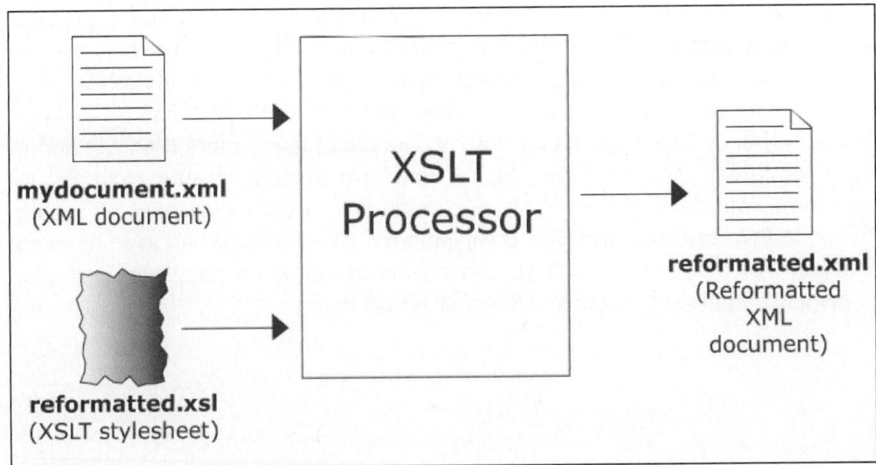

FIGURE 8.1 Using the XSLT Processor
The XSLT processor reads an XML file and an XSLT stylesheet, then outputs another file based on the instructions found in the stylesheet.

IMPORTANT

The W3C recognizes XSL as an industry standard. The first two parts of the language, XSLT and XPath, became a W3C Recommendation in November 1999. XML Formatting was added to the XSL Recommendation in October 2001.

Using XSLT to Transform XML Documents with XSL

XSLT has the most important role in the XSL standard. This is the part of XSL that can turn one XML document into another. Or you can transform an XML document into another format that can be recognized by a browser (like an XHTML document). Typically, XSLT does this by converting each XML element into an XHTML element.

XSLT is a template-based programming language. An XSLT template can also introduce new XML elements into the output document it creates, or remove others. It can change the order of elements and choose which to display and which to hide. You also can use XSLT to create multiple "views" of the same source document to let your data be displayed on a broad variety of devices, including Web-enabled cell phones or PDAs. In this way, XSLT lets different kinds of software applications exchange XML-enabled data with one another.

One way to think of this process is that XSL uses XSLT to transform an XML **source tree** into an XML **result tree** (Figure 8.2).

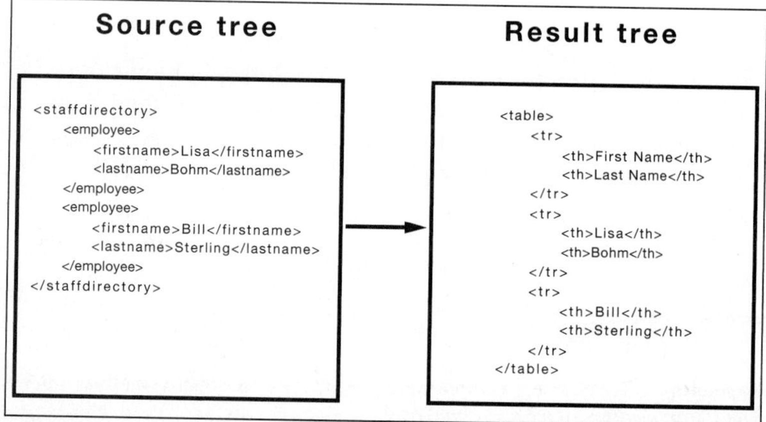

FIGURE 8.2 Using XSLT to Convert an XML Source Tree into an XML Result Tree

Now let's look at how this works. You need two starting documents for an XSLT transformation—an XML source document and an XSLT stylesheet—to create a single result document. The process starts when the XSLT stylesheet is applied to an XML document's source tree to generate a result tree, which is typically saved as an XML or HTML document.

In this process, XSLT uses XPath to define parts of the XML source document that match one or more predefined templates. Once a match is found, XSLT transforms the matching part of the source document into the result document. If any parts of the source document don't find an exact match in the templates, they will pass unmodified into the result document.

Learning the Details of XSL Stylesheets

Since an XSL stylesheet is an XML document in its own right, it must begin with an XML declaration:

```
<?xml version="1.0" encoding="ISO-8859-1"?>
```

Every XSL stylesheet needs to identify the **XSL namespace** (abbreviated as `xslns`) so that the parser knows what version of XSLT to use. Accordingly, the next line in an XSLT stylesheet statement defines a root element called `<xsl:stylesheet>` or `<xsl:transform>`. This might appear as

```
<xsl:stylesheet version="1.0"
  xmlns:xsl="http://www.w3.org/1999/XSL/Transform">
```

or

```
<xsl:transform version="1.0"
  xmlns:xsl="http://www.w3.org/1999/XSL/Transform">
```

You'll see that the namespace prefix `xsl:` is used throughout the rest of the XSL stylesheet to identify all XSL processing statements. If there's no `xsl:` at the beginning of a bracketed tag, that element is simply copied to the output file without any processing taking place. This is how you would add HTML tags to your output document.

IMPORTANT

The elements `<xsl:stylesheet>` and `<xsl:transform>` are identical; either can be used as a root element in an XSL stylesheet.

Using XSLT to Transform an XML Document

Let's use a hand's-on example to illustrate exactly how to convert an XML document into a formatted document that displays a small number of elements. In this example, we'll transform catalog data about computer games—including the game's title, manufacturer, genre, cost, and so on—into an XML document that displays each game's name and the manufacturer in a two-column list.

Listing 8.1 shows the details for one such game in the catalog.

LISTING 8.1 *gamecatalog.xml*

```
<?xml version="1.0" encoding="ISO-8859-1"?>
<catalog>
  <game>
    <title>Escape from Monkey Island</title>
    <manufacturer>Lucas Arts</manufacturer>
    <genre>Adventure</genre>
    <platform>Windows 95/98/ME</platform>
    <country>USA</country>
    <cost>9.99</cost>
    <year>2002</year>
  </game>
.
.
.
</catalog>
```

Next, you'll need to create an XSL stylesheet (called `gamecatalog.xsl` and shown in Listing 8.2) with a transformation template.

LISTING 8.2 *gamecatalog.xsl*

```
<?xml version="1.0" encoding="ISO-8859-1"?>
<xsl:stylesheet version="1.0"
xmlns:xsl="http://www.w3.org/1999/XSL/Transform">
<xsl:template match="/">
  <html>
  <body>
    <h2>My Game Auctions</h2>
    <table border="1">
    <tr bgcolor="#ffffcc">
      <th align="left">Title</th>
      <th align="left">Manufacturer</th>
    </tr>
    <xsl:for-each select="catalog/game">
    <tr>
      <td><xsl:value-of select="title"/></td>
```

```
        <td><xsl:value-of select="manufacturer"/></td>
      </tr>
      </xsl:for-each>
      </table>
    </body>
    </html>
  </xsl:template></xsl:stylesheet>
```

Now we're ready to link the XSL stylesheet to our original XML document (abbreviated in Listing 8.1). To do so, we need to add an XSL stylesheet reference to the `gamecatalog.xml` file. The line we've added appears in italics in Listing 8.3.

LISTING 8.3 The Updated `gamecatalog.xml`

```
<?xml version="1.0" encoding="ISO-8859-1"?>
<?xml-stylesheet type="text/xsl" href="gamecatalog.xsl"?>
<catalog>
  <game>
    <title>Escape from Monkey Island</title>
    <manufacturer>Lucas Arts</manufacturer>
    <genre>Adventure</genre>
    <platform>Windows 95/98/ME</platform>
    <country>USA</country>
    <cost>9.99</cost>
    <year>2002</year>
  </game>
.
.
.
</catalog>
```

Open the `gamecatalog.xml` document in your Web browser. Instead of seeing all of your catalog data, you should now see a two-column table, with one column headed "Title" and the other "Manufacturer," as shown in Figure 8.3. The background color on this title row is a medium green color. Next, you'll see a row that contains the pertinent information for the game's title and manufacturer. All other game information has been suppressed from display.

IMPORTANT

The `<xsl:value-of>` element does not take a closing tag. Instead, end the tag with a closing slash (/) followed by a closing bracket (>), as shown below:

```
<xsl:value-of select="title"/>
```

My Game Auctions	
Title	**Manufacturer**
Escape from Monkey Island	Lucas Arts
American Idol	Vivendi Universal Games
Doom III	id Software
Command & Conquer: Yuri's Revenge	Westwood Studio
Grom	CDV
Diablo 2	Blizzard
Prince of Persia 3D	Broderbund
Steel Panthers: World at War	Matrix Games
Star Wars: Rogue Squadron	Lucas Arts
Extreme Boards & Blades	Head Games
Homeworld: Cataclysm	Sierra

FIGURE 8.3 Viewing the `gamecatalog.xml` File in a Web Browser Once a Reference to an XSL Stylesheet Is Added

How XSL Uses Templates

Now let's examine how XSL was used to control the formatting of the XML document shown in Figure 8.3. Let's take another look at Listing 8.2. Immediately after the `<xsl:stylesheet>` root element, there's an `<xsl:template>` element:

```
<xsl:template match="/">
```

The `match` attribute within the `<xsl:template>` element indicates where to look for a match between the XML and XSL documents. In this case, the value "/" tells the processor to look for matches across the **root level,** or entirety of your XML document. As you'll see in later examples, the value for the `match` attribute could be the name of a single element you've defined in your XML document.

IMPORTANT

The template forms the basis of XSLT's rule-based architecture. You must have at least one template in your XSLT file.

Next, HTML tags are used to set up a headline for the document ("My Game Auctions") and add a two-column table structure. Table header tags (the `<th>` tags) in HTML are used to make the words "Title" and "Manufacturer" stand out; the green background color of those cells is controlled by the `<bgcolor>` attribute in the overall table row (using HTML's `<tr>` tag).

Now look at how the next tag, which indicates the XML data is going to be transformed in some way:

```
<xsl:for-each select="catalog/game">
```

The `<xsl:for-each>` element can be used to select every element in a particular **node,** or chosen set of elements. In this case, every `<game>` element within `<catalog>` will be examined. The `select` attribute is required; the value it takes is in the form of an **XPath expression.** In XPath expressions, the forward slash (/) indicates a hierarchical relationship. This is why the `select` attribute used here (`catalog/game`) denotes a search on every `game` element that is a child of a parent element called `catalog`.

Now that the processor knows where to look, what will it change? The answers are in the `<xsl:value-of>` elements. Find the following lines of code in Listing 8.2:

```
<tr>
  <td><xsl:value-of select="title"/></td>
  <td><xsl:value-of select="manufacturer"/></td>
</tr>
```

Within the table row and cell formatting indicated by the `<tr>` and `<td>` table tags, we have some selective data display taking place. For each `<game>` node, the title and manufacturer information are grabbed and displayed in separate table cells. If we had wanted to display additional information that we have stored for each game, we just need to modify the XSL stylesheet to display or suppress certain elements. This might be useful in a number of ways: A company may not want to reveal the pricing for all products on a Web page. Alternatively, you may collect private information in your records that you wouldn't want to release to the public. For example, you might want to publish an employee or class directory for your organization on the Web, but wouldn't want to release information like Social Security numbers or unlisted telephone numbers.

IMPORTANT

XPath also can conduct complex selection and search processes. For example, you can use XPath to manipulate data and perform numerical calculations.

Filtering

You can filter the output from an XML document by setting a criterion for the `select` attribute in the `<xsl:for-each>` element. For example, if you changed that line in Listing 8.2 from

```
<xsl:for-each select="catalog/game">
```

to

```
<xsl:for-each select="catalog/game[manufacturer=
  'Activision']]">
```

then the results listing would show only games that had been released from Activision.

You can filter your data using several **operators,** not just the equal (=) sign. These include

- = (equal)
- != (not equal)
- `<` (less than)
- `>` (greater than)

Sorting

To sort your output at the same time it's generated, you add an `<xsl:sort>` element within the `<xsl:for-each>` element in your XSL stylesheet:

```
<xsl:for-each select="catalog/game">
<xsl:sort select="manufacturer"/>
```

For example, we can update the XSL stylesheet we used in Listing 8.2 to alphabetize all of the games by title or by manufacturer when generating the output. This can make your data listings much more useful to readers who want to see at a glance if you have the information they need. Since it's a real timesaver to search an alphabetical or chronological listing, always consider how your audience may want or need to see the data you're presenting them with.

Listing 8.4 adds a single `<xsl:sort>` element to our `gamecatalog.xsl` file; it appears in boldface in the listing.

IMPORTANT

The `<xsl:sort>` element does not take a closing tag. Instead, end the tag with a closing slash (/) followed by a closing bracket (>).

LISTING 8.4 Adding Sorting Capabilities to *gamecatalog.xsl*

```
<?xml version="1.0" encoding="ISO-8859-1"?>
<xsl:stylesheet version="1.0"
  xmlns:xsl="http://www.w3.org/1999/XSL/Transform">
<xsl:template match="/">
  <html>
  <body>
    <h2>My Game Auctions</h2>
    <table border="1">
    <tr bgcolor="#ffffcc">
      <th align="left">Title</th>
      <th align="left">Manufacturer</th>
    </tr>
    <xsl:for-each select="catalog/game">
    <xsl:sort select="title"/>
    <tr>
      <td><xsl:value-of select="title"/></td>
      <td><xsl:value-of select="manufacturer"/></td>
    </tr>
    </xsl:for-each>
    </table>
  </body>
  </html>
</xsl:template></xsl:stylesheet>
```

Figure 8.4 shows how this sorting capability has made a difference in how the games listing now displays.

Creating Conditional Statements

You also can add a conditional statement to an XSL stylesheet. This tests your file's content with a straightforward true-false condition, applying a template only if that specified condition is true. You can use conditional statements to limit the display of data. It's not unlike a conditional statement in English; using our game catalog data, consider answering the question, "Show me all the games you have—if there are any that cost less than $30." Putting an `<xsl:if>` statement in your XSL stylesheet allows this kind of conditional testing to take place. The format looks like the following:

```
<xsl:if test="cost&lt;'30'">
.
.
.
</xsl:if>
```

The `test` attribute is where the criterion under evaluation is expressed. This is a required attribute.

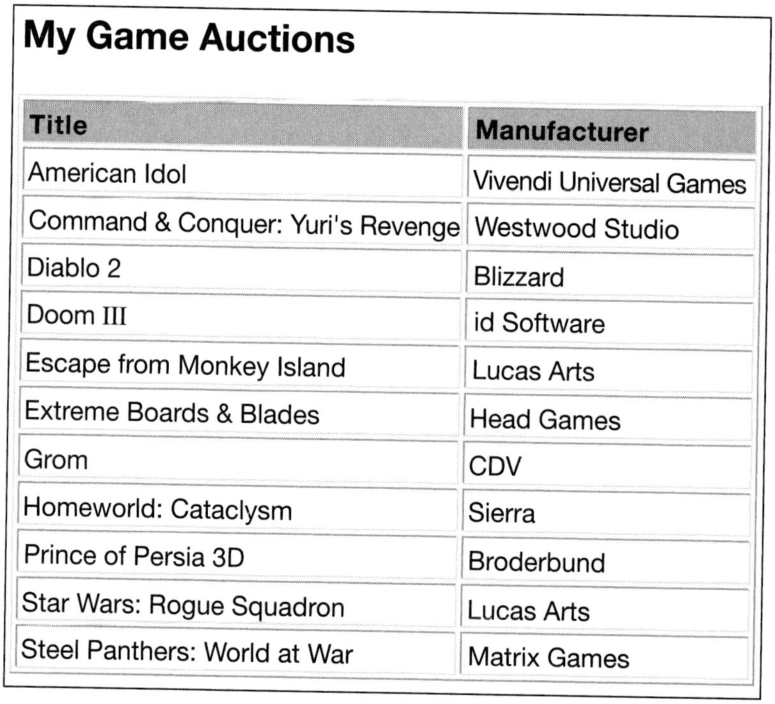

My Game Auctions

Title	Manufacturer
American Idol	Vivendi Universal Games
Command & Conquer: Yuri's Revenge	Westwood Studio
Diablo 2	Blizzard
Doom III	id Software
Escape from Monkey Island	Lucas Arts
Extreme Boards & Blades	Head Games
Grom	CDV
Homeworld: Cataclysm	Sierra
Prince of Persia 3D	Broderbund
Star Wars: Rogue Squadron	Lucas Arts
Steel Panthers: World at War	Matrix Games

FIGURE 8.4 Viewing the *gamecatalog.xml* File Once Sorting Capabilities Are Added to the XSL Stylesheet with *<xsl:sort>*

Listing 8.5 adds the opening and closing tags for the `<xsl:if>` element to the `gamecatalog.xsl` file, which appear in boldface in the listing.

LISTING 8.5 Adding Conditional Testing to *gamecatalog.xsl*

```
<?xml version="1.0" encoding="ISO-8859-1"?>
<xsl:stylesheet version="1.0"
xmlns:xsl="http://www.w3.org/1999/XSL/Transform">
<xsl:template match="/">
  <html>
  <body>
    <h2>My Game Auctions</h2>
    <table border="1">
    <tr bgcolor="#ffffcc">
      <th align="left">Title</th>
      <th align="left">Manufacturer</th>
    </tr>
    <xsl:for-each select="catalog/game">
    <xsl:if test="cost&lt;'30'">
    <tr>
      <td><xsl:value-of select="title"/></td>
```

```
            <td><xsl:value-of select="manufacturer"/></td>
          </tr>
          </xsl:if>
          </xsl:for-each>
          </table>
        </body>
        </html>
      </xsl:template></xsl:stylesheet>
```

Figure 8.5 shows how adding this conditional statement produces a difference in the output, listing only those games that cost less than $30.

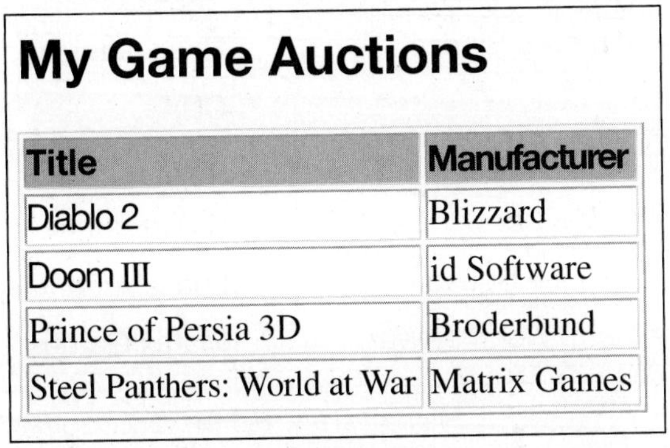

My Game Auctions

Title	Manufacturer
Diablo 2	Blizzard
Doom III	id Software
Prince of Persia 3D	Broderbund
Steel Panthers: World at War	Matrix Games

FIGURE 8.5 The Output of *gamecatalog.xml* Once a Condition about the Cost of the Games Is Put into Place

The game title and manufacturer only display if the games cost less than $30.

So far, we've only looked at a single condition and result. If a condition is met, content displays. But it gets better: you can set up multiple conditional tests so that one result happens if a condition is met and another result takes place otherwise. You can do this by using the `<xsl:choose>` element with its partnering `<xsl:when>` and `<xsl:otherwise>` elements. The general format is shown below:

```
<xsl:choose>
  <xsl:when test=”year&gt;’2002’”>
  .
  .
  .
  </xsl:when>
  <xsl:otherwise>
  .
  .
  .
```

```
</xsl:otherwise>
</xsl:choose>
```

In this example, the condition to be met is the year that the game was released; if the game was released after 2002, it should display differently than the other games. We'll implement that next in Listing 8.6, where the titles of games released after 2002 will appear with a graphic reading "New!" next to them.

LISTING 8.6 Adding a Multiple Conditional Statement to *gamecatalog.xsl*

```
<?xml version="1.0" encoding="ISO-8859-1"?>
<xsl:stylesheet version="1.0"
  xmlns:xsl="http://www.w3.org/1999/XSL/Transform">
<xsl:template match="/">
  <html>
  <body>
    <h2>My Game Auctions</h2>
    <table border="1">
    <tr bgcolor="#ffffcc">
      <th align="left">Title</th>
      <th align="left">Manufacturer</th>
    </tr>
    <xsl:for-each select="catalog/game">
<tr>
      <xsl:choose>
        <xsl:when test="year&gt;'2002'">
          <td><xsl:value-of select="title"/>
            <img src="new.gif"></td>
        </xsl:when>
        <xsl:otherwise>
          <td><xsl:value-of select="title"/></td>
        </xsl:otherwise>
      </xsl:choose>
          <td><xsl:value-of select="manufacturer"/></td>
      </tr>
      </xsl:for-each>
    </table>
  </body>
  </html>
</xsl:template>
</xsl:stylesheet>
```

Figure 8.6 shows how this conditional display has added the "New!" image after certain game titles.

My Game Auctions

Title	Manufacturer
American Idol	Vivendi Universal Games
Command & Conquer: Yuri's Revenge	Westwood Studio
Diablo 2	Blizzard
Doom III NEW!	id Software
Escape from Monkey Island	Lucas Arts
Extreme Boards & Blades	Head Games
Grom NEW!	CDV
Homeworld: Cataclysm	Sierra
Prince of Persia 3D	Broderbund
Star Wars: Rogue Squadron	Lucas Arts
Steel Panthers: World at War	Matrix Games

FIGURE 8.6 Applying a Multiple Conditional Statement to Indicate Which Items Are the Most Recent

Styling the Appearance of XML Elements with XSL

In order to distinguish XSL from CSS, the other stylesheet language you can use with XML, we've held off discussing how you can use XSL to apply template rules to style or format your XML elements or their child nodes. But our discussion of XSL wouldn't be complete without covering `<xsl:apply-templates>`, an element that lets you choose both the specific elements to format and the order in which they're processed.

Listing 8.7 shows a brief example in which an `<h2>` tag in HTML is applied to all `<subhead>` elements that are children of an element called `<essay>`.

IMPORTANT

The `<xsl:apply-template>` element is always found inside an `<xsl:template>` element.

LISTING 8.7 Applying Templates

```
<?xml version="1.0" encoding="ISO-8859-1"?>
<xsl:stylesheet version="1.0"
  xmlns:xsl="http://www.w3.org/1999/XSL/Transform">
  <xsl:template match="essay">
    <h2><xsl:apply-templates select="subhead"/></h2>
  </xsl:template>
</xsl:stylesheet>
```

Let's walk through what the code in Listing 8.7 does. The `select` attribute (`select=`) that appears in the `<xsl:apply-templates>` element processes only the child element that matches the value shown (in this case, `"subhead"`).

If the value is set to an asterisk (*), all child nodes of the current element (`essay`) would be selected, as shown below:

```
<xsl:template match="essay">
<h2><xsl:apply-templates select="*"/></h2>
</xsl:template>
```

If you want the `<xsl:apply-template>` instructions to process only certain child elements, you can separate them with a pipe (|) character:

```
<xsl:template match="/">
<strong><xsl:apply-templates select="client/name | client/
  address"/></strong>
</xsl:template>
```

Debugging XSLT

In the same way that a word processor's spell-checker can ensure there are no obvious misspellings in your writings, validators and debuggers are essential tools for programmers in reducing or eliminating errors in their code.

Often debuggers are built into suites of authoring tools, but you shouldn't need something that complex to check your own errors. For example, Macromedia's Dreamweaver is a sophisticated suite of tools for Web designers and developers. It happens to include an HTML validator. If all you want to do is ensure your code is error-free, though, you don't need Dreamweaver; for example, you can use one of several free online HTML validators (including one offered by the W3C at http://validator.w3c.org/).

Similarly, you can find debugging tools for troubleshooting XSL within a number of commercial tools for creating and maintaining XML documents. The more you experiment and advance with your XML projects, the more you'll want to double-check or troubleshoot your work with an XML debugger. You can download free trial versions of commercial XML tools like Altova's XMLSpy (see Figure 8.7) and eXcelon's Stylus Studio.

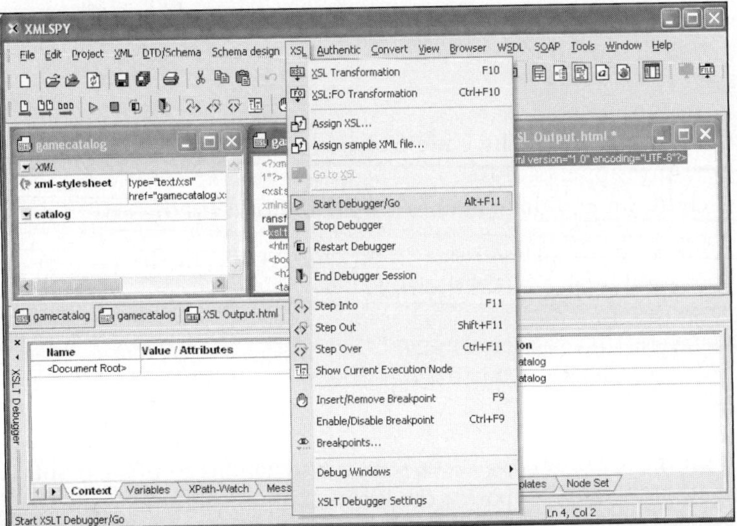

FIGURE 8.7 Using the XSLT Debugging Feature in Altova's XMLSpy Program

However, you don't need to invest in a commercial product just to troubleshoot your XSL. XSLDebugger (see Figure 8.8) is a free tool for debugging XSL transformations; it can be downloaded from http://www.vbxml.com/xsldebugger/. Visit http://www.xslt.com/ to stay up-to-date on new releases of XML/XSL editors and utilities, since new software programs, including freely distributed ones, continue to be released regularly.

There is also an `<xml:message>` element that can be used in an XSL document to issue error messages or warnings. However, not all XML parsers support `<xml:message>`. For a working example of how to use `<xml:message>` to debug your XSL stylesheets as you develop them, see the article "Debug XSLT on the Fly" on IBM's developerWorks site at http://www-106.ibm.com/developerworks/xml/library/x-debugxs.html.

XSL Element References

The XSL coding examples provided in this chapter should help you with experimenting, transforming, and customizing XML data. To help you brainstorm further, Table 8.2 summarizes the XSL elements covered in the W3C Recommendation for XSLT 1.0 and provides examples of each. Many of these

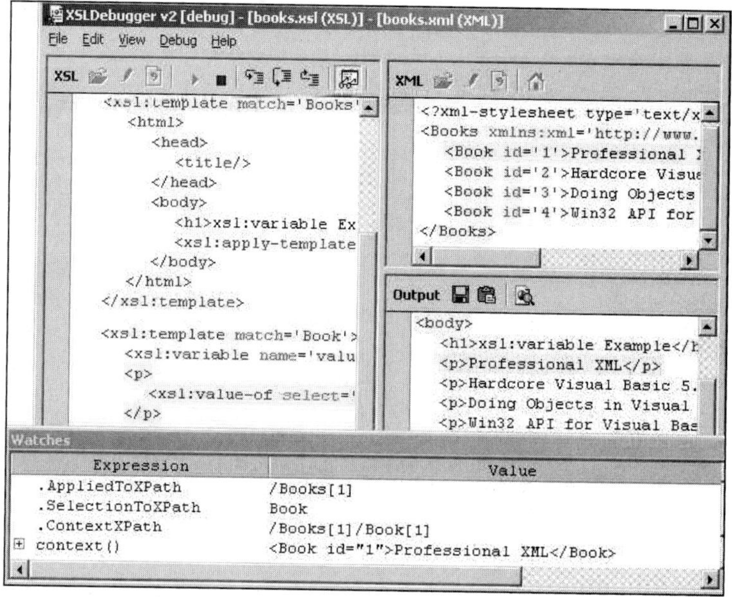

FIGURE 8.8 The Free XSLDebugger Program

elements are beyond the scope of the material covered in this introductory chapter, but do provide the syntax you can use for reference, especially as you examine sample XSL stylesheets offered by the content providers mentioned in the Case Study section at the end of this chapter.

TABLE 8.2 The XSLT Elements and How They Work

Element	What It Does	Code Example	Comments

`xsl:apply-imports`	Applies a template rule from an imported style sheet.	Assuming that a sample stylesheet (called `example.xsl`) includes a rule for an element called `chaptertitle`:
		`<xsl:template match="callout">`
		`<blockquote><xsl:apply-templates/>`
		`</blockquote>`
		`</xsl:template>`
		Another XSL stylesheet could import `example.xsl` (shown in italics below) and modify the `callout` element.
		`<xsl:import href="example.xsl"/>`
		`<xsl:template match="callout">`
		`<div style="border:solid red">`
		`<xsl:apply-imports/>`
		`</div>`
		`</xsl:template>`
			The result of using `<xsl:apply-import>` in the code example at left would produce the following:
			`<div style="border: solid red">`
			`<blockquote> . . . </blockquote></div>`

Continued

TABLE 8.2 The XSLT Elements and How They Work (continued)

Element	What It Does	Code Example	Comments

xsl:attribute	Lets you add an attribute to an element you create.	<img>
		  <xsl:attribute name="src">
		  <xsl:value-of select="@src"/>
		  </xsl:attribute>
		</img>
			This produces the output:
			<img src="sample.gif">

xsl:apply-templates	Applies a template rule to the current element or its child nodes.	<xsl:apply-templates select= "person/name"/>	If the select value is set to an asterisk (*), all child nodes of the current element are selected.

xsl:call-template	Requests a specific template when the processor finds an element matching the value given in the <xsl:template> element.	<xsl:template match="computer">
		  <xsl:call-template name=
		    "platform"/>
		</xsl:template>
			The name attribute is required.

xsl:choose	Used with <xsl:when> and <xsl:otherwise> to test multiple conditions. Defines a choice between alternatives.	<xsl:choose> <xsl:when test=*boolean* *expression*> <!--template body goes here--> </xsl:when> <xsl:otherwise> <!-- template body goes here --> </xsl:otherwise> </xsl:choose>	Contrasts with <xsl:if>, which only allows a single condition to be tested.
xsl:comment	Creates a comment node in the result document.	<xsl:comment>Revised: July 15. </xsl:comment>	There are no attributes associated with this element.

xsl:copy	Creates a copy of the current node, but without any child nodes or attributes.	This copies a node called review to the output document.
		<xsl:template match="review">
		  <xsl:copy>
		    <xsl:apply-templates/>
		  </xsl:copy>
		</xsl:template>
			Note that the child nodes and attributes of the current node are not automatically copied.

Continued

TABLE 8.2 The XSLT Elements and How They Work (continued)

Element	What It Does	Code Example	Comments
xsl:copy-of	Creates a copy of the current node—including child nodes and attributes.	This copies a node called review—and all child elements and attributes—to the output document. <xsl:copy-of select="$subhead"/>	You can use this element to place multiple copies of the same node into different places in the output.
xsl:decimal-format	Defines what characters and symbols are used when numbers are converted into strings using the format-number() function (not covered in this chapter).	The syntax for this element is as follows: <xsl:decimal-format name="name" decimal-separator="char" grouping-separator="char" infinity="string" minus-sign="char" NaN="string" percent="char" per-mille="char" zero-digit="char" digit="char" pattern-separator="char"/>	This is useful when distributing numeric data to many countries, which may use different characters for separating the decimals from integers. For example, in the U.S., a comma (,) typically is used in denoting the thousand sign (1,000), while a period is used in Europe.

xsl:element	Creates a new element node in the output document.	The example below creates an element called author that contains the value of each element formerly known as reporter:
		<xsl:template match="/">
		  <xsl:for-each select="magazine/
		    article">
		    <xsl:element name="author">
		      <xsl:value-of select=
		        "reporter" />
		    </xsl:element>
		
		  </xsl:for-each>
		</xsl:template>
			An optional namespace element can be set to an expression that is computed when accessed by the user, which is useful for indicating user variables such as country or language.

Continued

TABLE 8.2 The XSLT Elements and How They Work (continued)

Element	What It Does	Code Example	Comments
xsl:fallback	Specifies back-up, alternative code that should run if the XSL processor does not support an XSL element.	This example purports to loop through each "item" element with a made-up <xsl:imaginary> element. Since the XSL processor does not support this element, it uses the <xsl:for-each> element instead. <xsl:imaginary select="title"> <xsl:fallback> <xsl:for-each select="item"> <xsl:value-of select="."/> <xsl:/for-each> </xsl:fallback> </xsl:imaginary>	There are no attributes associated with this element.
xsl:for-each	Loops through each node in a specified set and processes the same instructions for all these elements.	<xsl:for-each select="magazine/title">	This statement finds all title elements contained in the magazine element context using the XPath expression magazine/title.
xsl:if	Applies a template only if a specified condition is met.	<xsl:if test="format='CD'"> . . . </xsl:if>	The test attribute is required.
xsl:import	Imports the contents of one XSL stylesheet into another.	See <xsl:apply-imports> above for a full code example. *<xsl:import href="example.xsl"/>* <xsl:template match="callout"> <div style="border:solid red"> <xsl:apply-imports/> </div> </xsl:template>	It's important to remember that an imported stylesheet has lower precedence than the importing stylesheet.
xsl:include	Includes the contents of one stylesheet in another.	<xsl:include href="URI"/>	<xsl:include> must appear as a child node of <xsl:stylesheet> or <xsl:transform>. It's important to note that an included stylesheet has the same precedence as the XSL stylesheet that includes it.

Continued

TABLE 8.2 The XSLT Elements and How They Work (continued)

Element	What It Does	Code Example	Comments

`xsl:key`	Declares a named key that can be used in the XSL stylesheet with the `key()` function (not covered in this chapter).	The syntax for this element is as follows:
		`<xsl:key`
		`name="name"`
		`match="pattern"`
		`use="expression"/>`
			All three of these attributes are required.

`xsl:message`	Writes a message to the output. This can be used to report errors.	This example code checks to see if the field for the customer's street address is empty. If it is, the XSL processor quits and displays an error message: `<xsl:template match="/">` `  <html>` `  <body>` `  <xsl:for-each select="address/` `    delivery">` `      <p>Customer Name:` `        <xsl:value-of select=` `          "name"/> ` `      Street Address:` `      <xsl:if` `        test="address1=''">` `        <xsl:message terminate=` `          "yes">` `          Error: The street address` `            is missing!` `        </xsl:message>` `      </xsl:if>` `    <xsl:value-of select=` `      "address1"/>` `    </p>` `  </xsl:for-each>` `  </body>` `  </html>` `</xsl:template>`	The `terminate` attribute provides an option to either quit or continue the processing when an error takes place.

Continued

TABLE 8.2 The XSLT Elements and How They Work (continued)

Element	What It Does	Code Example	Comments
xsl:namespace-alias	Replaces a namespace in an XSL stylesheet with a different namespace in the output (not covered in this chapter).	<xsl:namespace-alias stylesheet-prefix="wxsl" result-prefix="xsl"/>	<xsl:namespace-alias> is a top-level element. It must be a child node of <xsl:stylesheet> or <xsl:transform>.
xsl:number	Determines the integer position of the current node and formats a number.	The following example: <xsl:number value="750000" grouping-separator=","/> would produce the following output: 750,000 Here's the acceptable syntax for this element: <xsl:number count="expression" level="single|multiple|any" from="expression" value="expression" format="formatstring" lang="languagecode" letter-value="alphabetic|traditional" grouping-separator="character" grouping-size="number"/>	All of these attributes are optional.
xsl:otherwise	Specifies a default action for the <xsl:choose> element when a specified condition is not met.	<xsl:choose> <xsl:when test=*boolean expression*> <!-- template body goes here --> </xsl:when> <xsl:otherwise> <!-- template body goes here --> </xsl:otherwise> </xsl:choose>	If none of the <xsl:when> criteria are met, then the <xsl:otherwise> instructions are carried out.

Continued

TABLE 8.2 The XSLT Elements and How They Work (continued)

Element	What It Does	Code Example	Comments
xsl:output	Defines the format of the output document.	<xsl:output method="xml|html|text|name" version="string" encoding="string" omit-xml-declaration="yes|no" standalone="yes|no" doctype-public="string" doctype-system="string" cdata-section-elements="namelist" indent="yes|no" media-type="string"/>	<xsl:output> is a top-level element. It must be a child node of <xsl:stylesheet> or <xsl:transform>.
xsl:param	Declares a local or global parameter (which appears as an XPath expression).	<xsl:variable name="xx"> <html> <body> <xsl:call-template name= "display_review"> <xsl:with-param name= "title"/> </xsl:call-template> </body> </html> </xsl:variable> <xsl:template name=" display_ review " match="/"> *<xsl:param name="review" />* <xsl:for-each select="record/ employee"> <p>Title: <xsl:value-of select="review" /></p> </xsl:for-each> </xsl:template>	This parameter is global when it is declared as a top-level element. It also can be local if declared within an <xsl:template> expression.
xsl:preserve-space	Defines which elements should have whitespace preserved.	<xsl:preserve-space elements= "headline_text document_url"/>	Since preserving whitespace is the default setting, the <xsl:preserve-space> element is only needed if the <xsl:strip-space> element has been used.

Continued

TABLE 8.2 The XSLT Elements and How They Work (continued)

<table>
<tr><th>Element</th><th>What It Does</th><th>Code Example</th><th>Comments</th></tr>
<tr><td>xsl:processing-instruction</td><td>Writes a processing instruction to the output document.</td><td>This code:
<xsl:processing-instruction name="xml-stylesheet">
href="example.css" type="text/css"
</xsl:processing-instruction>
creates this tag:
<?xml-stylesheet href="example.css" type="text/css"?></td><td>The name attribute is required.</td></tr>
<tr><td>xsl:sort</td><td>Defines sort criteria for a given expression, then sorts the output.</td><td>Syntax is
<xsl:sort
select="expression"
lang="language-code"
data-type="text|number|name"
order="ascending|descending"
case-order="upper-first|lower-first"/>
Sample expression:
<xsl:sort
select="listprice" data-type="number" /></td><td><xsl:sort> always appears within <xsl:for-each> or <xsl:apply-templates>.</td></tr>
<tr><td>xsl:strip-space</td><td>Changes the default settings of preserving whitespace, defining the elements for which whitespace should be removed.</td><td><xsl:strip-space elements="country state school" /></td><td>See <xsl:preserve-space> above.</td></tr>
<tr><td>xsl:stylesheet</td><td>Defines the root element of an XSL stylesheet.</td><td><xsl:stylesheet xmlns:xsl="http://www.w3.org/1999/XSL/Transform"
version="1.0"></td><td>The value shown here is the most up-to-date reference for the XML namespace.</td></tr>
<tr><td>xsl:template</td><td>Indicates what rules to apply when a specified node is matched.</td><td><xsl:template match="/"></td><td>The match="/" attribute selects the entire document.</td></tr>
</table>

Continued

TABLE 8.2 The XSLT Elements and How They Work (continued)

Element	What It Does	Code Example	Comments
xsl:text	Writes actual text to the output document. To do so, it generates a text string from its content.	<xsl:attribute name="href"> <xsl:call-template name="file-of"/> *<xsl:text>#</xsl:text>* <xsl:call-template name="anchor-of"/> </xsl:attribute>	This element can contain literal text, entity references, and #PCDATA.
xsl:transform	Defines the root element of an XSL stylesheet. Synonymous with <xsl:stylesheet> above.	<xsl:transform xmlns:xsl="http://www.w3.org/1999/XSL/Transform" version="1.0">	See <xsl:stylesheet> above.
xsl:value-of	Extracts and copies to the output file the value stored in the selected element.	<xsl:value-of select="lastname"/>	Used with <xsl:for-each>.
xsl:variable	Lets you set a variable in your XSL stylesheet.	<xsl:variable name="country" select="'united states'"/>	You give the variable a name and then define its context (or string) using the select attribute.
xsl:when	Indicates an action for the <xsl:choose> element.	<xsl:choose> <xsl:when test=*boolean expression*> <!– template body goes here –> </xsl:when> <xsl:otherwise> <!-- template body goes here --> </xsl:otherwise> </xsl:choose>	There is no limit to the number of possible <xsl:when> instructions.

Continued

TABLE 8.2 The XSLT Elements and How They Work (continued)

Element	What It Does	Code Example	Comments

xsl:with-param	Defines the value of an XPath expression that will be passed into a template.	<xsl:variable name="xx">
		  <html>
		  <body>
		  <xsl:call-template name=
		    "display_review">
		    <xsl:with-param name="title" />
		  </xsl:call-template>
		  </body>
		  </html>
		</xsl:variable>
		<xsl:template name=" display_
		  review " match="/">
		  <xsl:param name="review" />
		  <xsl:for-each select="record/
		    employee">
		      <p>Title: <xsl:value-of
		        select="review" /></p>
		  </xsl:for-each>
		</xsl:template>
			The value of the `name` attribute in `<xsl:with-param>` must match one in an `<xsl:param>` element. Otherwise, `<xsl:with-param>` will be ignored.

In the next chapter, you'll learn about XLink, which lets you create links between XML resources, and XPointer, which lets you find and manipulate content within elements, attributes, and XML content. XLink and XPointer work with a little help from XPath, which you first saw here in this chapter as a means for specifying which elements or child nodes should be transformed.

Key Terms

node
operators
result tree
root level
source tree
template
XPath
XPath expression
XSL Formatting Objects
XSL namespace
XSL Transformations (XSLT)

Code Summary

1. **A sample XSL transformation template:**

```
<?xml version="1.0" encoding="ISO-8859-1"?>
<xsl:stylesheet version="1.0"
   xmlns:xsl="http://www.w3.org/1999/XSL/Transform">
<xsl:template match="/">
   <html>
   <body>
      <h2>My Game Auctions</h2>
      <table border="1">
      <tr bgcolor="#ffffcc">
         <th align="left">Title</th>
         <th align="left">Manufacturer</th>
      </tr>
      <xsl:for-each select="catalog/game">
      <tr>
         <td><xsl:value-of select="title"/></td>
         <td><xsl:value-of select="manufacturer"/></td>
      </tr>
      </xsl:for-each>
      </table>
   </body>
   </html>
</xsl:template></xsl:stylesheet>
```

2. **An XML document that links to an XSL stylesheet:**

```
<?xml version="1.0" encoding="ISO-8859-1"?>
<?xml-stylesheet type="text/xsl" href="gamecatalog.xsl"?>
<catalog>
   <game>
      <title>Escape from Monkey Island</title>
      <manufacturer>Lucas Arts</manufacturer>
      <genre>Adventure</genre>
      <platform>Windows 95/98/ME</platform>
      <country>USA</country>
      <cost>9.99</cost>
      <year>2002</year>
   </game>
.
.
.
</catalog>
```

3. **The `match` attribute:**

```
<xsl:template match="/">
```

4. **Filtering output with an XSL stylesheet:**

```
<xsl:for-each select="catalog/game[manufacturer='Activision']]">
```

5. **Sorting output with an XSL stylesheet:**

```
<?xml version="1.0" encoding="ISO-8859-1"?>
<xsl:stylesheet version="1.0"
xmlns:xsl="http://www.w3.org/1999/XSL/Transform">
<xsl:template match="/">
  <html>
  <body>
    <h2>My Game Auctions</h2>
    <table border="1">
    <tr bgcolor="#ffffcc">
      <th align="left">Title</th>
      <th align="left">Manufacturer</th>
    </tr>
    <xsl:for-each select="catalog/game">
    <xsl:sort select="title"/>
    <tr>
      <td><xsl:value-of select="title"/></td>
      <td><xsl:value-of select="manufacturer"/></td>
    </tr>
    </xsl:for-each>
    </table>
  </body>
  </html>
</xsl:template></xsl:stylesheet>
```

6. **Adding conditional testing with an XSL stylesheet:**

```
<?xml version="1.0" encoding="ISO-8859-1"?>
<xsl:stylesheet version="1.0"
xmlns:xsl="http://www.w3.org/1999/XSL/Transform">
<xsl:template match="/">
  <html>
  <body>
    <h2>My Game Auctions</h2>
    <table border="1">
    <tr bgcolor="#ffffcc">
      <th align="left">Title</th>
      <th align="left">Manufacturer</th>
    </tr>
    <xsl:for-each select="catalog/game">
    <xsl:if test="cost&lt;'30'">
    <tr>
      <td><xsl:value-of select="title"/></td>
```

```
          <td><xsl:value-of select="manufacturer"/></td>
       </tr>
       </xsl:if>
       </xsl:for-each>
       </table>
    </body>
    </html>
</xsl:template></xsl:stylesheet>
```

7. Adding a multiple conditional statement with an XSL stylesheet:

```
<?xml version="1.0" encoding="ISO-8859-1"?>
<xsl:stylesheet version="1.0"
xmlns:xsl="http://www.w3.org/1999/XSL/Transform">
<xsl:template match="/">
   <html>
   <body>
      <h2>My Game Auctions</h2>
      <table border="1">
      <tr bgcolor="#ffffcc">
         <th align="left">Title</th>
         <th align="left">Manufacturer</th>
      </tr>
      <xsl:for-each select="catalog/game">
<tr>
            <xsl:choose>
               <xsl:when test="year&gt;'2002'">
                  <td><xsl:value-of select="title"/><img src="new.gif"></td>
               </xsl:when>
               <xsl:otherwise>
                  <td><xsl:value-of select="title"/></td>
               </xsl:otherwise>
            </xsl:choose>
               <td><xsl:value-of select="manufacturer"/></td>
         </tr>
         </xsl:for-each>
      </table>
   </body>
   </html>
</xsl:template>
</xsl:stylesheet>
```

8. Applying templates to XML elements with an XSL stylesheet:

```
<?xml version="1.0" encoding="ISO-8859-1"?>
<xsl:stylesheet version="1.0" xmlns:xsl="http://www.w3.org/1999/XSL/Transform">
<xsl:template match="essay">
<h2><xsl:apply-templates select="subhead"/></h2>
</xsl:template>
</xsl:stylesheet>
```

Alerts and Advice

In order to successfully experiment with XSLT, you'll need a well-formed XML document, an XSL stylesheet that contains formatting and transformation templates, and an XSLT parser to finish the transformation.

Ensure that you are using an XSL-compatible Web browser when working on your own XSL projects. If you use MS Internet Explorer, you will need to upgrade to at least version 6.0. Earlier versions of Internet Explorer are not fully XSL-compatible. Netscape 6 does not fully support XSL.

There are several ways to view an XSL document in Internet Explorer. You can click on a link, enter the URL in the address bar, or double-click on the name of an XML file in a file folder listing. In Netscape 6, by contrast, you'll need to open the XSL file, then right-click within the XSL file and select `View Page Source`.

You've seen that you can use a slash (/) in a `select` or `match` attribute to indicate the hierarchical relationship between parent elements and child nodes:

```
<xsl:template match="/clothes/*/size">
```

In the above example, a match would be found in the `<size>` grandchild of the `<clothes>` element. Here, `<size>` could be a child element of `<shirts>` or `<pants>` within `<clothes>`.

You can also use two slashes (//) in a `select` or `match` attribute to find all elements with that name across the hierarchy. Zero or more levels may occur between the two slashes.

```
<xsl:template match="/recipe//amount">
```

Review Questions

1. What are the three parts that comprise XSL? Which of these parts has the most important role?
2. What is a query language?
3. Describe what a slash (/) means in an XPath expression.

Case Study

One of the practical ways that organizations leverage XML is by distributing their content through XML newsfeeds. They then encourage Web site managers to offer dynamically updating headlines on their sites by integrating their XML newsfeeds. The Web sites that integrate such readily available content often use XSL to customize the display of the XML newsfeeds to match the look and feel of their own Web sites.

Point your browser to FreeSticky.com (http://www.freesticky.com/stickyweb/section.asp?sectionname=newsheadlines) and browse the listing of sites that offer newsfeeds. Note which of these offer their newsfeeds in XML format; this short list includes NASA and SatireSearch, among others. Some of these sites also may offer a sample XSL stylesheet for you to modify.

Moreover.com is a site whose business is based on distributing real-time information via newsfeeds to major corporations. They offer free access to their newsfeeds to personal Web sites. Visit Moreover's page for Web developers at http://w.moreover.com/dev/xml/ to learn about the categories of newsfeeds that the company offers. One example is Moreover.com's listing of biotechnology headlines at http://p.moreover.com/cgi-local/page?c=Biotech%20news&o=xml. Examine the sample stylesheet at http://w.moreover.com/dev/xml/xsl/stylesheet_example.html and compare it against one or more of the downloadable XML newsfeed files. What changes would result if you changed some of the formatting details in the XSL file? How could you change the number of headlines that display?

For this project, you'll mark up your own repository of data, then use XSL to see how you can easily change what part of that data you choose to display—and how it looks when output.

1. Create a catalog listing of data, recording several pieces of information about each item. You could use a collection of books, CDs, games, baseball cards, recipes, or any other item that you may have in bulk. Refer to the code in Listing 8.1 to get started with saving this data as an XML document and identifying which elements you'd like to create (such as `<title>` or `<cost>`).
2. Now create an accompanying XSL stylesheet file to select which elements to display and what formatting to add to your resulting document.
3. Refer to your new XSL stylesheet file within the catalog's XML file. Remember the line that was added in Listing 8.3:

   ```
   <?xml-stylesheet type="text/xsl" href="gamecatalog.xsl"?>
   ```

   Remember to change `gamecatalog.xsl` to the name you've given to your XSL stylesheet.
4. Consider how you could sort or filter your data that would make your content more meaningful to your audience. A baseball card collection, for example, might be sorted by team or player's surname, then sorted by year. Modify the XSL document to add a sorting rule.
5. Now add a conditional statement to your XSL document that changes the display of the content depending on the value of the data in one field. A listing of books, for example, could highlight all titles released in 2003. Make sure that your formatting changes will style your content one way if a criterion is met, and uses another formatting approach if the condition is not met.

CHAPTER 9

Linking XML Documents

LEARNING OBJECTIVES

1. To learn how to use XLink to link between XML documents and specific parts within them.
2. To see how both single-direction links like those in HTML documents and multidirectional links can be added to XML documents.
3. To define XLink elements in an XML DTD.
4. To use XPointer to point to any part of a target document on local or remote Web servers.

When XML first began to gain prominence as a Web standard, many Web developers began to compare what was involved in using XML versus HTML to create Web documents—and immediately found some trade-offs. For example, HTML is a simple language with a fixed number of tags. By contrast, creating your own elements in XML is a more flexible but potentially more complex process. HTML tags have a certain amount of built-in formatting; with XML, you need a style sheet (using CSS or XSL) to indicate any formatting. HTML provides hyperlinking functionality with the **anchor tag** (the <a> element), while linking XML documents in a standardized way has been a long time coming. By now you've seen how XML is far more versatile and flexible than HTML.

In this chapter you'll learn the details of two leading XML linking technologies: XLink and XPointer. While linking has lagged further behind other XML technologies in terms of development, the XLink and XPointer specifications emerged to deal with making links work within XML documents:

- **XLink** lets you insert elements into XML documents in order to create links between XML documents. You can create HTML-like hyperlinks using XLink, but you also can do much more with it. XLink makes it easier to manage links as time goes by (and Web documents move), and create XML documents that consist of only links.

- **XPointer** provides a way to link into the internal structures of XML documents, including elements, attributes, and actual content. XPointer can be used to reach anywhere inside an XML file. This is very different from HTML, where you can only point to a specific location within a given HTML document if you can edit or update that targeted document.

Now let's examine how you can put XLink and XPointer to work for you.

Introducing XML Linking Language (XLink)

With the XML Linking Language, or XLink, you can add elements within XML documents that create and link not only to other XML documents, but also to many components that might appear in an XML document, such as images, query results, or even other types of files or applications.

The syntax used by XLink is reminiscent of HTML in many respects. Here's a quick example:

```
<anchor xlink:type="simple" href="index.xml">Index</anchor>
```

In the code above, we've created an element named `anchor`. The attribute that follows (`xlink:type="simple"`) is what identifies that this particular element will serve as a link. Next, the `href` attribute indicates where readers will go—that is, what document, image, or other file will be delivered—when they follow the link.

In HTML, you can essentially create two kinds of links. An **anchor link,** which uses the `<a>` tag, lets readers know that, if they click on this link, they will be transported to the targeted destination. You also can link to objects in HTML, through tags like `<img>` (to link to images) or `<embed>` (to link to audio or video clips).

But despite the power and appeal of hyperlinking across Web documents, there are limitations to what HTML links can do. For starters, it can be time-consuming to keep the links on a Web site pointing to the right places and to sites that are still active all the time. If you're a Web producer who redesigns your Web site from time to time, you may rename directories, or add or

IMPORTANT

XLink and XPointer are still such works-in-progress that few browsers implement many of their capabilities. The W3C posts an implementation chart at http://www.w3.org/XML/Linking that marks which features of XLink and XPointer have been implemented to date in various Web browsers.

remove levels of the directory hierarchy—and any of these name changes could inadvertently create broken links if you don't change all the hyperlinks to files that have moved.

Another challenge you may run into is not being able to link to the exact place in a document you'd like to. For example, you might want to link to a specific paragraph in a very long HTML document on another site so that visitors don't have to scroll down from the top of the page. However, if that target document is on another person's or company's site, you wouldn't have the appropriate level of access to edit that page and add what HTML calls a **named anchor,** a link that points directly to a specific section of a page. Figure 9.1 shows how a named anchor link takes the reader directly to that portion of the document. This figure depicts a question-and-answer column that features a list of questions at the top of the page. Clicking each hyperlinked question takes the reader further down the page to read the specific answer to that question.

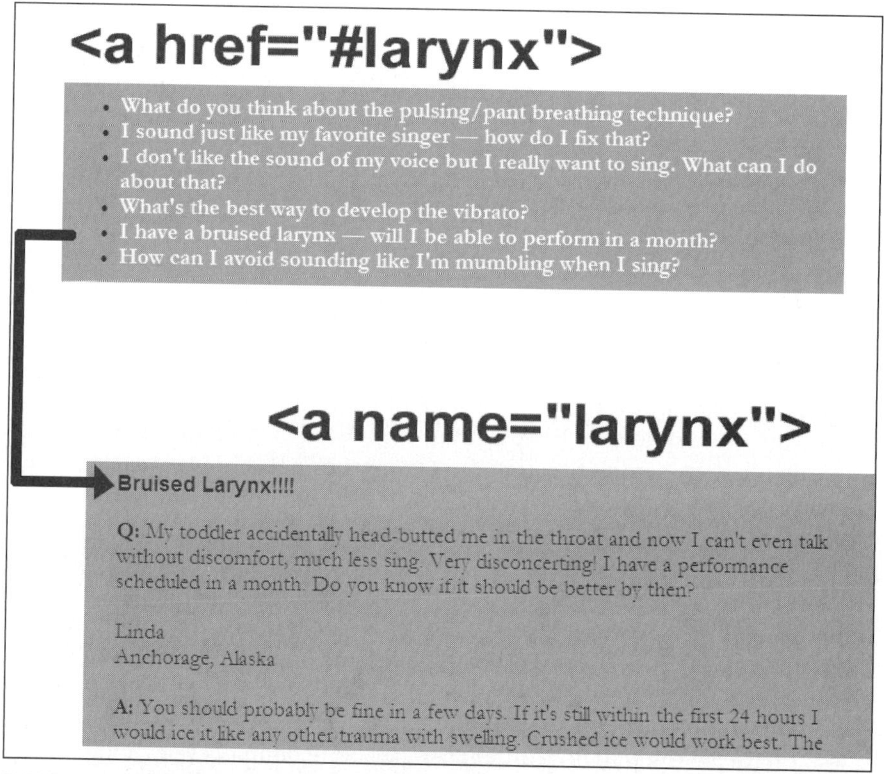

FIGURE 9.1 Hyperlinking within HTML Documents

XLink can help solve the linking problems in both of these scenarios. Here's how it works: With HTML, you enclose the initial linking text or graphic within an anchor tag (<a> and </a> tags) and then provide a Web address for the destination page. To do this, you have to be able to edit and update the page that contains the link. However, in XLink, you just provide a Web address for both the starting point (where the link gets placed) and the target destination (where you should wind up). See Figure 9.2 for an illustration of this. The Web address doesn't necessarily need to point to an XML document; the link could be intended for images, the results of a query, or other kinds of files and documents. For this reason, we will use the term **resource** extensively in this chapter to describe the Web address that is the target or destination of a link.

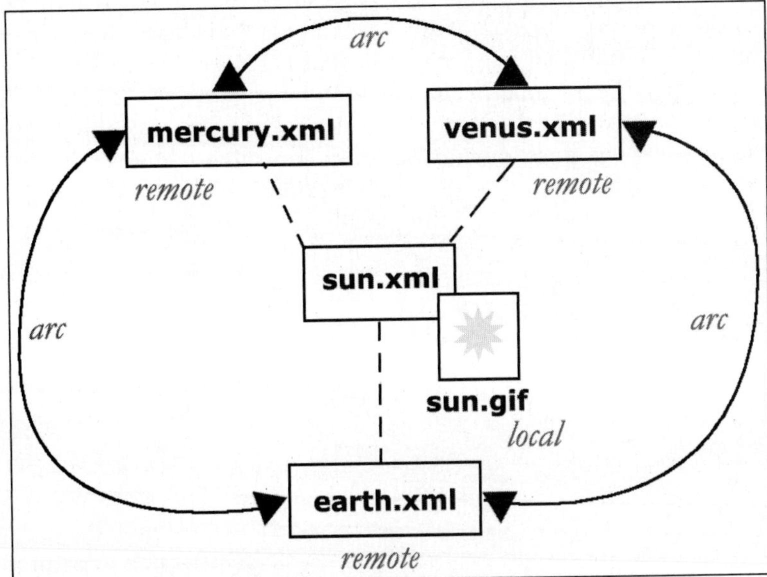

FIGURE 9.2 Hyperlinking in XML Documents

In this example, we've used a series of documents containing information about our solar system to demonstrate a number of relationships at work. Working from the assumption that the `sun.xml` information is at the core and the `sun.gif` image is a **local resource,** each XML document about the various planets (`mercury.xml` and so on) is a **remote resource.** Each planet document could be described in terms of its relationships with one another, and the solid lines represent that this is a two-way relationship between the planet pairs. The information that describes how resources (here, the different planet documents) relate to each other is called an **arc.** For example, we could create a new arc to describe the relationship between the document about Earth and one about Earth's moon. That Earth-moon relationship (or arc) doesn't have anything to do with `venus.xml`, for example, even though we've separately described how our Earth and Venus documents are related and created a separate Earth-Venus arc.

We haven't gone into any detail yet about how these links might behave. Should the `sun.gif` image automatically display, for example, when the `sun.xml` page is accessed? When you click from the `sun.xml` page to the `venus.xml` document, should the Venus page reload in the same browser window or open a new window? All of the details about what happens when a link is followed—or a resource is accessed—using XLink comes under the comprehensive term **traversal.**

Another useful XLink benefit is that you can create a collection of links for a series of documents in an ongoing database, known as a **linkbase,** which can be filtered or sorted as you desire.

In addition, it's possible to use XLink to import blocks of text or other markup into an XML document. This can help simplify your content maintenance. For example, you can readily insert updates into a news story, or insert a standard copyright notice in your content with a single XLink. There's no straightforward, equivalent tag in HTML to do that. Instead, in an HTML document you can accomplish this with a JavaScript script or employ a mechanism known as a **server-side include** (or **SSI**), which references a block of text or code. (You would need to ensure that the Web server that hosts your site supports SSIs, since not all do.) It's worth mentioning that this capability is native to XLink, because this function is very useful for managing updates to a common block of text or code in a single location while referring to it from multiple documents.

Table 9.1 shows at a glance the kinds of differences between linking in HTML documents and XML resources that we've discussed so far.

To create XLink-based links, you need to define a **linking element,** which is an XML element recognized as having linking powers. There are two types of linking elements you can create with XLink; these are designated **simple links** and **extended links.** In broad strokes, simple links are designed to point to one target page only. Extended links essentially offer a fork in the road: you could visit one of multiple potential destination pages. XLink elements can be one of six different types. Two of them are the linking elements (simple and extended) described just above. The other four elements furnish a means by which you can supply more sophisticated details about the linking relationship, which essentially let you construct a kind of "smart link." These include

- *Locator,* which locates an external resource, such as a different XML document.
- *Resource,* which identifies internal resources, such as a link to a section halfway down the same document.
- *Arc,* which describes what happens when the link is followed. For example, this can describe what relationships are established between different sets of data.
- *Title,* which designates a word or phrase to clarify the linking relationship in a way that's easy for people to understand.

XLink provides **global attributes** that you use to declare your links' details and special qualities. You've already seen one of them—the `type` attribute—discussed in detail, although we hadn't yet introduced its proper term. The six types of XLink elements discussed above (along with `none`) are all possible values for the `type` attribute, one of XLink's global attributes. Table 9.2 lists

TABLE 9.1 Comparing Links Implemented with HTML and XLink

Feature	HTML	XLink
Direction	Links go in one direction only, from a source document to a single destination.	Links can be either unidirectional or **multidirectional.** With multidirectional links, you can reach one document from the other, regardless of which one you started at first.
Destination	A link points to a single destination.	A link can point to multiple topics.
Where the link appears	You can define whether the new page appears in the same browser window or a new one.	You can display the target in a new window or embed it under the link, utilizing a "drop-down" effect.
Link databases	Not applicable.	You can store the links for a collection of documents in a linkbase for potential link filtering, sorting, analyzing, or processing.
Importing text and markup	Not available with a single HTML tag. Can be implemented with server-side includes, a capability implemented on many (but not all) Web servers that let you embed commands in an HTML file. Many HTML authors also accomplish this with JavaScript.	You can import text and other information from external documents.

TABLE 9.2 XLink's Global Attributes

Category	Attribute Name	Purpose of This Category
Type definition attribute	`type`	This value defines what type of element is in use.
Locator attribute	`href`	This value should be set to the Web address of the desired resource.
Semantic attributes	`role, arcrole, title`	These attributes provides a short description of the resource.
Behavior attributes	`show, actuate`	These attributes specify where and how a link is activated—for example, in a separate browser window and upon clicking (or automatically).
Traversal attributes	`label, from, to`	These attributes describe what activates a link, and includes what resources are participating in the link relationship.

XLink's global attributes by category and briefly describes their overall function.

The global attributes include `type`, `href`, `role`, `arcrole`, `title`, `show`, `actuate`, `label`, `from`, and `to`. Table 9.3 provides more details on how you can define an XLink element's behavior through these attributes, as well as some sample syntax when defining them in an XML document. We haven't covered the details of the attributes shown here yet, but a number of examples will appear later in this chapter.

TABLE 9.3 The Global Attributes Used in XLink

Attribute	XML Example	Notes
`type`	`xlink:type="simple"`	Identifies the link as a simple link, extended link, any of the four XLink elements (locator, arc, resource, title), or none.
`href`	`xlink:href="http://www.w3.org/TR/xptr"`	Contains the Web address that represents the target of this link.
`role`	`xlink:role="http://www.my-site.com/singerlist"`	Describes the link's content; the value for this attribute must be a Web address. For simple links, this could be used to style different kinds of links differently.
`arcrole`	`xlink:arcrole="reviewer"`	Describes the resource at the end of the `xlink:href` address. The value for this attribute must be a Web address. For simple links, this could be used to style different kinds of links differently.
`title`	`xlink:title="Index"`	Provides a title for the link that humans would understand.
`show`	`xlink:show="new"`	Possible values include `new` (appear in a new window), `embed` (include in text), and `replace` (appear in the current window) for the link content, as well as `other` and `none`.
`actuate`	`xlink:actuate="onLoad"`	Tells the parser when to activate the link: `onLoad` (automatically, when the page displays), `onRequest` (wait for visitors to click a link), `other`, and `none`.

Next, let's see how these global attributes are put to use in an XML DTD, and what they look like when defined in an XML document.

Writing an XLink Statement

It's a good idea to experiment first with the basics of simple links, since a variety of features using extended links are not yet implemented in the major Web browsers. Consider leveraging extended links in your XML documents only when the popular browsers have caught up with the XLink specification. Until then, it's useful to keep an eye on implementation developments for XLink.

Simple Links

Let's take a look at how you can use XLink to create an anchor link that operates much like the standard HTML `<a>` tag:

```
<publisher
  xmlns:xlink="http://www.w3.org/1999/xlink/"
  xlink:type="simple"
  xlink:href="http://www.mcgraw-hill.com/about/about.html"
  xlink:show="new"
  xlink:actuate="onRequest"
>About McGraw-Hill</publisher>
```

Now let's walk through how this works. First, we've created an element called `publisher`. Next, the `xmlns:xlink` attribute defines that this XML document will use the XML namespace, and points to the URL for the page where the W3C defines the XLink namespace. This is the page where XLink will pull its preset definitions from, as we have seen before with external DTDs. After that, the `xlink:type` attributes indicate that this is a simple link (as opposed to an extended link, which is not as well supported by current browsers). By setting the value for the `xlink:show` attribute to `new`, we're specifying that the target should launch in a new window.

The next attribute, `xlink:actuate`, tells the parser when to activate the link; the value `onRequest` means that visitors will need to click the link to go to that target location. The way the XML application should interpret that is that the link should be activated upon the request of the visitor, which is when they click.

Now let's examine how to use XLink to link to an object. In the example below, we create an element in an XML document called `my-image`:

```
<my-image
  xmlns:xlink="http://www.w3.org/1999/xlink/"
  xlink:type="simple"
  xlink:href="http://pics.ebay.com/aw/pics/
    ebay_my_button.gif"
  xlink:show="embed"
  xlink:actuate="onLoad"
/>
```

Just as in our previous XLink example, after naming the element `my-image`, we add an `xmlns:xlink` attribute pointing to the W3C's XLink specification page. Then, we use the `xlink:type` attribute to say that this is a simple link. The `xlink:href` attribute then appears, but points to the address of the file that we want to display inline in the document; in this example, we've used a "Shop at eBay" graphic. Next, the `xlink:show` attribute is set the value `embed`, which tells the parser to include the image in this page's display, to literally embed it in the page. Finally, the value for the `xlink:actuate` attribute is `onLoad`, which means that the image should display automatically when the page loads. Another way to look at that piece of code is that when the page loads (`onLoad`), display the image (`actuate`). Finally, there's an ending slash before the close of the tag (/>) since this is an empty tag; no closing `</my-image>` tag is necessary. Remember, empty tags don't contain any elements or free text within them; an element meant to display an image could readily use an empty tag.

Now let's turn to using XLink to link to an external file and import blocks of text or code markup. Let's create an element in an XML document called `imported-legal`:

```
<imported-legal
   xmlns:xlink="http://www.w3.org/1999/xlink/"
   xlink:type="simple"
   xlink:href="http://www.genuineclass.com/xml/legalese.html"
   xlink:show="onLoad"
   xlink:actuate="embed"
/>
```

As in the two previous examples, we start the tag with the element's name and then add an `xmlns:xlink` attribute. The `xlink:type` attribute indicates that this is a simple link. Now the `xlink:href` attribute references the address of the file whose contents we want to pull into the document. As you saw in the previous example, setting the value for the `xlink:show` attribute to `embed` tells the parser to include the image in this page's display (that is, embed it in the display). Lastly, the `onLoad` value for the `xlink:actuate` attribute will automatically pull in the specified external content when the page loads.

Extended Links

An extended link is intended to link to any number of resources. It defines a set of arcs—containing information about where links are used and where they should go—between several resources. An extended link is the only kind of XLink link that can have **inbound arcs** (linking a remote resource to a local resource, where the local resource is the "inbound" one) and **third-party arcs** (linking one remote resource to another, or sources "outside" the local resource).

It's typical for extended linking elements to be stored separately—in different documents, for instance—from the resources they associate. As a result,

IMPORTANT

Similarly, in an **outbound arc**, the source is a local resource and the destination a remote resource.

extended links are most important in situations where the participants have access to the resources under discussion. Updating a separate linking element also can be utilized as a cost-effective workaround in situations where modifying the actual resources is too cumbersome or costly to justify. Another potential use is when the resources appear in formats that don't typically allow for clickable, embedded links—for example, audio or video files.

Figure 9.3 shows an extended link that associates five remote resources. Imagine that this represents information about a singer and his discography. One resource would be a description of the singer himself, another describes the record company that publishes his works, two resources represent albums that the singer has released, and the last resource represents the album he is currently recording but has not yet released.

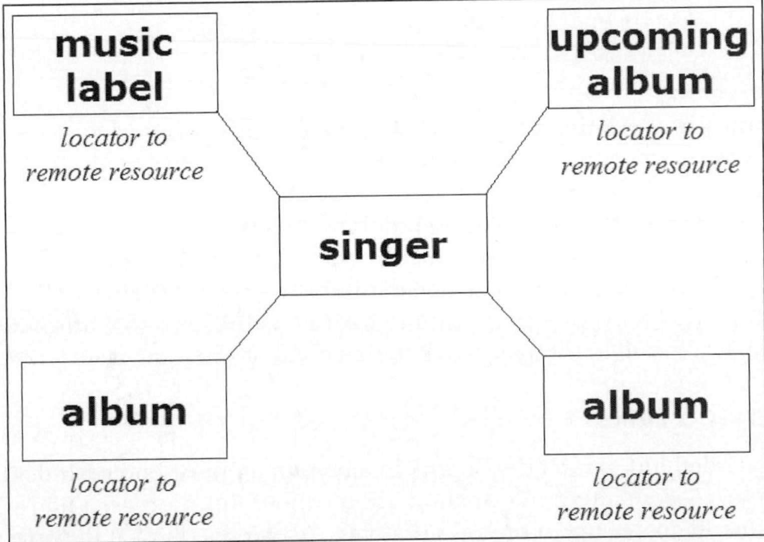

FIGURE 9.3 Remote Resources Connected through an Extended Link

To create an extended link, the value for that element's `type` attribute should be set to `extended`:

```
xlink:type="extended"
```

The extended-type element can contain child elements with any of the following type attributes:

- Locator-type elements, which list what remote resources are participating in the link.
- Arc-type elements, which provide traversal rules among the link's participating resources.
- Title-type elements, which apply labels to make it easy for people to understand what each link is for.
- Resource-type elements, which indicate the local resources that participate in the link.

The following markup shows how XML elements using these declarations might look.

```
<discography>

  <tooltip>Discography for Breck Bowie</tooltip>

  <singer
    xlink:href="singers/breckbowie.xml"
    xlink:label="singer_breck_bowie"
    xlink:role="http://www.sample-site.com/linkproperties/
      singer"
    xlink:title="Breck Bowie" />

  <musiclabel
    xlink:href="publisher/bmi.xml"
    xlink:label="publisher_bmi"
    xlink:role="http://www.sample-site.com/linkproperties/
      musiclabel"
    xlink:title="BMI Records" />
  <!-- more remote resources for recording companies,
    etc. -->

  <album
    xlink:href="albums/B00004sw4c.xml"
    xlink:label="ASIN-B00004SW4C"
    xlink:title="Hugging Rock Stars" />

  <album
    xlink:href="albums/B00003gpd1.xml"
    xlink:label="ASIN-B00003GPD1"
    xlink:title="Why Can't You" />

  <album
    xlink:href="albums/upcoming17.xml"
```

```
    xlink:label="Upcoming_Bowie2"
    xlink:title="Handspring Love" />
  <!-- more remote resources for additional albums,
    recordings, etc. -->

  <recorded
    xlink:from="ASIN-B00004SW4C"
    xlink:arcrole="http://www.sample-site.com/linkproperties/
      recorded"
    xlink:to="singer_bowie2"
    xlink:show="replace"
    xlink:actuate="onRequest"
    xlink:title="Breck Bowie, recorded works" />

  <recorded
    xlink:from="ASIN-B00003GPD1"
    xlink:arcrole="http://www.sample-site.com/linkproperties/
      recorded"
    xlink:to="singer_bowie2"
    xlink:show="replace"
    xlink:actuate="onRequest"
    xlink:title="Breck Bowie, current work-in-progress" />

  <recorded
    xlink:from="singer_bowie2"
    xlink:arcrole="http://www.sample-site.com/linkproperties/
      label"
    xlink:to="publisher_bmi"
    xlink:show="replace"
    xlink:actuate="onRequest"
    xlink:title="BMI Records, recording label" />

</discography>
```

The traversal attributes shown above—`label`, `from`, and `to`—define how information should be sent between resources that are connected in the same link. The `from` attribute defines the source document, while the `to` attribute defines the intended **sources** and target (or **destination**). The behavior attributes—`show` and `actuate`—specify how the end resources should display when the XLink-enabled applications reach them. Refer back to Table 9.2 to review the purpose of each of these attributes.

The semantic attributes—`role`, `arcrole`, and `title`—are where things get interesting. These describe the purpose of the arc's target in relation to its source. For example, Breck Bowie has BMI Records as his recording label. This role could change when taken outside the context of this particular arc. For example, consider the resource BMI Records. In the context of this particular arc, it would have the role of "recording label," while in the context of a different arc with another company it might have the role of "partner" or "customer."

Creating XLinks in DTDs

Before we can get started defining XLink-enabled elements in a DTD, you should first be aware of limitations on what attributes can be used with which elements. This is a very important distinction and will save you a lot of time later on.

XLink's attributes can only be combined with the various XLink types in certain ways. Table 9.4 shows how the W3C has specified which element types (in the vertical columns) each of the global attributes (in the horizontal rows) are allowed.

TABLE 9.4 The Attributes for XLink Types That Are Required and Those That Are Optional

	XLink type					
Attribute	Simple	Extended	Locator	Arc	Resource	Title
type	Required	Required	Required	Required	Required	Required
href	Optional		Required			
role	Optional	Optional	Optional		Optional	
arcrole	Optional			Optional		
title	Optional	Optional	Optional	Optional	Optional	
show	Optional			Optional		
actuate	Optional			Optional		
label			Optional		Optional	
from				Optional		
to				Optional		

Source: World Wide Web Consortium (W3C).

By extension, there are various XLink element types that have special meanings when they appear as child elements of other XLink element types. Table 9.5 summarizes the child element types that can play a large role in their parent element types.

Now let's construct a DTD that incorporates some of the XLink types. To do this, let's continue using an example of linking singers with the albums they've recorded.

TABLE 9.5 XLink Element Type Relationships, as Defined by the W3C

Parent Type	Significant Child Types
Simple	None
Extended	Locator, arc, resource, title
Locator	Title
Arc	Title
Resource	None
Title	None

Let's start by declaring a straightforward simple link element in a DTD. Previously, we looked at an XLink outside of an attribute. We are examining it now as an !ATTLIST component specifically because it is within a DTD:

```
<!ELEMENT schedule (#PCDATA)>
<!ATTLIST schedule
  xmlns:xlink    CDATA        #FIXED "http://www.w3.org/
                              1999/xlink"
  xlink:type     (simple)     #FIXED "simple"
  xlink:href     CDATA        #IMPLIED
  xlink:show     (new)        #FIXED "new"
  xlink:actuate  (onRequest)  #FIXED "onRequest">
```

So in your XML document, you might add a link as follows:

```
<schedule xlink:href="class_schedule.xml">Current class
  schedule</schedule>
```

Remember that the resources used by your links can be either local (resource-type elements) or remote (pointed to by locator-type elements). Resource-type elements are the equivalent of HTML's named anchor (<a name>) links. Locator-type elements are the counterparts of ordinary HTML anchor tags (<a href>).

Let's look at another example. Here, the following code declares a resource element in a DTD:

```
<!ELEMENT singer (first_name,surname)>
<!ATTLIST singer
  xlink:type    (resource)   #FIXED "resource"
  xlink:title   CDATA        #IMPLIED
  xlink:label   NMTOKEN      #IMPLIED>
  xlink:role    CDATA        #IMPLIED
```

The first attribute for this element is `type`, which indicates its function as a resource. Next, the semantic attribute `title` takes the character data (`CDATA`) entered and christens the resource with this new name. Recall in our earlier example that showed the links between Breck Bowie, his discography, and record label. The label of each of his albums used the ASIN number, assigned to help track sales; however, this number would make little sense to the casual reader. Accordingly, each album also had a title assigned to it, which corresponded to the album's title. The attribute `label` uses `NMTOKEN` (which is frequently used for either numerics or other programming language statements). It's good also for identifying Java classes, or when something has to be limited, like a state name instead of New York or NY to identify the element later, when arcs are put in place. Again, ASIN numbers (or, for books, ISBN numbers) are product identifiers useful for tracking sales and distribution, but are not very readable to the casual user. The final attribute, `role`, takes the literal data entered and uses it to describe a property of the document or other resource at hand. In our Breck Bowie example, the `role` attributes brought readers to information about the singer or the record label in that contextual role (and not, for example, in more generic roles as people or companies).

In an XML document, then, a singer element could look like the following:

```
<singer xlink:label="singer_bowie2">
  <first_name>Breck</first_name>
  <last_name>Bowie</surname>
</singer>
```

Since remote resources are pointed to by locators, we need to define a locator-type element in our DTD:

```
<!ELEMENT album EMPTY>
<!ATTLIST album
  xlink:type     (locator)    #FIXED "locator"
  xlink:title    CDATA        #IMPLIED
  xlink:role     CDATA        #IMPLIED
  xlink:label    NMTOKEN      #IMPLIED
  xlink:href     CDATA        #REQUIRED>
```

Here, the album element is empty because it contains no subelements; we're going to link to a variety of other resources to gain information about the

IMPORTANT

Note that the subelements of resource-type elements (here, the `first_name` and `last_name` elements) don't have any XLink-related meaning.

singer, the songs on the album, and so on. Locators can take the same attributes as resources, including `title`, `label`, and `role`, as well as the required semantic attribute `href`, which points to the remote resource. A locator album element will look like the following:

```
<album xlink:label="B00004SW4C" xlink:title="Hugging Rock
  Stars" xlink:href="albums/B00004sw4c.xml"/>
```

This means that the album starts the label (which is the album's cryptic-looking ASIN number, for product distribution and tracking), includes the actual album title in the `xlink:title` attribute, and ends with linking back to a document that contains all of the information about the album (e.g., song titles or lyrics). That document is `B00004sw.xml`.

As you saw earlier in this chapter, the relationships between resources in a link are specified with arcs, which are actually connectors. Arc-type elements use the `to` and `from` attributes to designate the starting and ending points of an arc:

```
<album xlink:type="arc" xlink:from="singer_breck_bowie"
  xlink:to="B00004SW4C"/>
```

This means that the album starts with the name of the singer and links back to the label.

The following DTD defines the above attributes in an arc-type element:

```
<!ELEMENT recorded EMPTY>
<!ATTLIST recorded
  xlink:type     (arc)                          #FIXED "arc"
  xlink:title    CDATA                          #IMPLIED
  xlink:show     (new | replace | embed |
                 other | none)                  #IMPLIED
  xlink:from     NMTOKEN                        #IMPLIED
  xlink:to       NMTOKEN                        #IMPLIED>
```

So now, let's connect our resource and locator examples with this arc and examine the resulting XML markup:

```
<!-- A local resource -->
<singer xlink:label="singer_breck_bowie">
  <first_name>Breck</first_name>
  <surname>Bowie</surname>
</singer>

<!-- A remote resource -->
<album xlink:label="B00004SW4C" xlink:href="b00004sw4c.
  xml"/>

<!-- An arc that connects the two -->
```

```
<recorded xlink:type="arc" xlink:from="singer_breck_bowie"
  xlink:to="b00004sw4c.xml"/>
```

An extended-type element could encompass these relationships.

Introducing XPointer

While XLink can be very useful, as you've seen, it only lets you refer to another document. It's likely that you may want to refer to a specific part within another document. XPointer allows you to do this with a capability similar to the concept of named anchors in HTML pages. This is especially useful for search engines and in cataloging large documents.

Here's one such example: In Chapter 4, you learned that elements can have an `ID` attribute, which is meant to be used for linking and pointing. The sample line of code below shows this `ID` attribute used in an element declaration:

```
<!ATTLIST cdcover CatalogNo ID #REQUIRED>
```

Now let's suppose we'd like to create a link to a certain part within the W3C's Technical Reports and Publications page at http://www.w3.org/TR/—specifically, to the Notes section more than halfway down this long document (see Figure 9.4). The ID assigned to this section is "Notes". An XPointer that specifically points the W3C Notes entry on this page would appear as follows:

```
http://www.w3.org/TR/#xpointer(id('Notes'))
```

This means that within the pages and pages of documents, the specific section tagged, in advance, as "Notes" would be referenced.

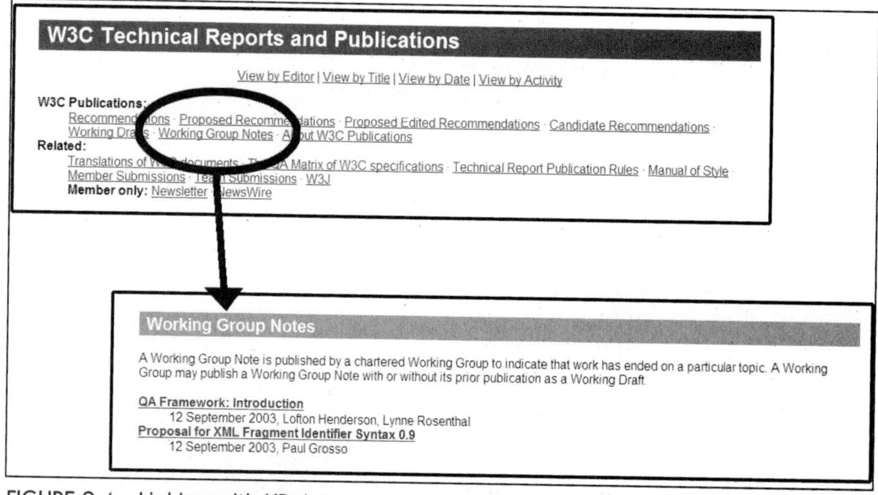

FIGURE 9.4 Linking with XPointer

However, you'll need to bear the following caveats in mind when linking with XPointer:

- *The resource you link to must be an XML document.* You can use XPointer to link to XHTML-compliant documents, but not to older HTML documents that are not XHTML-compliant.
- *The resource must remain online.* This sounds obvious, but bears articulating: If the document or other resource that you're linking to is no longer available, the link will break and cause an error.
- *The ID must not change.* If the value of the element's `ID` attribute changes, any links you've made using XPointer would need to be updated in kind; otherwise, the link will not work correctly.
- *The application has to support XPointer.* Browser support for XPointer has plodded along even further behind that for XLink.

Now that you've seen all the prerequisites for using XPointers, you're ready to delve into the details of how XPointers can be used to refer to specific parts of XML resources. XPointer's linking and addressing capabilities are actually an extension of XPath, which you saw in the previous chapter on XSL. When you see or use an XPointer link, you're connecting an XPath expression with a Web address.

XPath lets you locate a node (elements or character data), or set of nodes, at any level of an XML document tree using what's called a **location path.** A node, for example could be specific enough to include only one letter of a sentence, or could include a phrase, a paragraph, a document, or an entire title. A location path can be an **absolute path,** which describes a location in reference to the root node, or it could be a **relative path,** which means you can point to elements that are relative to other elements.

For example, let's look at a sample from a collection of favorite films called `filmdb.xml`. A typical entry looks like the following:

```
<?xml version="1.0"?>
<film id="284" genre="comedy">
  <title>Raising Arizona</title>
  <year>1987</year>
  <director>Joel Coen</director>
</film>
```

IMPORTANT

Since XPointer is not yet a standard, few tools are available that can process XPointers accurately. As a result, it will be difficult to actually test much of the material in this section. You will likely want to wait until the final W3C Recommendation emerges before beginning to use XPointers in your development activities.

IMPORTANT

Any special characters that appear in an XPointer expression—such as quote marks or an ampersand—must be converted to their character entity codes in order for the address to parse correctly. To include an ampersand (&) in a XPointer expression, for example, you would need to change it to `&`.

Now let's add a simple XLink to point to this information. An XPointer could link directly to the data for *Raising Arizona* via the film's `id` attribute:

```
<entry xlink:type="simple" xlink:href="filmdb.xml#xpointer
  (id('284'))">Raising Arizona</entry>
```

XPointer even lets you use further shortcuts in naming, largely to remain compatible with HTML's named anchor conventions (e.g., `#name`). In this way, the XPointer could consist only of a name and refer to any element that has an `id` attribute that matches:

```
xpointer(id('284'))
```

An XPointer could also contain a **child sequence** that uses an addressing scheme reminiscent of the directories in a Web address. You begin by identifying the document element and drill down, level by level, to the desired resource. Each level is separated from the next via a forward slash (`/`), and is defined in terms of integers rather than element names. For example:

```
xpointer(/1/1)
```

is an XPointer that refers to the first child element of the document element—which in this case is the film title (*Raising Arizona*). In the next chapter, you'll gain an overview of the current crop of XML parsers and information to bear in mind when you're validating your XML documents.

Key Terms

absolute path
anchor link
anchor tag
arc
child sequence
destination (in terms of traversal)
extended links
global attributes
inbound arcs
linkbase
linking element
local resource
location path
multidirectional
named anchor
outbound arc
relative path
remote resource
resource
server-side include (SSI)
simple links
source (in terms of traversal)
third-party arc
traversal
XLink
XPointer

Code Summary

1. **Syntax for XLink's global attributes:**

```
xlink:type="simple"
xlink:href="http://www.w3.org/TR/xptr"
xlink:role="http://www.my-site.com/singerlist"
xlink:arcrole="reviewer"
xlink:title="Index"
xlink:show="new"
xlink:actuate="onLoad"
```

2. **Syntax for creating a simple link in an XML document, using XLink to link to an object:**

```
<my-image
  xmlns:xlink="http://www.w3.org/1999/xlink/"
  xlink:type="simple"
  xlink:href="http://pics.ebay.com/aw/pics/ebay_my_button.gif"
  xlink:show="embed"
  xlink:actuate="onLoad"
/>
```

3. **Syntax for creating an extended link in an XML document:**

```
<recorded
  xlink:from="singer_bowie2"
  xlink:arcrole="http://www.sample-site.com/linkproperties/label"
  xlink:to="publisher_bmi"
  xlink:show="replace"
  xlink:actuate="onRequest"
  xlink:title="BMI Records, recording label" />
```

4. **Extended links:**

```
<discography>

<tooltip>Discography for Breck Bowie</tooltip>

<singer
  xlink:href="singers/breckbowie.xml"
  xlink:label="singer_breck_bowie"
```

```
   xlink:role="http://www.sample-site.com/linkproperties/singer"
   xlink:title="Breck Bowie" />

<musiclabel
   xlink:href="publisher/bmi.xml"
   xlink:label="publisher_bmi"
   xlink:role="http://www.sample-site.com/linkproperties/musiclabel"
   xlink:title="BMI Records" />
<!-- more remote resources for recording companies, etc. -->

<album
   xlink:href="albums/B00004sw4c.xml"
   xlink:label="ASIN-B00004SW4C"
   xlink:title="Hugging Rock Stars" />

<album
   xlink:href="albums/B00003gpd1.xml"
   xlink:label="ASIN-B00003GPD1"
   xlink:title="Why Can't You" />

<album
   xlink:href="albums/upcoming17.xml"
   xlink:label="Upcoming_Bowie2"
   xlink:title="Handspring Love" />
<!-- more remote resources for additional albums, recordings, etc. -->

<recorded
   xlink:from="ASIN-B00004SW4C"
   xlink:arcrole="http://www.sample-site.com/linkproperties/recorded"
   xlink:to="singer_bowie2"
   xlink:show="replace"
   xlink:actuate="onRequest"
   xlink:title="Breck Bowie, recorded works" />

<recorded
   xlink:from="ASIN-B00003GPD1"
   xlink:arcrole="http://www.sample-site.com/ linkproperties/recorded"
   xlink:to="singer_bowie2"
   xlink:show="replace"
   xlink:actuate="onRequest"
   xlink:title="Breck Bowie, current work-in-progress" />

<recorded
   xlink:from="singer_bowie2"
   xlink:arcrole="http://www.sample-site.com/linkproperties/label"
   xlink:to="publisher_bmi"
   xlink:show="replace"
   xlink:actuate="onRequest"
   xlink:title="BMI Records, recording label" />

</discography>
```

5. **Syntax for creating an XLink in a DTD:**

```
<!ELEMENT schedule (#PCDATA)>
<!ATTLIST schedule
```

```
    xmlns:xlink     CDATA          #FIXED "http://www.w3.org/1999/xlink"
    xlink:type      (simple)       #FIXED "simple"
    xlink:href      CDATA          #IMPLIED
    xlink:show      (new)          #FIXED "new"
    xlink:actuate   (onRequest)    #FIXED "onRequest">
```

In your XML document, you might then add a link as follows:

```
<schedule xlink:href="class_schedule.xml">Current class schedule</schedule>
```

6. **Syntax for an XPointer expression:**

```
xpointer(id('Notes'))
xpointer(string-range(//band, "Breck Bowie"))
```

7. **Simple links:**

```
<publisher
  xmlns:xlink="http://www.w3.org/1999/xlink/"
  xlink:type="simple"
  xlink:href="http://www.mcgraw-hill.com/about/about.html"
  xlink:show="new"
  xlink:actuate="onRequest"
>About McGraw-Hill</publisher>
```

8. **Using XLink to link to an external file:**

```
<imported-legal
  xmlns:xlink="http://www.w3.org/1999/xlink/"
  xlink:type="simple"
  xlink:href="http://www.genuineclass.com/xml/legalese.html"
  xlink:show="onLoad"
  xlink:actuate="embed"
/>
```

9. **Linking to data with XLink and XPointer:**

```
<entry xlink:type="simple" xlink:href="filmdb.xml#xpointer(id('284'))">Raising
  Arizona</entry>
```

Alerts and Advice

Since few applications offer support yet for XLinks and XPointers, consult the W3C's implementation chart (linked from http://www.w3.org/XML/Linking) to obtain the tools you'll need for testing and experimentation.

In addition to the six types of XLink elements—simple, extended, locator, resource, arc, and title—you also can set the type value to `none` via the `xlink:type` attribute.

For the latest developments on XLink and XPointer, visit the W3C's site at http://www.w3.org/TR/xlink/ and http://www.w3.org/TR/xptr/, respectively.

Remember that special characters in XPointer expressions—for example, quote marks or an ampersand—need to be converted to their character entity codes.

In July 2002, the W3C's XML Linking Working Group split the XPointer specification from one document into four separate specifications. The central specification is now called XPointer Framework; it outlines general XPointer syntax rules and levels of processor conformance.

Review Questions

1. What are some of the differences between hyperlinking in HTML versus XLink?
2. Which attribute is required for all types of XLink elements?
   a. `href`
   b. `role`
   c. `type`
   d. `title`
3. _______ links point to a single document, while _______ links can link to multiple destinations.
4. An _______ describes how to traverse a pair of resources, including the direction and how the link should display.
5. You can use an XPointer to link to any HTML document. True or False?
6. How would you design a simple flowchart to track an XLink statement? Show the step-by-step process you would employ.

Case Study

Read the following how-to column on IBM's developerWorks site at http://www-106.ibm.com/developerworks/xml/library/x-xdxlnk/index.html?dwzone=xml. This column uses an example of how a company could add XLink pointers to its invoices and create XLinks with a URL-addressable database. Examine the sample code and construct a similar example for your own purposes.

Hands On Project

In this exercise, you will create a series of XML documents that relate to movies. As you do, you'll add links to cross-reference the titles with any information you deem useful, from the directors to actors to the year of release.

1. Visit http://movieweb.com/movie/alltime.html, which is MovieWeb's listing of the top-grossing movies of all time. Decide on a theme for your movies page—you could create a page about your favorites, for example—and choose between 10 and 20 movies from this listing to include on your page. This page also lists the box-office gross and the year that the movie was released; consider whether this information is something you'd like to include or link to on your page.
2. The movie titles on MovieWeb's page are hyperlinks. Click through to browse the additional information collected here about each film.
3. Now let's start to put XLink to work. Start by adding simple links in your new XML document so that when users click the movie title in your document, they encounter more information on MovieWeb's site.
4. Now consider what extended links you could add to your set of pages. For example, you could create pages about different movie genres.

CHAPTER 10

Scripting with the DOM

LEARNING OBJECTIVES

1. To examine how the DOM represents one popular model for parsing XML.
2. To learn how the elements and attributes in your XML documents can be represented as objects.
3. To load and display XML data using JavaScript.
4. To manipulate XML data with DHTML.
5. To learn about browser support for the DOM.

In Chapters 7 and 8, you learned about displaying XML in a Web browser using two kinds of stylesheet technology: CSS and XSL. This approach lets you separate the content from the layout and styles used in your Web site, letting you control the site's look and feel. However, there is a second approach to marking up XML data for use in a Web browser: You can manipulate XML documents in the browser with the W3C's XML **Document Object Model** (or **DOM**) and a scripting language like JavaScript or VBScript. With this approach, XML carries your data in a way that makes it easily accessible to the rest of your code.

Scripting with the DOM—a technology that has been in development by the W3C since 1998—makes it possible for you to incorporate many kinds of features that can be updated on the fly on a Web site. These interactive capabilities could include dynamic navigation menus, randomly generated quotes, or random values for Web-based games (such as picking cards from a deck for a magic trick, online card game, or online tarot card reading). Many Web developers today are used to utilizing JavaScript alone to accomplish this kind of task, but this method tends to produce lengthy code with a lot of scripting errors. By scripting with the DOM instead, you can retrieve new XML data in a hierarchical fashion from your Web server without having to reload the page in your Web browser. It's meant to create a "write once, run everywhere" standard for Web page scripting, but the development technique is less efficient than other W3C-recommended technologies (such as SVG, SMIL, and XForms) that have emerged in more recent years.

In this chapter, we'll examine how the DOM can help you manipulate XML documents easily with **client-side** scripting—which means within a Web browser, without needing to go back to the Web server for **server-side** processing. When you can reduce how many times you need to go back to the Web server to refresh the page, you'll make a visible difference in how fast your Web application responds to the user.

An Overview of the DOM

Advice

Both the DOM and XPath make no distinction between elements and attributes and use the term *node* to apply to one or the other. A node is essentially a single item that contains data within the document tree.

The W3C XML DOM is a standardized set of programming interfaces, or objects, that can access XML data. What that means is that the DOM defines the way that programs and scripts can access XML documents and update them. The DOM is meant to be used with any operating system or programming language.

So how does it work? The DOM presents an XML document—which, in literal form, is really just a long string of alphanumeric characters—in a hierarchical diagram or a tree structure. It establishes the hierarchy that shows where elements and their attributes (which we'll collectively call **nodes** here) fall in the structured parent-child order of the document.

As an example, the XML markup shown in Listing 10.1 can be represented as the tree of nodes shown in Figure 10.1.

LISTING 10.1

```
<?xml version="1.0" encoding="UTF-8"?>
<restaurants>
<restaurant cuisine="French">Lutece</restaurant>
<restaurant cuisine="Seafood">Pescatore</restaurant>
<restaurant cuisine ="Vegetarian">Zen Palate</restaurant>
</restaurants>
```

DOM-Based Parsers

Advice

An XML parser may also be called an **XML processor.**

When the W3C developed its XML recommendation, it anticipated that XML documents would not be read just as plain text. Rather, a type of program called an XML parser (as you saw in Chapter 6) is needed to process the document's content and structure and move this information to an XML application (such as a browser). There are two basic models of XML parsers: **tree-based** and **event-based parsers.** Each parsing model has its own advantages for processing XML documents. Tree-based parsers are commonly referred to as **DOM-based parsers,** while event-based parsers are frequently called **SAX**

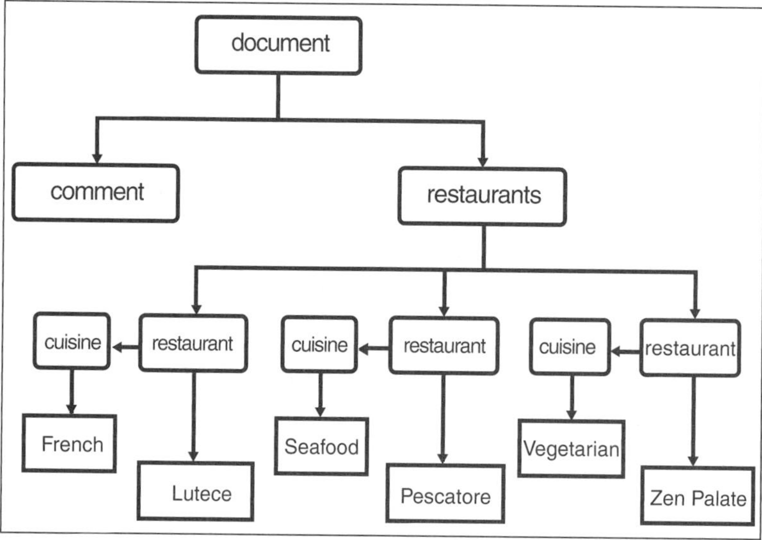

FIGURE 10.1 A DOM Representation of an XML Document

parsers. Many XML parsers, such as the Microsoft XML parser you read about in Chapter 6, can support both kinds of parsing.

Figure 10.2 shows how the intermediary XML parser takes the information from an XML document and passes it on to an XML application. The parser takes the information from an XML document and filters it before passing the data along to the application (such as a Web browser).

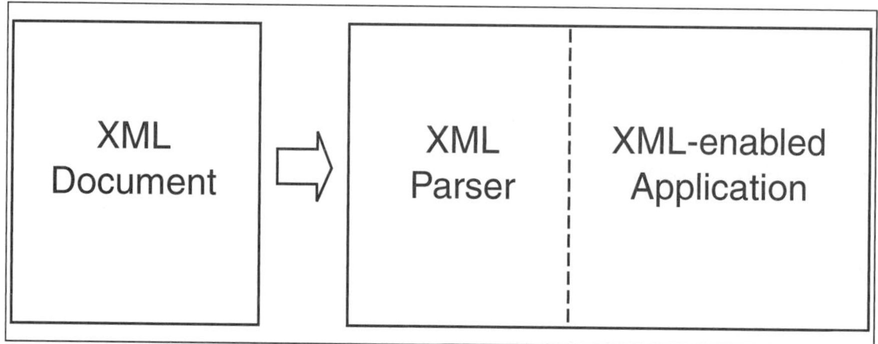

FIGURE 10.2 An XML Parser (or XML Processor) in Action

The DOM specification is intended to provide a standard **Application Programming Interface (API)** for manipulating XHTML documents and XML data through a programming language like Java or JavaScript. A program or scripting language (like JavaScript, for example) can utilize this API to manipulate this document: It can read information, add new nodes (including elements, attributes, and processing instructions), and rearrange and change existing nodes. The DOM has been approved as a W3 recommendation.

At this point, it's worth briefly describing the other major kind of XML processor besides DOM-based parsing. **SAX** (which stands for **Simple API for XML**) does not have the official status of a W3C recommendation like the DOM does, but it is already supported by many software companies and developers. A SAX-based parser processes an XML document in a sequential basis. It represents a document as a string of **events** (such as the beginning or end of an element) that a programmer writes **handlers** for. A handler is a piece of code that produces an appropriate action when triggered by specific events. As a result, SAX-based parsing is popular with programming languages that are good at event handling (such as Java or C++). However, SAX-based parsing is less appropriate for the commonly employed scripting languages on the Web (like JavaScript), so, for practical purposes, this chapter is focused on scripting using DOM-based parsing.

DOM-Based Parsing versus SAX-Based Parsing

There are benefits to both DOM-based parsing and SAX-based parsing. You can use a DOM-based parser to validate an XML document against a DTD or schema—which, as you've seen in Chapter 6, is invaluable for ensuring there are no mistakes in your XML documents. In doing so, however, a DOM-based parser loads the full XML document into memory. By comparison, a SAX-based parser does not need to load an entire XML document into memory. Since it operates on a sequential basis, a SAX-based parser processes one node at a time and discards it before processing the next node. As a result, a DOM-based parser tends to use more memory and processing power than a SAX-based parser. This is important to bear in mind if you're processing larger documents (several megabytes in size or larger, for example), because a DOM-based parser could require an excessive amount of memory to handle such large files.

The DOM's Design Levels

The W3C has split the DOM specification into three different implementation levels. Each supports a different level of functionality. These implementation levels include

- *DOM Level 1.* This is a core framework for navigating and manipulating HTML and XML documents. It was first released in 1998.
- *DOM Level 2.* A stylesheet object model and an event model are built into this level. Most of this specification was released in November 2000. Since the DOM Level 2 is incompatible with Level 1, the W3C now recommends that Web developers and authors conform to DOM Level 2 HTML, a recommendation approved in January 2003.
- *DOM Level 3.* This level focuses on loading and saving documents, along with content models like DTDs and schemas.

The Node Interface

In a document tree, nodes are shown in relationship to one another. A node may appear as a **parent, child, sibling, ancestor,** or **descendant** — much like the relationships represented on a family tree.

Understanding this concept of a tree structure is critical for understanding **object-oriented programming.** In order to simplify computer programming, developers of computer languages developed a system of organizing code into logical entities called **objects.** Further development along these lines led to expressing objects in terms of their relationships to one another in a hierarchical structure. In this way, a child object can inherit the properties of its parents, but still differentiate itself from its siblings.

For example, as Figure 10.3 shows, a class called *bicycle* could contain child objects like tricycle, mountain bike, or tandem. Each child object inherits certain properties from the bicycle class; each has handlebars, wheels, pedals, and so on. But the child objects can add variations to the properties that they inherit from the parent class. For example, a tricycle has a third wheel, tandem bicycles have two sets of handlebars and seats, and a mountain bike has an extra set of gears.

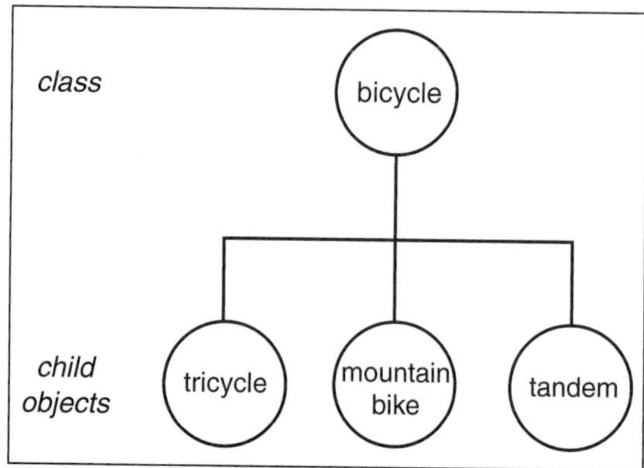

FIGURE 10.3 Classes and Inheritance

The DOM, therefore, is an API that lets you access XML and HTML documents through an object model. Accordingly, as we discuss each type of node in the node interface in this section, we may refer to them as node objects.

As we have said, the DOM defines a document as a hierarchical tree structure of nodes. A node can have child nodes beneath it in the hierarchy. A node also may appear as a **leaf,** which takes no children. Table 10.1 shows the node types that the W3C has stated that the DOM may use, as well as the child nodes each kind can take.

TABLE 10.1 The Hierarchy of Node Objects Used by the DOM

Node Type	Child Nodes

`Document`	`Element` (maximum of one)
	`ProcessingInstruction`
	`Comment`
	`DocumentType` (maximum of one)

`DocumentFragment`	`Element`
	`ProcessingInstruction`
	`Comment`
	`Text`
	`CDATASection`
	`EntityReference`

`DocumentType`	No children

`EntityReference`	`Element`
	`ProcessingInstruction`
	`Comment`
	`Text`
	`CDATASection`
	`EntityReference`

`Element`	`Element`
	`Text`
	`Comment`
	`ProcessingInstruction`
	`CDATASection`
	`EntityReference`

`Attr` (or `Attribute`)	`Text` `EntityReference`
`ProcessingInstruction`	No children
`Comment`	No children
`Text`	No children
`CDATASection`	No children

`Entity`	`Element`
	`ProcessingInstruction`
	`Comment`
	`Text`
	`CDATASection`
	`EntityReference`

`Notation`	No children

Source: W3C.

You have seen most of these types of nodes in use in the sample XML documents in previous chapters. This is really the first time, though, that we are explicitly identifying the most common methodology for writing XML programs—which you now know is called the Document Object Model (DOM).

Table 10.2 shows a few brief examples of the most commonly used node types.

Listing 10.2 shows another code example that demonstrates how you can project an XML document onto the DOM.

TABLE 10.2 Examples of Common Node Types Used in XML Documents

Node Type	Example
`DocumentType`	`<!DOCTYPE candy SYSTEM "candy.dtd">`
`Element`	`<chocolate type="bar">Hershey</chocolate>`
`Attr` (or `Attribute`)	`type="bar"`
`Text`	`Hershey`

LISTING 10.2

```
<?xml version="1.0"?>
<!-- in this listing, periodicals appear first, then books -->
<library xmlns="http://www.library.org/schemas/library">
  <periodical name="Rolling Stone">
    <writer>Jonathan Cott</writer>
    <writer>Cameron Crowe</writer>
    <writer>P.J. O'Rourke</writer>
  </periodical>
  <!-- insert next periodical here -->
</library>
```

The XML markup shown in Listing 10.2 can be represented as the tree of nodes shown in Figure 10.4.

Let's walk through the code in Listing 10.2 to articulate how each element and attribute is aligned with a node in the document tree. The topmost node in the tree structure is of type `Document`. The Document node has two child nodes related to the document information item's children property: a Comment node and an Element node (for the `library` element). This Element node has two child nodes corresponding to the children property: one Element node (for the `periodical` element) and one Comment node. That Element node, in turn, contains three Element nodes (each one is an element called `writer`) as children, again corresponding to the children property.

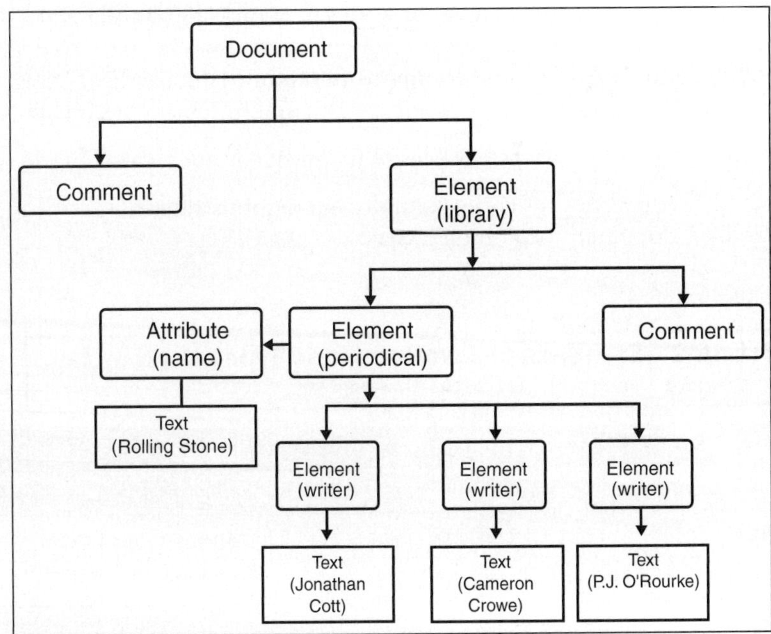

FIGURE 10.4 Associating an XML Document with the DOM

Parsing the DOM

> **Alert**
> To view the examples in this section, you will need a Web browser with a parser compatible with the Microsoft parser (MSXML), such as Microsoft Internet Explorer 5.0 or higher. Later in the chapter, when we discuss browser compatibility issues, we will show additional code examples that show how to extend these examples to make them more fully compatible with other parsers, like the one in the Mozilla browser.

Now let's turn our attention to our first actual scripting examples with the DOM. In the examples below, we will utilize JavaScript to load XML data and files into the parser. Typically, client-side JavaScript supplies objects to control a Web browser and its DOM. Here, we will use JavaScript to create an instance of the Microsoft parser to process the node objects from an XML file.

Don't worry if you've never used JavaScript before in your coding; we will step through each of the significant lines of code in each example.

You embed a JavaScript script within an XHTML document using opening and closing `<script>` tags:

```
<script type="text/javascript">
// The rest of the script goes here.
</script>
```

To add a comment to a JavaScript script—as shown in the second line of code just above—you add two slashes (`//`) to the beginning of the line. If you have a comment that breaks over several lines, you use `/*` to indicate the beginning of the comment and `*/` to indicate the end of the comment.

Using JavaScript, you can create an XML document object with the following code:

```
var xmlDoc = new ActiveXObject("Microsoft.XMLDOM")
```

This creates an instance of the Microsoft XML parser, using the variable name `xmlDoc`.

Now let's look at your first full sample JavaScript script for displaying XML data in Listing 10.3. We're going to load a sample XML file called `exchanges.xml`, which will contain contact information about financial exchanges around the world. Once the file is loaded, we will begin to manipulate the data and control its display.

LISTING 10.3

```
<script type="text/javascript">
var xmlDoc = new ActiveXObject("Microsoft.XMLDOM")
xmlDoc.async="false"
xmlDoc.load("exchanges.xml")
document.write ("The first XML element in this file
  consists of the following: ");
document.write(xmlDoc.documentElement.firstChild.text);
</script>
```

Alert

In the second line of Listing 10.3, the Microsoft parser uses an ActiveX component for scripting, which is not a standardized call in the DOM specification. (Microsoft's ActiveX technology lets programmers assemble reusable software components into applications and services.) Attempting to display this page in a browser that uses a parser that's not fully compatible with the Microsoft parser—the Mozilla browser, for example—would not be successful. Later in this chapter, in the "Browser Support for the DOM" section, we will show with additional code examples how to extend these examples to make them more fully compatible with other parsers, like the one in the Mozilla browser.

Let's examine what this code does. First, we create a new JavaScript script. Next, we create an instance of the Microsoft XML parser and call it `xmlDoc` so that we can refer to it more easily in our code. The second line of the script prevents the parser from executing until the document has been completely loaded. After that, the parser loads an XML document called `broadcast.xml`.

Next, one of the most common reasons for using JavaScript is to display text. JavaScript does this via an object called `document` and a method called `write`. The syntax for the `write` method of the `document` object is

```
document.write("String")
```

where *`String`* is replaced either by the literal text contained within the quotation marks or by the value returned by a JavaScript expression. The two `document.write` statements that follow demonstrate an example of each. First, a literal text phrase displays on the screen, containing the words "The first XML element in this file consists of the following: ".

The second `document.write` statement requires some more detailed explanation:

```
document.write(xmlDoc.documentElement.firstChild.text);
```

Here, `documentElement` is a property of the `document` object, which is really the parent object for the rest of your document. The `firstChild` property returns the first node in a listing (called the `NodeList` object) that contains all the child nodes at the next level down in the hierarchy. The `text` option displays the `Text` object for that node. Another way of displaying this same information is

```
document.write (xmlDoc.documentElement.childNodes.item(0).
  text);
```

Here, the `childNodes` property returns a `NodeList` object that contains all the child nodes at the next level down in the hierarchy. These child nodes are numbered beginning with 0 (not 1). So `xmlDoc.documentElement.childNodes.item(0)` refers to the first child node one level below the root node of the XML document.

Finally, we end the script with a closing `</script>` tag. But what actual results does this script produce? For that, we need to construct an XML file called `exchanges.xml`. We do that next in Listing 10.4.

Listing 10.4

```
<?xml version="1.0" ?>
<exchange>
  <name>New York Stock Exchange</name>
  <code>NYSE</code>
  <url>www.nyse.com</url>
  <phone>1-212-656-3000</phone>
  <fax>1-212-656-5557</fax>
</exchange>
```

The `documentElement` property would reveal that the top-level element in Listing 10.4 is `exchange`. Its `firstChild` property shows that the first child node of `exchange` is `name`; the text value of the `name` object here is `New York Stock Exchange`.

Figure 10.5 shows the results of displaying an XHTML document containing the markup shown in Listing 10.5. When the text displayed through both `document.write` statements is rendered, it appears as a single sentence onscreen: "The first XML element in this file contains: New York Stock Exchange". If this `name` object file is updated in the `exchanges.xml` file to another value (for example, London Stock Exchange), then this page's display will dynamically update as well.

LISTING 10.5

```
<html xmlns="http://www.w3.org/1999/xhtml" xml:lang="en"
  lang="en">
  <head>
    <title>Exchange Directory: Sample</title>
  </head>
  <body>
<script type="text/javascript">
var xmlDoc = new ActiveXObject("Microsoft.XMLDOM")
xmlDoc.async="false"
xmlDoc.load("exchanges.xml")
```

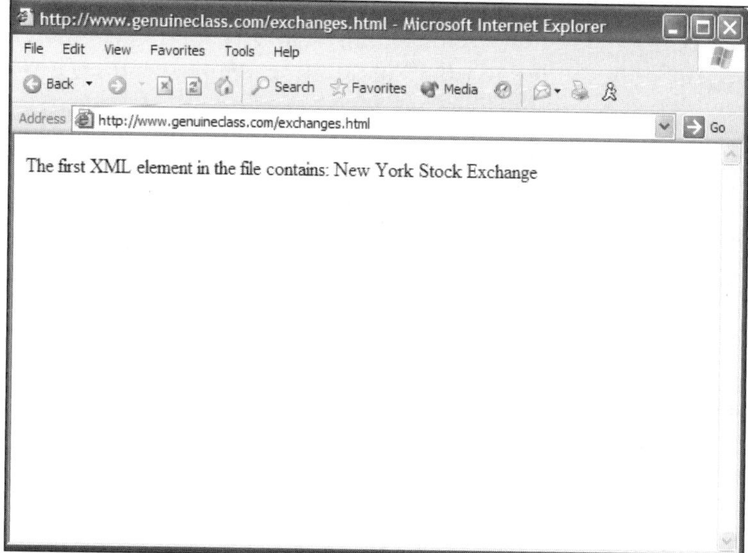

FIGURE 10.5 Our XHTML Document from Listing 10.5, Which Loads *exchange.xml*

```
document.write ("The first XML element in this file
  contains: ");
document.write(xmlDoc.documentFlement.firstChild.text);
</script>
  </body>
</html>
```

Now let's consider how else we could make this script more useful. For starters, you can control the order in which your scripts process data by using a **looping statement.** In our next example, we will display the text value of every child node for our root element. To do this, we'll need to create a simple loop that starts counting at the first child node, displays the text value, then increments the counter. This lets us repeatedly execute this line in the script until a certain condition is met—namely, until we run out of child nodes to count and display.

Earlier you saw that one way to display the first child node of the root element was

```
document.write (xmlDoc.documentElement.childNodes.item(0).
  text);
```

In our new variation of this script, which we'll show in Listing 10.6, we will replace this line with the following:

```
document.write (xmlDoc.documentElement.childNodes.item(n).
  text);
```

The only change we've made so far is to replace the numeric value (0) with a **variable** (represented by n). A variable is a named location in computer memory that JavaScript can use to store data while a script executes. The looping statement will consist of the following lines:

```
for (var n=0; n < xmlDoc.documentElement.childNodes.
  length; n++)
{
document.write (xmlDoc.documentElement.childNodes.
  item(n).text);
document.write ("<br />");
}
```

Advice

A `for` statement is a common **conditional statement** in JavaScript and other scripting languages (such as VBScript). The format is as follows: The loop consists of three optional expressions surrounded by parentheses and separated by semicolons, followed by a block of statements to be executed (enclosed by the { and } brackets). The first expression initializes the counter variable, the second expression (which is optional) provides a condition that is evaluated on each encounter through the loop, and the third updates (or **increments**) the counter variable.

The looping is defined through the `for` statement in the first line above. Here we're using JavaScript to create a variable called `n` and give it an initial value of 0. As long as the value of `n` is less than the total number of child nodes (which can be represented by `xmlDoc.documentElement.childNodes.length`), the script should continue to execute. The third expression (`n++`) means that the counter variable `n` should be incremented by 1. Thus, another pass through the loop is generated.

We need to update just a few lines of the code in Listing 10.5 to accommodate the additional text display of all the child nodes for the `<exchange>` element. We also have added a couple of comments—these are the lines beginning with //—to clarify the purpose of each of the parts of the script we've changed.

LISTING 10.6

```
<html xmlns="http://www.w3.org/1999/xhtml">
  <head>
    <title>Exchange Directory: Sample</title>
  </head>
  <body>
<script type="text/javascript">
var xmlDoc = new ActiveXObject("Microsoft.XMLDOM");
xmlDoc.async="false"
xmlDoc.load("exchanges.xml")

// We move up the literal text we want displayed, in order
  to precede the looping statement
document.write ("The values recorded for the first exchange
  listed in this file are as follows: <br /><br />");

// The looping statement appears here
for (var n=0; n < xmlDoc.documentElement.childNodes.
  length; n++)
```

```
{
document.write (xmlDoc.documentElement.childNodes.
  item(n).text);
document.write ("<br />");
}
</script>
  </body>
</html>
```

Figure 10.6 shows the results of displaying an XHTML document containing the markup shown in Listing 10.6.

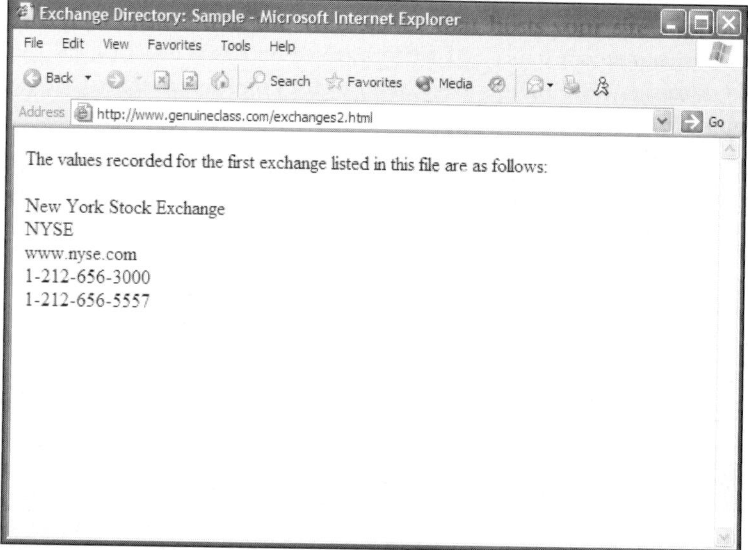

FIGURE 10.6 Resulting Display for Listing 10.6
Our XHTML document from Listing 10.6 displays the text value of all the child nodes of the root element in `exchange.xml`.

By now you've seen a few quick demonstrations of how you can use different properties and methods of various node objects to manipulate and display data from an XML file—some examples were the `documentElement` property and the `load()` method used with the Document node object. Table 10.3 shows a fuller listing of the properties and methods available to each of the major kinds of objects you will run across in your XML files. These descriptions may provide some inspiration for how you can creatively target, display, and manipulate certain types of data in your XML files. Since the properties and methods in Table 10.3 are provided by the W3C, the chart omits custom (but highly useful) extensions like the `load()` method for the Document object.

Table 10.3 Properties and Methods Available to Objects Used by the DOM

Object	Property or Method	What It Does
`Document`	`documentElement`	Returns the root element of the document
	`doctype`	Returns the DTD or schema for the document
	`implementation`	Returns the implementation object for this particular document
	`getElementsByTagName(tagName)`	Returns the specified node, and all its child nodes, as a `NodeList`
	`createElement(tagName)`	Creates an element with the specified `tagName`
	`createTextNode(text)`	Creates a text node containing the specified text
	`createAttribute(attributeName)`	Creates an attribute node with the specified attribute name
	`createCDATASection(text)`	Creates a `CDATASection` containing the specified text
	`createComment(text)`	Creates a comment node containing the specified text
	`createDocumentFragment()`	Creates an empty `documentFragment` object
	`createEntityReference (referenceName)`	Creates an `entityReference` with the specified `referenceName`
	`createProcessingInstruction (target,text)`	Creates a `processingInstruction` node containing the specified target and text
`Node`	`attributes`	Returns a `NamedNodeMap` containing all attributes for this node
	`parentNode`	Returns the parent node for this node
	`childNodes`	Returns a `NodeList` containing all the child nodes for this node
	`firstChild`	Returns the first child node for this node
	`lastChild`	Returns the last child node for this node
	`prevousSibling`	Returns the previous sibling node
	`nextSibling`	Returns the next sibling node

Continued

Table 10.3 Properties and Methods Available to Objects Used by the DOM (continued)

Object	Property or Method	What It Does
	`nodeName`	Returns the `nodeName`, depending on the type
	`nodeType`	Returns the `nodeType` as a number
	`nodeValue`	Returns, or sets, the value of this node, depending on the type
	`OwnerDocument`	Returns the root node of the document
	`hasChildNodes()`	This method returns a true or false value, indicating whether the node in question has children nodes
	`appendChild(newChild)`	Appends the node `newChild` at the end of the child nodes for this node
	`removeChild()`	Removes the specified node
	`removeChild(nodeName)`	Removes the specified node, `nodeName`
`NodeList`	`length`	Returns the number of nodes in a `NodeList`
	`item(index)`	Returns a specific node in the `NodeList`
`NamedNodeMap`	`getNamedItem(name)`	Returns the name of a Node object
	`removeNamedItem(name)`	Returns the Node that is removed
	`setNamedItem(newNode)`	Appends a Node to the end of the `namedNodeMap`

Source: W3C.

Browser Support for the DOM

In spite of outward appearances, the parser in Microsoft Internet Explorer is not fully compatible with that found in the Mozilla browser. This has happened because the browsers have added their own custom extensions to their implementation of the W3C XML DOM.

How, then, can you ensure your client-side scripting is compatible under both Microsoft Internet Explorer and Mozilla? One easy answer would be to avoid all custom extensions. However, this would eliminate some critical functionality for working with XML data; as you saw earlier, the `load()` method for loading an XML file is specific to the Microsoft parser. One workaround could be to create what's called a **wrapper** to make the parser that doesn't support the extensions act as though it does.

Another more practical workaround is to write a conditional statement in your script to test to see what parser is in use, and then produce compatible code for each situation.

For example, the earlier code listings in this chapter used the following lines of code to retrieve and load an XML file using the Microsoft parser:

```
var xmlDoc = new ActiveXObject("Microsoft.XMLDOM")
xmlDoc.async="false"
xmlDoc.load("exchanges.xml")
```

With the Mozilla browser, though, this code would fail to load. Listing 10.7 shows how you could instead provide one way of retrieving and loading the `exchanges.xml` file into browser memory if the Microsoft parser is in use, and another method that complies with the DOM specification (used by Netscape and the Mozilla browsers).

LISTING 10.7

```
if (window.ActiveXObject){
var xmlDoc = new ActiveXObject("Microsoft.XMLDOM");
xmlDoc.async=false; //Enforce download of XML file first.
  IE only.
}
else if (document.implementation && document.implementation.
  createDocument)
var xmlDoc= document.implementation.
  createDocument("","doc",null);
xmlDoc.load("exchanges.xml");
```

The `if . . . else` statement comprises the conditional statement in use here. If Microsoft Internet Explorer (which uses the ActiveXObject for scripting) is in use, then `xmlDoc` is created. Otherwise, you query the document's implementation with `document.implementation` (which works for Netscape or Mozilla, but not Internet Explorer) and create an XML document using the standard means—the `createDocument()` method—provided by the DOM. The `load()` method was an extension created by Microsoft, but it has been adopted by Mozilla to ensure consistency with the Microsoft parser. At this point, the `load()` method retrieves the `exchanges.xml` file and loads it into the new document.

Summary

The advantages of scripting with the DOM include its simple and straightforward implementation. The tree structure of an XML document matches directly with the DOM tree structure; the variety of properties and methods available to a document's objects give you a lot of control over accessing and manipulating your XML data. Despite the usefulness of scripting with the DOM, though, the W3C recommends that Web developers utilize alternative techniques whenever possible if their computer tasks allow. The next two chapters on SVG and SMIL provide examples of emerging Web standards that could be utilized for developing multimedia content.

Key Terms

ancestor
Application Programming Interface (API)
Document Object Model (DOM)
DOM-based parser
child
client-side
conditional statement
descendant
event
event-based parser
handler
increments
leaf
looping statement
node
object-oriented programming
objects
parent
SAX-based parser
server-side
sibling
Simple API for XML (SAX)
tree-based parser
variable
wrapper
XML processor

Code Summary

1. **Both elements (e.g., restaurant) and attributes (e.g., cuisine) appear as nodes in a document tree structure):**

```
<?xml version="1.0" encoding="UTF-8"?>
<restaurants>
<restaurant cuisine="French">Lutece</restaurant>
<restaurant cuisine="Seafood">Pescatore</restaurant>
<restaurant cuisine ="Vegetarian">Zen Palate</restaurant>
</restaurants>
```

2. **Creating an XML document object with JavaScript:**

```
var xmlDoc = new ActiveXObject("Microsoft.XMLDOM")
```

3. **Loading and displaying XML data using JavaScript:**

```
<script type="text/javascript">
var xmlDoc = new ActiveXObject("Microsoft.XMLDOM")
xmlDoc.async="false"
xmlDoc.load("exchanges.xml")
document.write ("The first XML element in this file consists of the following: ");
document.write(xmlDoc.documentElement.firstChild.text);
</script>
```

4. **A sample XML file for use with Code Summary Example 3 above:**

```
<?xml version="1.0" ?>
<exchange>
<name>New York Stock Exchange</name>
<code>NYSE</code>
```

```
<url>www.nyse.com</url>
<phone>1-212-656-3000</phone>
<fax>1-212-656-5557</fax>
</exchange>
```

5. **A sample XHTML file containing the JavaScript script from Code Summary Example 3 above:**

```
<html xmlns="http://www.w3.org/1999/xhtml" xml:lang="en" lang="en">
   <head>
      <title>Exchange Directory: Sample</title>
   </head>
   <body>
<script type="text/javascript">
var xmlDoc = new ActiveXObject("Microsoft.XMLDOM")
xmlDoc.async="false"
xmlDoc.load("exchanges.xml")
document.write ("The first XML element in this file consists of the following: ");
document.write(xmlDoc.documentElement.firstChild.text);
</script>
   </body>
</html>
```

6. **An XHTML file that uses a JavaScript script with a looping statement to count and display the text values for all child nodes of the root element (**<exchange>**):**

```
<html xmlns="http://www.w3.org/1999/xhtml" xml:lang="en" lang="en">
   <head>
      <title>Exchange Directory: Sample</title>
   </head>
   <body>
<script type="text/javascript">
var xmlDoc = new ActiveXObject("Microsoft.XMLDOM");
xmlDoc.async="false"
xmlDoc.load("exchanges.xml")

// We move up the literal text we want displayed, in order to precede the looping statement
document.write ("The values recorded for the first exchange listed in
   this file are as follows: <br /><br />");

// The looping statement appears here
for (var n=0; n < xmlDoc.documentElement.childNodes.length; n++)
{
document.write (xmlDoc.documentElement.childNodes.item(n).text);
document.write ("<br />");
}

</script>
   </body>
</html>
```

7. **Cross-browser code for loading an XML file:**

```
if (window.ActiveXObject){
var xmlDoc = new ActiveXObject("Microsoft.XMLDOM");
xmlDoc.async=false;
}
else if (document.implementation && document.implementation.createDocument)
var xmlDoc= document.implementation.createDocument("","doc",null);
xmlDoc.load("exchanges.xml");
```

Review Questions

1. What are the benefits of client-side scripting with the W3C XML DOM over just using JavaScript within HTML pages?
2. What is an API (Application Programming Interface)?
3. How does DOM-based parsing differ from SAX-based parsing?
4. What are the relative merits of DOM-based parsing and SAX-based parsing?
5. How would you distinguish DOM Level 1, DOM Level 2, and DOM Level 3?
6. Describe object-oriented programming.
7. What are some relationships that nodes can have to each other in a document tree?
8. How do you indicate a comment in a JavaScript script?
9. What is the syntax for a `for` statement in JavaScript?
10. How do you load an XML document using the Microsoft parser?
11. How do you load an XML document according to the W3C DOM specification?

Case Study

Dynamic Drive, an online library Web site that provides DHTML scripts, offers the DOM XML Ticker script shown in Listing 10.8 on its site. (At publication time, this script could be accessed from http://www.dynamicdrive.com/dynamicindex2/xmlticker2.htm). Listing 10.9 is the sample `ticker.xml` file used by the script in Listing 10.8. Place Listing 10.9, which should be saved in a file named `ticker.xml`, within a new XHTML file and modify the sample messages in Listing 10.9. The results you see should be similar to those found in Figure 10.7.

LISTING 10.8

```
<script language="JavaScript1.2">
/*
DOM XML ticker- © Dynamic Drive (www.dynamicdrive.com)
For full source code, 100's more DHTML scripts, and Terms Of Use,
   visit http://www.dynamicdrive.com
Credit MUST stay intact
*/
//Container for ticker. Modify the STYLE attribute to customize style:
var tickercontainer='<div id="container" style="background-color:
   #FFFFE1;width:150px;height:120px;font:normal 13px Verdana;">
   </div>'

//Specify path to xml file
var xmlsource="ticker.xml"

////No need to edit beyond here///////////
//load xml file
if (window.ActiveXObject)
var xmlDoc = new ActiveXObject("Microsoft.XMLDOM");
else if (document.implementation && document.implementation.
   createDocument)
var xmlDoc= document.implementation.createDocument("","doc",null);
if (typeof xmlDoc!="undefined"){
```

```
document.write(tickercontainer)
xmlDoc.load(xmlsource)
}

//Regular expression used to match any non-whitespace character
var notWhitespace = /\S/

function init_ticker(){
//Cache "messages" element of xml file
tickerobj=xmlDoc.getElementsByTagName("xmlticker")[0]

//REMOVE white spaces in XML file. Intended mainly for NS6/Mozilla
for (i=0;i<tickerobj.childNodes.length;i++){
if ((tickerobj.childNodes[i].nodeType == 3)&&(!notWhitespace.
   test(tickerobj.childNodes[i].nodeValue))) {
tickerobj.removeChild(tickerobj.childNodes[i])
i-
}
}
document.getElementById("container").innerHTML=tickerobj.childNodes[1].
   firstChild.nodeValue
msglength=tickerobj.childNodes.length
currentmsg=2
themessage="
setInterval("rotatemsg()",tickerobj.childNodes[0].firstChild.
   nodeValue)
}

function rotatemsg(){
var msgsobj=tickerobj.childNodes[currentmsg]
if (msgsobj.getAttribute("url")!=null){
themessage='<a href="'+msgsobj.getAttribute("url")+'"'
if (msgsobj.getAttribute("target")!=null)
themessage+=' target="'+msgsobj.getAttribute("target")+'"'
themessage+='>'
}
themessage+=msgsobj.firstChild.nodeValue
if (msgsobj.getAttribute("url")!=null)
themessage+='</a>'

//Rotate msg and display it in DIV:
document.getElementById("container").innerHTML=themessage
currentmsg=(currentmsg<msglength-1)? currentmsg+1 : 1
themessage="
}

function fetchxml(){
if (xmlDoc.readyState==4)
init_ticker()
else
setTimeout("fetchxml()",10)
}

if (window.ActiveXObject)
fetchxml()
```

```
else if (typeof xmlDoc!="undefined")
xmlDoc.onload=init_ticker

</script>
```

LISTING 10.9

```
<?xml version="1.0"?>
<xmlticker>
<pause>3000</pause>
<message>Welcome to Dynamic Drive</message>
<message url="http://www.dynamicdrive.com">Link to Dynamic Drive
  </message>
<message url="http://www.javascriptkit.com" target="_blank">Check out
  JavaScriptKit.com</message>
<message>This is a sample text message</message>
<message>This is another sample text message</message>
</xmlticker>
```

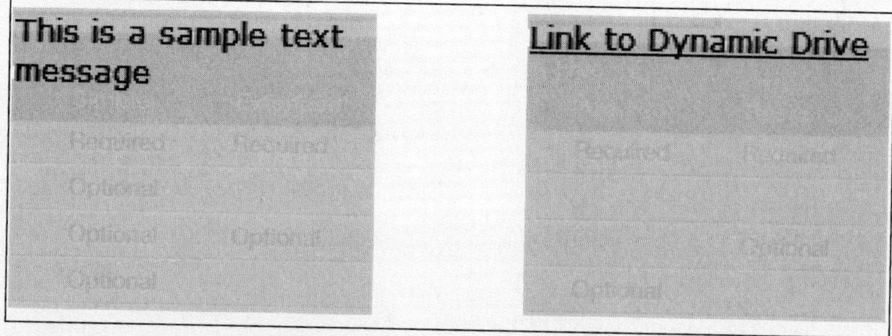

FIGURE 10.7 Retrieving and Displaying the Ticker Messages in Listing 10.9
You can control the style of the display within the XHTML with a stylesheet.

CHAPTER 11

Scalable Vector Graphics (SVG)

LEARNING OBJECTIVES

1. To learn the benefits of using SVG.
2. To create and render an image in the SVG Viewer.
3. To investigate the basic SVG syntax.
4. To create and style basic shapes.
5. To validate SVG and CSS.

So far we've looked at the core features of XML; for instance, schemas, DTDs, elements, attributes, and stylesheets, as well as XPath and XPointer among others. But XML is positioned to go far beyond just the raw exchange of information and data. With the introduction of Web services and wireless technologies, there are new uses for XML. The first one we will investigate is **SVG, or Scalable Vector Graphics.** Referencing specific mathematical algorithms to draw images in real time on a viewing screen creates an SVG image. This means these images can scale in real time and thus can be used in real time for different devices. And using different images in real time on different devices is going to become more commonplace in the future. The issue of creating two-dimensional images on the Web that renders the same on all browsers, and conceivably all devices, is problematic for designers and developers. If you are looking on a browser for your local news station and you want to see traffic and weather updates, it is relatively simple to click and have a pop-up window appear with that information. However, that same news Web page and pop-up would be problematic on a PDA or cell phone, where there is much less room to display information. So, in the case of weather, just a small screen with current temperature and forecast for that day would display, with the information extrapolated from the main Web site for the news station. CSS and XSL can only go so far in working around this problem. That is because, currently, images on the Web and most display devices are

Advice

SVG also can be used on a pocket PC mobile device using Windows CE from Microsoft and the **SVG Tiny** specification—http://www.w3.org/TR/SVGMobile/. You can take a look at this view at http://www.cmis.csiro.au/PocketSVG/. It allows users to view street maps, hand-held navigation systems, and even architectural maps on a portable device. You can even download the pocket SVG demo: http://www.cmis.csiro.au/PocketSVG/Download.htm.

bitmapped graphic (also referred to as raster) images. These images are composed of thousands of **pixels** that carry information about color, almost like the dots that make up newspaper images, except much smaller. The images do not compress very well in terms of how much information they must display and there is a constant trade-off between download time and image quality. Also, the bitmapped images do not scale well and render differently on different browsers.

SVG, which is based on a mathematical formula and coordinate system, is not constrained by pixel size. Using an internal, preset graph, vectors plot a series of coordinate points and instruct browsers on how to render these points as an image by using straight lines and curves through the use of **paths.** SVG also works with different basic shapes and can have many special effects and filters. You can easily animate images with it as well. Because SVG is derived from XML, it enjoys all the advantages of XML like portability and cross-platform compatibility. So let's take a look at what this means.

Advantages of SVG

SVG is the result of developments in XML by W3C. It is both **vector** and text based and combines graphics with programming that allows control not possible in standard Web-based graphics formats like .gif, .jpg, .png, and .bmp formats, which are bitmapped. Table 11.1 shows the differences between vector and bitmapped graphics.

TABLE 11.1 Vector versus Bitmapped Graphics

SVG	Bitmapped Graphics
Vector-based mathematical algorithm and XML code	Pixel based; each pixel contains color information
File extension: .svg	File extensions: .gif, .jpg, .png, .bmp
Not resolution dependent	Resolution dependent with fixed number of pixels
Does not lose resolution upon zooming image	Loses resolution upon zooming image
Keeps file size small and has a quick load time	File size over 50 KB can be problematic with slow load time

Because SVG is not dependent on resolution, one of the most important advantages it offers is a saving on bandwidth, critical in underserved geographic areas like rural farming communities or in using large interactive graphics like maps. It also calls upon a "color profile" so it can render color more accurately and with more consistency across different browsers and devices. The difference in color of pixel rendering between just Netscape and IE has caused many a Web designer in the past to pull an all-nighter trying to tweak a site to perfection. Other advantages of SVG are numerous. They include

- It is part of the official standard at W3C and therefore compatible with all XML standards.
- It is written in an XML-derived language.
- It is open source and interested committees can add on new facets of the standards.
- SVG is text-based and therefore can be edited by individuals.
- It is cross-browser compatible.
- Search engines can look for specific information.
- People with visual disabilities can access it.
- It is dynamic and can be updated.
- The graphics can be animated.
- Images can use **filters,** transformations, clips, and masks.
- Images can work with layers of transparency.
- Individual text can be copied, indexed, or, with **VoiceML,** spoken by the computer.
- SVG files can be exported from Illustrator, CorelDraw, WebDraw, and other packages.
- It can be used for both Web graphics and print medium.

SVG versus Flash

Web animation is an essential part of the normal way we all experience the Internet on an almost daily basis. Most people commonly think of Macromedia's Flash program as the leading program to use for animation. But SVG can create animation as well. Fortunately both are vector-based. Flash uses .swf files instead of SVG's .svg files. Some other compatibilities are that both allow hyperlinking, can connect to databases, and are scriptable, though Flash's Actionscript is proprietary, meaning it belongs only to Flash and cannot be opened or edited. So what is the big deal about SVG? The fact that it is **open source** is a huge advantage. This means the code can be read and edited by any user with access, and it is text-based as well. Flash code is binary and readable by machines only. And since SVG is a subset of XML, it is really not in competition with Flash to begin with. This means that SVG works perfectly

Advice

A complete list of native SVG editors can be found at the W3C's site: http://www.w3.org/Graphics/SVG/SVG-Implementations.htm8#svgedit.

Advice

SVG uses an XML DOM that can be scripted for interaction through JavaScript. Sometimes JavaScript in an SVG document can interact with JavaScript in the host Web page. This means client-side animations are possible.

Tech Tip

Older versions of browsers do not support SVG, including Opera 5.0 and Netscape 6.0 and 6.01. Oddly enough, Netscape 4.0 through 4.75 do support SVG. IE 4.0 and higher are supported as well. In Macintosh Systems versions 8.6 through 9.2 and 10.1, though not 10.0 through 10.0.4, support SVG. Netscape Navigator and Communicator versions 4.5 through 4.78 and Internet Explorer 5.0 or higher (unscripted SVG only) do support SVG. Netscape 6 for Macintosh is not supported for viewing SVG.

with XLink, XPointer, CSS2, or XSLT and even has its own DOM. It is compatible with Unicode and XHTML as well.

SVG Versions

SVG already exists as version 1.0 and that is the version we will be using. However, SVG 1.1 is now a recommended version and version 1.2 is being reviewed. There is also an SVG Mobile profile for mobile devices, and SVG Tiny for handheld devices.

SVG Viewer

There is currently no native browser support for SVG in the most popular browsers such as Netscape, IE, and Opera. However, that will change in the near future. There are a few open-source browsers that do support SVG like Mozilla (www.mozilla.org/projects/svg/) and X-Smiles, a Java-based viewer (www.x-smiles.org). Right now the common way to view SVG files is with a plug-in.

There are a number of common plug-ins available, but the most common one is the Adobe **SVG Viewer.** Batik, an open-source project, and IBM also offer viewers. For this chapter, we will be using the freely available Adobe SVG Reader. The link for the Adobe SVG Reader for both PCs and Macintosh, as of this writing, is version 3.0 and is available at http://www.adobe.com/support/downloads/main.html. After you have downloaded and installed your viewer, you will be ready to look at an SVG-enabled image.

Images rendered on a screen are actually all **bitmaps.** However, the most important point of any program is at which point the image becomes a bitmap. A program like Adobe Photoshop does the job for you and all you have to figure out is if the image should be a GIF or JPEG.

SVG keeps the code text-based and easily editable until it renders as a bitmap from the machine of the person viewing the image, or the "client" machine. So the SVG Viewer takes the responsibility of rendering the image, not a separate program.

Figure 11.1 shows a blank SVG **viewport,** which is the most basic blank area inside an SVG workspace. When first setting up the root `<svg>` element, at the same time a rectangular viewing area is set up called the *viewport.* It is possible to have more than one `<svg>` element in a document, but each time that is done, a new viewport is created. The size of the viewport is controlled by attributes such as `height` and `width`. A viewport is like looking at an empty window frame or canvas. In a moment we will start adding figures.

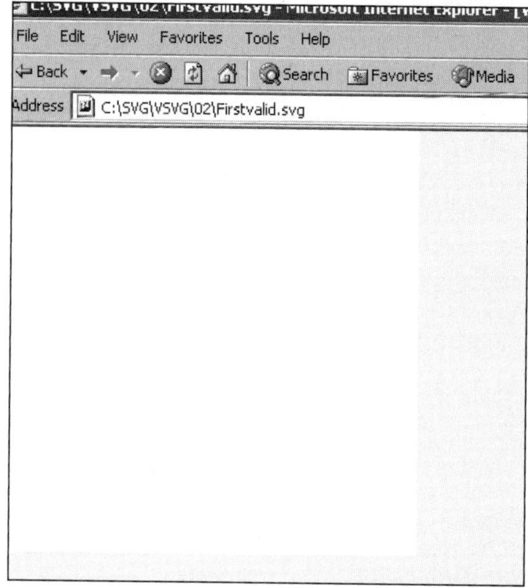

FIGURE 11.1 A Look at an Empty SVG Working Area Called the Viewport
Notice that it is a white box inside a slightly light gray area.

Introducing SVG Syntax

SVG syntax is very similar to XML syntax, except it works with many graphical terms. For those of you who are Web designers, you will find it easy to adapt. For non-Web designers, the code is easy to familiarize yourself with.

LISTING 11.1

```
<?xml version="1.0" standalone="no"?>
<!DOCTYPE svg PUBLIC "-//W3C//DTD SVG 1.0//EN"
"http://www.w3.org/TR/2001/REC-SVG-20010904/DTD/
  svg10.dtd">
<svg width="300" height="300">
<circle cx="150" cy="150" r="70" style="fill:green;
stroke:black; stroke-width:2;"/>
</svg>
```

Listing 11.1 begins with the standard XML processing instruction and `standalone` is set to `"no"`. The `svg10.dtd` is referenced from the site of W3C, an external DTD. The root SVG statement `<svg>` starts the beginning

Alert

In SVG all attribute values must be in either single or double quotes or the image will not render correctly. Therefore, `attribute=value` is incorrect, but `attribute="value"` is correct and `attribute='value'` is also correct. It does not matter which one you use, but you must use the same single or double quote to start and finish an attribute value.

of the SVG code. Elements describe the kinds of objects to place inside a file. The `width` and `height` attributes here set up a standard viewport, or viewing area. A circle is created using the circle elements with `cx` and `cy` attributes. In order to further control the attributes, they are given values. These attributes describe the *x* and *y* coordinates of the circle, hence the `cx` and `cy` with `r` being the radius. The value units are in pixels, though other units of measurement can be used such as inches or centimeters. The default value in SVG is pixels. The style attribute comes next with the values of `fill`, `stroke`, and `stroke-width`, and all of these have a further specifier such as `green`, `black`, or `2`. The root SVG statement is then closed with the `</svg>` tag. It is really that simple. (See Figure 11.2.)

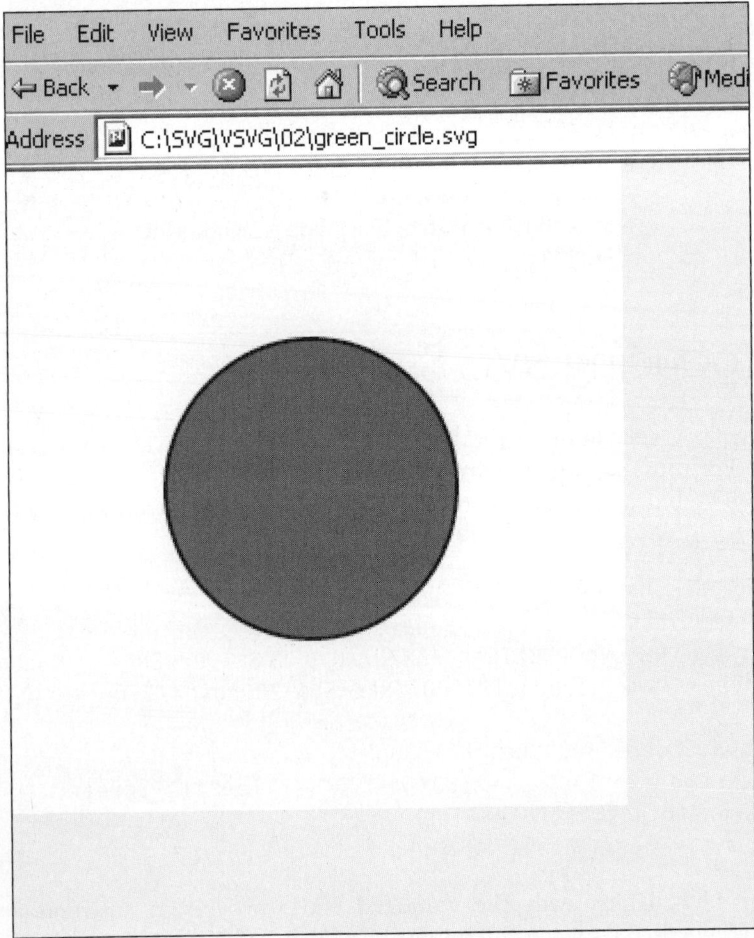

FIGURE 11.2 A Simple Circle in SVG

The SVG Viewport

When you start an SVG statement with the root SVG element `<svg>`, at the same time, due to the internal structure of SVG, you are setting up a specialized rectangular viewing area that graphics and text will appear within. We saw this in Figure 11.1 as the blank white square inside the gray area. Again, as mentioned above, this is called the viewport.

Tech Tip

You can have more than one `<svg>` element in an SVG statement. However, each time you have a new `<svg>` element, a new viewport will be created at the same time.

Viewport Defaults

As a default, the SVG Viewer makes the viewport 100 percent of the width and height of the browser. That is why it is so important to set the width and height attributes. If no `x` or `y` coordinates are specified for an element, the default is "0, 0". This is true with one exception. It does not apply to the attributes of the root `<svg>` element. The `x` coordinate starts in the upper left corner of the viewport.

Tech Tip

The `x` and `y` attributes of the root `<svg>` element are always set at "0,0".

Nested Viewports

SVG can have nested viewports by having `<svg>` elements nested inside one another. The main reason is to allow you to space information inside of each one the way you choose to.

The code for the centered **nested viewport** in Figure 11.3 is shown in Listing 11.2.

LISTING 11.2

```
<?xml version="1.0" standalone="no"?>
<!DOCTYPE svg PUBLIC "-//W3C//DTD SVG 1.0//EN"
"http://www.w3.org/TR/2001/REC-SVG-20010904/DTD/
  svg10.dtd">
<svg width="500" height="400" x="0" y="0">
<svg width="300" height="300" x="100" y="50">
<rect x="0" y="0" width="300" height="300" style=
  "stroke:red; stroke-width:2; fill:blue;
    fill-opacity:.25"/>
<text x="30" y="50" style="font-family:arial;
  font-size:28; fill:red">
Centered Viewport</text>
</svg>
</svg>
```

We start with the root `<svg>` element with a `width` of 500 pixels and a `height` of 400 pixels. Because it is the root element, it also sets up the viewport. The `x` and `y` coordinates of the root element are not set, because, as we said above, the root element's `x` and `y` coordinates always default to 0,0. Then

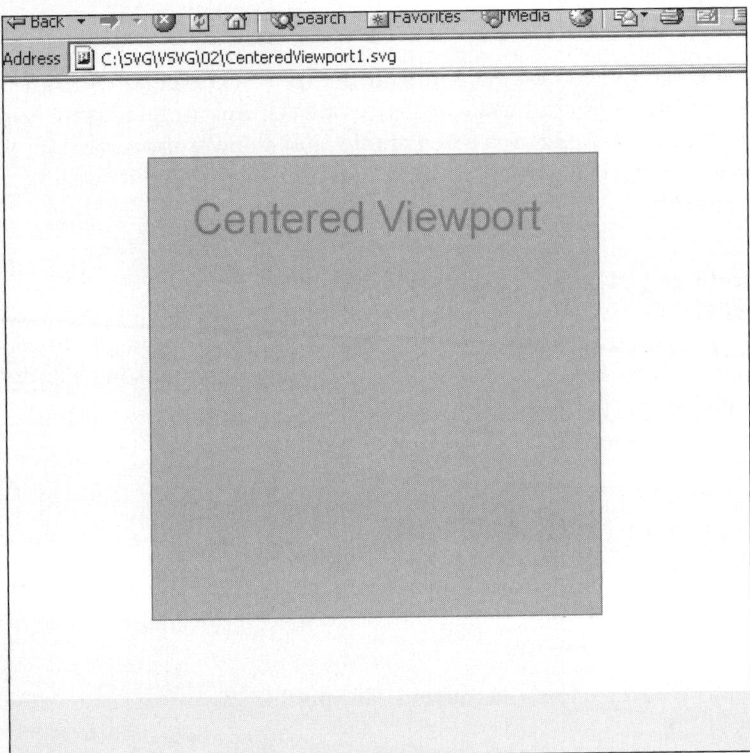

FIGURE 11.3 A Centered Nested Viewport

a second <svg> element follows the first. It has a smaller width and height of 300 by 300 pixels. Setting it at the `x` coordinate of 100 and `y` coordinate of 50 nests it right in the middle of the larger root <svg> element's viewport.

Now we make a rectangle exactly the same dimension as the inner viewport with a `width` and `height` of 300 respectively as well. The rectangle's `x` and `y` coordinates are also set to 0. The rectangle is set at the top left corner of the inner viewport. The `style` attribute of the rectangle is used and outlined in red. Then it is filled in blue with an **opacity,** or degree of fading in an image, of .25. For this example, it is important to have some text, so the `x` and `y` coordinates of the `text` are set at 30, 50. It has a `font-family` of Arial and a `font-size` of 28 points. The text is also filled in with the color red. The first </svg> tag closes the nested <svg> element and the next </svg> tag closes the root <svg> element.

The *preserveAspectRatio* Attribute

One of the great things about SVG is that it snaps to the size of the browser or device it uses for display purposes. This is very important when planning multiple uses. For instance, what if your TV station had the weather report on its

Web site, and then you wanted to have the small display of the storm moving into your area downloaded onto your wireless PDA. These scenarios are going to become more and more common in the future, as made clear by the CSIRO viewer and SVG Tiny and looking at weather reports and roadmaps on a small mobile device. The **preserveAspectRatio** attribute works in conjunction with the `viewBox` attribute to allow control over an image to keep its original proportions or distort them into the viewing area.

Tech Tip

`preserveAspectRatio` will only work when the `viewBox` attribute is also used on an element.

`viewBox` attribute So let's take a quick look at the `viewBox` attribute, which is necessary to use with `preserveAspectRatio`. Think of it as a *moveable* window. The size of an SVG canvas viewing area is potentially infinite. The `viewBox` attribute narrows it down to specific measurements. In Listing 11.3 you can see the code.

Alert

Be careful not to confuse the `viewBox` with the viewport.

LISTING 11.3

```
<?xml version="1.0" standalone="no"?>
<!DOCTYPE svg PUBLIC "-//W3C//DTD SVG 1.0//EN"
"http://www.w3.org/TR/2001/REC-SVG-20010904/DTD/
  svg10.dtd">
```

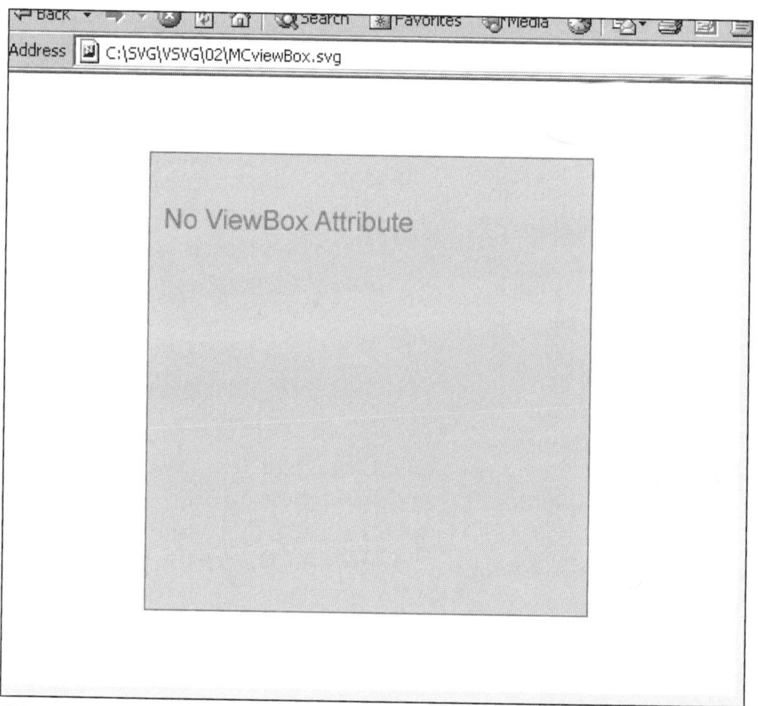

FIGURE 11.4 A Nested Viewport without *viewBox* Attribute Applied

```
<svg width="500" height="400" x="0" y="0" >
<svg width="300" height="300" x="100" y="50" >
<rect x="0" y="0" width="300" height="300"
style="stroke:red; stroke-width:2; fill:grey;
  fill-opacity:.25"/>
<text x="10" y="50" style="font-size:18;
  font-family:arial; fill:red">
No ViewBox Attribute </text>
</svg>
</svg>
```

Figure 11.4 is a nested viewport similar to Figure 11.3. Now let's look at the same viewport with the same code, but with the `viewBox` attribute applied to the outmost <svg> element (see Figure 11.5).

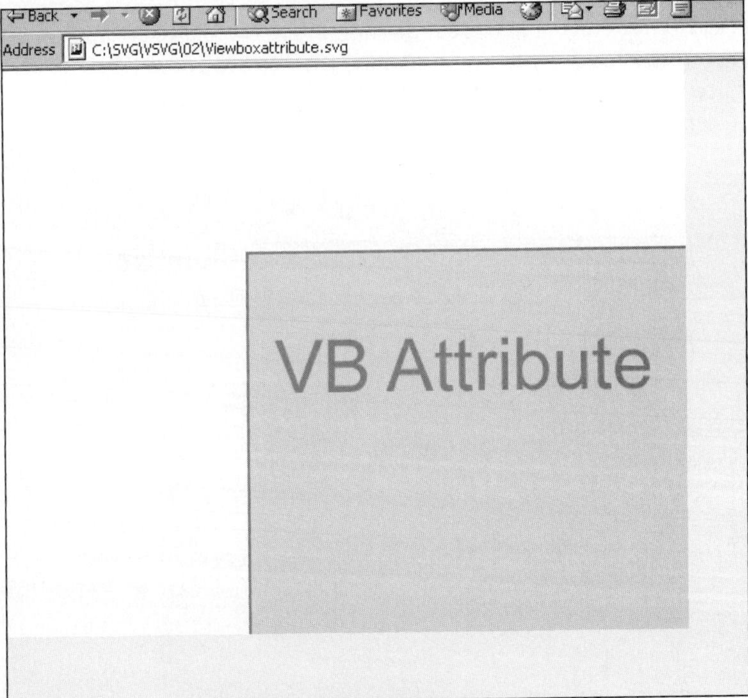

FIGURE 11.5 Viewport with *viewBox* Attribute

Here it looks like we've zoomed in on the upper left corner of the image and the text inside that image. Well, that is true. But what we don't see is that the `viewBox` attribute created a separate rectangular area using number (4 in this case, as it is a rectangle) that we have specified. Let's look at the code in Listing 11.4.

LISTING 11.4

```
<?xml version="1.0" standalone="no"?>
<!DOCTYPE svg PUBLIC "-//W3C//DTD SVG 1.0//EN"
"http://www.w3.org/TR/2001/REC-SVG-20010904/
  DTD/svg10.dtd">
<svg width="500" height="400" x="0" y="0"
  <?xml version="1.0" standalone="no"?>
<!DOCTYPE svg PUBLIC "-//W3C//DTD SVG 1.0//EN"
"http://www.w3.org/TR/2001/REC-SVG-20010904/
  DTD/svg10.dtd">
<svg width="500" height="400" x="0" y="0"
  viewBox="10 10 250 150”>
<svg width="300" height="300" x="100" y="50">
<rect x="0" y="0" width="300" height="300"
style=”stroke:red; stroke-width:2; fill:grey;
  fill-opacity:.25"/>
<text x="10" y="50" style="font-size:26;
  font-family:arial; fill:red">
VB Attribute</text>
</svg>
</svg>
<svg width="300" height="300" x="100" y="50">
<rect x="0" y="0" width="300" height="300"
style="stroke:red; stroke-width:2; fill:grey;
  fill-opacity:.25"/>
<text x="10" y="50" style="font-size:26;
  font-family:arial; fill:red">
VB Attribute</text>
</svg>
</svg>
```

Comparing the two codes, the only difference is the insertion, after the <svg> root element of `viewBox="10 10 250 150"`. The numbers (10 10 250 150) mean the following: The first two (10 10) are the `x` and `y` coordinates of the upper left corner of the `viewBox`. The second set of numbers (250 150) define the lower right corner of the `viewbox`. This area is smaller than the area of the viewport.

Creating the preserveAspectRatio `PreserveAspectRatio` is used with the viewBox attribute for a very important purpose—the combination allows sized drawings to fit in any viewing area. Even more important, it allows control of the drawing as to whether it keeps its original proportions or distorts to fit in the viewing area. Figure 11.6 is an image of an ellipse with the text “STRETChIT”; the code is in Listing 11.5.

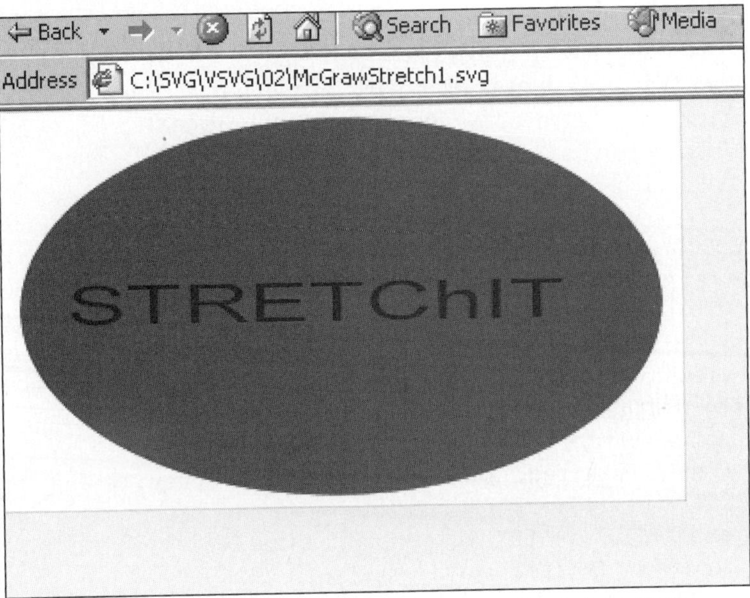

FIGURE 11.6 Viewport with a *width* of 350 and a height of 200

LISTING 11.5

```
<?xml version="1.0" standalone="no"?>
<!DOCTYPE svg PUBLIC "-//W3C//DTD SVG 1.0//EN"
"http://www.w3.org/TR/2001/REC-SVG-20010904/
  DTD/svg10.dtd">
<svg width="350" height="200" viewBox="0 0 1500 1500"
  preserveAspectRatio="none">
<rect x="0" y="0" width="1500" height="1500" style=
  "stroke:red; stroke-width:2; fill:none"/>
<circle cx="750" cy="750" r="700" style="fill:blue;
  stroke:navy; stroke-width:3"/>
<text x="150" y="800" style="font-size:200;
  font-family:arial; fill:black">
STRETChIT</text>
</svg>
```

Now we will change the viewport size and keep the `preserveAspectRatio`, which is currently set to `"none"` (see Figure 11.7).

With the viewport sized smaller, and the `preserveAspectRatio` set to `none`, the image squeezes, which means it is not sized uniformly. The only thing changed from the code above is the size of the viewport. Think of this happening with an image migrating from your computer to your cell phone. It could be quite problematic in the way that it scales down in size. Listed in Tables 11.2 and 11.3 are different ways to preserve the aspect ratio.

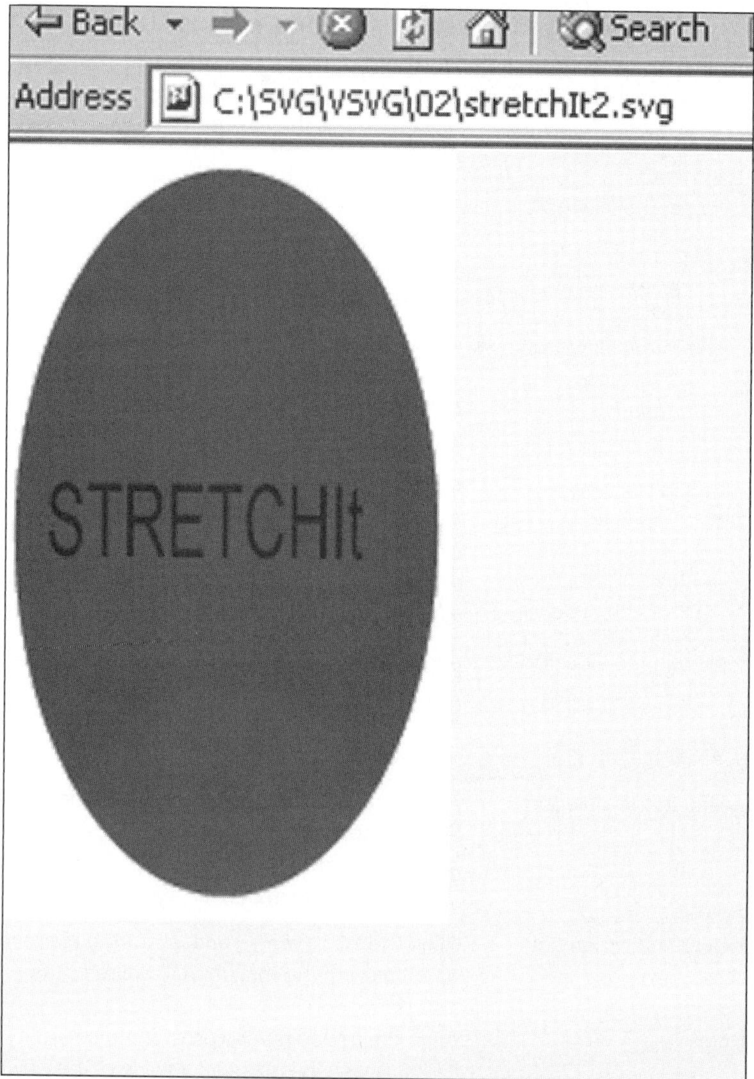

FIGURE 11.7 Viewport with a *width* of 150 and a height of 250

Let's take a look at using <meet>. The viewport in Figure 11.8 has the same dimensions as in Figure 11.7, 150 pixels wide by 250 pixels high. The meet attribute scales the image uniformly inside the viewport. The new code for this is as follows:

```
<svg width="150" height="250" viewBox="0 0 1500 1500"
  preserveAspectRatio="xMinYMin meet">
```

TABLE 11.2 *preserveAspectRatio* **Attribute Parameters and Options Using** *<align>*

Options	Scale	Description
none	Will not scale objects within the viewport	Objects will fill the viewport no matter what their size.
xMinYMin	Forces uniform scaling in the viewport	Align the <min-x> of the element's viewBox with the smallest X value of the viewport. Align the <min-y> of the element's viewBox with the smallest Y value of the viewport.
xMidYMin	Forces uniform scaling in the viewport	Align the midpoint X value of the element's viewBox with the midpoint X value of the viewport. Align the <min-y> of the element's viewBox with the smallest Y value of the viewport.
xMaxYMin	Forces uniform scaling in the viewport	Align the <min-x>+<width> of the element's viewBox with the maximum X value of the viewport. Align the <min-y> of the element's viewBox with the smallest Y value of the viewport.
xMinYMid	Forces uniform scaling in the viewport	Align the <min-x> of the element's viewBox with the smallest X value of the viewport. Align the midpoint Y value of the element's viewBox with the midpoint Y value of the viewport.
xMidYMid	Forces uniform scaling in the viewport	Align the midpoint X value of the element's viewBox with the midpoint X value of the viewport. Align the midpoint Y value of the element's viewBox with the midpoint Y value of the viewport.
xMaxYMid	Forces uniform scaling in the viewport	Align the <min-x>+<width> of the element's viewBox with the maximum X value of the viewport. Align the midpoint Y value of the element's viewBox with the midpoint Y value of the viewport.
xMinYMax	Forces uniform scaling in the viewport	Align the <min-x> of the element's viewBox with the smallest X value of the viewport. Align the <min-y>+<height> of the element's viewBox with the maximum Y value of the viewport.
xMidYMax	Forces uniform scaling in the viewport	Align the midpoint X value of the element's viewBox with the midpoint X value of the viewport. Align the <min-y>+<height> of the element's viewBox with the maximum Y value of the viewport.

Source : W3C.org.

TABLE 11.3 *preserveAspectRatio* **Attribute Parameters and Options Using** *<meetOrSlice>*

Options	Scale	Description
meet	Forces uniform scaling in the viewport	Keeps the image intact and sizes it by making it only as large as the entire viewBox
slice	Forces uniform scaling in the viewport	Does not keep the image intact and slices off parts of the image that extend outside the viewBox

Source: W3C.org.

Tech Tip

The <meetOrSlice> attribute is optional and should be separated from <align> by one or more spaces.

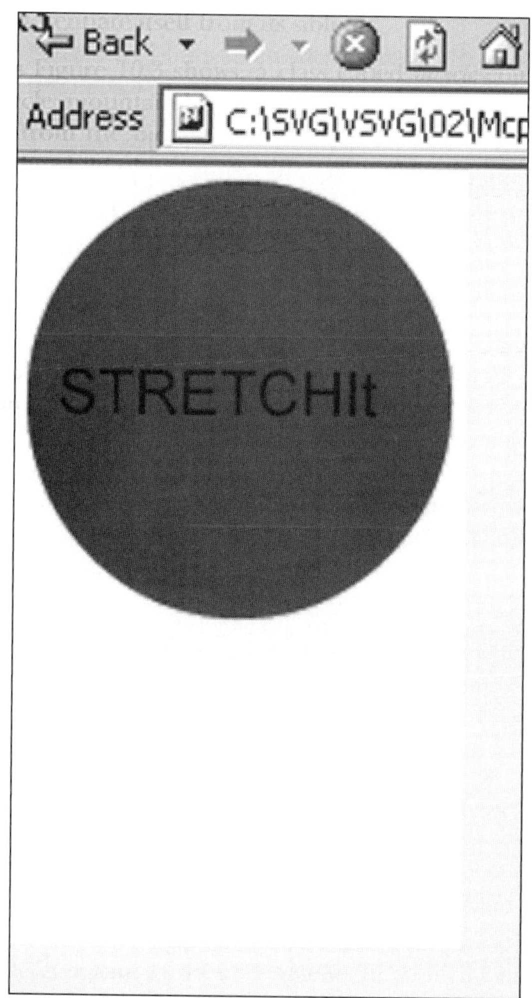

FIGURE 11.8 Using *<meet>* to Scale an Image Uniformly within the Viewport

Notice also that `meet` takes on `xMinYMin`. This means it scales uniformly no matter what size the viewport is, and `meet` will stretch to fit the edges.

Basic Shapes

SVG works with just a few basic shapes. They are

- Circles `<circle>`
- Ellipse `<ellipse>`
- Lines `<line>`
- Rectangles (including with rounded corners) `<rect>`
- Polygons `<polygon>`
- Polylines `<polyline>`

Polygons are closed shapes made up of straight line segments. **Polylines** are open shapes consisting of straight line segments defined by a series of numbers. All shapes can be stroked, filled, and used as part of a clipping path. Stroking paints along the outline of a shape, filling fills the inside of a shape, and clipping is the same as in CSS2, in that it defines what part of a shape is going to be made visible. We will look at stroking, filling, and more shapes shortly.

Table 11.4 gives the basic shapes and their attributes.

The <g> Group Element

Grouping images together is a very common graphic trick that takes two or more graphic objects and makes them into one object (see Figure 11.9). The <g> or **group element** is referred to as a **container element,** which means it can contain other elements or groups of elements. Container elements also help streamline code, as you can see in Listing 11.6.

LISTING 11.6

```
<?xml version="1.0" standalone="no"?>
<!DOCTYPE svg PUBLIC "-//W3C//DTD SVG 1.0//EN"
"http://www.w3.org/TR/2001/REC-SVG-20010904/
  DTD/svg10.dtd">
<svg width="500" height="500">
<g id="3littleRectangles">
<desc>Group of 3 rectangles</desc>
<rect x="120" y="120" width="120" height="70"
style="fill:blue; stroke:rgb(0,0,128);
stroke-width:3; opacity:0.5"/>
<rect x="160" y="160" width="120" height="70"
style="fill:blue; stroke:rgb(0,0,128);
stroke-width:3; opacity:0.75"/>
<rect x="200" y="200" width="120" height="70"
```

TABLE 11.4 Basic Shape Elements and Attributes

Element	Attribute	Description
`<circle>`	cx	x coordinate position of center point of circle
	cy	y coordinate position of center point of circle
	r	Radius of the circle
`<ellipse>`	cx	x coordinate position of center point of circle
	cy	y coordinate position of center point of circle
	rx	x axis (horizontal) radius of ellipse
	ry	y axis (vertical) radius of ellipse
`<line>`	x1	x coordinate position of the beginning of the line
	y1	y coordinate position of the beginning of the line
	x2	x coordinate position of the end of the line
	y2	y coordinate position of the end of the line
`<rect>`	x	x coordinate position of upper left corner
	y	y coordinate position of upper left corner
	rx	Rounded rectangle only; x axis radius of ellipse to round corner
	ry	Rounded rectangle only; y axis radius of ellipse to round corner
	width	Width of rectangle
	height	Height of rectangle

```
style="fill:blue; stroke:rgb(0,0,128);
stroke-width:3; opacity:1"/>
</g>
</svg>
```

The code begins with the XML declaration and `Doctype`, the standard SVG 1.0 DTD. The `width` and `height` of the viewport are set to 500 pixels each. Then the group element begins using the `<g>` tag. Anything that is inside of this `<g>` element is grouped together as one element. If we ever want to use this group again (a good idea for long-term code reuse), it is given the `id` attribute of `3little Rectangles`.

The `<desc>` Description Element This is a new element, the **description element.** It is similar to a comment, but there is one important difference. The `<desc>` element is set up to allow rendering into other forms such as Braille

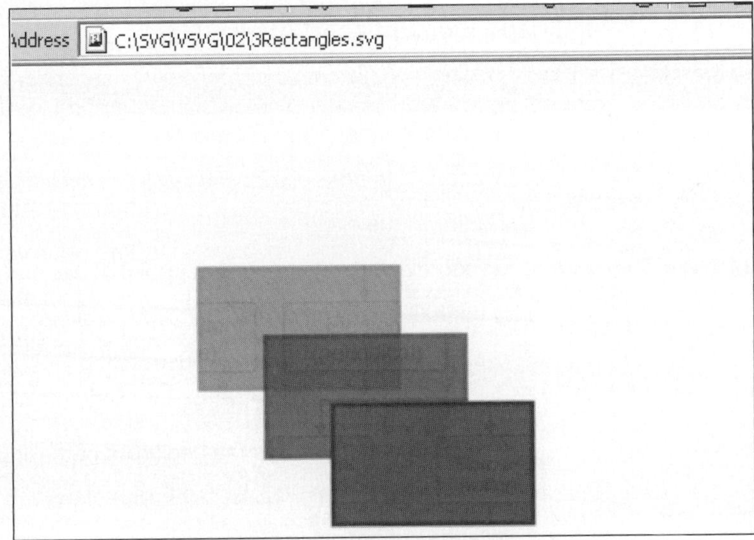

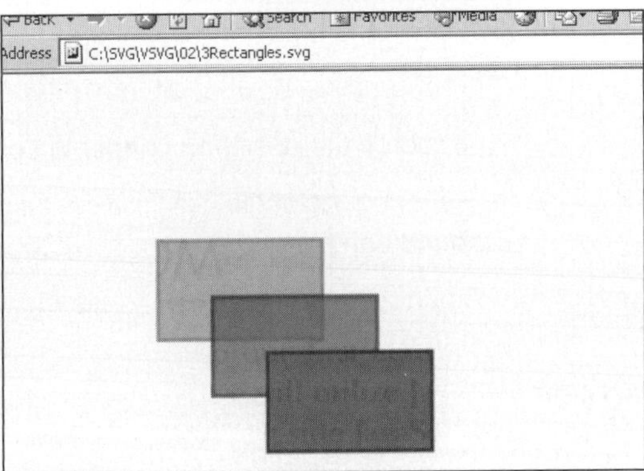

FIGURE 11.9 Three Rectangles Used to Make a Group

or VoiceML, a speech recognition XML. This makes it ideal for people with disabilities. However, <desc>, like a comment, does not render in a browser.

The <rect> tag begins the first of the three rectangles, which share the same color, size, and outline width. The `width, 120 pixels, and height`, 70 pixels, stay consistent. The `x` and `y` coordinate points change from 120 to 160 to 200 pixels and have different opacities. `opacity` can be set between 0, which is completely transparent, and 1, completely opaque. The first `opacity` is 0.5, which is half transparent. The next is set to .75 and the final one is set to 1. The `fill` is set to an SVG-enabled color, `blue`, but the `stroke` uses an **RGB value** as part of the `style` attribute. </g> closes the group and </svg> closes the root SVG element and ends the document.

Alert

You can use both SVG colors and RGB values together in a statement to have a wider range to choose from.

A Small Word About Color Color is a huge topic in SVG. The way SVG vector graphics render colors is more accurate than the way bitmaps using hex equivalents of RGB render color because SVG uses the guidelines of the International Color Consortium (ICC), http://www.color.org/, a cross-platform device specification. The actual site where you can see a list of recognized color keyword names and their associative RGB values for SVG is at http://www.w3.org/TR/SVG/types.html#ColorKeywords.

Filling, Stroking, and Opacity The way you are able to actually see color in SVG is to either `fill` an object, which paints the inside of it, or `stroke` an object, which colors the outline of the object's shape. Objects are painted in the order they appear in code, with the first instance being laid down on the bottom and other instances layering on top. This is important to keep in mind when making intricate shapes. Also, the `fill` is always painted first, and the `stroke` comes after it. `opacity` is a number from 0 to 1, with 0 being totally transparent and 1 being totally opaque. The default is opaque.

```
style="fill:blue; stroke:rgb(0,0,128);
stroke-width:3; opacity:0.5"/>
```

This code example is taken from the three rectangles we previously used. The `style` element usually, but not always has the `fill`, `stroke`, and other attribute values such as `stroke-width` (very important or you can't see the `stroke`) and, if called for, `opacity`.

`Transform` Attributes The `transform` **attribute** transforms or shifts an original coordinate system from one location in a viewport to another location along an `xy` coordinate system. The `transform` attribute does not transform separate elements but actually creates a new coordinate system and viewport within the original viewport. When you move a coordinate system to new `x` and `y` coordinate points, the new system's upper left corner is at the new `x`, `y` point instead of the old coordinate system's default of (0,0). This change is referred to as the `translate` value of the `transform` attribute. That way the unique spatial relationships are maintained.

Suppose you had a circle and wanted to make it larger. This size change could potentially disturb the circle's relationship to all the other objects in a drawing. The correct way to apply transformations to objects is by using the `<g>` element, which we learned about above. In fact, that is the main reason for the `<g>` element. It is set up to function as much more than just a simple group tag.

Table 11.5 gives the values for the `transform` attributes.

The `translate` Transformation Translate really means "move." The `translate` attribute creates a new coordinate system that moves the old coordinate

TABLE 11.5 `transform` **Attributes and Values**

Attribute	Syntax	Definition
`rotate`	`transform="rotate(degrees)"`	Rotates a new coordinate system by the amount of degrees specified inside the parentheses.
`scale`	`transform="scale(value)"` `transform="scale(x scale value, y scale value)"`	Scales a new coordinate system. It does this by multiplying all the coordinates by the number inside the parentheses (if only one number) or the x coordinates by the first number and the y coordinates by the second number.
`skewX`	`transform="skewX (degrees of skew)"`	Skews the x axis by the degree in the parentheses.
`skewY`	`transform="skewY (degrees of skew)"`	Skews the y axis by the degree in the parentheses.
`translate`	`transform="translate (x coordinate, y coordinate)"`	Moves the new coordinate system to the x and y coordinates specified by the numbers in parentheses.

system to the new x and y coordinates. Listing 11.7 gives the original code for an image and its new location through the `translate` **transformation.**

LISTING 11.7

```
<?xml version="1.0" standalone="no"?>
<!DOCTYPE svg PUBLIC "-//W3C//DTD SVG 1.0//EN"
"http://www.w3.org/TR/2001/REC-SVG-20010904/
  DTD/svg10.dtd">
<svg width="400" height="200">
<desc>Original coordinate system</desc>
<g style="fill:none; stroke:black; stroke-width:2">
<desc>How to draw x and y axes showing the
  dimensions of the original coordinate system</desc>
<line x1="3" y1="3" x2="400" y2="3"/>
<line x1="3" y1="3" x2="3" y2="200"/>
</g>
<g><ellipse cx="130" cy="50" rx="100" ry="40"
style="fill:blue; fill-opacity:.5; stroke:purple;
  stroke-width:2"/>
<text>
  <tspan x="85" y="45" style="font-size:20;
```

```
font-family:ariel; fill:#dedeba; stroke:#dedeba">
Original</tspan> <tspan x="45" y="70" style=
  "font-size:20;
font-family:arial; fill:#dedeba; stroke:#dedeba">
Coordinates</tspan>
</text>
</g>
<!--New coordinate system, moved to 150 x and 95 y-->
<g transform="translate(150,95)">
<g style="fill:none; stroke:black; stroke-width:2">
<!-- draw new axis lines to show the difference -->
  <line x1="0" y1="0" x2="100" y2="0"/>
  <line x1="0" y1="0" x2="0" y2="100"/>
</g>
  <ellipse cx="130" cy="50" rx="100" ry="40"
  style="fill:blue; fill-opacity:.5;
  stroke:purple; stroke-width:2"/>
  <text>
  <tspan x="85" y="45" style="font-size:20;
  font-family:ariel; fill:#dedeba; stroke:#dedeba">
  New</tspan> <tspan x="45" y="70" style="font-size:20;
    font-family:arial; fill:#dedeba; stroke:#dedeba">
  Coordinates</tspan>
  </text>
</g>
</svg>
```

The text that is italicized is the original code, the image of the ellipse in the left-hand side of Figure 11.10. The plain text is all of the new code and the image on the right side of the figure. Notice how, after the <desc> element, the group element <g> is used. Everything that is between the <g> and </g> tags is part of the group. This includes the attributes of style. In this case, the style is fill:blue, fill-opacity:.5, stroke:purple, and stroke-width:2. Two lines are drawn, one for the x **axis** and one for the y **axis.**

```
<line x1="3" y1="3" x2="400" y2="3"/>
<line x1="3" y1="3" x2="3" y2="200"/>
```

The first line is the x axis and is a black horizontal line on the top that reaches to the end of the x coordinate, which is the <svg> width of 400. The next line draws the y axis, a vertical line along the left side. The coordinates are given the number 3 so you can see them; if they were given the number 0, you couldn't really see them. Also, because the lines are included within the <g> element, they reference the style attributes of the <g> tag.

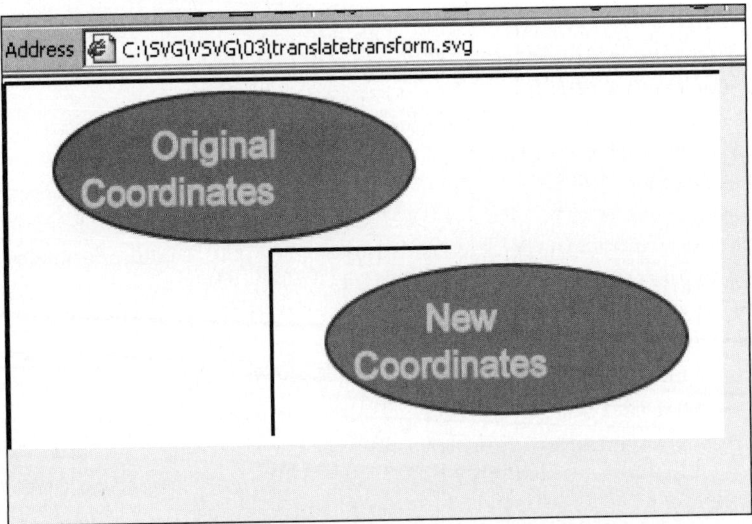

FIGURE 11.10 Original Coordinate System and a New One That Uses `transform="translate(150,95)"` to Move the Image to a New Location

A second <g> tag opens up another group in the original image, but this one has no `style` attributes because there are no styles common to all the elements in this <g> group. An `ellipse` element is added with `style` attributes. The `cx` and `cy` attributes set the center of the ellipse at 130x and 150y.

```
ellipse cx="130" cy="50" rx="100" ry="40"
```

Without going into <tspan> very deeply because since there is only one chapter on SVG, we can say that the <tspan> element adjusts text properties inside of a <text> element. Here it creates the text "Original Coordinates" and places it into the ellipse.

We create a second ellipse and move it to new coordinates with the following code inside the group element:

```
g transform="translate(150,95)"
```

And this moves it to the new coordinates of 150 and 95.

More Element Shapes: Circle Element

The basic difference between a rectangle, like we used in the group rectangle example previously, and a circle is a radius. A circle needs center `x` and `y` coordinates as well as a radius or center point. A rectangle starts in the upper left corner. A circle starts at a center point. If no `cx` and `cy` values are set in a circle, SVG assigns them the default value of zero. That means the center point of the circle will be set in the upper left corner of the viewport, as you can see in Listing 11.8.

LISTING 11.8

```
<?xml version="1.0" standalone="no"?>
<!DOCTYPE svg PUBLIC "-//W3C//DTD SVG 1.0//EN"
"http://www.w3.org/TR/2001/REC-SVG-20010904/DTD/
  svg10.dtd">
<svg width="400" height="400">
<rect x="50" y="50" width="300" height="300"
style="fill:peachpuff; fill-opacity:.75; stroke:orange;
  stroke-width:4"/>
<circle cx="200" cy="200" r="50" style="fill:gold"/>
</svg>
```

With just a few simple lines of code after the XML declaration, we were able to create an SVG viewport of 400 pixels by 400 pixels, a rectangle with `x` and `y` values of 50 and `height` and `width` of 300. It is styled with a peachpuff-colored `fill`, an `opacity` of .75 that has an orange `stroke` with a `stroke-width` of 4. Inside of the rectangle, we have a circle with a radius of 50 pixels and `cx` and `cy` values of 200 with a gold `fill` (it may appear middle gray in your book, but not in your browser). See Figure 11.11.

SVG and CSS Stylesheets

So far, styles have been used to style only individual objects. As you have seen in Chapter 7 on CSS, stylesheets are essential when working with large projects that require multiple styling changes and transformations. Styling allows the user to separate the presentational aspects of an element from the strictly structural aspects of the element in a separate document, usually a CSS document. Styles have properties that are defined by values, such as a color property being defined by an RGB value. The properties are separated by semicolons (;).

The `style` element in SVG allows a CSS to be embedded within the document. Different elements can be assigned different styles by using a **class selector** and **class attribute.** A class selector is defined within the actual stylesheet. Then it is referenced in the class attribute of an element.

LISTING 11.9

```
<?xml version="1.0" standalone="no"?>
<!DOCTYPE svg PUBLIC "-//W3C//DTD SVG 1.0//EN"
"http://www.w3.org/TR/2001/REC-SVG-20010904/DTD/
  svg10.dtd">
<svg width="500" height="500">
<defs> <style type="text/css">
<![CDATA[
  circle.newStyle {
```

FIGURE 11.11 Circle Nested Inside a Rectangle with *stroke* and *fill*

```
    fill:blue;
    stroke:red;
    stroke-width:4
    }
    ]]></style>
  </defs>
  <circle cx="200" cy="200" r="70" class="newStyle"/>
  </svg>
```

Now let's examine the code in Listing 11.9 (the output is displayed in Figure 11.12). Starting after the `<defs>` element, the `style` element is assigned a `type`, because without it the browser cannot recognize the stylesheet. It is called `"text/css"` so the browser knows it is a CSS as per the W3C. Next the stylesheet is put inside a `<![CDATA[. . .]]>` block. This is used so the processor does not confuse the internal tags as delimiters. Then the selector

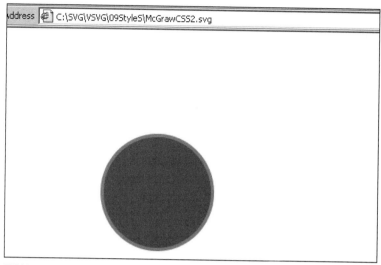

FIGURE 11.12 *circle* and *stroke* Used as a CSS Style with a Class Selector and Class Attribute

`circle.newStyle` is used. This is a new type of syntax that uses the period as the class selector within the stylesheet. It has a `fill` of blue, a `stroke` of red, and a `stroke-width` of 4. For our example here, the `circle.newStyle` would apply to all circles in the stylesheet. The class selector is closed, then the `CDATA` statement is closed, and, finally, the `style` element is closed as well. The class attribute "`newStyle`" is then referenced in the circle. Here we used an internal stylesheet. It is also possible to reference an external stylesheet that resides in either the local directory, or even links to an external directory on the Web.

Ensuring Your SVG Is Valid

SVG is XML after all, so a robust development tool like XML Spy works very well with SVG. However, there are other commercial and freeware products, though they are constantly changing. Some of the more popular editors are Amaya, a W3C editor and browser, and Jasc Webdraw, a commercial product. They can read and modify SVG files without converting them first to another format. Other editors, such as Adobe Illustrator and Corel Draw, can only export SVG files. Still other programs are specific to just SVG conversions, like Apache Batik or JPEG to SVG encoders. For a full list of the developing roster of tools available in beta, freeware, and commercial implementations, go to http://www.w3.org/Graphics/SVG/SVG-Implementations#edit.

Key Terms

bitmap
class attribute
class selector
container element
`cx`
`cy`
description element
`fill`
filter
group element
`meet`
nested viewport
`opacity`
open source
path
pixel
polygon
polyline
`preserveAspectRatio`
`r`
RGB value
Scalable Vector Graphics (SVG)
`stroke`
`stroke-width`
SVG Tiny
SVG Viewer
`transform` attribute
`translate` transformation
vector
`viewBox`
viewport
VoiceML
x axis
y axis

Code Summary

1. **Listing 11.1:**

```
<?xml version="1.0" standalone="no"?>
<!DOCTYPE svg PUBLIC "-//W3C//DTD SVG 1.0//EN"
"http://www.w3.org/TR/2001/REC-SVG-20010904/DTD/svg10.dtd">
<svg width="300" height="300">
<circle cx="150" cy="150" r="70" style="fill:green; stroke:black;
  stroke-width:2;"/>
</svg>
```

2. **Listing 11.2:**

```
<?xml version="1.0" standalone="no"?>
<!DOCTYPE svg PUBLIC "-//W3C//DTD SVG 1.0//EN"
"http://www.w3.org/TR/2001/REC-SVG-20010904/DTD/svg10.dtd">
<svg width="500" height="400" x="0" y="0">
<svg width="300" height="300" x="100" y="50">
<rect x="0" y="0" width="300" height="300" style="stroke:red;
  stroke-width:2; fill:blue; fill-opacity:.25"/>
<text x="30" y="50" style="font-family:arial; font-size:28; fill:red">
Centered Viewport</text>
</svg>
</svg>
```

3. **Listing 11.3:**

```
<?xml version="1.0" standalone="no"?>
<!DOCTYPE svg PUBLIC "-//W3C//DTD SVG 1.0//EN"
"http://www.w3.org/TR/2001/REC-SVG-20010904/DTD/svg10.dtd">
<svg width="500" height="400" x="0" y="0" >
<svg width="300" height="300" x="100" y="50" >
<rect x="0" y="0" width="300" height="300"
style="stroke:red; stroke-width:2; fill:grey; fill-opacity:.25"/>
<text x="10" y="50" style="font-size:18; font-family:arial;
  fill:red">
No ViewBox Attribute </text>
</svg>
</svg>
```

4. **Listing 11.4:**

```
<?xml version="1.0" standalone="no"?>
<!DOCTYPE svg PUBLIC "-//W3C//DTD SVG 1.0//EN"
"http://www.w3.org/TR/2001/REC-SVG-20010904/DTD/svg10.dtd">
<svg width="500" height="400" x="0" y="0" <?xml version="1.0"
  standalone="no"?>
<!DOCTYPE svg PUBLIC "-//W3C//DTD SVG 1.0//EN"
"http://www.w3.org/TR/2001/REC-SVG-20010904/DTD/svg10.dtd">
<svg width="500" height="400" x="0" y="0" viewBox="10 10 250 150">
<svg width="300" height="300" x="100" y="50">
<rect x="0" y="0" width="300" height="300"
style="stroke:red; stroke-width:2; fill:grey; fill-opacity:.25"/>
<text x="10" y="50" style="font-size:26; font-family:arial;
  fill:red">
VB Attribute</text>
</svg>
</svg>
<svg width="300" height="300" x="100" y="50">
<rect x="0" y="0" width="300" height="300"
style="stroke:red; stroke-width:2; fill:grey; fill-opacity:.25"/>
<text x="10" y="50" style="font-size:26; font-family:arial;
  fill:red">
VB Attribute</text>
</svg>
</svg>
```

5. **Listing 11.5:**

```
<?xml version="1.0" standalone="no"?>
<!DOCTYPE svg PUBLIC "-//W3C//DTD SVG 1.0//EN"
"http://www.w3.org/TR/2001/REC-SVG-20010904/DTD/svg10.dtd">
<svg width="350" height="200" viewBox="0 0 1500 1500"
preserveAspectRatio="none">
<rect x="0" y="0" width="1500" height="1500" style="stroke:red;
  stroke-width:2; fill:none"/>
<circle cx="750" cy="750" r="700" style="fill:blue; stroke:navy;
  stroke-width:3"/>
<text x="150" y="800" style="font-size:200; font-family:arial;
  fill:black">
STRETChIT</text>
</svg>
```

6. **Listing 11.6:**

```
<?xml version="1.0" standalone="no"?>
<!DOCTYPE svg PUBLIC "-//W3C//DTD SVG 1.0//EN"
"http://www.w3.org/TR/2001/REC-SVG-20010904/DTD/svg10.dtd">
<svg width="500" height="500">
<g id="3littleRectangles">
<desc>Group of 3 rectangles</desc>
<rect x="120" y="120" width="120" height="70"
style="fill:blue; stroke:rgb(0,0,128);
stroke-width:3; opacity:0.5"/>
<rect x="160" y="160" width="120" height="70"
style="fill:blue; stroke:rgb(0,0,128);
stroke-width:3; opacity:0.75"/>
<rect x="200" y="200" width="120" height="70"
```

```
style="fill:blue; stroke:rgb(0,0,128);
stroke-width:3; opacity:1"/>
</g>
</svg>
```

7. **Listing 11.7:**

```
<?xml version="1.0" standalone="no"?>
<!DOCTYPE svg PUBLIC "-//W3C//DTD SVG 1.0//EN"
"http://www.w3.org/TR/2001/REC-SVG-20010904/DTD/svg10.dtd">
<svg width="400" height="200">
<desc>Original coordinate system</desc>
<g style="fill:none; stroke:black; stroke-width:2">
<desc>How to draw x and y axes showing the
dimensions of the original coordinate system</desc>
<line x1="3" y1="3" x2="400" y2="3"/>
<line x1="3" y1="3" x2="3" y2="200"/>
</g>
<g><ellipse cx="130" cy="50" rx="100" ry="40"
style="fill:blue; fill-opacity:.5; stroke:purple; stroke-width:2"/>
<text>
<tspan x="85" y="45" style="font-size:20;font-family:arial; fill:#dedeba;
   stroke:#dedeba">
Original</tspan> <tspan x="45" y="70" style="font-size:20;
font-family:arial; fill:#dedeba; stroke:#dedeba">
Coordinates</tspan>
</text>
</g>
<!-New coordinate system, moved to 150 x and 95 y->
<g transform="translate(150,95)">
<g style="fill:none; stroke:black; stroke-width:2">
<!- draw new axes lines to show the difference ->
<line x1="0" y1="0" x2="100" y2="0"/>
<line x1="0" y1="0" x2="0" y2="100"/>
</g>
<ellipse cx="130" cy="50" rx="100" ry="40"
style="fill:blue; fill-opacity:.5;
stroke:purple; stroke-width:2"/>
<text>
<tspan x="85" y="45" style="font-size:20;
font-family:arial; fill:#dedeba; stroke:#dedeba">
New</tspan> <tspan x="45" y="70" style="font-size:20;
font-family:arial; fill:#dedeba; stroke:#dedeba">
Coordinates</tspan>
</text>
</g>
</svg>
```

8. **Listing 11.8:**

```
<?xml version="1.0" standalone="no"?>
<!DOCTYPE svg PUBLIC "-//W3C//DTD SVG 1.0//EN"
"http://www.w3.org/TR/2001/REC-SVG-20010904/DTD/svg10.dtd">
<svg width="400" height="400">
<rect x="50" y="50" width="300" height="300"
```

```
style="fill:peachpuff; fill-opacity:.75; stroke:orange;
   stroke-width:4"/>
<circle cx="200" cy="200" r="50" style="fill:gold"/>
</svg>
```

9. **Listing 11.9:**

```
<?xml version="1.0" standalone="no"?>
<!DOCTYPE svg PUBLIC "-//W3C//DTD SVG 1.0//EN"
"http://www.w3.org/TR/2001/REC-SVG-20010904/DTD/svg10.dtd">
<svg width="500" height="500">
<defs> <style type="text/css">
<![CDATA[
   circle.newStyle {
   fill:blue;
   stroke:red;
   stroke-width:4
   }
   ]]></style>
</defs>
<circle cx="200" cy="200" r="70" class="newStyle"/>
</svg>
```

Review Questions

1. What is necessary to start an SVG statement?
2. What is the basic difference between a vector and a pixel image?
3. You can edit Flash files. True or False?
4. SVG can be used for a mobile device. True or False?
5. What is the default measurement value used by SVG?
6. What is a viewport? How is it different from a `viewBox`?
7. SVG syntax is similar to XML syntax. What is the difference?
8. What does `preserveAspectRatio` actually do? How would you use it?
9. What is the difference between `<meet>` and `<slice>`?
10. How many basic shapes are there in SVG?
11. What do container elements do?
12. What is the difference between `<desc>` and a comment?
13. Putting together RGB values and SVG color values in the same statement is not allowed. True or False?
14. What four values do you need to create a rectangle?
15. An `rz` value is necessary for a circle. True or False?
16. What is the purpose of `transform=translate`?
17. What is the difference between a class selector and a class attribute?

Case Study

Go to Jasc.com and download the latest version of WebDraw, which allows a free, 30-day trial use. Create a new document (`File | New`) using the default 500 pixels by 500 pixels for the document window. There are three tabs: `Canvas`, `Source`, and `Preview`. Click on `Source`. You will see an SVG statement already set up for input. Save the file with the name `WDExercise` and notice that it automatically saves itself as an .svg file.

Using the circle tool on the left, draw an ellipse with the following values: `cx="287" cy="235.5" rx="90" ry="71.5"`. Have the `style` be a medium blue. The `style` code should have the following values: `style="fill:rgb(0,0,192); stroke:rgb (0,0,0); stroke-width:1"`. After you have drawn the ellipse and you are not sure of its size, go into the `Source` tab and edit the code to conform to the above example. If necessary, edit the `style` as well. As you can see, in SVG you can edit directly into the source code. Go back to the `Canvas` tab and select the ellipse and click `Edit | Copy`. Paste the ellipse two times so it resembles the three little rectangles graphic from the group, with one ellipse on top of the other. (See Figure 11.13.) Note the DOM, or Document Object Model, in the side panel.

Using the text tool (the capital letter `A`), draw the numbers 1, 2, and 3, respectively, in the ellipses. Go into the `Source` tab next to the `Canvas` tab and make the font size for number 1 "36", for number 2 "38", and for number 3 "40" (see Figure 11.14). Note the `transform=translate` code for the ellipses. Now go to the `style` element for the ellipse and insert `opacity` values of .25, .50, and .75, respectively, into the code.

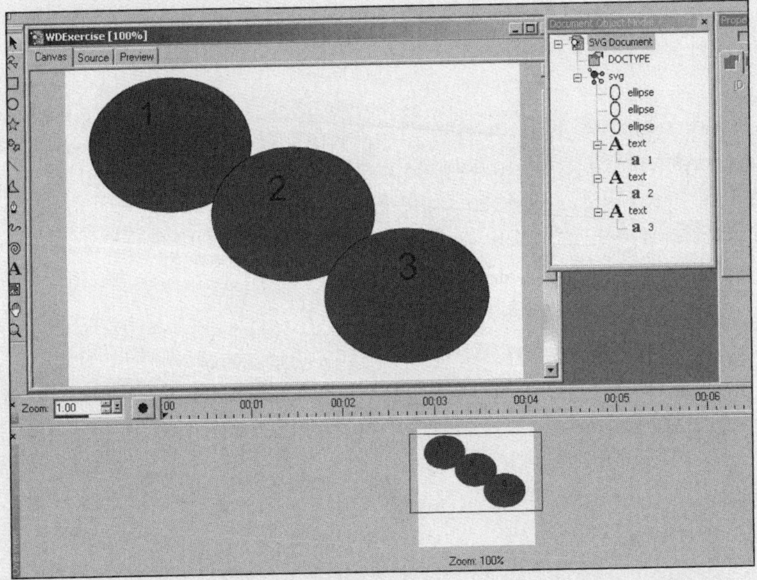

FIGURE 11.13 Drawing of Three Circles

FIGURE 11.14 Source View for Drawing of Three Circles

For a detailed discussion of the benefits and drawbacks of SVG versus Flash point your browser to http://www.carto.net/papers/svg/comparison flash svg.html.

1. Take the code of Listing 11.2, which is for Figure 11.3, and type it into the text editor of your choice. Try moving the rectangle and the text of the inner <svg> element. The way you can do this is to first type in a new coordinate for the inner rectangle, save your file with a .svg three-letter extension and an encoding of UTF-8, and name it `mynewrect`. Open it up in your browser. Now go back to your code and change the `x` and `y` coordinates of the inner <svg> element. Save the file again and open it in your browser. Notice the rectangle and text keep their spacing in reference to one another.

2. Take the code from Listing 11.4, which is for Figure 11.5, and type it into the editor of your choice. Using the `viewBox=` statement, try putting in different numbers for the `x` and `y` coordinates defining the upper left corner, the first set. Also change the coordinates for the `x` and `y` coordinates for the second set. See what part of the `viewBox` statement goes beyond the viewport by varying the numbers. See what part of the `viewBox` statement stays within the confines of the viewport.

3. In Figure 11.7 using the same code, look at Figure 11.8, the <meet> option. Try instead using the <slice> option. Also try variations on the `xMinYMin` with one of the other attribute options.

4. Using the code from Listing 11.6, which is for Figure 11.9, change the following: first, change the `fill` color to any of these standard SVG colors: green, pink, red, brown. As you do this, change the `opacity` of just one of the rectangles. For example, if an `opacity` is .75, change it to .25, or .10, or .85. As you vary both colors and `opacity`, see the different ways it renders in your browser.

   EXTRA CREDIT: Go to the Color Keywords SVG site, http://www.w3.org/TR/SVG/types.html#ColorKeywords, and substitute an RGB value for a color keyword. For example, use the color keyword `magenta`, then substitute the RGB value `rgb(255, 0, 255)` .

5. Using Figure 11.10 as a model, draw another figure inside the root `<svg>` element with an `opacity` of .25 and a `fill` color and `stroke-width` of your choice. Make it either another circle or another rectangle. Place it either after the rectangle or after the circle element. View it in your browser.

6. To see an example of an SVG map in action, point your IE browser to http://www.rgs.ca/renfrew.htm, the Ruffled Grouse Society of Canada. Click on the country map. Deselect `Tenure` and then select it again. Deselect other different check boxes as well. You must have the SVG Viewer from Adobe installed to see this map properly. Scroll down the code and see the SVG class and attribute statements. Notice that SVG is combined here with extensive JavaScript.

CHAPTER 12

SMIL

LEARNING OBJECTIVES

1. To investigate SMIL in terms of both multimedia and XML development.
2. To interpret the critical differences between SMIL 1.0 and SMIL 2.0 and the correct ways to view them.
3. To assemble the components of a basic SMIL statement.
4. To link multimedia within a SMIL presentation.

SMIL (Synchronized Multimedia Integration Language—pronounced "smile") lets one write interactive audiovisual presentations under the umbrella of XML-enabled standards of the W3C. Partially it was developed to work around the issues of bandwidth limitations and partially it was developed to stitch together sound, text, video, and images in a simple format. Another of its features is to allow presentations to be **synchronized,** meaning you can program start and end times for each aspect of a presentation. These presentations are then streamed individually from a server to a client, but appear, because of single timeline technologies, to be one continuous presentation occurring in real time.

Streaming is when media is streamed or brought in to a client for viewing in real time from a very specific server. The file is not downloaded onto the client's computer and the presentation is automatically synched to the connection speed of the client to deliver the best quality available. **Pseudo streaming** is when streamed information and content come from a Web server, and it does not occur in real time. Delivery time is delayed by the protocols in use and playback begins when enough of the content is delivered so it does not break up. This is also known as **buffering.** The presentation downloads onto the computer of the client and is dependent on the bandwidth of the user.

> **Advice**
> SMIL is constantly being updated and improved upon. To keep up with the latest developments, point your browser to http://www.w3.org/AudioVideo/.

Another forward-looking feature of SMIL is that it can be created and subsequently stored in different languages, bandwidths, sounds, and other versions, making it a viable content provider capable of true internationalization. It also does not require a complex programming language like Java, though it can incorporate Java servlets or CGI scripts to access information stored in a database.

See Figure 12.1 for an example of a SMIL presentation.

FIGURE 12.1 A RealOne Player SMIL Presentation on the Getty Museum
Notice the architectural plans in the background; the two slide screens, one for text and one for images (they can fade into one another and become new images as well); the header, which says "The Getty Museum – POP Mul..."; and the audio buttons at the bottom. This presentation is audio enabled and if you look in the upper right-hand corner, you will see the timing notations.

A Word on SMIL versus Flash

It is true that Flash can create smart-looking vector animations and has great tools to do that. However, Flash has two drawbacks in terms of coordinating media types. The first, as we saw in Chapter 11 on SVG, is that Flash files are not text editable. And the second is that Flash is not as nimble in terms of adapting to bandwidth and constraints with coordinated media. Plus, as mentioned above, SMIL is fully compatible with other XML-based standards, which Flash is not.

A Brief History of SMIL

SMIL 1.0

The first SMIL recommendation came out from the W3C in June 1998 and allowed for a quick paste up of generic multimedia presentations. It focused around issues such as how media was delivered over time with tags like <seq> for sequence (one unit played after another) and <par> for parallel (units playing together). The recommendation also allowed a basic layout control **<layout>** to place elements in a viewing area (similar to the SVG viewport, but called *region*) and allowed linking of Web elements. As a bonus, it even threw in the element **<switch>**, which allowed for different languages to be used and different data rates to be tailored to different audiences, all with only one DTD. Interestingly enough, Real Networks was an early supporter of SMIL but Microsoft was not, and wanted to incorporate SMIL into standard HTML.

Advice

To see the first SMIL recommendation, go to http://www.w3.org/TR/REC-smil/. To look at the actual DTD, go to http://www.w3.org/TR/REC-smil/#smil-dtd.

SMIL 2.0

The second version of SMIL was endorsed by W3C in August 2001, though work on it started as early as 1999. It was written to expand the capabilities of version 1.0. Instead of just one DTD, it now contained 10. These DTDs function as **modules,** part of the official specification, and contain many more new elements and attributes. The original SMIL spec was only 30 pages long; SMIL 2.0 is 540 pages long. Real Networks and MacroMedia, the multimedia powerhouses, were involved in its development and even Microsoft came back on board. The modules are

Animation
Content Control
Layout
Linking
Media Objects
Metainformation
Structure
Timing and Synchronization
Time Manipulations
Transition Effects

But SMIL even goes beyond modules to think about cross-device development to create profiles that allow for seamless playback of presentations. The main

Advice

To see everything you wanted to know about SMIL 2.0, go to http://www.w3.org/TR/smil20/, and to see the actual SMIL schema, take a look at http://www.w3.org/TR/smil20/smil-SCHEMA.html#language. To access the SMIL 2.0 Language Profile, go to http://www.w3.org/TR/smil20/smil20-profile.html.

Alert

Right now, SMIL files use the extension .smi, but, in the future, that may change to .smil. So it is a good idea to code your files with .smil.

Alert

SMIL 2.0 needs the SMIL namespace specification in the prologue statement.

Tech Tip

If a SMIL 1.0 presentation was created for an earlier version of the RealPlayer, it can play in the RealOne Player just by updating the `<smil>` 1.0 tag to a SMIL 2.0 tag using the following declaration: `<smil xmlns=http://www.w3.org/2001/SMIL20/Language>`.

Tech Tip

The SMIL 2.0 DTD is extremely unstable and, as of this writing, will not validate in most parsers. W3C has attempted to correct this by issuing a version with changes at http://www.w3.org/2001/07/REC-SMIL20-20010731-errata. But this has not corrected all the problems. However, this does not mean that SMIL 2.0 does not work. RealPlayer converts SMIL 2.0 files very well with its proprietary system. Figure 12.2 shows how XML Spy cannot locate the SMIL 2.0 DTD even though it is located at a perfectly valid address. This is because of structural problems, in the process of being corrected by W3C, of the DTD.

profile, the **SMIL 2.0 Language Profile,** details how these 10 modules are integrated. It uses the root `<smil>` element but is also backward compatible with SMIL 1.0, very important for legacy applications built using that standard, and it supports CSS2 color names. The SMIL 2.0 Basic Language Profile, a subset of the main profile, is a simplified version that can be used with mobile phones, PDAs, and even MP3 players. The XHTML + SMIL Profile is under development in order to incorporate it into a Web page, and thus do away with the root `<smil>` element. It will apply timing to a text-based display and have an XHTML layout. A simple but important change between SMIL 1.0 and 2.0 is its syntax change. An attribute such as `audio-begin` was changed to a more facile `audioBegin`. Another advantage of SMIL 2.0 is clips can be stored on different servers and played simultaneously.

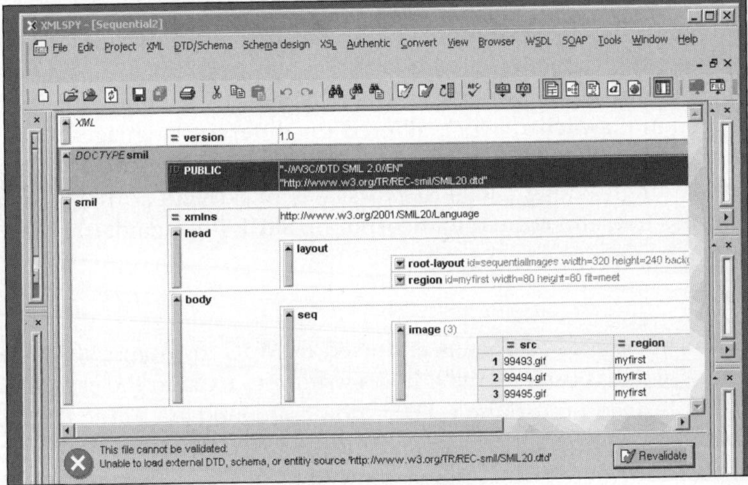

FIGURE 12.2 Validation Problems with SMIL 2.0

How to SMIL

The best way to actually see a SMIL file, especially a SMIL 2.0 file, in action is by using the RealPlayer from Real Networks. It works across multiple platforms and has kept pace with the ongoing developments in SMIL by supporting many formats that play simultaneously. The only reason the RealPlayer wasn't an actual Web browser was its lack of support for HTML, but that has changed with the release of the **RealOne Player,** and in effect it has become a minibrowser. To download the free version of the player (make sure you don't accidentally choose the paid version), go to http://www.real.com/realoneplayer.html?pp=home&src=022703realhome_2 and install it on your computer. SMIL 1.0 worked with different versions of the RealPlayer, such as G2 and Real 8, which are no longer available for download on the RealPlayer site. This is one of the drawbacks of working with a rapidly emerging standard.

One of the pluses is to see how well a new standard quickly incorporates new formats.

Real has its own formats to handle SMIL content that differs slightly from strict SMIL coding. They are **RealPix** (.rp) and **RealText** (.rt). RealPix is used for streaming images with transition and motion effects and is good for intensive multimedia using low bandwidth. RealText is actually a hypertext format that offers specific text support such as scrolling and captioning. Both can be composed in a simple text editor and saved as separate documents that SMIL can reference: RealVideo, RealAudio (.rm), and RealFlash.

Apple Computer has the QuickTime multimedia player that can be used on both Macs and PCs. QuickTime supports more than 200 digital media formats and SMIL capabilities first appeared in version 4.1. As of this writing, the version is 6.0 and you can get it at http://www.apple.com/quicktime/download/.

It should be noted that RealNetworks, QuickTime, and IE all deliver SMIL presentations in their own unique manner, and what you will learn in this chapter are the overarching, general principles of SMIL. How files are formatted, uploaded, and streamed from a server are different for each player, and you will need to consult their Web sites and manuals for specifications.

Advice

RealOne requires using its own proprietary Real Server in order to view files. For the purpose of the exercises in this book, we will not be creating and uploading RealOne files to a Real Server. Real has recently announced its Helix multimedia server, which will supersede its basic Real Server architecture.

Tech Tip

QuickTime uses Apple's own version of the SMIL namespace instead of W3C's version that RealPlayer uses. The QuickTime statement is `<smil xmlns:qt=http://www.apple.com/quicktime/resources/smilextensions>`.

Other Ways to SMIL

Internet Explorer also can use SMIL though its HTML+TIME (Timed Interactive Multimedia Extensions for HTML) SMIL-like language, which was first introduced in IE 5. Another player is Oratrix's GRiNS player, available at http://www.oratrix.com/Products/G2P. The GRiNS player is not free. Also, the Adobe SVG Viewer that you used in Chapter 11 also can support limited SMIL animation.

Another Way to View SMIL

Because RealOne Player, Apple QuickTime, and IE all require their own proprietary changes to basic SMIL, and because some of them even require using *only* their servers, we will use a generic player, X-Smiles, to view some of our code examples. Although not feature rich, it does show basic aspects of SMIL. Go to http://www.xsmiles.org/ to download and install the latest version of X-Smiles in your local directory of choice.

Tech Tip

There is a free SMIL validating tool on the Web to check your code. Point your browser to http://www.oratrix.com/Links/visitExtSite?get_link=3 and just follow the instructions. You don't need to download anything. It validates against the SMIL 1.0 DTD.

Basic SMIL

Core Elements

The three core SMIL elements are `<smil>`, `<head>`, and `<body>` and they also compose the basic SMIL 2.0 structure module. `<smil>` opens and closes the actual `<smil>` statement and is the root element. **<head>** is always contained within the root element and must contain either a `<layout>` element

Alert

Never apply an attribute to a closing element in SMIL. This will freeze your presentation.

or a <switch> element as well as other elements that define appearance, layout, and meta information. The header also defines the structure of the presentation. The <**body**> element defines the content and timing and, if appropriate, linking information. All of these elements follow XML dual tag conventions <> . . . </>. All of these elements have attributes associated with them (see Table 12.1) and all elements listed apply to SMIL 1.0 and 2.0, with a backward compatibility.

TABLE 12.1 Basic *<smil>* Elements and Attributes

Attribute	Element	Code	Description	Version
class	<smil> <head> <body>	class="smil-media"	Assigns a class name to the element. Similar to id=". . ." but allows for any number of names.	2.0
id	<smil> <head> <body>	id="firstsmil"	Gives a unique id name for different content types.	1.0, 2.0
profile	<head>	http://www.w3.org/TR/2000/WD-smil20-20000921/smil-DTD.html#smilbasic-model-1	Identifies the DTD the SMIL document is matched to. Not all DTDs are used for all documents.	1.0, 2.0
title	<smil> <head> <body>	title="My First SMIL Presentation"	Gives a page title for the title bar. This is optional and display depends on the viewer.	2.0
xml:lang	<smil> <head> <body>	xml:lang="en"	Language attribute from XML also seen in Unicode.	2.0
xmlns	<smil>	http://www.w3.org/2001/SMIL20/	Identifies the origin of all elements used in SMIL through their namespaces. Use this attribute as many times as there are element origins	2.0

Media Elements

So what media elements or id types are allowed in SMIL? After all, that is why it exists, to play multimedia presentations.

- <animation>: Animation (.swf, .anim).
- <audio>: Audio (.rm, .wav, .mp3, .aiff).
- <img>: Image (.jpg, .gif, .png).
- <ref>: Reference, points to anything not covered in the list (for example, .rp).

- <text>: Text (.txt, .html).
- <textstream>: Streaming text (.rt, .mov).
- <video>: Video (.rm, .mpg, .mov).

The syntax for these types would look like the examples in Listing 12.1.

LISTING 12.1

```
<animation src="bartsimpson.anim" . . . />
<audio src="grammyhits.wav" . . . />
<img src="stockmarketgraph.jpg" . . . />
<ref src="anyotherobject" . . . />
<text src="openingtitle.html" . . . />
<textstream src="rtsp://www.CNN.com/mediaheadlines.rt" . . . />
<video src="mtvvideo.mpg" . . . />
```

Alert

If the URI is local, the syntax is `file ://`.

The `src=` attribute defines a URI for locating the appropriate data, which can be local or off a specified server. The data type is determined by a variety of factors, including `type=attribute`, which declares the mime type of the data, the filename suffix, and the type information communicated by different Internet protocols.

Tech Tip

Remember, just like XML, SMIL is case-sensitive, and any mixing of case, except in a specified attribute, will cause problems in your presentation. It is best to use lowercase.

So how do all of these components come together to make a presentation? Figure 12.3 gives a diagram that represents the interaction of all the parts. The <body> element mostly controls the timing and content.

LISTING 12.2 Anatomy of SMIL Code

```
<?xml version="1.0" encoding="UTF-8"?>
<!DOCTYPE smil PUBLIC "-//W3C//DTD SMIL 2.0//EN"
"http://www.w3.org/TR/REC-smil/SMIL20.dtd">
<smil xmlns="http://www.w3.org/2001/SMIL20/Language">
<!---Simply edited in NotePad--->
<smil id="MyVeryFirst”>
  <head id="schoolpresentation">
    <metaname=”cool_animation.smil” content=
      "schoolcontents"/>
  <layout>
    <root-layout width="400" height="280"/>
    <region id=audio_1/>
    <region id=image_1>
  </layout>
  </head>
  <body>
    <t:audio> . . . </t:audio>
    <t:text> . . . </t:text>
    <t:video> . . . </t:video>
```

Alert

The <header> section is optional (but usually necessary), but the <body> section is mandatory for SMIL 2.0. We can see this more closely in Listing 12.2.

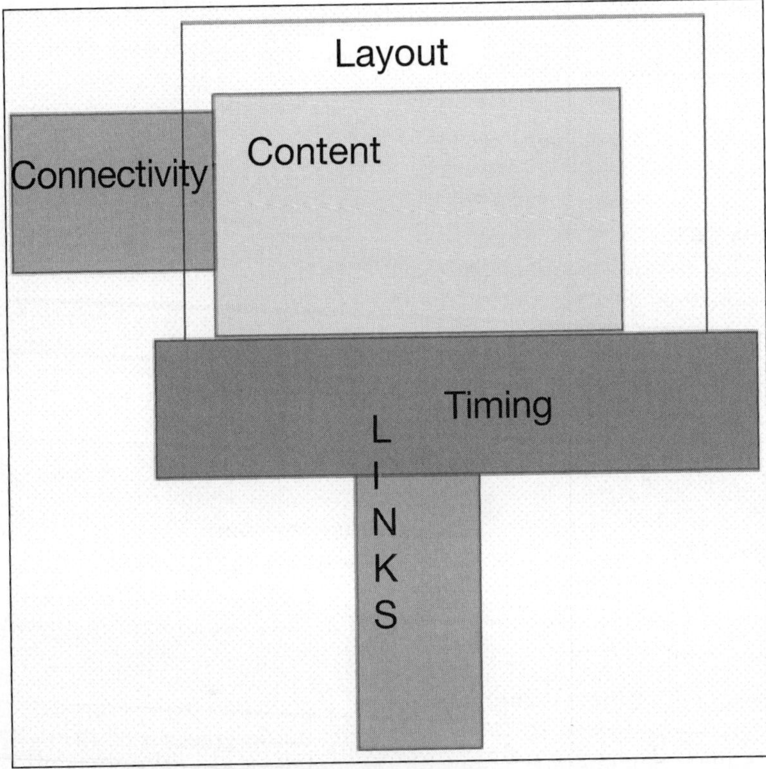

FIGURE 12.3 SMIL Components Overview

```
  </body>
</smil>
```

A SMIL statement begins with an XML PI declaration and encoding type, in this case UTF-8. The full DTD declaration is stated, and it is pulled from an external source maintained on the W3C site. It is then followed by smil xmlns, or the SMIL (XML) namespace. smil xmlns is only attached to the <smil> root element. This entire group is known as the prologue.

The SMIL root element begins the next part of the statement, <smil>. Here we use an id attribute of "MyVeryFirst". The head element <head> contains within it all the layout information. It also contains the <**meta**> element, or information about the information. <meta> also provides information such as a title for the presentation. Here the <layout> element is part of the structure and deals with the arrangements of media objects in the viewport. <layout> has two child elements: <root-layout> and then <**region**>.

The <body> element is the container for all the actual content and timing functions and no SMIL file can exist without it. It tells the object that will display the SMIL code what aspects of the presentation—such as audio, text, video, images, and so forth—should be displayed in what part of the presentation and when they should stop. It has many different child elements and attributes, specifies what clips and groups should be used, and presents the basic sequence of how content is displayed. Table 12.2 is a basic overview of the attributes and elements of a SMIL statement.

TABLE 12.2 *<head>* **Elements and Attributes—An Overview**

Element	Child Elements	Attributes	Values	Notes
<head>	<layout> <meta> <switch> <transition>	class Id Title xml:lang	Appropriate for their type	Describes layout capabilities such as where on the screen a presentation will appear
<layout>	<region> <regPoint> <root-layout> <topLayout>	type		Must be inside <head> element
		type	text/smil-basic-layout text/css	
	<region>	backgroundColor background-color bottom fit id height left region regionName right showBackground soundLevel top width z-index		
		fit	fill hidden meet scroll slice	

Continued

TABLE 12.2 <head> Elements and Attributes—An Overview (continued)

Element	Child Elements	Attributes	Values	Notes
		showBackground	Always whenActive	
		soundLevel	Nonnegative percentages	
	<regPoint>	bottom left regAlign right top		
		regAlign	bottomLeft bottomMid bottomRight center midLeft midRight topLeft topMid topRight	
	<root-layout>	backgroundColor background-color height width	Smil 2.0 syntax Smil 1.0 syntax	Only one <root-layout> allowed
		height width	Dependent on parent element usage	Also for region, topLayout
	<topLayout>	backgroundColor close height open width		
		open	onStart whenActive	
		backgroundColor	inherit Keyword colors RGB colors Hexadecimal colors transparent	

Continued

TABLE 12.2 <head> **Elements and Attributes—An Overview (continued)**

Element	Child Elements	Attributes	Values	Notes
		bottom left right top	Percentages Pixel auto	
		close	onRequest whenNotActive	
<meta>		content id name skip-content		SMIL 1.0, 2.0
		name	base label pics PICS-Label title	
<metadata>				Used for resources, properties, and statements in SMIL 2.0; good for machine-to-machine information exchange; like the <meta> element in HTML
<switch>				Used mostly in the <body> element
<transition>	<param>	borderColor borderWidth direction dur endProgress fadeColor horzRepeat id startProgress subtype vertRepeat		

The *<layout>* Module

Though contained within the <head> section of a SMIL document, layout elements and attributes give a name to, and define the position of, windows and regions for media presentation. The <layout> module is not essential in a SMIL presentation, but if it is not included, the location of visual elements falls into the default position of the viewer upon which they are being presented, a situation that does not utilize the robust capabilities of SMIL and leaves your presentation looking weird. Besides the BasicLayout module, SMIL 2.0 adds three other submodules: AudioLayout, MultiwindowLayout, and HierarchicalLayout.

<layout> states a group of regions where media elements are displayed through their position, size, and scale. This is done through the <region> attribute. Regions can take CSS2 proprieties like height, width, left, top, and backgroundColor. These properties are defined by a type attribute.

A basic syntax for the <layout> element is shown in the example in Listing 12.3.

LISTING 12.3

```
<layout>
<root-layout backgroundColor="blue" width="300" height="350"/>
<region id="PlaceItHere" top="20" left="30" width="80" height=
  "100"/>
</layout>
```

In this code snipped, <root-layout> creates the presentation window with a color of blue and a width of 300 and height of 350 pixels, the default. <region> acts essentially as a placeholder and doesn't contain any content, but defines a bounding box. Then a specific media object locates the region by its id name and targets it as the site for playback inside of the region's bounding box.

The next code example, in Listing 12.4, shows how different regions are defined (see Figure 12.4). Every visual media element has to be set to a specific region, but only one element can be displayed in that region at any time. However, multiple regions can cover the same screen area and overlap.

LISTING 12.4

```
<smil>
<head>
<layout>
<root-layout backgroundColor="blue"
  height="180"
  width="180"/>
<region id="Region1"
  left="41"
  top="40"
  height="100"
  width="100"
  z-index="1"
```

```
        backgroundColor="yellow"/>
      <region id="Region2"
        left="0"
        top="0"
        height="180"
        width="180"
        z-index="0"
        backgroundColor="red"/>
      </layout>
      </head>
    </smil>
```

Let's take a look at this code in X-Smiles.

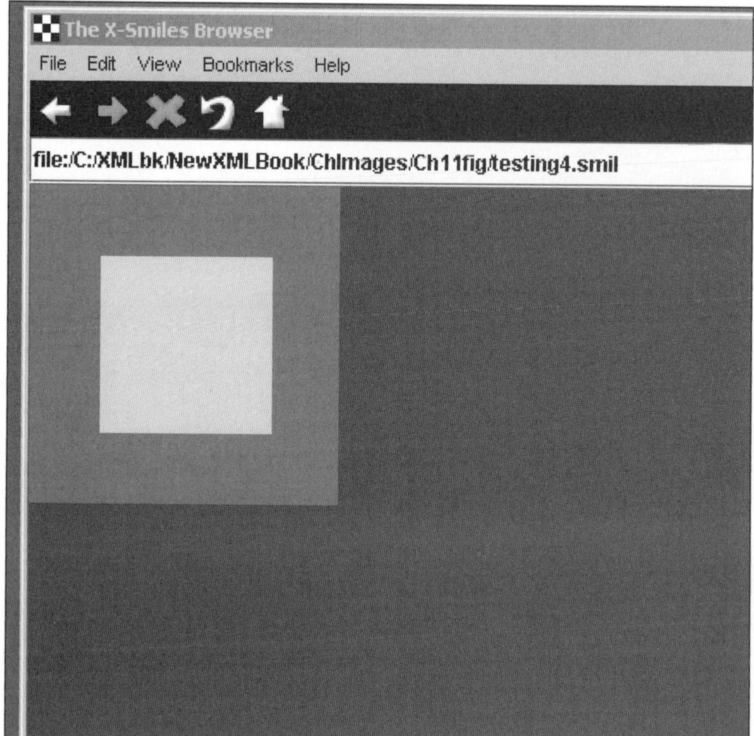

FIGURE 12.4 Root Layout and Regions

The `root-layout` background color is blue, and that is the color that fills the entire bounding box. `Region1` is the yellow inner square with a height and width both of 100 pixels and left and top coordinates of (41, 40) in relation to the bounding box. `Region2` is the red middle-sized square of 180 × 180 pixels, and because the left and top coordinates are both set to 0, it lines up with the left and top corners of the object's bounding box. The colors will appear in

Tech Tip

You can try validating basic SMIL code with a free validator at http://www.cwi.nl/%7Emedia/symm/validator/. See Figure 12.5.

your black-and-white textbook as different shades of gray, with yellow being the lightest.

The `z-index` attribute is similar to the `z-index` CSS property. When regions overlap, `z-index` shows which region appears on top and which ones are either hidden or partially hidden via their stacking order. The higher the number, the closer to the top of the stack an object appears.

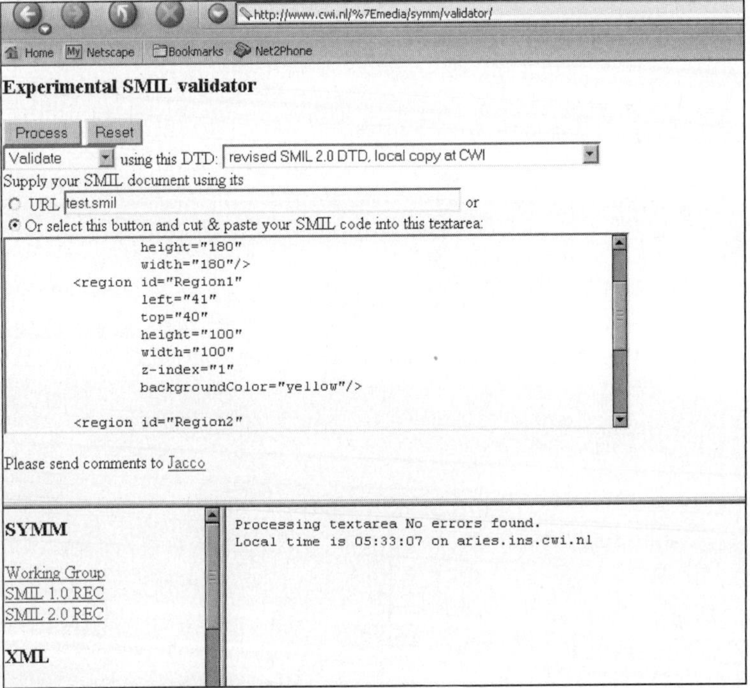

FIGURE 12.5 Simple Validator

The *<body>* Element

The <body> element indicates what media elements to present as well as what regions they should be presented in, and also what the timeline should be for the different aspects. Things that happen, or elements present, occur in two distinct ways. First, events that show up one after the other, or in sequence, with one ending and the next beginning, are referred to as **sequential elements** and are defined by the child element or tag <seq> . . . </seq> (see Listing 12.5). We also take a look at allowed <body> elements and their child elements in Table 12.3.

LISTING 12.5

```
<seq>
<audio src="NumberThreeHit.mp3"/>
<audio src="NumberTwoHit.mp3"/>
```

```
<audio src="NumberOneHit.mp3"/>
<seq>
```

TABLE 12.3 *<body>* **Elements—An Overview**

Element	Child Elements	Description
<body>	<a> <animate> <animateMotion> <animateColor> <audio> <brush> <excl> <img> <par> <priorityClass> <ref> <seq> <switch> <text> <textstream> <transition> <transitionFilter> <video>	The amount of attributes for each child element is much too numerous to list and can be seen in the SMIL 2.0 specification from W3C

Listing 12.5 is an example of three hits being played in a countdown order. Since there is only audio in this sample, no regions need to be defined, and their play order, because of <seq>, is NumberThreeHit plays first, ends, then NumberTwoHit plays, and then NumberOneHit plays.

However, other media has duration, even if it is a still image. You can choose to display a .gif or .jpg for 10 seconds or 5 seconds, as shown in Listing 12.6.

LISTING 12.6

```
    <seq>
    <image src="beautifulSunset.jpg" region="FirstRegion"
      dur="10 sec"/>
    <image src="beautifulMoonrise.jpg" region="FirstRegion"
      dur="5 sec"/>
  </seq>
```

In Listing 12.6, an image of a beautiful sunset is displayed in a region called "FirstRegion" for 10 seconds. After the sunset ends, a beautiful moonrise is displayed in the same region, but this time for only 5 seconds.

The second way events can occur is with **parallel elements,** or concurrent presentations, with the <par> and </par> tags, as seen in Listing 12.7. They can display at the same time, but they don't have to end at the same time, though they can.

LISTING 12.7

```
      <par>
      <image src="MyGreatVacation.jpg" region="FirstRegion"
        dur="15 sec" />
      <image src="MyGreatVacation.txt" region="SecondRegion"
        dur="15 sec" />
  </par>
```

Here, `MyGreatVacation` pictures and text display in two different regions for 15 seconds each. Of course, their region `id` dimensions must be set up in advance.

Sequential and parallel durations can be combined within a SMIL statement.

The <*switch*> Attribute

Different elements can be presented to different viewers with <`switch`>. The attributes under it are color depth, language, maximum data rate, and language, which you can see in Listing 12.8.

LISTING 12.8

```
    <switch>
    <audio src="dutch.aiff" system-language="nl"/>
    <audio src="french.aiff" system-language="fr"/>
    <audio src="english.aiff" system-language="en"/>
    </switch
```

The first audio would be in Dutch, the next in French, and the third in English. Or, if a default language needs to be designated, that would be the final one without a language attribute. As shown in Listing 12.9, it would fall back to English if no other choice is made.

LISTING 12.9

```
    <switch>
    <audio src="dutch.aiff" system-language="nl"/>
    <audio src="french.aiff" system-language="fr"/>
    <audio src="english.aiff" />
    </switch
```

Another use for `switch` that is very important is for overseas connections where people tend to have lower bandwidth. This uses the attribute `system-bitrate` and it is best to list the speeds from highest to lowest, as you can see in Listing 12.10.

LISTING 12.10

```
<switch>
<audio src="192k.aif" system-bitrate="192000"/>
<audio src="128k.aif" system-bitrate="128000"/>
</switch>
```

Here users with higher speed connections can play a sound file at 192 Kbits/sec or for those with slower systems, they get to hear it at 128 Kbits/sec. However, SMIL servers like the RealServer protocol (RTSP) have their own proprietary system of content negotiation that can work instead of `<switch>`.

Linking Module

Within a SMIL presentation, it is usual and customary to link to other SMIL or non-SMIL objects or plug-ins. This also means different servers can be accessed simultaneously, both locally and externally. Links are unidirectional, which means they are enabled to work in only one direction, target to source. Also, SMIL elements try to conform to the same language as XLink with some differences depending on the type of media, as well as XHTML.

<a> Linking

The <**a**> element, part of the SMIL 2.0 linking module, and also a part of SMIL 1.0, is the basis for hyperlinking in SMIL. It ties together a link with any kind of media-enabled visual object. These links, which must at least have the `href` attribute (similar to HTML's `href` statement), can link to either other SMIL internal and external presentations, Web pages, or XML documents. The `<a>` element may not be nested. In SMIL 2.0, the linking can be set off by a variety of events that are user defined (like clickthrough) or even a specialized access or hot key.

An example of this is shown in Listing 12.11.

LISTING 12.11

```
<a href="NumberOneHit.mp3">
<ref id="NumberOne" . . . />
</a>
```

Here is a link to the recording of a number one hit record that is activated when a user clicks on the Number One media object that has the `id` of `NumberOne`. This is also a statement that can be written for SMIL 1.0 or SMIL 2.0.

In SMIL 2.0, there are new user attributes like `actuate`, which is followed by specific values such as `onRequest` (meaning if the information is requested) or `onLoad` (when the action loads). That means the user does not necessarily have to trigger the event. The `<a>` element is not involved in synchronization or timing but can load into a presentation at a set time as determined by the coder.

LISTING 12.12

```
<a href="NumberOneHit.mp3" actuate="onLoad">
<ref id="NumberOne" . . . />
</a>
```

The example in Listing 12.12 means a link is followed when the media object is activated. `NumberOne` activates when requested. The link to the Number One Hit .mp3 will follow when `NumberOne` activates.

In SMIL 2.0, other child elements of <a> are

- `<animation>`
- `<brush>`
- `<img>`
- `<ref>`
- `<text>`
- `<textstream>`
- `<video>`

Possible attributes of these elements are

- `accesskey`
- `actuate`
- `alt`
- `destinationLevel`
- `destinationPlaystate`
- `external`
- `show`
- `sourcePlaystate`
- `tabindex`
- `target`

<anchor> and *<area>* Elements

In SMIL 1.0, <**anchor**> defined just a part of a media object's display area to activate. In SMIL 2.0, this was expanded to include <**area**>. `<area>` in SMIL 2.0 is most useful in defining just a part or section of the presentation, something `<anchor>` could not do. See Table 12.4 `<anchor>` and `<area>` attributes.

An example of this might be as shown in Listing 12.13.

LISTING 12.13

```
<video src="NumberOneHit.mov" height="300" width="300">
<area id="NumberOneToday" shape="rect" cords="0,0, 200,
  250"
```

TABLE 12.4 *<anchor>* **and** *<area>* **Elements and Attributes—An Overview**

Element	Parent Elements	Attributes	Values
<anchor>	<animation> <img> <ref> <text> <textstream> <video>	cords href show	Appropriate for their type
<area>	<animation> <brush> <img> <ref> <text> <textstream> <video>	accesskey actuate alt cords destinationLevel destinationPlaystate external fragment href nohref shape show sourceLevel sourcePlaystate tabindex target	Appropriate for their type

```
href="HitMovie.html"/>
</video>
```

Here the video source is NumberOneHit movie, and the bounding box is 300 × 300 pixels. The area id that is targeted is NumberOneToday in a rectangular shape with coordinates of 0,0, (which place it in the upper left-hand side of the bounding box) by 200 × 250 pixels. It also pulls up the Web page HitMovie.html to pull the movie from. <area> is also set up to handle different spatial and temporal arrangements, something <anchor> could not do, as shown in Listing 12.14.

LISTING 12.14

```
<smil>
<head>
<layout>
<root-layout backgroundColor="blue" width="300"
  height="350"/>
```

```
<region id="PlaceItHere" top="20" left="30" width="80"
  height="100"/>
</layout>
</head>
<body>
<img region="PlaceItHere" src="JumpingUpDown.jpg"/>
</img>
</body>
</smil>
```

Key Terms

<a>
<anchor>
<area>
<body>
buffering
<head>
<layout>
<meta>
modules
parallel elements
pseudo streaming
Real
RealOne Player
RealPix
RealText
<region>
sequential elements
SMIL 2.0 Language Profile
streaming
<switch>
synchronized
Synchronized Multimedia Integration Language (SMIL)

Code Summary

1. **Listing 12.1:**

```
<animation src="bartsimpson.anim" . . . />
<audio src="grammyhits.wav" . . . />
<img src="stockmarketgraph.jpg" . . . />
<ref src="anyotherobject" . . . />
<text src="openingtitle.html" . . . />
<textstream src="rtsp://www.CNN.com/mediaheadlines.rt" . . . />
<video src="mtvvideo.mpg" . . . />
```

2. **Listing 12.2:**

```
<?xml version="1.0" encoding="UTF-8"?>
<!DOCTYPE smil PUBLIC "-//W3C//DTD SMIL 2.0//EN"
"http://www.w3.org/TR/REC-smil/SMIL20.dtd">
<smil xmlns="http://www.w3.org/2001/SMIL20/Language">
<!---Simply edited in NotePad--->
<smil id="MyVeryFirst">
  <head id="schoolpresentation">
    <metaname="cool_animation.smil" content="schoolcontents"/>
  <layout>
    <root-layout width="400" height="280"/>
```

```
    <region id=audio_1/>
    <region id=image_1>
  </layout>
  </head>
  <body>
    <t:audio> . . . </t:audio>
    <t:text> . . . </t:text>
    <t:video> . . . </t:video>
  </body>
</smil>
```

3. **Listing 12.3:**

```
<layout>
<root-layout backgroundColor="blue" width="300" height="350"/>
<region id="PlaceItHere" top="20" left="30" width="80" height="100"/>
</layout>
```

4. **Listing 12.4:**

```
  <smil>
  <head>
  <layout>
  <root-layout backgroundColor="blue"
    height="180"
    width="180"/>
  <region id="Region1"
    left="41"
    top="40"
    height="100"
    width="100"
    z-index="1"
    backgroundColor="yellow"/>
  <region id="Region2"
    left="0"
    top="0"
    height="180"
    width="180"
    z-index="0"
    backgroundColor="red"/>
  </layout>
  </head>
</smil>
```

5. **Listing 12.5:**

```
<seq>
<audio src="NumberThreeHit.mp3"/>
<audio src="NumberTwoHit.mp3"/>
<audio src="NumberOneHit.mp3"/>
</seq>
```

6. **Listing 12.6:**

```
<seq>
  <image src="beautifulSunset.jpg" region="FirstRegion" dur=10 sec"/>
  <image src="beautifulMoonrise.jpg" region="FirstRegio" dur=5 sec"/>
</seq>
```

7. **Listing 12.7:**

```
<par>
  <image src="MyGreatVacation.jpg" region="FirstRegion" dur="15 sec" />
  <image src="MyGreatVacation.txt" region="SecondRegion" dur="15 sec" />
</par>
```

8. **Listing 12.8:**

```
<switch>
<audio src="dutch.aiff" system-language="nl"/>
<audio src="french.aiff" system-language="fr"/>
<audio src="english.aiff" system-language="en"/>
</switch
```

9. **Listing 12.9:**

```
<switch>
<audio src="dutch.aiff" system-language="nl"/>
<audio src="French.aiff" system-language="fr"/>
<audio src="english.aiff" />
</switch
```

10. **Listing 12.10:**

```
<switch>
<audio src="192k.aif" system-bitrate="192000"/>
<audio src="128k.aif" system-bitrate="128000"/>
</switch>
```

11. **Listing 12.11:**

```
<a href="NumberOneHit.mp3">
<ref id="NumberOne" . . . />
</a>
```

12. **Listing 12.12:**

```
<a href="NumberOneHit.mp3" actuate="onLoad">
<ref id="NumberOne" . . . />
</a>
```

13. **Listing 12.13:**

```
<video src="NumberOneHit.mov" height="300" width="300">
<area id="NumberOneToday" shape="rect" cords="0,0, 200, 250"
href="HitMovie.html"/>
</video>
```

14. **Listing 12.14:**

```
<smil>
<head>
<layout>
<root-layout backgroundColor="blue" width="300" height="350"/>
<region id="PlaceItHere" top="20" left="30" width="80" height="100"/>
</layout>
</head>
<body>
<img region="PlaceItHere" src="JumpingUpDown.jpg"/>
</img>
</body>
</smil>
```

Review Questions

1. What is the basic difference between SMIL 1.0 and SMIL 2.0?
2. What is synchronization and what is streaming?
3. The three core SMIL elements are (pick three)
   <head> <id> <body> <profile> <title> <smil>
4. How many media types are allowed in SMIL?
5. What are the three basic components of a SMIL statement?
6. `src= attribute` can be pulled from how many locations?
7. <region> acts as a
   a. color code
   b. video loop
   c. placeholder
   d. sound file
8. How does <seq> present media? In what order? How does <par> present media? In what order?
9. Is the SMIL 2.0 DTD correct or incorrect?
10. What is HTML+TIME? Who uses it? What is its purpose?
11. What is the difference between .smi and .smil?
12. What are the three core SMIL elements?
13. What is a SMIL module? How are some modules used?
14. Name some media elements used in SMIL.
15. How is <region> used in SMIL?
16. What is the difference between <layout> and <root-layout>?
17. In the `z-index` attribute, what does a higher number mean?
18. What is the difference between sequential and parallel tags?
19. What are some of the things a <switch> tag can do?
20. Are SMIL links unidirectional or bidirectional?

Case Study

Much research is being done in the fields of Medical Image Analysis, Surgery Simulation, and Medical Robotics throughout the world. Often surgeons and other medical personnel cannot be present to learn about important advances in their field. The INRIA Epidaure group decided to deal with this problem by recording both a live video stream of a seminar along with the slides and text. It was preserved in SMIL format. In order to view this, go to http://www.inria.fr/multimedia/Didactheque/4-Docmnt-Didact/0002/MEDIM.HTM. Click on `the 68 mn presentation in XML/SMIL with slides, audio and video included`. Go to the section on `Surgery simulation`. The RealOne Player is launched and Dr. Nicholas Ayache is presented talking in a video stream that loads without buffering or snags on the left side of the player, and on the right side are text and slides. Underneath the video stream is a text layout of Dr. Ayache's speech; you can click on any subtopic and jump right ahead or back to that specific topic. The amount and types of visual information are of the highest quality.

In the RealOne Player, go to the `File` pull-down menu, select `Clip Properties` and then `Clip Source`. Scroll through the code and notice how many of the elements and declarations you recognize. Notice also that this was built using SMIL 1.0 only.

First, you must have the RealOne Player installed and be using the Internet.

1. Go to http://www.oratrix.com/Links/visitExtSite?get_link=4. Download the file `custom1.zip` 984KB, which is also viewed as http://www.geocities.com/ramirez_j2001/custom1/custom1.zip. Using an unzip utility, unzip the file. It should unzip to a folder called `Custom`. Open the folder and you will see a Real file `custom1` and another folder called `media`.
2. Open `custom1` and launch the RealOne Player presentation. You will be asked to select one presentation. Select the `piano` audio presentation, and then select the `Mission San Juan Capistrano` image. Watch and listen to the presentation.
3. Then go to the `File` pull-down menu in the RealOne Player, select `Clip Properties` and then `Clip Source`. Examine the code, which begins with the root element `<smil>`. After scrolling through the code, close the `Clip Source` window.
4. Go back to the folder `media` and open it. Click on the Real audio file `piano_1/`. The audio file will launch in the RealOne Player. Go back to the `media` folder and open `juan_5c`. It should be an image of the bell from the presentation. Also try opening the other `juan` files. Also open the text file `select_a_1`, which should give you the text choice `select audio`.
5. Now go back to `custom1` and play the file again, and if you want, select another audio and visual track. Look again at the code through the `Clip Source` window. Identify the individual audio, visual, and text files you opened from the `media` file and take a look at the coding for how these files fade and transition into each other.

Next, look at a SMIL file written for IE6.

1. Open the Web page http://www.oratrix.com/Links/visitExtSite?get_link=4 in IE and, on the right-side, click `Green is in!` an XHTML+SMIL presentation. Depending on your bandwidth connection, it could take about a minute or more to load into your browser, so be patient.
2. After the presentation plays, go into `View | Source` in your browser. As you can see, the code begins with `<html>` and ends with `</html>` and looks nothing like the RealOne file you looked at, even though it is a SMIL file.

To See the Difference between the Same Presentation in SMIL and XHTM+SMIL

In this example, you will also need to have the Adobe SVG Viewer 3 downloaded and installed on your computer.

1. If you need to, go to Adobe.com, select `Support`, `Other Downloads`, and then under `Readers` choose the SVG Viewer for either PC or Mac.
2. Then on http://www.oratrix.com/Links/visitExtSite?get_link=4, select the link on the right-side for `The Multifaceted Transition Element of SMIL 2.0`. Examine the transition codes that appear in your browser, and then scroll to the bottom of the page. On the left side, it says "View this SMIL 2.0 profile example". If you click this, you will see the presentation in the RealOne Player. After viewing it in the Player, go to `File`, `Clip Properties`, and then `Clip Source` and look at the clip in SMIL. Close the `Clip Source` window. Close the RealOne Player.
3. Now on the Web page with the transition code, go to the right-side and click on the HTML+SMIL version and look at the same presentation in IE. After it plays, go to `View` and then `Source` and notice the difference in coding from the RealOne Player presentation. Notice how XHTM+SMIL turns it into HTML through the rendering engine in the Microsoft browser.

X-SMILS Viewer

The X-Smils Viewer comes with an excellent XML parser to check errors.

1. Using the code example from the `regions` example (the blue, red, and yellow squares), save it under the name `examples2.smil` and delete the end > tag on `layout`. Run it through the parser and see the error message you get. Now put back the end > tag and see the difference.
2. Next, add another region and call it `Region3`. Give it `left` and `top` values of 60 and `height` and `width` of 140. The background color should be set to green. Change all the `z-index` settings so green is 0, red is 1, and yellow is 2. Save the file and view it. Then change the `z-index` for yellow to 0, red to 1, and green to 2. Again save it and view it. Now make the red `z-index` 0, and yellow and green both 1. Save the file and view it.

HTML+TIME

Using IE, go to http://msdn.microsoft.com/library/default.asp?url=/workshop/author/behaviors/time.asp. Start at `HTML+TIME: a Roadmap`, which you can click on in the left-side of the Web page. On the right-side, an example says, "You can spice up a presentation using HTML+TIME transitions" and below there is a blue box that says, "Show me". Click on that box. A popup appears showing examples. With your mouse over the popup box, right-click and select `View Source` from the shortcut menu. See Figure 12.6.

1. Notice the very first tag is `<HTML>`, which means it is an HTML file. There is no SMIL DTD or SMIL element and no layout element like there is in SMIL. Next, the line `xmlns:t = "urn:schemas-microsoft-com:time">` appears that declares the SMIL namespace (`xmlns:t`), which is a proprietary one reserved for the HTML+TIME code and a valid XML namespace designation. A schema is drawn from `microsoft-com` that is called `:time`.
2. `<?import namespace = t urn = "urn:schemas-microsoft-com:time" implementation = "#default#time2" />` is an `import` processing instruction that maps a SMIL media object element using the `t` namespace to tie in to the HTML1TIME statement. Then the `time2` behavior element is used to aid in definitively establishing `t` as the XML/SMIL namespace.

```
<STYLE>
   .time    {behavior: url(#default#time2);}
   .caption {font-size:medium}
</STYLE>
```

3. The `STYLE` statement above declares an internal stylesheet and establishes `time2` as a class attribute. Then it is linked to another stylesheet called `samples`.

```
<LINK REL="stylesheet" HREF="/workshop/samples/samples.css" TYPE="text/css">
</HEAD>
<BODY >
```

4. Next, many transition filters with targeted elements are listed that showed the short video in the popup box.
5. The `<DIV CLASS="time" dur="22"` and the rest of the statements until `</DIV>` has the text embedded inside of the document using the HTML `<DIV>` element.

```
<!- Copyright ->
<A class="copyright"
HREF="http://www.microsoft.com/isapi/gomscom.asp?TARGET=/info/cpyright.htm"
   TARGET="_top">
&copy; 2002 Microsoft Corporation. All rights reserved. Terms of use.
</A>
```

6. The <A> anchor links different elements and combines with the `HREF` statement to pull a specific URL.

   It is clear from this example that Microsoft has a very different view of SMIL than a program like XML Spy or RealPlayer One does. However, this link does provide a very good starting point for looking at HTML+TIME. If you want to write HTML+TIME code, you can do so in XML Spy by naming it an HTML file and using the examples from Microsoft as templates. Of course, you will have to create your own audio, image, text, and video files to use.

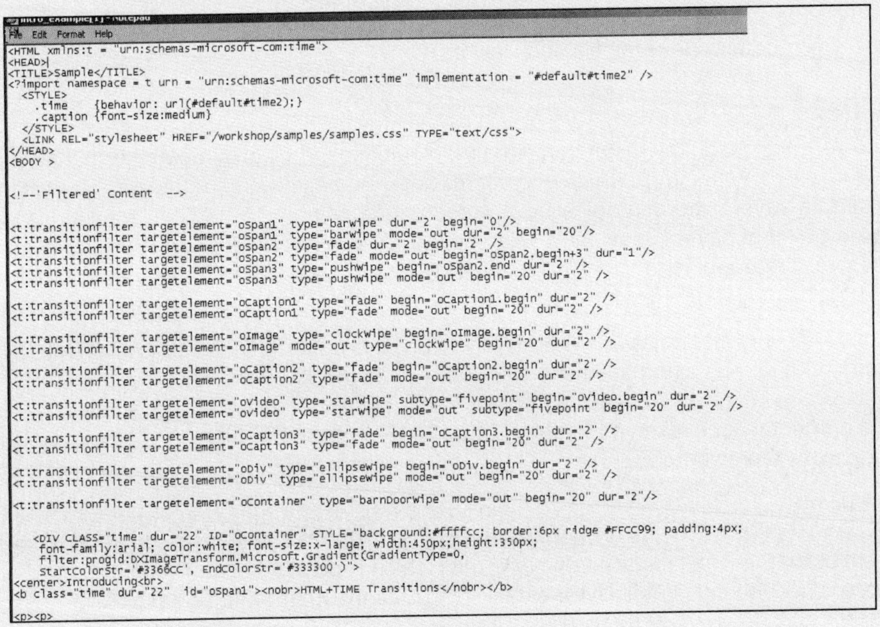

```
File Edit Format Help
<HTML xmlns:t = "urn:schemas-microsoft-com:time">
<HEAD>
<TITLE>Sample</TITLE>
<?import namespace = t urn = "urn:schemas-microsoft-com:time" implementation = "#default#time2" />
  <STYLE>
    .time     {behavior: url(#default#time2);}
    .caption {font-size:medium}
  </STYLE>
  <LINK REL="stylesheet" HREF="/workshop/samples/samples.css" TYPE="text/css">
</HEAD>
<BODY >


<!--'Filtered' Content  -->


<t:transitionfilter targetelement="oSpan1" type="barwipe" dur="2" begin="0"/>
<t:transitionfilter targetelement="oSpan1" type="barwipe" mode="out" dur="2" begin="20"/>
<t:transitionfilter targetelement="oSpan2" type="fade" dur="2" begin="2" />
<t:transitionfilter targetelement="oSpan2" type="fade" mode="out" begin="oSpan2.begin+3" dur="1"/>
<t:transitionfilter targetelement="oSpan3" type="pushwipe" begin="oSpan2.end" dur="2" />
<t:transitionfilter targetelement="oSpan3" type="pushwipe" mode="out" begin="20" dur="2" />

<t:transitionfilter targetelement="oCaption1" type="fade" begin="oCaption1.begin" dur="2" />
<t:transitionfilter targetelement="oCaption1" type="fade" mode="out" begin="20" dur="2" />

<t:transitionfilter targetelement="oImage" type="clockwipe" begin="oImage.begin" dur="2" />
<t:transitionfilter targetelement="oImage" mode="out" type="clockwipe" begin="20" dur="2" />

<t:transitionfilter targetelement="oCaption2" type="fade" begin="oCaption2.begin" dur="2" />
<t:transitionfilter targetelement="oCaption2" type="fade" mode="out" begin="20" dur="2" />

<t:transitionfilter targetelement="oVideo" type="starwipe" subtype="fivepoint" begin="oVideo.begin" dur="2" />
<t:transitionfilter targetelement="oVideo" type="starwipe" mode="out" subtype="fivepoint" begin="20" dur="2" />

<t:transitionfilter targetelement="oCaption3" type="fade" begin="oCaption3.begin" dur="2" />
<t:transitionfilter targetelement="oCaption3" type="fade" mode="out" begin="20" dur="2" />

<t:transitionfilter targetelement="oDiv" type="ellipsewipe" begin="oDiv.begin" dur="2" />
<t:transitionfilter targetelement="oDiv" type="ellipsewipe" mode="out" begin="20" dur="2" />

<t:transitionfilter targetelement="oContainer" type="barnDoorWipe" mode="out" begin="20" dur="2"/>


   <DIV CLASS="time" dur="22" ID="oContainer" STYLE="background:#ffffcc; border:6px ridge #FFCC99; padding:4px;
    font-family:arial; color:white; font-size:x-large; width:450px;height:350px;
    filter:progid:DXImageTransform.Microsoft.Gradient(GradientType=0,
    StartColorStr='#3366CC', EndColorStr='#333300')">
<center>Introducing<br>
<b class="time" dur="22"  id="oSpan1"><nobr>HTML+TIME Transitions</nobr></b>

<p><p>
```

FIGURE 12.6 HTML+TIME Code in IE

CHAPTER 13

Integrating Databases with XML

LEARNING OBJECTIVES

1. To understand the differences between focusing on data versus documents when working with databases and XML.
2. To discover how to use XML with relational databases.
3. To learn what a native XML database is.
4. To know when to use a native XML database.
5. To gain familiarity with how database vendors utilize XML.

Throughout the earlier chapters in this book, we've described using XML to manipulate and display simple collections of data—for example, for recipes, travel information, or music collections. Up until now, though, we haven't discussed how you might use XML to interact with an actual database. Storing all of your data within an XML document instead of a full-fledged database may work well for small amounts of information—say, an address book, a collection of Web links, or other personal data. However, when it comes to scaling up the performance of these collections—for example, to share catalog information with potential customers worldwide—you'll want to ensure that your data is available immediately upon request even if a large number of users request the same data simultaneously. That's where integrating a database with your XML content is useful and can help.

Let's examine some situations in which you might like to or want to use a database. For starters, you may find yourself working with an organization that has a great deal of information in files or databases. This stored information may date all the way back to when your company first began operations, perhaps even using data formats that are not in popular use anymore. This kind of historical information is also called **legacy data**. If you want to make use of such legacy data, pulling it into a database for reference on demand is a good way to make it available.

An Introduction to Using Databases with XML

The tasks that your data is used for should influence what kind of database you need. If you have built a Web site based on a number of long, wordy XML documents, you could use a database to manage the Web site or allow users to search its documents. For example, a print magazine or newspaper could use a Web site to showcase articles from its back issues. A human resources department could place its employee manual on an intranet where employees can search its contents for benefits information. In these cases, searching for and displaying full documents is an important business requirement. Using XML could be an integral component of managing these documents; on a Web site, for example, you could code these documents in XHTML to ensure that they are in a consistent format and are searchable. This is an example of **document-centric XML.** The type of database best suited for this task would likely be a **native XML database** or a **content management system** (also known as a **content management framework**), which we'll describe in more detail later in this chapter.

As another example, your company may utilize an e-commerce application for taking orders and completing online credit card transactions. This application could use XML as a **data transport**—in other words, to transfer the data containing order details and credit card numbers and store it in the company's ordering systems. In this case, the individual pieces of data are what's important—the product numbers, the quantities of items purchased, sizes, credit card number, and expiration date, for example. Here, XML is only used for messaging, to transfer the data back and forth from the database to any documents (for example, to an order receipt). This is an example of **data-centric XML.** In this case, you could use a traditional database and software that would enable the transfer of information between XML documents and the database. We will describe how to make this work in detail later in this chapter.

Traditional databases that can work with XML are also known as **XML-enabled databases** because they have been developed to transfer data seamlessly between their data stores and XML documents. Major commercial vendors of database software and servers have all developed extensive sets of components or solutions to work with XML-related information in their databases.

Let's now review examples of data-centric XML as opposed to document-centric XML.

Data-Centric XML

In data-centric XML, data is pulled from a database to be used in an XML document. Flight schedules, sales receipts, or stock quotes are all examples of data-centric documents. The actual information retrieval with XML is usually done by computers with little or no human intervention. Human readers are more interested in the resulting XML document that includes the information of relevance to them—the details of their recent online purchase, their flight particulars, or their stock portfolio's current net worth—than in the overall database.

Data-centric documents usually have consistently structured data. For example, every entry in a flight schedule will show that flight's number, originating point, destination point, time of departure, and so on. XML can transfer the data in both directions, either from a database to an XML document or from an outside source into a database. For example, a company's human resources IT department could use XML to generate a payroll list for all managers that shows how much each employee in that group earned during that pay period. In turn, when new employees join the firm, their personal information could be entered into a data entry system, where it's converted into XML and added to the payroll system database.

For example, the following abridged description of a public recreational facility provided by Recreation.gov is an example of data-centric XML:

```
<Facility>
  <ID>3</ID>
  <AgencyName>Bureau of Reclamation</AgencyName>
  <RecGovURL>http://www.recreation.gov/
    detail.cfm?ID=(3)</RecGovURL>
  <JurisdictionType>Federal</JurisdictionType>
  <FacilityName>Canyon Lake</FacilityName>
  <FacilityURL>http://www.fs.fed.us/r3/
    tonto</FacilityURL>
  <Latitude>-1.05878e+006</Latitude>
  <Longitude>-1.20003e+006</Longitude>
  <StreetAddress1>Tonto National Forest</StreetAddress1>
  <StreetAddress2>2324 E. McDowall Road</StreetAddress2>
  <StreetAddress3>P.O. Box 5348</StreetAddress3>
  <City>Phoenix</City>
  <State_Territory_Provence>AZ</State_Territory_Provence>
  <PostalCode>85010</PostalCode>
  <Country>USA</Country>
  <Phone>602-225-5200</Phone>
  <States>AZ</States>
</Facility>
```

In the facility listing above, each element contains a very specific piece of information. A directory filled with such listings wouldn't make for very fascinating reading. Rather, it would be more useful as a reference—for example, if you knew you wanted to take a vacation in Arizona and decided to search for nature trails in a certain area. But with some effort, you could construct a more prose-like Web page that contains the information about each individual facility that's pulled in from the database. Here's an example sentence using several of the element names used in the recreational facilities example above:

```
<FacilityName>Canyon Lake</FacilityName> is a
  recreational facility located near
  <City>Phoenix</City>, <State_Territory_
  Provence>AZ</State_Territory_Provence>.
```

To dynamically construct sentences like this, you would use an XSL stylesheet to standardize the text and punctuation that separates the values for the `<FacilityName>`, `<City>`, and `<State_Territory_Provence>` elements. Here are the relevant lines from a sample XSL stylesheet that would produce the code above:

```
<xsl:value-of select="Facility/FacilityName"/> is a
  recreational facility located near <xsl:value-of
  select="Facility/City"/>, <xsl:value-of select=
  "Facility/State_Territory_Provence"/>.<br />
```

Document-Centric XML

As the name implies, document-centric XML describes documents that are meant for humans to browse and read through. Articles, books, brochures, and almost any large amount of prose stored in XHTML documents are good examples. In broad strokes, document-centric XML documents are less structured than data-centric XML documents. Document-centric documents frequently hold elements that in turn contain both free-form text and other elements, which is known as **mixed content.** Here is an example of document-centric XML that contains mixed content:

```
<Class>

<Introduction>
<ClassName>Choosing and Using Consumer Electronics
  </ClassName> is taught by <Instructor>Ross
  Rubin</Instructor>. When school is in session, this
  class is held every <Weekday>Monday</Weekday> from
  <StartTime>6:00 p.m.</StartTime> until <EndTime>
  8:30 p.m.</EndTime>.
</Introduction>

<Description>

<Para>Digital cameras, color printers and scanners, and
  a bevy of personal computers are now widely available to
  consumers. But how can you be confident you're getting
  what you paid for and making the most of it? In this
```

```
  class you'll gain an overview of the latest in video
  cameras, color scanners, color printers, and other
  consumer technology products. </Para>

<Para>You'll also learn:</Para>

<List>
<LineItem>How to brainstorm ways to put your new equipment
  to use</LineItem>
<LineItem>When to upgrade and when to invest in a new
  model</LineItem>
<LineItem>What sales channels offer the best deals, and
  which to avoid</LineItem>
</List>

</Description>

</Class>
```

In the example above, the <Introduction> element provides one example of mixed content because it contains both text and other elements (the <ClassName>, <StartTime>, and <EndTime>).

We mentioned earlier that data-centric XML is usually retrieved from a database. By contrast, the data in document-centric XML is rarely created in a database. It's usually generated by human authors and coded in an electronic format. The authors could create either XML or XHTML documents, or documents in another format (such as PDF or RTF) that are converted to XML.

Going from Data and Documents to Databases

In the real world, you may not find such clear-cut differences between data-centric and document-centric XML documents. For example, the data-centric example from Recreation.gov we used that summarized a recreational facility could just as easily contain a wordy description about the grounds themselves. The expanded example below shows our recreational facility listing with a text-heavy element called <FacilityDirections>, which contains directions to get there:

```
<Facility>
  <ID>3</ID>
  <AgencyName>Bureau of Reclamation</AgencyName>
  <RecGovURL>http://www.recreation.gov/detail.
    cfm?ID=(3)</RecGovURL>
  <JurisdictionType>Federal</JurisdictionType>
  <FacilityName>Canyon Lake</FacilityName>
  <FacilityURL>http://www.fs.fed.us/r3/
    tonto</FacilityURL>
```

```
    <FacilityDirections>There is only one way to Canyon
      Lake - the scenic Apache Trail (Highway 88) from
      Apache Junction. The 15 miles to the lake are fully
      paved and wind through some of the most colorful
      desert scenery in central Arizona. Drive with care -
      there are many sharp turns. The route used to be a
      construction road during the building of Roosevelt
      Dam.</FacilityDirections>
    <Latitude>-1.05878e+006</Latitude>
    <Longitude>-1.20003e+006</Longitude>
    <StreetAddress1>Tonto National Forest</StreetAddress1>
    <StreetAddress2>2324 E. McDowall Road</StreetAddress2>
    <StreetAddress3>P.O. Box 5348</StreetAddress3>
    <City>Phoenix</City>
    <State_Territory_Provence>AZ</State_Territory_Provence>
    <PostalCode>85010</PostalCode>
    <Country>USA</Country>
    <Phone>602-225-5200</Phone>
    <States>AZ</States>
  </Facility>
```

By the same token, document-centric documents like legal depositions or medical reports could still contain regularly structured data—for example, a client's name or relevant dates. In the computer class description example shown above, the information is very document-centric but also contains regular, structured information like a class title and instructor name that could conceivably be found in all class offerings.

Tech Tip

There are no hard-and-fast rules that dictate what kind of database must be used to store specific kinds of XML documents. It is possible to store data-centric XML in native XML databases. It's also possible to store document-centric XML in traditional databases if necessary. Vendors of traditional databases are increasingly adding native XML capabilities to their products, especially in regards to relational databases.

In any event, deciding whether your documents are truly data-centric or document-centric can help you determine what kind of database to use to store your XML data. Data-centric documents lend themselves well to storage in traditional kinds of databases. Some kinds of traditional databases are relational databases, **object-oriented databases,** and hierarchical databases; in the next section, we will examine what distinguishes these different kinds of traditional databases. Transferring data to and from a traditional database with XML may be accomplished with **middleware,** a term for software that's designed to connect applications in order to exchange data. You also can directly transfer data to and from a traditional database with XML, without middleware, if the database has its own built-in capabilities for doing so. If a database has such capabilities, it is said to be XML-enabled.

Document-centric documents are best stored in either a native XML database, which is a database specifically designed for holding XML content, or a content management system, which is an application that's built on a native XML database that's intended solely for managing documents.

Now let's examine the specifics of storing and retrieving data in traditional databases, followed by how to do the same for data in native XML databases.

Transferring Information between Traditional Databases and XML

A database is essentially a computerized system for recordkeeping. A database might be as simple as an electronic collection of recipes or business cards you store on your home PC, or as sophisticated as a banking institution's account tracking methods to oversee the continually updated accounts of their customers. A database is typically associated with the software that's used to update and query the database. A small business owner might use a database product like Microsoft Access to maintain business records; a large firm might use Oracle or Microsoft SQL Server as the underlying database for the applications it uses or builds.

Traditional databases come in a variety of flavors, from relational databases and object-oriented databases to hierarchical databases and information network databases.

The bulk of this chapter's discussion of using traditional databases with XML will focus on relational databases, largely because most instances of traditional databases you'll see transferring data with data-centric XML documents are likely to be relational databases. Relational databases and XML documents share a set of similarities that simplify associating specific data with the XML depiction of that data.

Relational Databases

A **relational database** is a database in which related information is stored in tables, and data is linked between tables. Each individual item and the information collected about it are known as a **record.** Each record is described in its own row in a table of rows and columns, with the various columns used to assign the specific kinds of information. Each record should be assigned a unique number. A record in a database of addresses, for example, might contain columns displaying the unique record number, name, address, city, state, telephone number, fax number, and so on. Relational databases contain more than one table. A retail firm, for example, would maintain tables with customer information, product information, sales history, supplier information, and a price list table. To track individual sales orders, the firm would create a new table that would refer to the other tables through the unique record number, pulling in the sales order's information from the sales history table

Advice

Practicing with Databases

The two tables shown in Figure 13.1 are part of the sample Northwinds database that's packaged with the Microsoft Access program. Experimenting with the sample Northwinds database included with Microsoft Access is an excellent way to gain hands-on experience with databases, even if you don't have any database information of your own to work with.

and the customer details from the customer information table. Figure 13.1 shows a product table and suppliers table, which share a column of data containing the supplier names. Retrieving a full listing of product and supplier information would require what's called a **join,** which is a query that combines rows from two or more tables or views.

A relational database implements a standardized set of operations—such as comparing data or inserting information—on its stored data using a programming language called **Structured Query Language (SQL).** SQL provides an interface that's intended to be much easier to learn than most programming languages. You can use SQL to manipulate data in database systems like Microsoft Access, Oracle, DB2, Sybase, Informix, and Microsoft SQL Server, among others.

A Brief Introduction to SQL

SQL lets you explicitly select data from the tables located in a database. The keywords used in the most basic SQL statement reflect that you want to `SELECT` information `FROM` a table:

```
SELECT "column_name" FROM "table_name"
```

As an example, let's select data from the table called `Employee_Information`. This employee table, shown in Table 13.1, is part of the Northwinds database included with Microsoft Access, so if you have Access, you can view this data onscreen.

The SQL statement that will select all the employees in this table is

```
SELECT Last_Name FROM Employee_Information
```

This will produce the following results:

```
Last_Name

Buchanan
Callahan
Davolio
Dodsworth
Fuller
King
Leverling
Peacock
Suyama
```

You can select multiple column names with a SQL statement, as well as multiple table names. You also can add conditions to your search requests. For example, to retrieve a list of all sales representatives, you would need a SQL statement like the following:

Products : Table

Product ID	Product Name	Supplier
1	Chai	Exotic Liquids
2	Chang	Exotic Liquids
3	Aniseed Syrup	Exotic Liquids
4	Chef Anton's Cajun Seasoning	New Orleans Cajun Delights
5	Chef Anton's Gumbo Mix	New Orleans Cajun Delights
6	Grandma's Boysenberry Spread	Grandma Kelly's Homestead
7	Uncle Bob's Organic Dried Pears	Grandma Kelly's Homestead
8	Northwoods Cranberry Sauce	Grandma Kelly's Homestead
9	Mishi Kobe Niku	Tokyo Traders
10	Ikura	Tokyo Traders
11	Queso Cabrales	Cooperativa de Quesos 'Las Cabras'
12	Queso Manchego La Pastora	Cooperativa de Quesos 'Las Cabras'
13	Konbu	Mayumi's
14	Tofu	Mayumi's
15	Genen Shouyu	Mayumi's
16	Pavlova	Pavlova, Ltd.
17	Alice Mutton	Pavlova, Ltd.
18	Carnarvon Tigers	Pavlova, Ltd.
19	Teatime Chocolate Biscuits	Specialty Biscuits, Ltd.
20	Sir Rodney's Marmalade	Specialty Biscuits, Ltd.

Record: 1 of 77

Suppliers : Table

Supplier ID	Company Name	Contact Name	Contact Title
1	Exotic Liquids	Charlotte Cooper	Purchasing Manager
2	New Orleans Cajun Delights	Shelley Burke	Order Administrator
3	Grandma Kelly's Homestead	Regina Murphy	Sales Representative
4	Tokyo Traders	Yoshi Nagase	Marketing Manager
5	Cooperativa de Quesos 'Las Cabras'	Antonio del Valle Saavedra	Export Administrator
6	Mayumi's	Mayumi Ohno	Marketing Representative
7	Pavlova, Ltd.	Ian Devling	Marketing Manager
8	Specialty Biscuits, Ltd.	Peter Wilson	Sales Representative
9	PB Knäckebröd AB	Lars Peterson	Sales Agent
10	Refrescos Americanas LTDA	Carlos Diaz	Marketing Manager
11	Heli Süßwaren GmbH & Co. KG	Petra Winkler	Sales Manager
12	Plutzer Lebensmittelgroßmärkte AG	Martin Bein	International Marketing Mgr.
13	Nord-Ost-Fisch Handelsgesellschaft mbH	Sven Petersen	Coordinator Foreign Markets
14	Formaggi Fortini s.r.l.	Elio Rossi	Sales Representative
15	Norske Meierier	Beate Vileid	Marketing Manager
16	Bigfoot Breweries	Cheryl Saylor	Regional Account Rep.
17	Svensk Sjöföda AB	Michael Björn	Sales Representative
18	Aux joyeux ecclésiastiques	Guylène Nodier	Sales Manager
19	New England Seafood Cannery	Robb Merchant	Wholesale Account Agent
20	Leka Trading	Chandra Leka	Owner

Record: 1 of 29

FIGURE 13.1 A Relational Database

```
SELECT Last_Name
FROM Employee_Information
WHERE Title = 'Sales Representative'
```

TABLE 13.1 A Sample Employee Table in Microsoft Access

Last_Name	First_Name	Title	Hire_Date
Buchanan	Steven	Sales Manager	17-Oct-1993
Callahan	Laura	Inside Sales Coordinator	05-Mar-1994
Davolio	Nancy	Sales Representative	01-May-1992
Dodsworth	Anne	Sales Representative	15-Nov-1994
Fuller	Andrew	Vice President, Sales	14-Aug-1992
King	Robert	Sales Representative	02-Jan-1994
Leverling	Janet	Sales Representative	01-Apr-1992
Peacock	Margaret	Sales Representative	03-May-1993
Suyama	Michael	Sales Representative	17-Oct-1993

This would produce a subset of the full employee table:

```
Last_Name

Buchanan
Davolio
Dodsworth
King
Leverling
Peacock
Suyama
```

Employees Callahan and Fuller are omitted because neither has the title of "Sales Representative." Later in this chapter, we'll take SQL queries a step further and show how they're used when the data results should be retrieved in XML.

What's Next: Mapping and Querying

To transfer data smoothly between XML documents and a database, you'll need to ensure that each element in your XML documents—as defined either through a DTD or XML Schema, for example—has an equivalent in the database's own schema. This requires a **mapping** of the XML document schema to the database schema. The database software then references this mapping as it transfers data.

The software that's used to transfer this data may utilize **querying**—with an XML query language, such as XPath or XQuery—in order to transfer data this way. Alternatively, the software that's used may directly transfer data. To directly map the data on a one-to-one basis, data transfer software usually uses XSLT to transform the document to a structure that the database expects and vice versa. Now let's examine what's involved in mapping an XML document schema to a database schema. After that, we'll examine the querying and direct transfer methods of actually transferring the data.

Mapping Document Schemas to Database Schemas

What gets mapped between XML documents and database schemas usually includes elements, attributes, and text. Other parts of XML documents are often left out; these include entities (blocks of text, especially those sourced from other documents), `CDATA` sections, and processing instructions, comments, and the ordering of elements and `PCDATA`.

Why are so many parts of an XML document left out when mapping XML documents to database schemas? Although the omitted information is important to XML documents, only the data is really of any relevance to a database. For example, to go back to the recreational facilities example earlier, it doesn't matter in the database if the ID number is stored before or after the facility name.

There are two kinds of mappings most frequently used to connect an XML document schema to traditional kinds of databases. One is called a **table-based mapping** and the other is known as an **object-relational mapping.**

Table-Based Mapping

Table-based mapping represents XML documents as a series of tables. Many middleware vendors utilize table-based mapping in their software for transferring data back and forth between XML documents and a relational database. Figure 13.2 shows how this process can start with a series of tables. We're once more referring to a set of tables in the sample Northwinds database; these tables show the firm's product categories, actual product offerings, and sales orders.

The code in Listing 13.1 shows how table-based mapping could represent the data from the series of tables in Figure 13.2 as an XML document.

LISTING 13.1

```
<SalesHistoryDB>
  <CategoryTable>
    <Category id="1">
      <Name>Beverages</Name>
      <Description>Soft drinks, coffees, teas, beers, and
        ales</Description>
    </Category>
    <Category id="2">
      <Name>Condiments</Name>
      <Description>Sweet and savory sauces, relishes,
        spreads, and seasonings</Description>
```

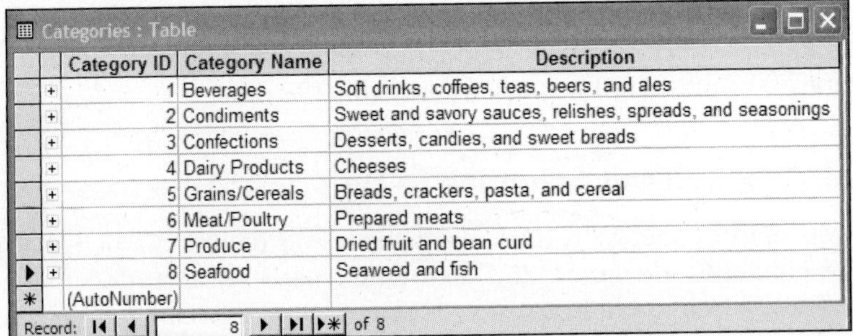

Categories : Table

Category ID	Category Name	Description
1	Beverages	Soft drinks, coffees, teas, beers, and ales
2	Condiments	Sweet and savory sauces, relishes, spreads, and seasonings
3	Confections	Desserts, candies, and sweet breads
4	Dairy Products	Cheeses
5	Grains/Cereals	Breads, crackers, pasta, and cereal
6	Meat/Poultry	Prepared meats
7	Produce	Dried fruit and bean curd
8	Seafood	Seaweed and fish
(AutoNumber)		

Record: 8 of 8

Products : Table

Proc	Product Name	Supplier	Category	Quantity Per Unit	Unit Price	Units In Stock	Units On Order
17	Alice Mutton	Pavlova, Ltd.	Meat/Poultry	20 - 1 kg tins	$39.00	0	0
3	Aniseed Syrup	Exotic Liquids	Condiments	12 - 550 ml bottles	$10.00	13	70
40	Boston Crab Meat	New England Seafood	Seafood	24 - 4 oz tins	$18.40	123	0
60	Camembert Pierrot	Gai pâturage	Dairy Products	15 - 300 g rounds	$34.00	19	0
18	Carnarvon Tigers	Pavlova, Ltd.	Seafood	16 kg pkg.	$62.50	42	0
1	Chai	Exotic Liquids	Beverages	10 boxes x 20 bags	$18.00	39	0
2	Chang	Exotic Liquids	Beverages	24 - 12 oz bottles	$19.00	17	40
39	Chartreuse verte	Aux joyeux ecclésiasti	Beverages	750 cc per bottle	$18.00	69	0
4	Chef Anton's Cajun Sea	New Orleans Cajun De	Condiments	48 - 6 oz jars	$22.00	53	0
5	Chef Anton's Gumbo Mi	New Orleans Cajun De	Condiments	36 boxes	$21.35	0	0

Record: 1 of 77

Orders : Table

Order ID	Customer	Employee	Order Date	Required Date	Shipped Date	Ship Via	Freight
10643	Alfreds Futterkiste	Suyama, Michael	25-Aug-1997	22-Sep-1997	02-Sep-1997	Speedy Express	$29.46
10952	Alfreds Futterkiste	Davolio, Nancy	16-Mar-1998	27-Apr-1998	24-Mar-1998	Speedy Express	$40.42
10625	Ana Trujillo Emparedados y hel:	Leverling, Janet	08-Aug-1997	05-Sep-1997	14-Aug-1997	Speedy Express	$43.90
10759	Ana Trujillo Emparedados y hel:	Leverling, Janet	28-Nov-1997	26-Dec-1997	12-Dec-1997	Federal Shipping	$11.99
10856	Antonio Moreno Taquería	Leverling, Janet	28-Jan-1998	25-Feb-1998	10-Feb-1998	United Package	$58.43
10573	Antonio Moreno Taquería	King, Robert	19-Jun-1997	17-Jul-1997	20-Jun-1997	Federal Shipping	$84.84
10920	Around the Horn	Peacock, Margaret	03-Mar-1998	31-Mar-1998	09-Mar-1998	United Package	$29.61
10383	Around the Horn	Callahan, Laura	16-Dec-1996	13-Jan-1997	18-Dec-1996	Federal Shipping	$34.24
10837	Berglunds snabbköp	Dodsworth, Anne	16-Jan-1998	13-Feb-1998	23-Jan-1998	Federal Shipping	$13.32
10733	Berglunds snabbköp	Davolio, Nancy	07-Nov-1997	05-Dec-1997	10-Nov-1997	Federal Shipping	$110.11
10444	Berglunds snabbköp	Leverling, Janet	12-Feb-1997	12-Mar-1997	21-Feb-1997	Federal Shipping	$3.50

Record: 4 of 808

FIGURE 13.2 A Series of Tables in a Relational Database
You can use table-based mapping to represent this information in an XML document.

```
    </Category>
    <Category id="3">
      <Name>Confections</Name>
      <Description>Desserts, candies, and sweet breads
</Description>
    </Category>
      . . .
  </CategoryTable>

  <ProductTable>
    <Product id="17">
      <Name>Alice Mutton</Name>
      <Supplier>Pavlova, Ltd.</Supplier>
        <Category>Meat/Poultry</Category>
        <QuantityPerUnit>20 - 1 kg tins</QuantityPerUnit>
        <UnitPrice>$39.00</UnitPrice>
```

```
        <InStock>0</InStock>
        <OnOrder>0</OnOrder>
        <ReorderLevel>0</ReorderLevel>
        <Discontinued>1</Discontinued>
    </Product >
    <Product id="3">
      <Name>Aniseed Syrup</Name>
      <Supplier>Exotic Liquids</Supplier>
        <Category>Condiments</Category>
        <QuantityPerUnit>12 - 550 ml bottles
          </QuantityPerUnit>
        <UnitPrice>$10.00</UnitPrice>
        <InStock>13</InStock>
        <OnOrder>70</OnOrder>
        <ReorderLevel>25</ReorderLevel>
        <Discontinued>0</Discontinued>
    </Product >
      . . .
  </ProductTable>
  <OrderTable>
    <Order id="10643">
      <Customer>Alfreds Futterkiste</Customer>
        <OrderDate>25-Aug-1997</OrderDate>
        <RequiredDate>22-Sep-1997</RequiredDate>
        <ShippedDate>02-Sep-1997</ShippedDate>
        <FreightMethod>Speedy Express</FreightMethod>
        <Freight>$29.46</Freight>
        <ShipName>Alfreds Futterkiste</ShipName>
        <ShipAddress>Obere Str. 57</ShipAddress>
        <ShipCity>Berlin</ShipCity>
        <ShipRegion></ShipRegion>
        <ShipPostalCode>12209</ShipPostalCode>
        <ShipCountry>Germany</ShipCountry>
    </Order>
    <Order id="10952">
      <Customer>Alfreds Futterkiste</Customer>
        <OrderDate>16-Mar-1998</OrderDate>
        <RequiredDate>27-Apr-1998</RequiredDate>
        <ShippedDate>24-Mar-1998</ShippedDate>
        <FreightMethod>Speedy Express</FreightMethod>
        <Freight>$40.42</Freight>
        <ShipName>Alfreds Futterkiste</ShipName>
        <ShipAddress>Obere Str. 57</ShipAddress>
        <ShipCity>Berlin</ShipCity>
        <ShipRegion></ShipRegion>
        <ShipPostalCode>12209</ShipPostalCode>
```

```
        <ShipCountry>Germany</ShipCountry>
    </Order>
        <Order id="10625">
      <Customer>Ana Trujillo Emparedados y
        helados</Customer>
        <OrderDate>08-Aug-1997</OrderDate>
        <RequiredDate>05-Sep-1997</RequiredDate>
        <ShippedDate>14-Aug-1997</ShippedDate>
        <FreightMethod>Speedy Express</FreightMethod>
        <Freight>$43.90</Freight>
        <ShipName>Ana Trujillo Emparedados y
          helados</ShipName>
        <ShipAddress>Avda. de la Constitución</
          ShipAddress>
        <ShipCity>2222  México D.F.</ShipCity>
        <ShipRegion></ShipRegion>
        <ShipPostalCode>05021</ShipPostalCode>
        <ShipCountry>Mexico</ShipCountry>
    </Order>
      ...
   </OrderTable>
 </SalesHistoryDB >
```

Object-Relational Mapping

The object-relational mapping method represents your data as a branching tree of objects—that is, each real-world item is represented by a corresponding item in the database. XML-enabled relational databases can all use this model, and so do some middleware products.

Object-relational mapping distinguishes between elements that XML Schema defines as complex types and simple types. Object-relational mapping correlates complex-type elements to tables and simple-type elements to columns. To review from Chapter 5's discussion of XML Schema, `complexType` elements may contain other elements, attributes, or parsed character data

IMPORTANT

The term *table* is used rather loosely in this discussion of mapping data between a relational database and an XML document. When you're transferring data from a relational database to XML, the "table" can refer to any set of resulting data. When you transfer data from XML to a relational database, the "table" can refer to an actual table in the database or to any view of the data that you'd like to see and update readily.

IMPORTANT

Although this mapping method is called object-relational mapping, it is not meant only for use with object-relational databases. In fact, most of the database products that use this method employ relational databases. Some middleware products that map to object-oriented and hierarchical databases do use object-oriented mapping as well.

(`PCDATA`) in their content; `simpleType` elements can only contain `PCDATA` within their contents.

For example, the sales history document shown in Listing 13.1 could be modeled as a tree of objects that include, among other elements, objects for the Category, Product, and Order. Each of these areas represents a complex-type element, which makes sense since the original database included a category table, a product table, and an order table. The simple-type elements that each complex-type element contains—such as the customer name and shipping address information in the order details—can be found mapped as individual columns in the order table.

The example shown in Figure 13.3 is a very straightforward example, but often the structure of an XML document can be very different from the structure of the database that the document's data needs to be transferred to. In such cases, XSLT is often used by many database products. XSLT lets you

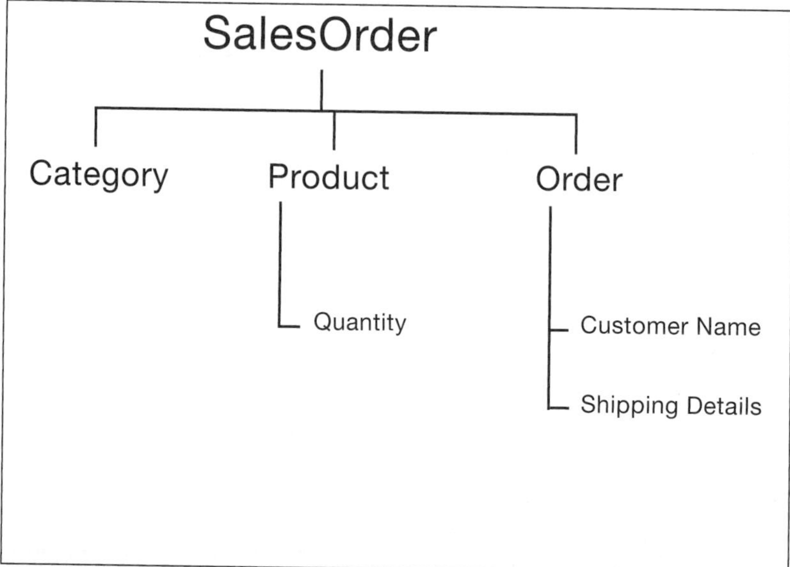

FIGURE 13.3 Object-Relational Mapping

convert a document to the structure that the database model requires and vice versa. This transformation takes place before any data transfer actually takes place. Since XSLT processing adds time and effort to data transfers, IT departments need to take these additional costs into consideration when determining the best way to implement data transfers between XML documents and databases.

Querying XML Documents to Transfer Data to Databases

Using a query language to retrieve data in XML from a database is a developing approach that is gaining in popularity among database vendors. Here's how one current implementation works: First, an XML document needs to contain queries embedded in templates. When the document is processed, the resulting data is returned within the template, thereby producing valid XML.

Similarly, there are SQL-based query languages that use standardized SQL statements in querying the database; the results returned from the database are then transformed to XML. Several SQL-based languages are in use that are proprietary—that is, specific to the companies that developed them. A group of other companies is working to develop standardized XML extensions to SQL; this undertaking is called SQL/XML and would no doubt hold greater appeal in theory than a proprietary solution.

Here is an example of what a sample SQL-based query would look like:

```
SELECT XMLElement("Invoice",
  XMLAttributes(IDNumber),
  XMLElement("Date", Date),
  XMLElement("Client", Client),
  XMLElement("ScopeOfWork", ScopeOfWork)) AS xmlresults
FROM Invoices WHERE IDNumber ="ZDM018"
```

This query would produce the XML document below in a column labeled `xmlresults`:

```
<Invoice IDNumber="ZDM018">
  <Date>08/31/2003</Date>
  <Client>Ziff Davis Media</Client>
  <ScopeOfWork>Provided computer instruction to writers
    at Baseline magazine.</ScopeOfWork >
</Invoice>
```

One potential application for SQL-based queries like this would be a Web-based accounts payable application. Different queries could be used to look up the status of a given invoice and display onscreen all invoices submitted for a particular client or from a specific vendor.

Directly Transferring Data to Databases

XML has the potential to be a far more sophisticated language for data models underlying many relational databases. As a result, storing your XML data in a SQL database can be more complicated than retrieving XML results back from a database. The most difficult part can be identifying a workable mapping from the nested data structures in XML documents to flat relational tables with rows and columns.

As an example, let's look at a straightforward collection of subscriber contact information stored by a newspaper formatted in XML in anticipation of storing in a database:

```
<Subscriber>
  <Name>Gertrude Sorensen</Name>
  <Address>
    <Street1>6220 Saunders Street</Street1>
    <Street2></Street2>
    <City>Flushing</City>
    <State>NY</State>
    <ZipCode>11374</ZipCode>
  </Address>
</Subscriber>
```

The child elements nested within the `<Address>` element would likely generate a table for addresses that's separate from the table for subscribers. In this case, and often more broadly, it would be more logical to keep the address within the subscriber table instead of as its own table.

This `<Address>` element provides an example of what's known as a **wrapper element.** Wrapper elements provide two functions. First, they add a naming structure that simplifies understanding of the other elements in the document. We would have realized anyway that the `<Street1>`, `<Street2>`, `<City>`, `<State>`, and `<ZipCode>` data compressed address information, but the `<Address>` wrapper element provides an identifying label. Next, wrapper elements are frequently used as a means of **data typing,** which means identifying the business purpose of the elements contained therein. In short, data typing classifies data from a semantic point of view rather than a programmer's perspective.

Although wrapper elements can be most helpful for classifying your XML data, they impose an extra layer of structure when the elements in your XML documents get mapped to the database. You could remove them from your document, but unless the overall DTD is updated as well, there could still be problems with mapping the XML documents and those expected by the data transfer software if the wrapper elements are omitted. In this situation, XSLT can provide the best solution by transforming the documents before and after the data transfer. XSLT can remove the wrapper elements before data is transferred to the database and then insert them again once data is transferred back from the database.

Transferring Information between Native XML Databases and XML Documents

> **Advice**
>
> **Caveats Regarding Performance of Native XML Databases**
>
> Note that any speed improvements in accessing data from an XML native database are enjoyed only when the data is retrieved in the same order in which it's stored in the database. If you need to change the view, the database performance will be slower than a relational database would have been. Accordingly, a good rule of thumb is that storing data in a native XML database will improve performance only when you're using a single view of your data for most retrieval purposes.

Now let's take a look at how you can store information from XML documents in a native XML database. As mentioned earlier in this chapter, one good reason to do this is to manage large numbers of document-centric XML documents. Ideally, these documents should each have a certain amount of structure—for example, all documents may have a title, author name, or publication date, among other characteristics by which they could be categorized. While you may store such partially structured documents in an object-oriented or hierarchical database, it would be more efficient from a data storage perspective to maintain them in a native XML database.

A native XML database also may retrieve data much more quickly than a relational database can because of how it stores the documents together in the database. As an example, consider the Northwinds sales order data we saw in Figure 13.2. As you see from this relational database, the data is stored in separate tables for category information, product information, customer information, and more. Retrieving the full sales order history would require using joins—which, as mentioned earlier, are queries that pull data in from multiple tables or views. By contrast, a native XML database would likely store the full document in a single place, simplifying retrieving any part of the information to a single pass at searching the database. In contrast, retrieving the data from a relational database requires a lookup in each table—the category table, product table, customer table, and so on—and separate data retrievals for each. All of these are time-consuming, which makes a native XML database a more logical choice when large document repositories are going to require frequent searches and data retrievals.

Database Vendors

Now let's take a look at some examples of how XML and some of the leading databases can be used together. Free evaluation versions of the products discussed here can be downloaded from the manufacturers' Web sites. Browsing the XML extensions offered by these vendors will help give you a better understanding of what capabilities are available and how to evaluate the best solution for a real-world database.

Using XML with Oracle

Oracle has XML-enabled database technology built into its Oracle9i database server. It has extensive documentation on storing and managing XML data with Oracle9i available on the company Web site at http://otn.oracle.com/documentation/. You'll also find an overview of the company's XML strategy at http://otn.oracle.com/tech/xml.

Oracle processes XML documents in one of two ways:

- **Composed** XML documents, which are stored as a Large Object (LOB).
- **Decomposed** XML documents, which are stored in relational tables. The XML tags are mapped to corresponding tables in the database's tables. These decomposed XML documents can then later be restored to composed XML documents.

An earlier version of Oracle's database server, Oracle8i, supports a limited number of LOBs.

In addition, Oracle has created an Oracle XML Developer's Kit (XDK) that would be of interest to anyone developing an XML-enabled application that needs to interact with an Oracle database.

Using XML with Microsoft's SQL Server 2000

Microsoft has added XML functionality to its SQL Server 2000 database server that lets you view your whole relational database as XML. This, in turn, gives you the ability to write full XML applications to interact with your data.

These capabilities are intended to let you work with your SQL Server 2000 data as a series of XML documents, although the underlying data is untouched. This preserves the functionality of any existing applications that use your database.

With SQL Server 2000, you can develop XPath queries that would be much shorter than the equivalent SQL statements, which should simplify development.

Using XML with IBM's DB2

IBM has developed extensive initiatives for building XML support into DB2. One research project IBM makes available on alphaWorks, its site for developers, is an XML Registry/Repository (XRR) package for storing and managing XML data. More information about this development tool is available at http://www.alphaworks.ibm.com/tech/xrr.

XRR includes five separate services. The first is a registry for groups to submit DTDs, schemas, or stylesheets. Once these documents are approved, they become registered objects within the system. A separate registration service for organizations themselves is next in order to become legitimate submitters of documents to the system. Next, a search service lets users search the registry for registered objects. An administration service manages the status of users and overall registry content. Finally, an access service lets users download registered objects from the registry.

Going forward, these vendors will likely add more sophisticated functionality to their XML offerings in order to remain competitive. Their offerings also will likely become easier to implement over time as actual usage increases and customers demand easier-to-use features. The continuing development of XML standards from the W3C also will have a huge impact on these continually evolving database products as well.

Key Terms

composed
content management framework
content management system
data transport
data typing
data-centric XML
decomposed
document-centric XML
join
legacy data
mapping
middleware
mixed content
native XML database
object-oriented database
object-relational mapping
querying
record
relational database
Structured Query Language (SQL)
table-based mapping
wrapper element
XML-enabled database

Code Summary

1. **Data-centric XML (Source: Recreation.gov):**

```
<Facility>
  <ID>3</ID>
  <AgencyName>Bureau of Reclamation</AgencyName>
  <RecGovURL>http://www.recreation.gov/detail.cfm?ID=(3)</RecGovURL>
  <JurisdictionType>Federal</JurisdictionType>
  <FacilityName>Canyon Lake</FacilityName>
  <FacilityURL>http://www.fs.fed.us/r3/tonto</FacilityURL>
  <Latitude>-1.05878e+006</Latitude>
  <Longitude>-1.20003e+006</Longitude>
  <StreetAddress1>Tonto National Forest</StreetAddress1>
  <StreetAddress2>2324 E. McDowall Road</StreetAddress2>
  <StreetAddress3>P.O. Box 5348</StreetAddress3>
  <City>Phoenix</City>
  <State_Territory_Provence>AZ</State_Territory_Provence>
  <PostalCode>85010</PostalCode>
  <Country>USA</Country>
  <Phone>602-225-5200</Phone>
  <States>AZ</States>
</Facility>
```

2. Document-centric XML:

```
<Class>

<Introduction>
<ClassName>Choosing and Using Consumer Electronics</ClassName> is
   taught by <Instructor>Ross Rubin</Instructor>. When school is in session, this class
   is held every <Weekday>Monday</Weekday> from <StartTime>6:00 p.m.</StartTime> until
   <EndTime>8:30 p.m.
   </EndTime>.
</Introduction>

<Description>

<Para>Digital cameras, color printers and scanners, and a bevy of
   personal computers are now widely available to consumers. But how can you be confident
   you're getting what you paid for and making the most of it? In this class you'll gain
   an overview of the latest in video cameras, color scanners, color printers, and other
   consumer technology products. </Para>

<Para>You'll also learn:</Para>

<List>
<Item> How to brainstorm ways to put your new equipment to use</Item>
<Item>When to upgrade and when to invest in a new model</Item>
<Item>What sales channels offer the best deals, and which to
   avoid</Item>
</List>

</Description>

</Class>
```

3. `SELECT` **statement in SQL:**

```
SELECT "column_name" FROM "table_name"
```

4. A conditional SQL query:

```
SELECT Last_Name
FROM Employee_Information
WHERE Title = "Sales Representative"
```

5. A SQL query producing XML results:

```
SELECT XMLElement("Invoice",
   XMLAttributes(IDNumber),
   XMLElement("Date", Date),
   XMLElement("Client", Client),
   XMLElement("ScopeOfWork", ScopeOfWork)) AS xmlresults
FROM Invoices WHERE IDNumber ="ZDM018"
```

which produces the following XML elements and data:

```
<Invoice IDNumber="ZDM018">
   <Date>08/31/2003</Date>
   <Client>Ziff Davis Media</Client>
```

```
    <ScopeOfWork>Provided computer instruction to writers at Baseline
      magazine.</ScopeOfWork >
  </Invoice>
```

6. **XML containing a wrapper element (<Address>):**

```
<Subscriber>
   <Name>Gertrude Sorensen</Name>
   <Address>
      <Street1>6220 Saunders Street</Street1>
      <Street2></Street2>
      <City>Flushing</City>
      <State>NY</State>
      <ZipCode>11374</ZipCode>
   </Address>
</Subscriber>
```

Review Questions

1. What are some characteristics of a data-centric document?
2. What are some characteristics of a document-centric document?
3. What is mixed content?
4. What is a database?
5. Describe what kind of database is typically used to store data-centric XML.
6. Describe what kind of database is typically used to store document-centric XML.
7. Name and describe several kinds of traditional databases.
8. What are the two kinds of mappings used to map an XML document schema to a database schema?
9. Give an example of a SQL query.
10. What would be the syntax for adding a condition to a SQL query?
11. When might a native XML database perform more slowly than a traditional database?

Case Study

Launch your Web browser and visit Recreation.gov at http://www.recreation.gov/. This government initiative in widely sharing data on public recreational facilities is intended to simplify enabling any interested Web site to provide reliable information to visitors. Read the associated documentation to learn how you could freely provide access to this data on a Web site of your own. Now consider how you would exchange data with Recreation.gov if you wanted to upload a personal database of facilities information to the overall database. What would you need to do to make this happen? Also consider how the system's subcategories may need to develop further. What would be needed, for example, to add new categories to the listing of activities?

For additional background, please read Ron Bourret's well-documented and frequently syndicated articles on XML and databases. They are hosted on his individual Web site at http://www.rpbourret.com/; we also have included specific links in this chapter's list of online links.

With this material in mind, please launch Microsoft Access and the sample Northwinds company database included with the program. We will use the program's wizards to generate the SQL syntax used for these hands-on queries.

1. When you open a database in Microsoft Access, the database window shown in Figure 13.4 displays. Open the Orders table to view the sample database's complete list of orders by ID, listing the customer name and other order details.

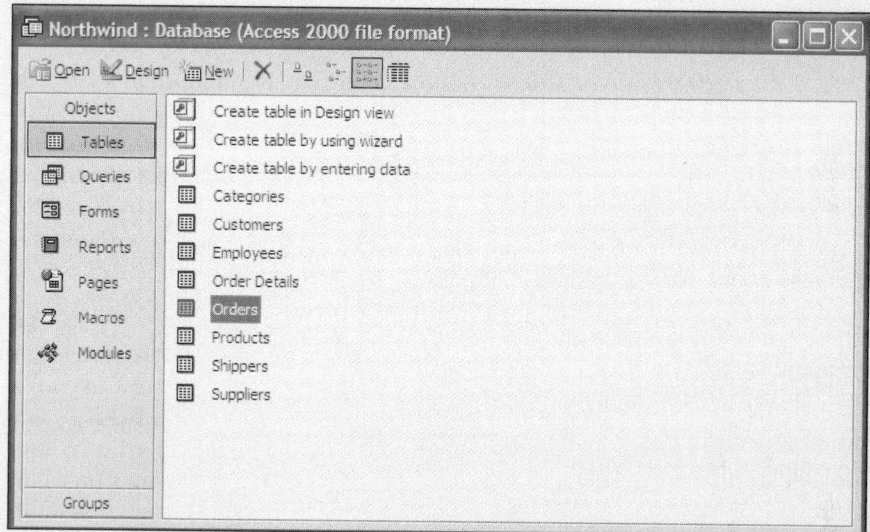

FIGURE 13.4 Opening the Orders Table in the Northwinds Database, a Sample Company Database Included with Microsoft Access

2. Now let's construct a query to display all sales orders from a particular customer. Consider what columns of data—and from which tables—would be most relevant to include for this instance. Microsoft Access's Simple Select Query Wizard can help you create queries that retrieve data from the fields you specify in one or more tables or queries. To access this wizard, click `Queries` in the left side of the database window. See Figure 13.5.

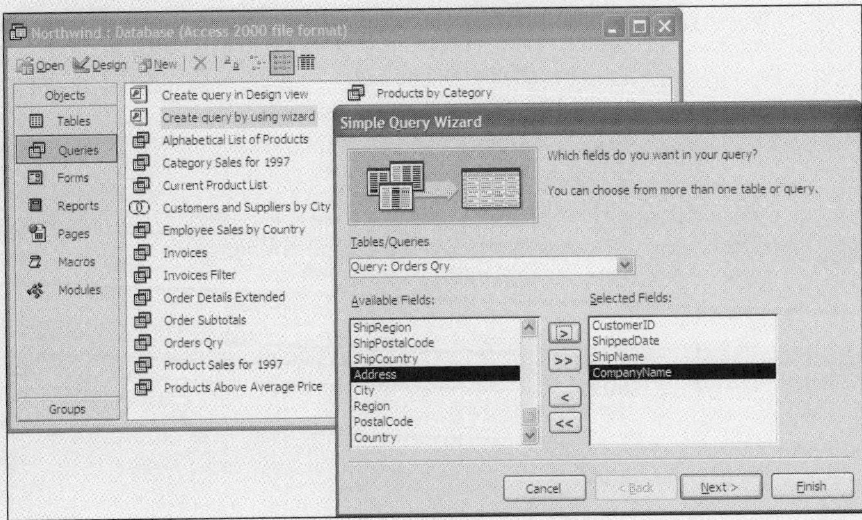

FIGURE 13.5 Accessing the Simple Select Query Wizard

3. The Simple Query Wizard displays. From the `Query` drop-down menu, choose `Query: Orders Qry`. Pick and choose the fields that you would like to display in your results—for example, the customer name and ID, the order date, and so on. Proceed to use the wizard until you're asked if you want to open the query or modify the query's design. See Figure 13.6.

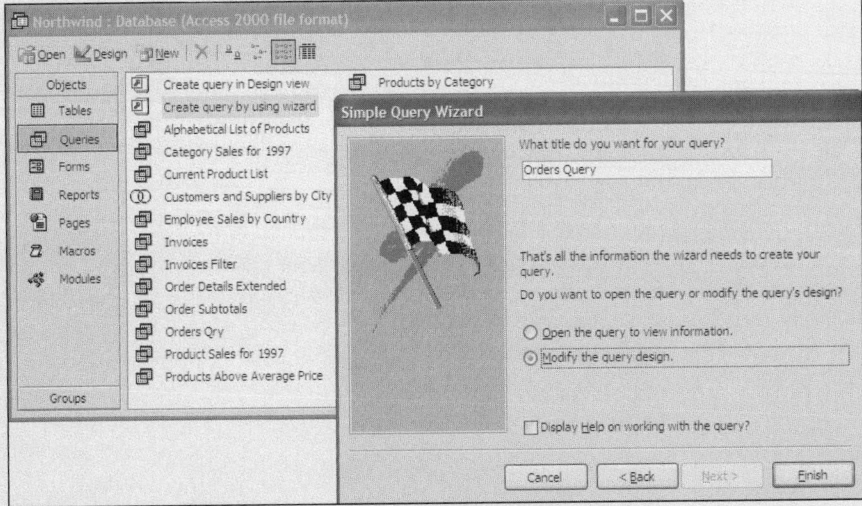

FIGURE 13.6 The Simple Query Wizard

4. Now let's construct a query to display all sales orders between a certain range of dates—for example, a single year. When the wizard asks if you want to open the query or modify the query's design, click the check box next to "Modify the query design."

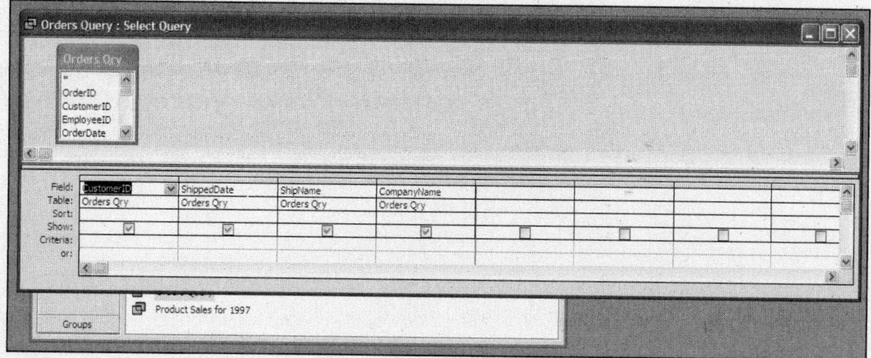

FIGURE 13.7 Modifying the Query Design Lets You Add Specify Criteria to Your Query

Your current query displays in a new window. (See Figure 13.7.) To see all sales orders placed in 1996, for example, you add the following expression to the criteria field:

```
Between #1/1/96# And #12/31/96#
```

This is the equivalent of using a SQL `between . . . and` clause in a `where` clause in a standard SQL query.

5. Create a stylesheet for displaying these sales order results.

CHAPTER 14

Web Services

LEARNING OBJECTIVES

1. To understand what Web Services are.
2. To investigate SOAP and how it works as a wrapper for XML messages.
3. To see how UDDI maintains a registry for business services.
4. To look at WSDL as a specific XML language to describe business services and the message groups it uses.
5. To view a simple Web Services Model: "publish, find, and bind."
6. To look at the way SOAP sends and receives messages.
7. To examine the way WSDL structures a statement.

As the Web grows, it is increasingly being employed for back-end application-to-application communication whether it be e-commerce, large financial transactions, medical information, or credit card data. We have already seen examples with XPath, Xlink, and XML's use of databases and external links. However, new programming concepts are being developed, along with resultant technologies, grouped together under the nomenclature Web Services. XML was included as part of the Web Services Activity statement of W3C in January 2002.

XML, XML namespaces, and XML schemas are now stabilized and commonly used together in distributed environments. XML now combines with SOAP (Simple Object Access Protocol), UDDI (Universal Description, Discovery and Integration), and WSDL (Web Services Description Language) (more on these in a moment) technologies to create intricate functionality and services in the XML-based sphere using a combination of distributed objects and B2B utilizing the Web. Distributed objects are part of a computing paradigm that allows objects to be distributed across a network, yet operates as a unified whole, usually, but not always, though object-oriented programming. This allows a basic exchange of

messages, a description of actual Web Services and a way to publish and find out about Web Service descriptions, also known as publish, find, and bind.

What Are Web Services?

Tech Tip

The W3C defines Web Services as "a software system identified by a URI, whose public interfaces and bindings are defined and described using XML. Its definition can be discovered by other software systems. These systems may then interact with the Web service in a manner prescribed by its definition, using XML based messages conveyed by Internet protocols."

Web Services are a group of services and technologies working together to ensure seamless information exchange and delivery. They consist of a core group of programming and data that work together in relational ways. Web Services reside on a Web server and organizations and individuals who provide these services are known as application service providers. These services can perform functions as simple as monitoring bids on auction items or furnishing up-to-date financial data, or manage complex storage of data and information and customer relation management (CRM) software.

Although Web Services do reside on specific servers, they also can be accessed through a peer-to-peer arrangement (p2p) (one person's computer to another person's computer). Before there were Web Services, EDI (electronic data interchange) was used to handle a very complex relationship of procedures and data that was proprietary and usually owned by a specific company.

Web Services are innately set up to work with the **Semantic Web,** which works with real-world objects linking data to programs. The inventor of the Web, Tim Berners-Lee, felt that although search engines returned results, they did not really select the specific links or pages a user might really want; they only returned keyword matches. Thus, he put forth the idea of the Semantic Web, or a Web that presented itself the same way that people spoke. Working with the idea of self-description, he aimed to improve programs so that they could understand actual context. The Semantic Web itself doesn't follow a physical document, but models itself after real things in the world by using XML. It then employs basic syntax using words and URIs, not software programs and their cumbersome logic, to name things. This advances the relational database model of finding information, making the Web resemble more of a flexible database with an associative, context-sensitive structure. (See Figure 14.1.)

The core of Web Services always uses XML. Web Services consist of

- XML
- SOAP
- UDDI
- WSDL
- XSD

SOAP (Simple Object Access Protocol) is a wrapper for XML messages. SOAP allows a program that functions under one type of operating system, say Mac, to communicate with another system—for instance, Linux—using HTTP

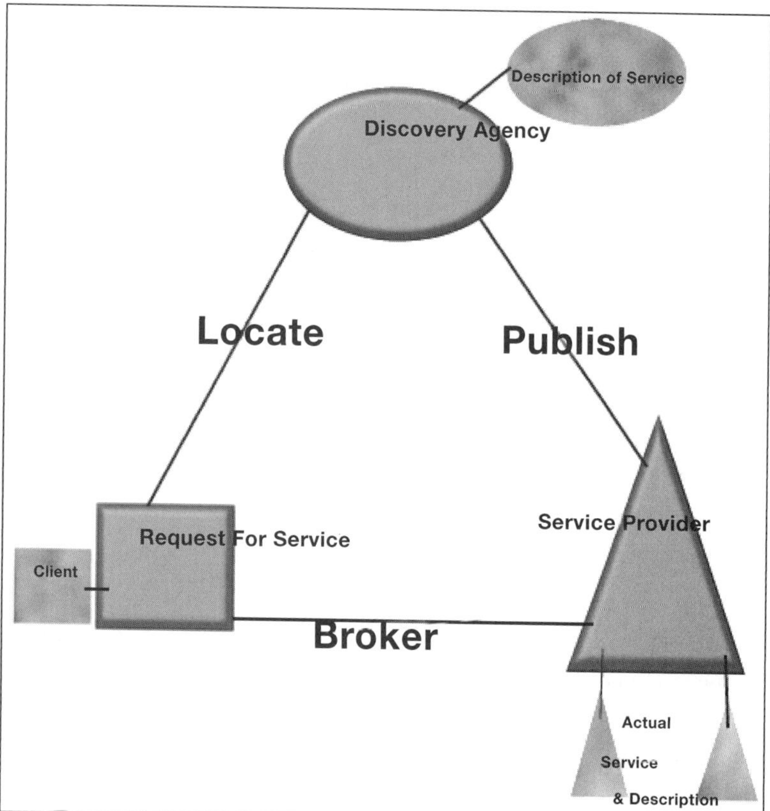

FIGURE 14.1 An Overview of Web Services

Advice

To view the SVG code for the diagram in Figure 14.1, see Appendix C. We have decided to use your knowledge of SVG, learned in Chapter 11, to enhance your understanding of how to make visual diagrams and reinforce your coding skills.

(and other protocols) over the Internet. Since SOAP is a high-level protocol, it is independent of what lies underneath it, so it can work over HTTP, IMS (Instant Messaging Service), or simple mail transport protocols. It concerns itself with communicating pure content and does not deal with what is in the content of a transmission from a sender to a receiver. SOAP concerns itself primarily with encoding the HTTP header with an enabled XML file so one program can pass that XML information to another program. It also sets parameters for how one program is allowed to respond back to the other program primarily using pure function calls. SOAP involves not only request/response behaviors, but it solicits responses and allows one-way asynchronous messaging and even event notification. However, one of the best things about SOAP is it can usually get through most firewalls. This was not its first intention, as SOAP, designed in 1998, was at first made to be compatible with scripting environments, which at that time had HTTP support as part of their design. Most firewalls, that is, programs that block unnecessary intrusions, leave open the standard HTTP port 80 on a network. SOAP uses HTTP as its primary transport medium and HTTP is allowed to pass through most firewalls.

UDDI (Universal Description, Discovery and Integration) is a registry of XML-enabled business worldwide. Think of it as a specialized Yellow Pages registry. Businesses and services can list by either the type of Web Service they offer, their product, name, or location. You can access the specifications of UDDI at http://www.uddi.org/. Large commercial vendors are involved in creating the registry including Hewlett-Packard, Oracle, Intel, SAO AG, Ariba, IBM, Microsoft, Sun Microsystems, VeriSign, Fujitsu, and others. The actual site to register is at http://www.uddi.org/register.html, which points one toward the appropriate node URLs.

WSDL (Web Services Description Language) is at the core of UDDI and is an XML language that describes what kind of services a business might offer, how it is able to communicate, how other businesses and individuals can use those services, and where the services reside on the network. It does this by describing endpoints on SOAP messages that give either document or procedural instructions. This is because SOAP never really explains what type of message is being relayed since it is basically an envelope wrapper. WDSL actually breaks messages into groups. These basic groups are conveyed in the specific order of

1. Import
2. Types
3. Message
4. PortType
5. Binding
6. Service

The **Import** part of Web Services lets different elements of a particular service be broken into different documents, which can be imported into a service as needed. **Types** is where data types are described. Using the basic XML `Schema:Datatypes` we talked about in Chapter 5, it sets up a way to host a variety of type definitions based on that schema. **Message** defines a message description component, which contains its local name and breaks the message into parts. A **PortType** talks about the location where messages are received from and sent to for a service. **Binding** is an important part of messaging. It lays out the format of the message and the underlying protocol for messages assigned to a specific PortType. A **Service** defines a `serviceType` component description. This means it has descriptions locally of the `serviceType`, a namespace referring back to W3C's WSDL specification, as well as a local port type. A `serviceType` groups a set of `portTypes`.

XSD, which we have seen in Chapter 5, is used for XML Schema Definition and enables institutions, organizations, and businesses to transfer elements, attributes, values, data types, structure, and standards. XSD is also used as a basis for Web Services.

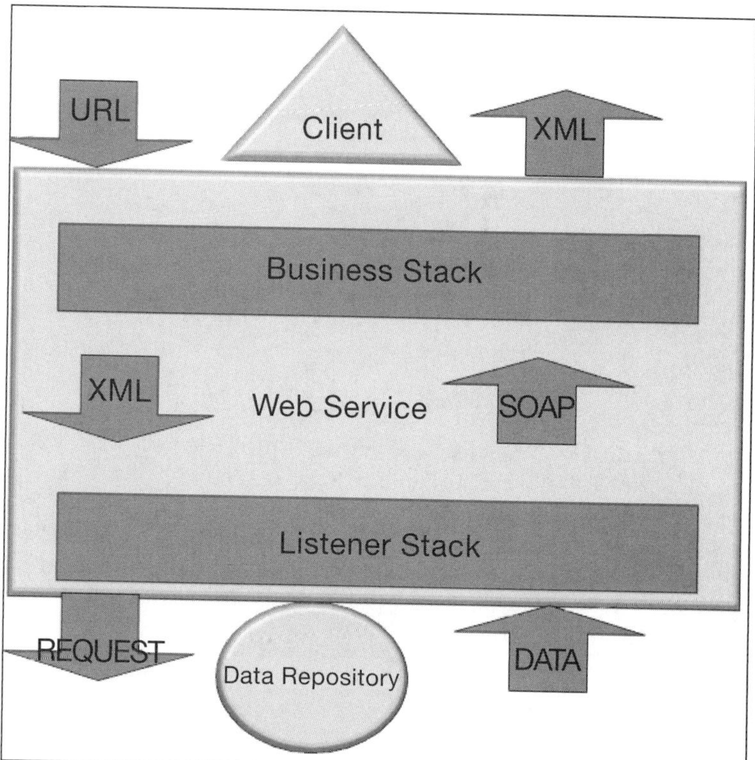

FIGURE 14.2 A Representation of the Flow of Web Services Structures

Advice

To view the SVG code for the diagram in Figure 14.2, see Appendix C.

A Simple Web Services Model

So let's take a further look into what flows around a Web Service by looking at Figure 14.2. How would a Web Service initiate? Well, the client (you) or the client application has to ask for information about something—like a service or a piece of data. The server that is hosting the Web Service processes and then invokes the Web Service from this request by searching for it on the Web Services registry. When the appropriate Web Service is located, it is sent back to the client application.

This further breaks down into "publish, find, and bind," which we mentioned previously. Part of the Web Service model makes it necessary to **publish** the service with a service registry. The service registry **finds** the requested service, or one like it, and the details of the Web Service go back to the initiating client and, if appropriate, invoke the service itself. One of the details it includes is the binding information, which means how the request and its application **bind** to the Web Service. Other details are the location of the Web Service and the type of functionality it renders. The service itself contains the code that invokes the service. You can see this displayed in Figure 14.3.

Advice

To view the SVG code for the diagram in Figure 14.3, see Appendix C.

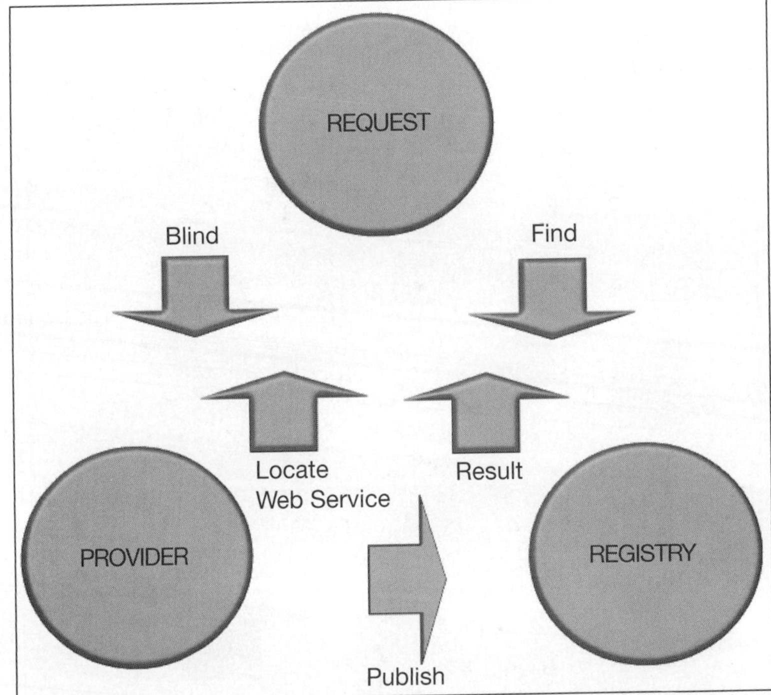

FIGURE 14.3 A Representation of the Flow of Web Services Structures

Because Web Services have expanding functionality, there are some basic XML Schema namespaces that are used to reference it as a standard. These basic namespaces are shown in Table 14.1.

TABLE 14.1 Basic Web Services Namespace URLS

Type	URL	Description
http	http://www.w3.org/2003/01/wsdl/http	XML Schema namespace for http
mime	http://www.w3.org/2003/01/wsdl/mime	XML Schema namespace for mime
soap	http://www.w3.org/2002/06/soap-envelope	XML Schema SOAP envelope
soap	http://www.w3.org/2003/01/wsdl/soap12	XML Schema WSDL namespace for SOAP
soap	http://www.w3.org/2002/06/soap-rpc	XML Schema SOAP RPC
wsdl	http://www.w3.org/2003/01/wsdl	XML Schema namespace for WSDL
xsd	http://www.w3.org/2001/XMLSchema	XML Schema namespace
xsi	http://www.w3.org/2001/XMLSchema-instance	XML Schema namespace for schema structures

A Little Bit of SOAP

The SOAP protocol uses XML by encoding its text data and distributing it in a decentralized environment. It does not mandate that a message be sent from requestor to server in a single "hop" and intermediaries can be used so the network can be truly virtual. Since the XML data is text, and is self-describing, it is not terribly difficult to interpret. SOAP version 1.2 became a W3C official recommendation on May 7, 2003, and consists of four parts: **Messaging Framework, Adjuncts, Primer and Assertions,** and **Test Collection.** It works with Java, .NET, Perl, Python, Visual Basic, and Visual C#. Surprisingly, even though SOAP can pass through firewalls, it is secure, because it lends itself to protocols like HTTP, SMTP, TCP, IM, and even FTP. When those protocols are encrypted, it follows that the SOAP message is encrypted as well. Listing 14.1 contains a very simple SOAP statement.

LISTING 14.1

```
<?xml version="1.0" ?>
<env:Envelope xmlns:env="http://www.w3.org/2002/06/
  soap-envelope">
  <env:Body>
    <r:NewsInfoHeadline xmlns:r="http://mcgrawhill.
      com/2003/09/headlines">
      <r:Head1>BreakingNews</r:Head1>
      <r:Head2>New 4U Every 10 Minutes</r:Head2>
    </r:NewsInfoHeadline>
  </env:Body>
</env:Envelope>
```

The SOAP message has a namespace, **Envelope**, that maps to the w3.org's specifications of an XML Schema. It also has `Body` and `Header` elements. Here, a sender is sending a message without an acknowledgement to a single receiver. This is done using the "fire-and-forget" feature that is included in a SOAP message. This means it doesn't really need a message back that it was received, since the content is only an update of a news header. If the update was to be sent using a multicast distribution scenario, it could happen, but the underlying transport layer would need to support it.

Tech Tip

The `Envelope` namespace must be included in a SOAP message.

To identify the message by giving the header an ID number or other way of tracking it, look at the code in Listing 14.2. Note that here the message is asking for an acknowledgment, or **requestresponse**, which is quite different than "fire and forget."

LISTING 14.2

```
<?xml version="1.0" ?>
<env:Envelope xmlns:env="http://www.w3.org/2002/06/
  soap-envelope">
  <env:Header>
```

```
    <n:MsgHeader xmlns:n="http://mcgrawhill.com/
      requestresponse">
      <n:MessageId>uuid:Series200310-04</n:MessageId>
    </n:MsgHeader>
  </env:Header>
  <env:Body>
      . . .
  </env:Body>
</env:Envelope>
```

So what would a response to this request look like? See Listing 14.3. Here the message ID and the message response ID are given identifying characteristics that we made up. Anything can be used if the messaging parties agree upon it.

LISTING 14.3

```
<?xml version="1.0" ?>
<env:Envelope xmlns:env="http://www.w3.org/2002/06/
  soap-envelope">
  <env:Header>
    <n:MsgHeader xmlns:n="http://mcgrawhill.com/
      requestresponse">
      <n:MessageId>uuid:Series200310-04</n:MessageId>
      <n:ResponseTo>uuid:Series200310-04-H1234</n:
        ResponseTo>
    </n:MsgHeader>
  </env:Header>
  <env:Body>
      . . .
  </env:Body>
</env:Envelope>
```

Sometimes a procedure needs to be called up that lives on a remote computer. When calling up the remote procedure, certain parameters must be passed to it using a `call` statement. This whole process is called **RPC (remote procedure call).** You can see it in Listing 14.4 with the RPC request message concerning foreign news headlines. The RPC response message to the RPC request message is shown in Listing 14.5.

LISTING 14.4

```
<?xml version="1.0" ?>
<env:Envelope xmlns:env="http://www.w3.org/2002/06/
  soap-envelope">
  <env:Body>
    <r:GetForeignNews env:encodingStyle=
      "http://www.w3.org/2002/06/soap-encoding"
      xmlns:r="http://mcgrawhill.com/2003/09/headlines">
```

```
        <r:ForeignHead>Today's Overseas Headlines</r:
          ForeignHead>
      </r:GetForeignNews>
    </env:Body>
  </env:Envelope>
```

LISTING 14.5

```
<?xml version="1.0" ?>
<env:Envelope xmlns:env="http://www.w3.org/2002/06/
  soap-envelope">
  <env:Body>
    <r:GetForeignNewsResponse env:encodingStyle=
      "http://www.w3.org/2002/06/soap-encoding"
      xmlns:r="http://mcgrawhill.com/2003/09/headlines"
      xmlns:rpc="http://www.w3.org/2002/06/soap-rpc">
        <rpc:Result>It's A Sunny Day in
          Antarctica</rpc:Result>
    </r:GetForeignNewsResponse>
  </env:Body>
</env:Envelope>
```

Limitations

The XML message in SOAP has to be extracted by an XML parser. This makes the developer extremely responsible for making sure the extraction works and everything is coded properly. It also requires a lot of space and processing ability, and if there are massive amounts of data to be exchanged, the performance won't be optimal. Errors only show up in run time, not during the compiling stage, which is another drawback for programmers. And all organizations must agree upon common XML Schemas to exchange information. Unfortunately, that is not always the case.

UDDI

What if you wanted to buy a compact disk. You, the client, would need a UDDI Registry to point you toward a descriptive service that lets you find it (see Figure 14.4). Plus you, the developer, would need to know how to encode it. This is all done in the registry. One registry for UDDI is maintained at http://www.microsoft.com (see Figure 14.5). All registries are maintained for free.

UDDI's main purpose is to allow B2B and other commerce easy descriptive access of how they define their business, find other businesses, and share information with each other. It allows one to look up, for free, both the Web Services of others and technical specifications of those services. This includes such simple information as inventory, billing, marketing, management, and

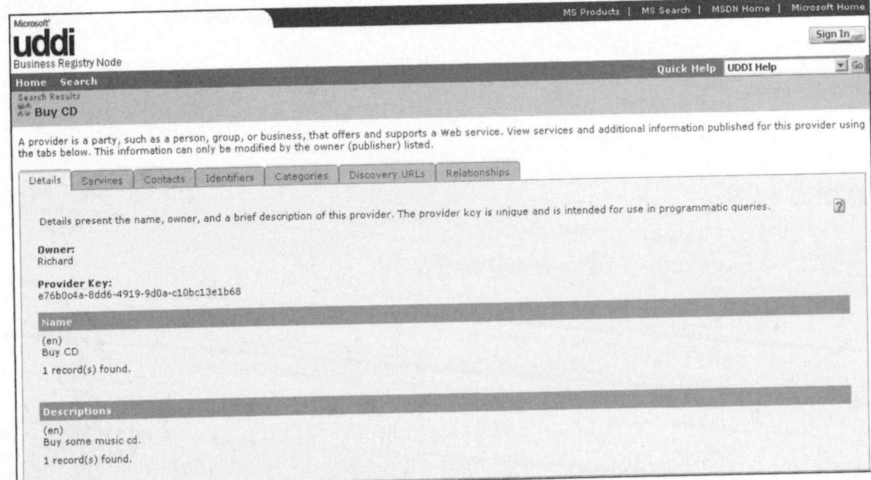

FIGURE 14.4 A Buy CD UDDI Provider

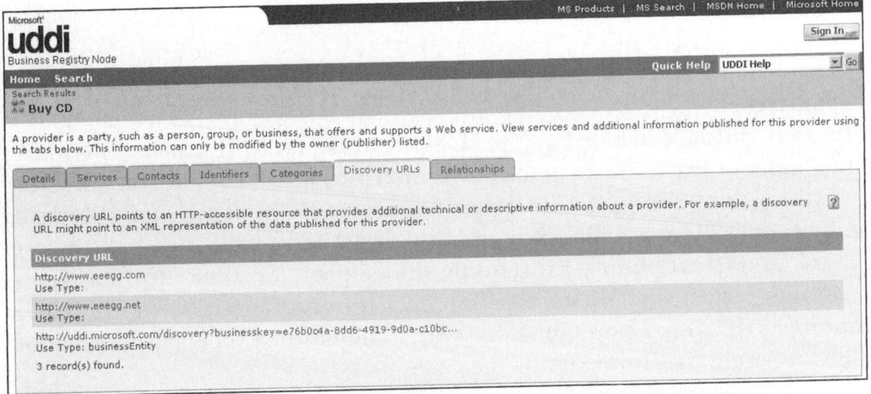

FIGURE 14.5 A Buy CD UDDI Provider Description of HTTP-Accessible URLs

ordering. It uses specifications derived from W3C and the **Internet Engineering Task Force (IETF)** as well as XML, HTTP, the **DNS (Domain Name System),** and SOAP. Searches are conducted on UDDI registry nodes, so far operated by Ariba, IBM, and Microsoft. If a company registers on one node, all three nodes display the information. Over 80 major developers and vendors are supporting registering with these nodes.

In theory, this solves a lot of problems with emerging Web Services. If there are millions of businesses online, this narrows the field to just the specific few you may be looking for. And once you or your organization does choose a business to work with, a common transaction parameter is established. UDDI is set up to work globally, so ordering widgets from India should become easier. But UDDI will work with much more than widgets. Some of the companies gearing up to use it are

- Distributors
- ERP vendors
- Global 2000 businesses
- Financial institutions
- Fortune 500 companies
- Health care providers
- ISVs (independent software vendors) and integrators
- Manufacturers
- Retailers
- Systems integrators

Known identifiers will be used to categorize companies such as D-U-N-S® Number, Keywords, RealNames, Thomas Supplier, and different Taxonomies. To see a good list of the types of industries looking to set up these categories, go to http://www.oasis-open.org/committees/committees.php (see Figure 14.6).

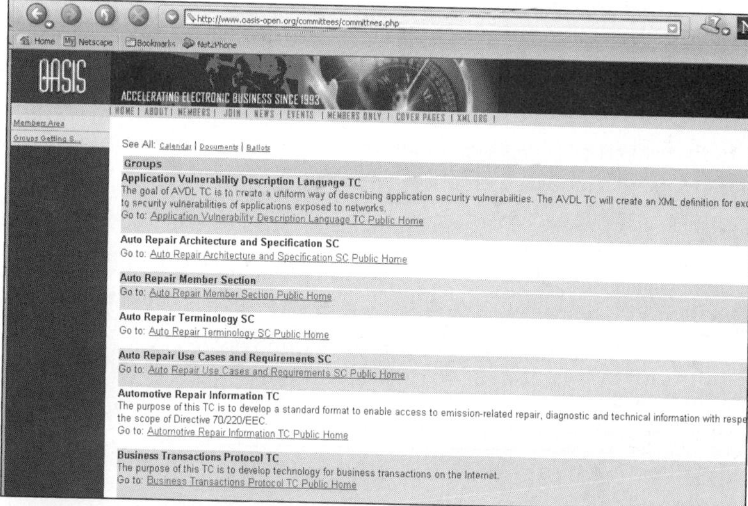

FIGURE 14.6 Some UDDI Groups to Set Up Common Terminology from the Oasis-Open.org Site

WDSL

Now that you have seen that a UDDI registry exists where businesses can register their services, how can information be provided about the Web Service itself, such as where it resides and the methods it uses to make itself accessible? Everyone must agree upon a format for these descriptions. This gave way to the WDSL standard. The current version is WSDL 1.2, which became a

W3C working draft in March 2003. Before that the standard was WSDL Standard 1.1, written in March 2001. Both standards use an XML format and distinguish between what is referred to as the abstract functionality of the service and the pragmatic "how" and "where." Types of abstract functionality might be data types, actual messages, and the way those messages are joined for request/response pairs in RPC operations. More pragmatic or concrete functionality would be how an actual message is sent using a specific protocol like HTTP-GET or SOAP. In other words, the standards describe where to get a Web Service and what set of protocols to use to do it.

Alert

When creating a Web Service, it is necessary to create a corresponding WSDL file as well, with an extension of .wsdl.

A WDSL statement begins with describing the messages between the Web Service provider and the Web Service requestor. The messages are bound to an actual network protocol with a message format. This exchange of messages is called an **operation.** A group of operations is referred to as a *port type.* A collection of ports is called a *service,* and each port launches a `portType`, which contains all the necessary details to interact between provider and service. `portType` also can be thought of as an interface.

TABLE 14.2 Mapping between Definitions and XML

Type	Mapping
{bindings}	Maps to `binding` element information items plus imported definitions.
{element declarations}	Maps to children of `type` element information item plus element declarations defined by XML Schema element information.
{messages}	Maps to `message` element information plus its children and imported definitions.
{port types}	Maps to all `portType` elements and children plus any imported definitions.
{services}	Maps to `service` element, children, and imported definitions.
{type definitions}	Maps to type definitions and children plus imported definitions. Uses the XML Schema `simpleType` and `complexType` element information.

Simple Sample of WSDL

Now let's look at the actual code for a WSDL file made up to resemble a file about this McGraw-Hill XML book (see Listing 14.6).

LISTING 14.6

```
<?xml version="1.0" encoding="UTF-8" ?>
<definitions name="McGrawHillXMLBook"
targetNamespace="http://McGrawHill.com/wsdl/"
xmlns:wsdlns="http://McGrawHill.com/wsdl/"
xmlns:typens="http://McGrawHill.com/xsd"
```

```
xmlns:xsd="http://www.w3.org/2001/XMLSchema"
xmlns:soap="http://schemas.xmlsoap.org/wsdl/soap/"
xmlns="http://schemas.xmlsoap.org/wsdl/">

<types>
<schema targetNamespace="http://McGrawHill.com/xsd"
xmlns="http://www.w3.org/2001/XMLSchema"
xmlns:SOAP-ENC="http://schemas.xmlsoap.org/soap/encoding/"
xmlns:wsdl="http://schemas.xmlsoap.org/wsdl/"
elementFormDefault="qualified" >
</schema>
</types>

<message name="First.try">
<part name="arg" type="xsd:int"/>
</message>

<message name="First.tryResponse">
<part name="result" type="xsd:int"/>
</message>

<portType name="SimplePortType">
<operation name="Try" parameterOrder="arg" >
<input message="wsdlns:First.try"/>
<output message="wsdlns:First.tryResponse"/>
</operation>
</portType>

<binding name="SimpleBinding" type="wsdlns:SimplePortType">
<stk:binding preferredEncoding="UTF-8" />
<soap:binding style="rpc"transport="http://schemas.
  xmlsoap.org/soap/http"/>
<operation name="try">
<soap:operation soapAction="http://McGrawHill.
  com/action/First.try"/>
<input>
<soap:body use="encoded" namespace="http://McGrawHill.
  com/message/"encodingStyle="http://schemas.xmlsoap.org/
  soap/encoding/" />
</input>
<output>
<soap:body use="encoded" namespace="http://McGrawHill.
  com/message/"encodingStyle="http://schemas.xmlsoap.
  org/soap/encoding/" />
</output>
</operation>
```

```
</binding>

<service name="TRYSAMPLEService">
<port name="SimplePort" binding="wsdlns:SimpleBinding">
<soap:address location="http://ellen:4040bbbb/TrySample/
  TrySample.asp"/>
</port>
</service>
</definitions>
```

The first line sets up the XML statement and the next, the `definitions name`, is the root element. Different namespace attributes are given as well as the XML Schema namespace. The `targetNamespace` definition is made up: `schema targetNamespace="http://McGrawHill.com/xsd"`. Next follows a `types` section, but because this is a made-up document, there are no real types, just specific placeholders for a namespace. Next the `message` element, `First.try`, begins that section. Input and output parameters are defined in the `message` and the output message gets a response. WSDL can describe in a `message` element what the name of the document is that is being sent and received.

There are four types of basic operations that WSDL uses. The first is one-way, which is just what it says: a message travels from one endpoint to another. The next is a notification operation. It is like one-way but with a notice. The third type we have also seen in SOAP, a request-response. The client sends a request to the provider. The request is processed and sent back to the client. It contains both input and output elements. The fourth one is solicit-response, which is very similar to request-response. Though not commonly used in Web Services, it sends a message to the client and gets a message back.

The `portType` element is actually the most critical WSDL element. This is because it does many things. First, it defines the Web Service. Then it specifies what operations can be performed and finally it shows what the messages are that it used. It can be zero, one, or more. Here there is just one `portType`, though if an abstract `portType` is used, it can be put in a separate file. The `operation` element is called `try`, and it is equivalent to a function name. This specific element can have up to three child elements and those elements can have attributes. The bindings section follows, and it can have zero, one, or more elements. Bindings specify how each operation call and response are sent. Services also can have zero, one, or more service elements, and port elements. Each of those refers back to a `binding` element in the bindings section. This is because the port defines the actual connection point to the Web Service. If you are familiar with any programming language, it is like the function library in a class or module.

A `binding` element contains two attributes. First it has a `name` attribute, which can be anything, and then a `type` attribute, which points to a specific port for the binding. The `soap:binding` element itself has two specific attributes. The first is the `style` attribute, which can be `"rpc"` or `"document"`. The next is the `transport` attribute, which defines which SOAP protocol to use. Then the `operation` element specifies the operation that the port uses. This is because, for each operation launched, a corresponding SOAP action has to be defined. It is also important to be specific about how the input and output of the action is defined.

Advice

A detailed list of Web Services tools is located at http://www-106.ibm.com/developerworks/views/webservices/tools.jsp, with an extensive list of code at http://www-106.ibm.com/developerworks/views/webservices/code.jsp. Also, see a list of Web Services standards at http://www-106.ibm.com/developerworks/views/webservices/standards.jsp.

Building a Real Web Service

In order to construct an actual Web Service, it is necessary to use a third-party application, like the Microsoft **SOAP Toolkit,** Visual Studio.NET, or IBM Websphere, with its own Web Services toolkit. It also helps to know ASP.NET or Java as well as C++. To learn more, try looking at *MCAD/MCSD XML Web Services and Server Components Development with Visual Basic .NET Study Guide,* by Kenneth Lind (New York: McGraw-Hill Osborne Media, 2003).

Key Terms

Adjuncts
bind
Binding
Domain Name System (DNS)
`Envelope`
find
Import
Internet Engineering Task Force (IETF)
mapping
Message
Messaging Framework
operation
PortType
Primer and Assertions
publish
publish, find, and bind
`requestresponse`
remote procedure call (RPC)
Semantic Web
Service
Simple Object Access Protocol (SOAP)
SOAP Toolkit
Test Collection
Types
Universal Description, Discovery and Integration (UDDI)
Web Services
Web Services Description Language (WSDL)

1. **Listing 14.1:**
```
<?xml version="1.0" ?>
<env:Envelope xmlns:env="http://www.w3.org/2002/06/soap-envelope">
  <env:Body>
    <r:NewsInfoHeadline xmlns:r="http://mcgrawhill.com/2003/09/
      headlines">
      <r:Head1>BreakingNews</r:Head1>
      <r:Head2>New 4U Every 10 Minutes</r:Head2>
    </r:NewsInfoHeadline>
  </env:Body>
</env:Envelope>
```

2. **Listing 14.2:**
```
<?xml version="1.0" ?>
<env:Envelope xmlns:env="http://www.w3.org/2002/06/soap-envelope">
  <env:Header>
    <n:MsgHeader xmlns:n="http://mcgrawhill.com/requestresponse">
      <n:MessageId>uuid:Series200310-04</n:MessageId>
    </n:MsgHeader>
  </env:Header>
  <env:Body>
    . . .
  </env:Body>
</env:Envelope>
```

3. **Listing 14.3:**
```
<?xml version="1.0" ?>
<env:Envelope xmlns:env="http://www.w3.org/2002/06/soap-envelope">
  <env:Header>
    <n:MsgHeader xmlns:n="http://mcgrawhill.com/requestresponse">
      <n:MessageId>uuid:Series200310-04</n:MessageId>
      <n:ResponseTo>uuid:Series200310-04-H1234</n:ResponseTo>
    </n:MsgHeader>
  </env:Header>
  <env:Body>
    . . .
  </env:Body>
</env:Envelope>
```

4. **Listing 14.4:**
```
<?xml version="1.0" ?>
<env:Envelope xmlns:env="http://www.w3.org/2002/06/soap-envelope">
  <env:Body>
    <r:GetForeignNews env:encodingStyle="http://www.w3.org/2002/06/
      soap-encoding"xmlns:r="http://mcgrawhill.com/2003/09/
      headlines">
      <r:ForeignHead>Today's Overseas Headlines</r:ForeignHead>
    </r:GetForeignNews>
  </env:Body>
</env:Envelope>
```

5. **Listing 14.5:**
```
<?xml version="1.0" ?>
<env:Envelope xmlns:env="http://www.w3.org/2002/06/soap-envelope">
```

```
  <env:Body>
    <r:GetForeignNewsResponse env:encodingStyle="http://www.w3.org/
      2002/06/soap-encoding"xmlns:r="http://mcgrawhill.com/2003/09/
      headlines"xmlns:rpc="http://www.w3.org/2002/06/soap-rpc">
      <rpc:Result>It's A Sunny Day in Antarctica</rpc:Result>
    </r:GetForeignNewsResponse>
  </env:Body>
</env:Envelope>
```

6. **Listing 14.6:**

```
<?xml version="1.0" encoding="UTF-8" ?>
<definitions name="McGrawHillXMLBook"
targetNamespace="http://McGrawHill.com/wsdl/"
xmlns:wsdlns="http://McGrawHill.com/wsdl/"
xmlns:typens="http://McGrawHill.com/xsd"
xmlns:xsd="http://www.w3.org/2001/XMLSchema"
xmlns:soap="http://schemas.xmlsoap.org/wsdl/soap/"
xmlns="http://schemas.xmlsoap.org/wsdl/">

<types>
<schema targetNamespace="http://McGrawHill.com/xsd"
xmlns="http://www.w3.org/2001/XMLSchema"
xmlns:SOAP-ENC="http://schemas.xmlsoap.org/soap/encoding/"
xmlns:wsdl="http://schemas.xmlsoap.org/wsdl/"
elementFormDefault="qualified" >
</schema>
</types>

<message name="First.try">
<part name="arg" type="xsd:int"/>
</message>

<message name="First.tryResponse">
<part name="result" type="xsd:int"/>
</message>

<portType name="SimplePortType">
<operation name="Try" parameterOrder="arg" >
<input message="wsdlns:First.try"/>
<output message="wsdlns:First.tryResponse"/>
</operation>
</portType>

<binding name="SimpleBinding" type="wsdlns:SimplePortType">
<stk:binding preferredEncoding="UTF-8" />
<soap:binding style="rpc"transport="http://schemas.xmlsoap.org/
  soap/http"/>
<operation name="try">
<soap:operation
soapAction="http://McGrawHill.com/action/First.try"/>
<input>
<soap:body use="encoded" namespace="http://McGrawHill.com/message/"
encodingStyle="http://schemas.xmlsoap.org/soap/encoding/" />
</input>
<output>
```

```
<soap:body use="encoded" namespace="http://McGrawHill.com/message/"
encodingStyle="http://schemas.xmlsoap.org/soap/encoding/" />
</output>
</operation>
</binding>

<service name="TRYSAMPLEService">
<port name="SimplePort" binding="wsdlns:SimpleBinding">
<soap:address location="http://ellen:4040bbbb/TrySample/TrySample.asp"/>
</port>
</service>
</definitions>
```

Review Questions

1. Define application-to-application communication.
2. Define distributed objects.
3. The term "publish, find, and discover" is commonly used in Web Services. True or False?
4. Web Services are communications and protocols working together. True or False?
5. What is the Semantic Web? Why is it important?
6. Web Services use five different technologies. What are they?
7. SOAP is an envelope. True or False?
8. Can SOAP work over a wireless network?
9. What technology is a registry of XML-enabled businesses?
10. What technology is at the core of UDDI?
11. Describe how a Web Service would find a service.
12. SOAP can penetrate firewalls. True or False?
13. Explain "fire and forget."
14. What does RPC mean?
15. A UDDI Registry costs money to use. True or False?
16. What types of organizations will use UDDI?
17. What does WSDL stand for?
18. What is an "operation" in terms of Web Services?
19. Basic WSDL operations use three types. True or False?
20. What is the most critical WSDL element?
21. What do bindings specify?

Case Study

Here are a variety of case studies on Web Services.

1. http://www.alphaworks.ibm.com/tech/wstkmd. This site examines a Web Services tool for mobile devices in run-time environments. It is a Java-enabled kit that supports PocketPC, Palm, and BlackBerry handhelds. It also mentions a C version of the toolkit and is interesting to view in terms of future uses of Web Services.
2. http://www-3.ibm.com/software/ebusiness/jstart/casestudies/pointserve.html. PointServe's mission was to enable a Web Service from any device connected to the Internet. Working with IBM, they streamlined their supply chain, the details of which are on this site.
3. http://www-3.ibm.com/software/ebusiness/jstart/casestudies/webservices.html. This site offers a multitude of case studies of Web Services, IBM architecture, and real-world solutions.
4. http://www.cio.com/archive/040102/real_content.html. The department store Nordstrom's; a health club chain, Life Time Fitness; and a Web Services prescription business are all profiled here.
5. http://www.fawcette.com/dotnetmag/2002_04/magazine/columns/casestudies/jsalas/. This looks at Microsoft's .NET platform and how it was used to connect schools serving underprivileged children in Chicago.
6. http://www.fawcette.com/dotnetmag/2002_01/magazine/departments/casestudy_1/. This site shows how a financial services company uses legacy data by integrating XML, Web Services, SOAP, and ASP.NET.

Hands On Project

Here we will examine an actual SOAP file to see how it is structured.

1. Open up XML Spy. Click on the pull-down menu that says `SOAP` and select `Create New Soap Request`. You will get a prompt that says "Please enter the WSDL file location".
2. Click on the button that says `Window`, *not* the button that says `browse`. A `Select File` two-window-pane dialogue box will open. The lower pane says `Project files` and `Examples`.
3. Scroll down until you come to the WSDL Editor. Choose `TimeService.wsdl`. Then a window appears that says "Please select a SOAP operation name".
4. Choose `getTimeZoneTime (get TimeZoneTime parameters)`, the second from the last choice. Click OK.
5. Go to the `View` pull-down menu in XML Spy and look at the WSDL statement first in `Enhanced Grid` (which you should currently be in). Then choose `text view` and after that choose `browser view`. Look at the code and locate the SOAP elements. Then go back to `Enhanced Grid` and look at the differences between the `xsi` and `xsd` namespaces that are laid out before you.
6. Open up another WSDL file from the menu, using the same process, and compare the differences between how different WSDL files are coded.

As you can see, all the basic structures of XML statements are used in a SOAP file.

ASCII Characters

Char	Oct	Dec	Hex	Key	Action
NUL	0	0	0	^@	Null character
SOH	1	1	1	^A	Start of heading, console interrupt
STX	2	2	2	^B	Start of text, maintenance mode on HP console
ETX	3	3	3	^C	End of text
EOT	4	4	4	^D	End of transmission, not the same as ETB
ENQ	5	5	5	^E	Enquiry, goes with ACK; old HP flow control
ACK	6	6	6	^F	Acknowledge, clears ENQ logon hand
BEL	7	7	7	^G	Bell, rings the bell
BS	10	8	8	^H	Backspace, works on HP terminals/computers
HT	11	9	9	^I	Horizontal tab, move to next tab stop
LF	12	10	a	^J	Line feed
VT	13	11	b	^K	Vertical tab
FF	14	12	c	^L	Form feed, page eject
CR	15	13	d	^M	Carriage return
SO	16	14	e	^N	Shift out, alternate character set
SI	17	15	f	^O	Shift in, resume default character set
DLE	20	16	10	^P	Data link escape
DC1	21	17	11	^Q	XON, with XOFF to pause listings; ":okay to send"
DC2	22	18	12	^R	Device control 2, block-mode flow control
DC3	23	19	13	^S	XOFF, with XON is TERM=18 flow control
DC4	24	20	14	^T	Device control 4

Continued

Char	Oct	Dec	Hex	Key	Action
NAK	25	21	15	^U	Negative acknowledge
SYN	26	22	16	^V	Synchronous idle
ETB	27	23	17	^W	End transmission block, not the same as EOT
CAN	30	24	17	^X	Cancel line, MPE echoes!!!
EM	31	25	19	^Y	End of medium, Control-Y interrupt
SUB	32	26	1a	^Z	Substitute
ESC	33	27	1b	^[	Escape, next character is not echoed
FS	34	28	1c	^\	File separator
GS	35	29	1d	^]	Group separator
RS	36	30	1e	^^	Record separator, block-mode terminator
US	37	31	1f	^_	Unit separator

Printing Characters				
Char	Octal	Dec	Hex	Description
SP	40	32	20	Space
!	41	33	21	Exclamation mark
"	42	34	22	Quotation mark (" in HTML)
#	43	35	23	Cross hatch (number sign)
$	44	36	24	Dollar sign
%	45	37	25	Percent sign
&	46	38	26	Ampersand
'	47	39	27	Closing single quote (apostrophe)
(	50	40	28	Opening parenthesis
)	51	41	29	Closing parenthesis
*	52	42	2a	Asterisk (star, multiply)
+	53	43	2b	Plus
,	54	44	2c	Comma
-	55	45	2d	Hyphen, dash, minus
.	56	46	2e	Period
/	57	47	2f	Slant (forward slash, divide)
0	60	48	30	Zero

Continued

Char	Octal	Dec	Hex	Description
1	61	49	31	One
2	62	50	32	Two
3	63	51	33	Three
4	64	52	34	Four
5	65	53	35	Five
6	66	54	36	Six
7	67	55	37	Seven
8	70	56	38	Eight
9	71	57	39	Nine
:	72	58	3a	Colon
;	73	59	3b	Semicolon
<	74	60	3c	Less than sign (`<` in HTML)
=	75	61	3d	Equals sign
>	76	62	3e	Greater than sign (`>` in HTML)
?	77	63	3f	Question mark
@	100	64	40	At-sign
A	101	65	41	Uppercase A
B	102	66	42	Uppercase B
C	103	67	43	Uppercase C
D	104	68	44	Uppercase D
E	105	69	45	Uppercase E
F	106	70	46	Uppercase F
G	107	71	47	Uppercase G
H	110	72	48	Uppercase H
I	111	73	49	Uppercase I
J	112	74	4a	Uppercase J
K	113	75	4b	Uppercase K
L	114	76	4c	Uppercase L
M	115	77	4d	Uppercase M
N	116	78	4e	Uppercase N

Continued

Char	Octal	Dec	Hex	Description
O	117	79	4f	Uppercase O
P	120	80	50	Uppercase P
Q	121	81	51	Uppercase Q
R	122	82	52	Uppercase R
S	123	83	53	Uppercase S
T	124	84	54	Uppercase T
U	125	85	55	Uppercase U
V	126	86	56	Uppercase V
W	127	87	57	Uppercase W
X	130	88	58	Uppercase X
Y	131	89	59	Uppercase Y
Z	132	90	5a	Uppercase Z
[	133	91	5b	Opening square bracket
\	134	92	5c	Reverse slant (backslash)
]	135	93	5d	Closing square bracket
^	136	94	5e	Caret (circumflex)
_	137	95	5f	Underscore
`	140	96	60	Grave accent
a	141	97	61	Lowercase a
b	142	98	62	Lowercase b
c	143	99	63	Lowercase c
d	144	100	64	Lowercase d
e	145	101	65	Lowercase e
f	146	102	66	Lowercase f
g	147	103	67	Lowercase g
h	150	104	68	Lowercase h
i	151	105	69	Lowercase i
j	152	106	6a	Lowercase j
k	153	107	6b	Lowercase k
l	154	108	6c	Lowercase l

Continued

Char	Octal	Dec	Hex	Description
m	155	109	6d	Lowercase m
n	156	110	6e	Lowercase n
o	157	111	6f	Lowercase o
p	160	112	70	Lowercase p
q	161	113	71	Lowercase q
r	162	114	72	Lowercase r
s	163	115	73	Lowercase s
t	164	116	74	Lowercase t
u	165	117	75	Lowercase u
v	166	118	76	Lowercase v
w	167	119	77	Lowercase w
x	170	120	78	Lowercase x
y	171	121	79	Lowercase y
z	172	122	7a	Lowercase z
{	173	123	7b	Opening curly brace
|	174	124	7c	Vertical line
}	175	125	7d	Closing curly brace
~	176	126	7e	Tilde (approximate)
DEL	177	127	7f	Delete (rubout), cross-hatch box

APPENDIX B

International Standards Organization (ISO) English Country Names and Code Elements

This list states 239 country names (official short names, in English), in alphabetical order, and their code elements.

Afghanistan	AF
Albania	AL
Algeria	DZ
American Samoa	AS
Andorra	AD
Angola	AO
Anguilla	AI
Antarctica	AQ
Antigua and Barbuda	AG
Argentina	AR
Armenia	AM
Aruba	AW
Australia	AU

Continued

Austria	AT
Azerbaijan	AZ
Bahamas	BS
Bahrain	BH
Bangladesh	BD
Barbados	BB
Belarus	BY
Belgium	BE
Belize	BZ
Benin	BJ
Bermuda	BM
Bhutan	BT
Bolivia	BO
Bosnia and Herzegovina	BA
Botswana	BW
Bouvet Island	BV
Brazil	BR
British Indian Ocean Territory	IO
Brunei Darussalam	BN
Bulgaria	BG
Burkina Faso	BF
Burundi	BI
Cambodia	KH
Cameroon	CM
Canada	CA
Cape Verde	CV
Cayman Islands	KY
Central African Republic	CF
Chad	TD
Chile	CL
China	CN
Christmas Island	CX

Continued

Cocos (Keeling) Islands	CC
Colombia	CO
Comoros	KM
Congo	CG
Congo, The Democratic Republic of the	CD
Cook Islands	CK
Costa Rica	CR
Côte D'ivoire	CI
Croatia	HR
Cuba	CU
Cyprus	CY
Czech Republic	CZ
Denmark	DK
Djibouti	DJ
Dominica	DM
Dominican Republic	DO
Ecuador	EC
Egypt	EG
El Salvador	SV
Equatorial Guinea	GQ
Eritrea	ER
Estonia	EE
Ethiopia	ET
Falkland Islands (Malvinas)	FK
Faroe Islands	FO
Fiji	FJ
Finland	FI
France	FR
French Guiana	GF
French Polynesia	PF
French Southern Territories	TF
Gabon	GA

iContinued

Gambia	GM
Georgia	GE
Germany	DE
Ghana	GH
Gibraltar	GI
Greece	GR
Greenland	GL
Grenada	GD
Guadeloupe	GP
Guam	GU
Guatemala	GT
Guinea	GN
Guinea-Bissau	GW
Guyana	GY
Haiti	HT
Heard Island and McDonald Islands	HM
Holy See (Vatican City State)	VA
Honduras	HN
Hong Kong	HK
Hungary	HU
Iceland	IS
India	IN
Indonesia	ID
Iran, Islamic Republic of	IR
Iraq	IQ
Ireland	IE
Israel	IL
Italy	IT
Jamaica	JM
Japan	JP
Jordan	JO
Kazakhstan	KZ

Continued

Kenya	KE
Kiribati	KI
Korea, Democratic People's Republic of	KP
Korea, Republic of	KR
Kuwait	KW
Kyrgyzstan	KG
Lao People's Democratic Republic	LA
Latvia	LV
Lebanon	LB
Lesotho	LS
Liberia	LR
Libyan Arab Jamahiriya	LY
Liechtenstein	LI
Lithuania	LT
Luxembourg	LU
Macao	MO
Macedonia, The Former Yugoslav Republic of	MK
Madagascar	MG
Malawi	MW
Malaysia	MY
Maldives	MV
Mali	ML
Malta	MT
Marshall Islands	MH
Martinique	MQ
Mauritania	MR
Mauritius	MU
Mayotte	YT
Mexico	MX
Micronesia, Federated States of	FM
Moldova, Republic of	MD
Monaco	MC

Continued

Mongolia	MN
Montserrat	MS
Morocco	MA
Mozambique	MZ
Myanmar	MM
Namibia	NA
Nauru	NR
Nepal	NP
Netherlands	NL
Netherlands Antilles	AN
New Caledonia	NC
New Zealand	NZ
Nicaragua	NI
Niger	NE
Nigeria	NG
Niue	NU
Norfolk Island	NF
Northern Mariana Islands	MP
Norway	NO
Oman	OM
Pakistan	PK
Palau	PW
Palestinian Territory, Occupied	PS
Panama	PA
Papua New Guinea	PG
Paraguay	PY
Peru	PE
Philippines	PH
Pitcairn	PN
Poland	PL
Portugal	PT
Puerto Rico	PR

Continued

Qatar	QA
Réunion	RE
Romania	RO
Russian Federation	RU
Rwanda	RW
Saint Helena	SH
Saint Kitts and Nevis	KN
Saint Lucia	LC
Saint Pierre and Miquelon	PM
Saint Vincent and the Grenadines	VC
Samoa	WS
San Marino	SM
Sao Tome and Principe	ST
Saudi Arabia	SA
Senegal	SN
Seychelles	SC
Sierra Leone	SL
Singapore	SG
Slovakia	SK
Slovenia	SI
Solomon Islands	SB
Somalia	SO
South Africa	ZA
South Georgia and the South Sandwich Islands	GS
Spain	ES
Sri Lanka	LK
Sudan	SD
Suriname	SR
Svalbard and Jan Mayen	SJ
Swaziland	SZ
Sweden	SE
Switzerland	CH

Continued

Syrian Arab Republic	SY
Taiwan, Province of China	TW
Tajikistan	TJ
Tanzania, United Republic of	TZ
Thailand	TH
Timor-Leste	TL
Togo	TG
Tokelau	TK
Tonga	TO
Trinidad and Tobago	TT
Tunisia	TN
Turkey	TR
Turkmenistan	TM
Turks and Caicos Islands	TC
Tuvalu	TV
Uganda	UG
Ukraine	UA
United Arab Emirates	AE
United Kingdom	GB
United States	US
United States Minor Outlying Islands	UM
Uruguay	UY
Uzbekistan	UZ
Vanuatu	VU
Vatican City State. See Holy See	
Venezuela	VE
Viet Nam	VN
Virgin Islands, British	VG
Virgin Islands, U.S.	VI
Wallis and Futuna	WF
Western Sahara	EH

Continued

Yemen	YE
Yugoslavia	YU
Zaire. See Congo, The Democratic Republic of the	
Zambia	ZM
Zimbabwe	ZW

UDDI (Universal Description, Discovery and Integration) is a registry of XML and a business community. Think of it as a specialized Yellow Pages registry; businesses and services can list by either the type of Web Service they offer, [illegible]. The specifications of UDDI [illegible] vendors are involved in creating the registry including Hewlett-Packard, Oracle, Intel, SAP AG, Ariba, IBM, Microsoft, Sun Microsystems, VeriSign, Fujitsu, and others. The actual site for registry is at http://www.uddi.org/register.html, which points one toward the appropriate node URLs.

WSDL (Web Services Description Language) is at the core of UDDI and is an XML language that describes what kind of services a business might offer, how it is able to communicate, how other businesses and individuals can use those services, and where the services reside on the network. It does this by describing endpoints on SOAP messages that give either document or procedural instructions. This is because SOAP never really explains what type of message it is sending, since it is basically an envelope wrapper. WSDL actually [illegible] into base groups. These base groups are separated in the specific [illegible]

1. Import
2. Types
3. Message
4. PortType
5. Binding
6. Service

The **Import** part of Web Services is different elements of a particular Web Service broken into different documents, which can be imported into a service as needed. **Types** is where data types are described. Using the basic XML **Schema Datatypes** we talked about in Chapter 5, it sets up a way to host a variety of type definitions based on that schema. **Message** defines a message component, which contains its local name, and breaks the message into parts. A **PortType** talks about the location where messages are received from and sent to for a service. **Binding** is an important part of messaging. It lays out the format of the messages and the underlying protocol for messages [illegible] specific PortType. A **Service** defines a **serviceType** component [illegible]. This means it has descriptions locally of the **serviceType**, a [illegible] for referring back to W3C's WSDL specification, as well as a local port [illegible] **serviceType** [illegible] set of **portTypes**.

XSD, which we have seen in Chapter 5, is used for XML Schema Definition and enables institutions, organizations, and businesses to transfer elements, attributes, values, data types, structure, and standards. XSD is also used as a [illegible]

APPENDIX C

Code for Chapter 14 Figures

SVG Code for Figure 14.1

```
<!DOCTYPE svg PUBLIC "-//W3C//DTD SVG 1.0//EN"
  "http://www.w3.org/TR/2001/REC-SVG-20010904/DTD/svg10.dtd">
<svg width="500" height="500">
  <defs>
    <filter id="Clouds" filterUnits="objectBoundingBox"
      x="-10%" y="-10%" width="150%" height="150%">
      <feTurbulence type="fractalNoise" baseFrequency=
        "0.02" numOctaves="3" result="I1a0"/>
      <feDisplacementMap in="I1a0" in2="I1a0" scale="50"
        xChannelSelector="R" yChannelSelector="G" result="I1a"/>
      <feColorMatrix in="I1a" type="matrix" values="0 0 0
        1 0 0 0 0 1 0 0 0 0 1 0 0 0 0 0 1" result="I2"/>
      <feComposite operator="in" in="I2" in2="SourceAlpha"
        result="I3"/>
      <feComposite operator="arithmetic" in="I3" in2=
        "SourceGraphic" k2="1" k3="1" result="I5"/>
      <feComposite operator="in" in="I5" in2="SourceAlpha"
        result="I6"/>
    </filter>
    <filter id="Bumpy_1" filterUnits="objectBoundingBox"
      x="-10%" y="-10%" width="150%" height="150%">
      <feTurbulence type="turbulence" baseFrequency=
        "0.15" numOctaves="1" result="image0"/>
      <feGaussianBlur stdDeviation="3" in="image0" result=
        "image1"/>
      <feDiffuseLighting in="image1" surfaceScale="10"
        diffuseConstant="1" result="image3" style=
        "lighting-color:rgb(255,255,255)">
        <feDistantLight azimuth="0" elevation="45"/>
```

```
  </feDiffuseLighting>
  <feComposite in="image3" in2="SourceGraphic" operator=
    "arithmetic" k2="0.5" k3="0.5" result="image4"/>
  <feComposite in="image4" in2="SourceGraphic" operator=
    "in" result="image5"/>
</filter>
<filter id="Bumpy" filterUnits="objectBoundingBox"
  x="-10%" y="-10%" width="150%" height="150%">
  <feTurbulence type="turbulence" baseFrequency=
    "0.15" numOctaves="1" result="image0"/>
  <feGaussianBlur stdDeviation="3" in="image0" result=
    "image1"/>
  <feDiffuseLighting in="image1" surfaceScale="10"
    diffuseConstant="1"result="image3" style=
    "lighting-color:rgb(255,255,255)">
    <feDistantLight azimuth="0" elevation="45"/>
  </feDiffuseLighting>
  <feComposite in="image3" in2="SourceGraphic" operator=
    "arithmetic" k2="0.5" k3="0.5" result="image4"/>
  <feComposite in="image4" in2="SourceGraphic" operator=
    "in" result="image5"/>
</filter>
<filter id="Bevel_1" filterUnits="objectBoundingBox"
  x="-10%" y="-10%" width="150%" height="150%">
  <feGaussianBlur in="SourceAlpha" stdDeviation="3"
    result="blur"/>
  <feSpecularLighting in="blur" surfaceScale="5"
    specularConstant="0.5" specularExponent="10"
    result="specOut" style="lighting-color:
    rgb(0,0,0)">
    <fePointLight x="-5000" y="-10000" z="20000"/>
  </feSpecularLighting>
  <feComposite in="specOut" in2="SourceAlpha" operator=
    "in" result="specOut2"/>
  <feComposite in="SourceGraphic" in2="specOut2"
    operator="arithmetic" k1="0" k2="1" k3="1"
    k4="0" result="litPaint"/>
</filter>
<filter id="Bevel" filterUnits="objectBoundingBox"
  x="-10%" y="-10%" width="150%" height="150%">
  <feGaussianBlur in="SourceAlpha" stdDeviation="3"
    result="blur"/>
  <feSpecularLighting in="blur" surfaceScale="5"
    specularConstant="0.5" specularExponent="10"
    result="specOut" style="lighting-color:
    rgb(255,255,255)">
```

```
        <fePointLight x="-5000" y="-10000" z="20000"/>
      </feSpecularLighting>
      <feComposite in="specOut" in2="SourceAlpha" operator=
        "in" result="specOut2"/>
      <feComposite in="SourceGraphic" in2="specOut2"
        operator="arithmetic" k1="0" k2="1" k3="1" k4="0"
        result="litPaint"/>
    </filter>
  </defs>
  <rect x="59" y="303" width="87" height="77"
    style="fill:rgb(0,0,255);stroke:rgb(0,0,0);
    stroke-width:1;filter:url(#Bevel)"/>
  <rect x="28" y="332" width="27" height="30" style=
    "filter:url(#Bumpy);fill:rgb(0,0,255);
    stroke:rgb(0,0,0);stroke-width:1" transform=
    "translate(55 347) scale(1.77778 1) translate
    (-55 -347) translate(41.5 332) scale(1 1.5)
    translate(-41.5 -332)"/>
  <rect x="53" y="361" width="1" height="1" style=
    "fill:rgb(0,0,255);stroke:rgb(0,0,0);stroke-width:1"/>
  <ellipse cx="248.5" cy="90" rx="72.5" ry="47" style=
    "fill:rgb(0,0,192);stroke:rgb(0,0,0);stroke-width:
    1;filter:url(#Bevel)"/>
  <ellipse cx="347.5" cy="41.5" rx="29.5" ry="16.5" style=
    "filter:url(#Bumpy_1);fill:rgb(0,0,192);stroke:
    rgb(0,0,0);stroke-width:1" transform="translate(347.5 58)
    scale(1 1.42424) translate(-347.5 -58) translate(318 41.5)
    scale(1.59322 1) translate(-318 -41.5) translate(347.5 58)
    scale(1 1.23404) translate(-347.5 -58) translate(318 41.5)
    scale(1.19149 1) translate(-318 -41.5) translate(347.5 25)
    scale(1 1.10345) translate(-347.5 -25)"/>
  <polygon points="413,274.503 469,371.497 357,371.497"
    transform="matrix(1 0 0 1.62895 0 -203.152)
    translate(3 0)" style="fill:rgb(0,0,255);
    stroke:rgb(0,0,0);stroke-width:1;filter:url(#Bevel)"/>
  <polygon points="381,433.278 398,462.722 364,462.722"
    transform="matrix(1 0 0 2.10563 0 -495.322)" style=
    "filter:url(#Clouds);fill:rgb(0,0,255);stroke:
    rgb(0,0,0);stroke-width:1"/>
  <polygon points="462,434.046 481,466.954 443,466.954"
    transform="matrix(1 0 0 1.79282 6.39377e-013 -357.167)
    translate(462 466.954) scale(1 1) translate
    (-462 -466.954)" style="filter:url(#Clouds);
    fill:rgb(0,0,255);stroke:rgb(0,0,0);stroke-width:1"/>
  <line x1="91" y1="304" x2="192" y2="119" style="fill:
    none;stroke:rgb(0,0,0);stroke-width:2"/>
```

```
<line x1="301" y1="123" x2="405" y2="269" style="fill:
  none;stroke:rgb(0,0,0);stroke-width:2" transform=
  "translate(301 123) scale(1.03846 1.0411) translate
  (-301 -123)"/>
<line x1="365" y1="373" x2="146" y2="373" style="fill:
  none;stroke:rgb(0,0,0);stroke-width:2"transform=
  "translate(146 373) scale(0.972603 1) translate
  (-146 -373) translate(146 373) scale(1.11268 1)
  translate(-146 -373) translate(146 373) scale
  (0.92827 1) translate(-146 -373) translate(146 373)
  scale(1.04545 1) translate(-146 -373)"/>
<text x="85px" y="326px" style="filter:url(#Bevel_1);
  fill:rgb(0,0,0);font-size:14;font-family:@MingLiU"
  transform="translate(0 0)">Request For Service</text>
<text x="18px" y="349px" style="fill:rgb(0,0,0);
  font-size:10;font-family:@MingLiU">Client</text>
<text x="227px" y="73px" style="fill:rgb(0,0,0);
  font-size:14;font-family:@MingLiU">Discovery
  Agency</text>
<text x="323px" y="38px" style="fill:rgb(0,0,0);
  font-size:10;font-family:@MingLiU">Description of
  Service</text>
<text x="339px" y="314px" style="fill:rgb(0,0,0);
  font-size:14;font-family:@MingLiU">Service
  Provider</text>
<text x="381px" y="462px" style="fill:rgb(0,0,0);
  font-size:10;font-family:@MingLiU">Service</text>
<text x="395px" y="437px" style="fill:rgb(0,0,0);
  font-size:10;font-family:@MingLiU">Actual</text>
<text x="389px" y="485px" style="fill:rgb(0,0,0);
  font-size:10;font-family:@MingLiU">&amp;
  Description</text>
<text x="123px" y="205px" transform="translate(-2 -3)"
  style="fill:rgb(0,0,0);font-size:24;font-family:
  @MingLiU">Locate</text>
<text x="186px" y="388px" transform="translate(12 1)"
  style="fill:rgb(0,0,0);font-size:24;font-family:
  @MingLiU">Broker</text>
<text x="316px" y="192px" transform="translate(0 13)"
  style="fill:rgb(0,0,0);font-size:24;font-family:
  @MingLiU">Publish</text>
<line x1="51" y1="356" x2="67" y2="356" style=
  "fill:none;stroke:rgb(0,0,0);stroke-width:2"/>
```

```
  <line x1="380" y1="432" x2="382" y2="388" transform=
    "translate(382 410) scale(0.5 1) translate(-382 -410)
    translate(382 410) scale(1 1) translate(-382 -410)"
    style="fill:none;stroke:rgb(0,0,0);stroke-width:2"/>
  <line x1="490" y1="432" x2="491" y2="433" style=
    "fill:none;stroke:rgb(0,0,0);stroke-width:2"/>
  <line x1="462" y1="436" x2="460" y2="391" style=
    "fill:none;stroke:rgb(0,0,0);stroke-width:2"/>
  <line x1="292" y1="62" x2="325" y2="36" transform=
    "translate(-5 -7)" style="fill:none;stroke:rgb(0,0,0);
    stroke-width:2"/>
  <line x1="364" y1="98" x2="365" y2="99" style="fill:
    none;stroke:rgb(0,0,0);stroke-width:2"/>
</svg>
```

SVG Code for Figure 14.2

```
<?xml version="1.0" standalone="no"?>
<!DOCTYPE svg PUBLIC "-//W3C//DTD SVG 1.0//EN"
  "http://www.w3.org/TR/2001/REC-SVG-20010904/DTD/svg10.dtd">
<svg width="800" height="800">
  <defs>
    <filter id="Bevel" filterUnits="objectBoundingBox"
      x="-10%" y="-10%" width="150%" height="150%">
      <feGaussianBlur in="SourceAlpha" stdDeviation="3"
        result="blur"/>
      <feSpecularLighting in="blur" surfaceScale="5"
        specularConstant="0.5" specularExponent="10"
        result="specOut" style="lighting-color:
        rgb(255,255,255)">
        <fePointLight x="-5000" y="-10000" z="20000"/>
      </feSpecularLighting>
      <feComposite in="specOut" in2="SourceAlpha"
        operator="in" result="specOut2"/>
      <feComposite in="SourceGraphic" in2="specOut2"
        operator="arithmetic" k1="0" k2="1" k3="1" k4="0"
        result="litPaint"/>
    </filter>
  </defs>
```

```
<ellipse cx="426.5" cy="738.5" rx="76.5" ry="58.5"
  transform="translate(-60.5634 0) translate
  (-22.5352 -105.634) translate(0 71.831)
  translate(2.8169 18.3099) translate(2 4)
  translate(-7 6) translate(0 -15) translate(-5 -85)"
  style="fill:rgb(0,0,192);stroke:rgb(0,0,0);
  stroke-width:1;filter:url(#Bevel)"/>
<polygon points="365,13 448.138,157 281.862,157"
  transform="matrix(1.1547 0 0 1 -56.4657 0)
  translate(-19.5161 1.40845) translate(9.52628 75)
  translate(365 157) scale(1 0.743056)
  translate(-365 -157)" style="fill:rgb(0,0,255);
  stroke:rgb(0,0,0);stroke-width:1;filter:url(#Bevel)"/>
<rect x="92" y="242" width="585" height="333"
  style="fill:rgb(0,0,255);stroke:rgb(0,0,0);
  stroke-width:1;filter:url(#Bevel)"/>
<text x="305px" y="723px" transform="translate(12.6761
  2.8169) translate(-69 11) translate(25 -4)
  translate(-6 -98)" style="fill:rgb(0,0,0);
  font-size:18;font-family:@MingLiU">Data
  Repository</text>
<text x="309px" y="139px" style="fill:rgb(0,0,0);
  font-size:24;font-family:@MingLiU" transform=
  "translate(6 49) translate(-4 2) translate(101 -37)
  translate(-92 61)">Client</text>
<text x="216px" y="466px" transform="translate(76 -35)"
  style="fill:rgb(0,0,0);font-size:24;font-family:
  @MingLiU">Web Service</text>
<rect x="131" y="284" width="511" height="68" transform=
  "translate(-2 1)" style="fill:rgb(0,0,255);stroke:
  rgb(0,0,0);stroke-width:1"/>
<rect x="114" y="251" width="511" height="68"
  transform="translate(6 243) translate(11 0)"
  style="fill:rgb(0,0,255);stroke:rgb(0,0,0);
  stroke-width:1"/>
<rect x="702" y="48" width="0" height="1" style=
  "fill:rgb(0,0,255);stroke:rgb(0,0,0);stroke-width:1"/>
<rect x="709" y="370" width="1" height="1" style=
  "fill:rgb(0,0,255);stroke:rgb(0,0,0);stroke-width:1"/>
<text x="206px" y="308px" transform="translate(57 12)"
  style="fill:rgb(0,0,0);font-size:24;font-family:
  @MingLiU">Business Stack</text>
<text x="187px" y="527px" transform="translate(68 3)
  translate(11 12)" style="fill:rgb(0,0,0);
  font-size:24;font-family:@MingLiU">Listner
  Stack</text>
```

```
<polygon points="337.49,621.309 414.49,599.51
  491.49,621.309 444.686,621.309 444.686,666.51
  382.784,666.51 382.784,621.309" transform=
  "translate(114 27) translate(-3 -53)" style=
  "fill:rgb(0,0,255);stroke:rgb(0,0,0);stroke-width:1"/>
<polygon points="292.49,502.309 369.49,480.51
  446.49,502.309 399.686,502.309 399.686,547.51
  337.784,547.51 337.784,502.309" transform=
  "translate(144 -99)" style="fill:rgb(0,0,255);
  stroke:rgb(0,0,0);stroke-width:1"/>
<polygon points="292.49,502.309 369.49,480.51
  446.49,502.309 399.686,502.309 399.686,547.51
  337.784,547.51 337.784,502.309" transform=
  "matrix(1 0 0 1 0 -229) translate(158 -97)
  translate(5 19)" style="fill:rgb(0,0,255);
  stroke:rgb(0,0,0);stroke-width:1"/>
<polygon points="292.49,502.309 369.49,480.51
  446.49,502.309 399.686,502.309 399.686,547.51
  337.784,547.51 337.784,502.309" transform=
  "matrix(-1 3.67382e-016 -3.67382e-016 -1 526.98 698)
  translate(-1 0) translate(0 -23)" style="fill:
  rgb(0,0,255);stroke:rgb(0,0,0);stroke-width:1"/>
<polygon points="292.49,502.309 369.49,480.51
  446.49,502.309 399.686,502.309 399.686,547.51
  337.784,547.51 337.784,502.309" transform=
  "matrix(-1 3.67382e-016 -3.67382e-016 -1 738.98 800)
  translate(191 -134)" style="fill:rgb(0,0,255);
  stroke:rgb(0,0,0);stroke-width:1"/>
<polygon points="292.49,502.309 369.49,480.51
  446.49,502.309 399.686,502.309 399.686,547.51
  337.784,547.51 337.784,502.309" transform=
  "matrix(-1 3.67382e-016 -3.67382e-016 -1 738.98 1029)
  translate(224 -151) translate(-4 7) translate(0 1)
  translate(-1 49) translate(-11 0) translate(-4 4)"
  style="fill:rgb(0,0,255);stroke:rgb(0,0,0);
  stroke-width:1"/>
<text x="501px" y="686px" transform="translate(3 2)
  translate(-6 -60)" style="fill:rgb(0,0,0);
  font-size:24;font-family:@MingLiU">DATA</text>
<text x="490px" y="436px" transform="translate(-9 1)"
  style="fill:rgb(0,0,0);font-size:24;font-family:
  @MingLiU">SOAP</text>
<text x="501px" y="212px" transform="translate(9 0)
  translate(-10 0) translate(17 4)" style="fill:
  rgb(0,0,0);font-size:24;font-family:
  @MingLiU">XML</text>
```

```
  <text x="133px" y="178px" transform="translate(6 12)
    translate(-1 17)" style="fill:rgb(0,0,0);
    font-size:24;font-family:@MingLiU">URL</text>
  <text x="160px" y="425px" style="fill:rgb(0,0,0);
    font-size:24;font-family:@MingLiU">XML</text>
  <text x="125px" y="661px" transform="translate(-21 18)
    translate(2 5) translate(4 -10) translate(5 0)
    translate(-8 -48) translate(13 0) translate(-5 0)
    translate(13 0)" style="fill:rgb(0,0,0);font-size:24;
    font-family:@MingLiU">REQUEST</text>
</svg>
```

SVG Code for Figure 14.3

```
<?xml version="1.0" standalone="no"?>
<!DOCTYPE svg PUBLIC "-//W3C//DTD SVG 1.0//EN"
  "http://www.w3.org/TR/2001/REC-SVG-20010904/
  DTD/svg10.dtd">
<svg width="800" height="800">
  <defs>
    <filter id="Bevel_1" filterUnits="objectBoundingBox"
      x="-10%" y="-10%" width="150%" height="150%">
      <feGaussianBlur in="SourceAlpha" stdDeviation="3"
        result="blur"/>
      <feSpecularLighting in="blur" surfaceScale="5"
        specularConstant="0.5" specularExponent="10"
        result="specOut" style="lighting-color:
        rgb(255,255,255)">
        <fePointLight x="-5000" y="-10000" z="20000"/>
      </feSpecularLighting>
      <feComposite in="specOut" in2="SourceAlpha"
        operator="in" result="specOut2"/>
      <feComposite in="SourceGraphic" in2="specOut2"
        operator="arithmetic" k1="0" k2="1" k3="1" k4="0"
        result="litPaint"/>
    </filter>
    <filter id="Bevel" filterUnits="objectBoundingBox"
      x="-10%" y="-10%" width="150%" height="150%">
      <feGaussianBlur in="SourceAlpha" stdDeviation="3"
        result="blur"/>
```

```
    <feSpecularLighting in="blur" surfaceScale="5"
      specularConstant="0.5" specularExponent="10"
      result="specOut" style="lighting-color:
      rgb(255,255,255)">
      <fePointLight x="-5000" y="-10000" z="20000"/>
    </feSpecularLighting>
    <feComposite in="specOut" in2="SourceAlpha"
      operator="in" result="specOut2"/>
    <feComposite in="SourceGraphic" in2="specOut2"
      operator="arithmetic" k1="0" k2="1" k3="1" k4="0"
      result="litPaint"/>
  </filter>
</defs>
<ellipse cx="379" cy="164.5" rx="103" ry="95.5"
  transform="translate(-14.6667 41.3333)" style=
  "fill:rgb(0,0,192);stroke:rgb(0,0,0);stroke-width:1;
  filter:url(#Bevel)"/>
<ellipse cx="401" cy="400.5" rx="103" ry="95.5"
  transform="translate(180 197.333) translate(17.3333 -
  18.6667)" style="fill:rgb(0,0,192);stroke:
  rgb(0,0,0);stroke-width:1;filter:url(#Bevel)"/>
<ellipse cx="400" cy="400.5" rx="103" ry="95.5"
  transform="translate(-244 160) translate(-9.33333
  14.6667)" style="fill:rgb(0,0,192);stroke:
  rgb(0,0,0);stroke-width:1;filter:url(#Bevel)"/>
<text x="278px" y="195px" style="fill:rgb(0,0,0);
  font-size:24;font-family:@MingLiU" transform=
  "translate(45 15)">REQUEST</text>
<text x="65px" y="581px" style="fill:rgb(0,0,0);
  font-size:24;font-family:@MingLiU" transform=
  "translate(30 1)">PROVIDER</text>
<text x="525px" y="586px" style="fill:rgb(0,0,0);
  font-size:24;font-family:@MingLiU" transform=
  "translate(24 0)">REGISTRY</text>
<text x="161px" y="582px" style="fill:rgb(0,0,0);
  font-size:24;font-family:@MingLiU">
</text>
<polygon points="287.011,380.539 213.511,402.989
  140.011,380.539 184.688,380.539 184.688,333.989
  243.776,333.989 243.776,380.539" style="filter:
  url(#Bevel_1);fill:rgb(0,0,255);stroke:rgb(0,0,0);
  stroke-width:1" transform="translate(-1 -1)
  translate(-13 -27) translate(2 11)"/>
```

```
<polygon points="374.011,312.539 300.511,334.989
  227.011,312.539 271.688,312.539 271.688,265.989
  330.776,265.989 330.776,312.539" style="filter:
  url(#Bevel_1);fill:rgb(0,0,255);stroke:rgb(0,0,0);
  stroke-width:1" transform="translate(208 50)
  translate(-3 21) translate(-89 -6) translate(101 -7)"/>
<polygon points="374.011,312.539 300.511,334.989
  227.011,312.539 271.688,312.539 271.688,265.989
  330.776,265.989 330.776,312.539" style="filter:
  url(#Bevel_1);fill:rgb(0,0,255);stroke:rgb(0,0,0);
  stroke-width:1" transform="matrix(-1.83691e-016
  -1 1 -1.83691e-016 33.0106 910.011) translate(-15 2)
  translate(0 51) translate(26 0)"/>
<polygon points="374.011,312.539 300.511,334.989
  227.011,312.539 271.688,312.539 271.688,265.989
  330.776,265.989 330.776,312.539" style="filter:
  url(#Bevel_1);fill:rgb(0,0,255);stroke:rgb(0,0,0);
  stroke-width:1" transform="matrix(-1 3.67382e-016
  -3.67382e-016 -1 958.022 677.001) translate(-2 15)
  translate(-1 6) translate(-1 -53) translate(203 -47)"/>
<text x="497px" y="310px" style="fill:rgb(0,0,0);
  font-size:24;font-family:@MingLiU">Find</text>
<text x="633px" y="420px" style="fill:rgb(0,0,0);
  font-size:24;font-family:@MingLiU" transform=
  "translate(-4 48) translate(-201 46)">Result</text>
<text x="176px" y="305px" style="fill:rgb(0,0,0);
  font-size:24;font-family:@MingLiU">Bind</text>
<polygon points="287.011,380.539 213.511,402.989
  140.011,380.539 184.688,380.539 184.688,333.989
  243.776,333.989 243.776,380.539" style="filter:
  url(#Bevel_1);fill:rgb(0,0,255);stroke:rgb(0,0,0);
  stroke-width:1" transform="matrix(-1 3.67382e-016
  -3.67382e-016 -1 493.022 820.001)"/>
<text x="255px" y="510px" style="fill:rgb(0,0,0);
  font-size:24;font-family:@MingLiU">Locate</text>
<text x="259px" y="538px" style="fill:rgb(0,0,0);
  font-size:24;font-family:@MingLiU">Web Service</text>
<text x="299px" y="719px" style="fill:rgb(0,0,0);
  font-size:24;font-family:@MingLiU" transform=
  "translate(46 -1) translate(-7 -28)">Publish</text>
</svg>
```

APPENDIX D

XML Spy

XML Spy, the XML advanced editing and parsing program by Altova, is available for a free, 30-day download at http://www.xmlspy.com/.

Click on the red download tab on the XML Spy homepage and choose XML Spy Professional Edition (see Figure D.1). Next, select the Windows version you will use it with. Note that XML Spy Professional Edition does not work with MacIntosh computers. After checking off the appropriate selections, choose the drive path specification of your choice, or, for convenience, you can save it to your desktop.

Note: The author used a licensed copy of XML Spy Enterprise Edition to create the examples in this book.

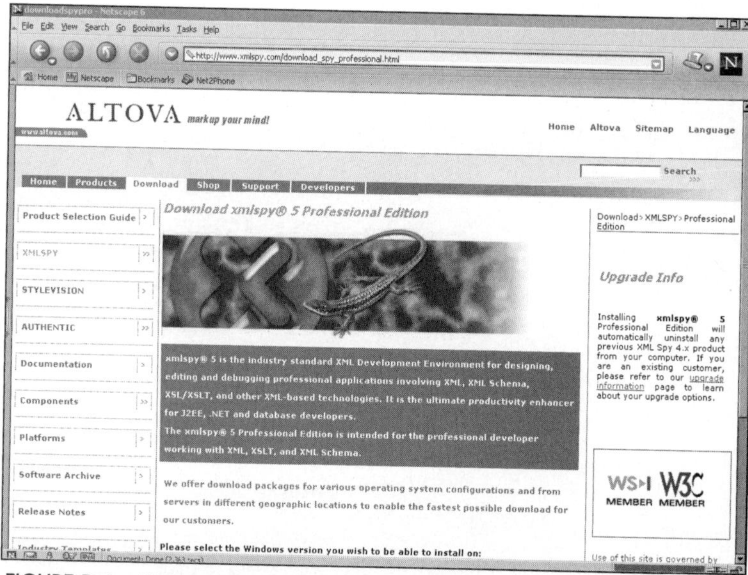

FIGURE D.1 XML Spy Professional Edition Web Page

Go to the File pull-down menu and select File and New. You will get a dialogue box where you should choose XML Document (see Figure D.2).

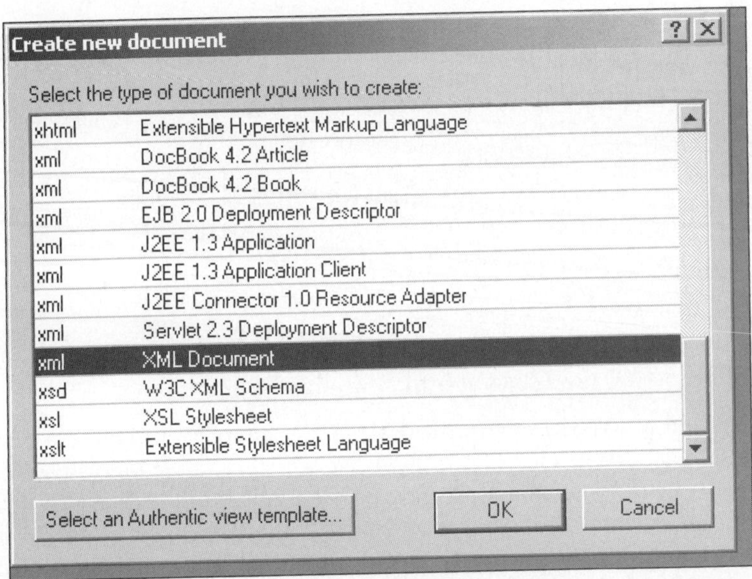

FIGURE D.2 Choosing to Make a New XML Document

You will get a dialogue box asking if you intend to base it on an already existing DTD or schema (see Figure D.3). Click Cancel as you will not be using an existing file at this time.

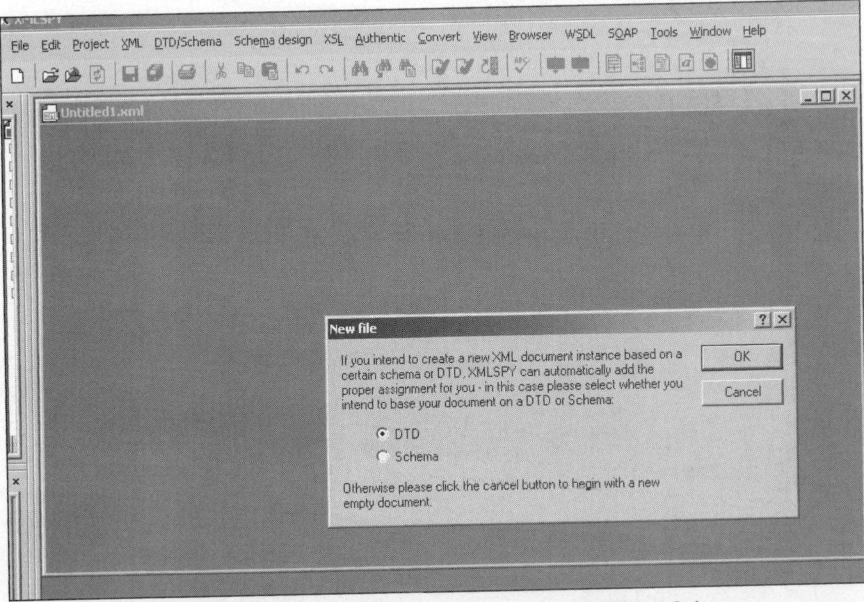

FIGURE D.3 Choosing Whether to Use an Existing or New DTD or Schema

Even though nothing has been programmed yet, note that there are a number of views you can use to see the information the program has inserted. The first is `Enhanced Grid` view, which is the default (see Figure D.4).

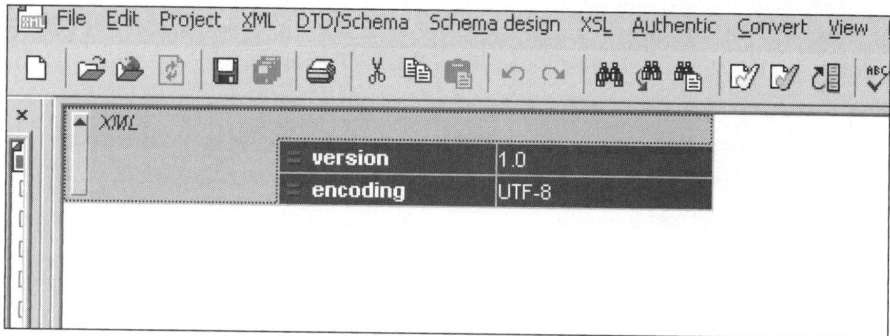

FIGURE D.4 Enhanced Grid View

Next, go to the `View` pull-down menu and select `Text view`. Note that a UTF-8 encoding has automatically been inserted by the program. Now switch back to `Enhanced Grid` view.

Now go to the `XML` pull down menu and choose `Insert` and `Comment`.

Follow with another comment, and then insert a `DOCTYPE` and various elements as you see listed in Figure D.5.

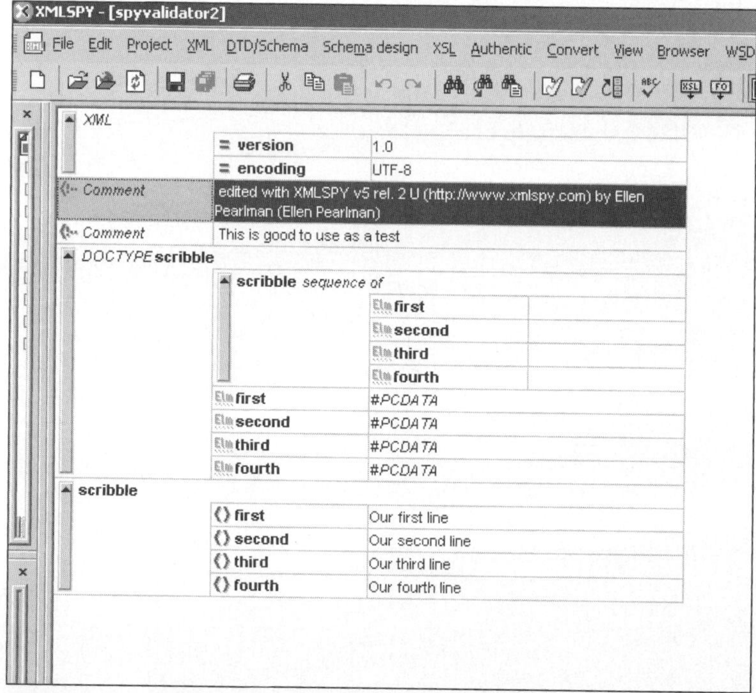

FIGURE D.5 Inserted Comments, `DOCTYPES`, and Elements in XML Spy

Change the view to `Text view` to see the final XML statement. Then change the view to `Browser view` to see another view. Make sure to change it back to `Text view`.

Hit the yellow-checked `Well formed` button on the toolbar. Then hit the green-checked `Valid` button on the toolbar. If you have entered the information correctly, the file should be both well formed and valid (see Figure D.6).

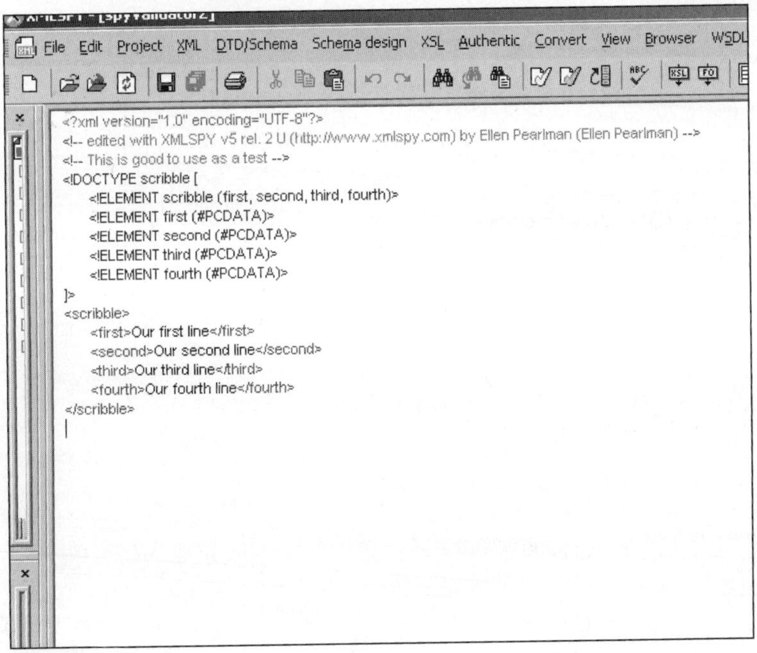

```
<?xml version="1.0" encoding="UTF-8"?>
<!-- edited with XMLSPY v5 rel. 2 U (http://www.xmlspy.com) by Ellen Pearlman (Ellen Pearlman) -->
<!-- This is good to use as a test -->
<!DOCTYPE scribble [
    <!ELEMENT scribble (first, second, third, fourth)>
    <!ELEMENT first (#PCDATA)>
    <!ELEMENT second (#PCDATA)>
    <!ELEMENT third (#PCDATA)>
    <!ELEMENT fourth (#PCDATA)>
]>
<scribble>
    <first>Our first line</first>
    <second>Our second line</second>
    <third>Our third line</third>
    <fourth>Our fourth line</fourth>
</scribble>
```

FIGURE D.6 An Example of a Valid XML File

Index

E

F

G

H

I

J

Q

R

S

T

U

V

W

X

Y

Z